RAMSGATE
DOVER
FOLKESTONE
CALAIS

The shortest route to good living.
    For your first taste of France take the shortest and
fastest crossing—via Calais. Traditional landfall on the
Continent for gourmets and travellers for centuries and
the logical route today.

**By far the <u>fastest</u> and the <u>best</u> way
to go and come back.**

THE A–Z GASTRONOMIQUE

A Dictionary of French Food & Wine

Fay Sharman and Brian Chadwick

Consultant editor
Klaus Boehm

Designed and illustrated by
Bryan Reading

PAPERMAC

First published 1982 by Macmillan Reference Books

First published in paperback 1983 by
PAPERMAC
a division of Macmillan Publishers Limited
4 Little Essex Street London WC2R 3LF
and Basingstoke

Reprinted 1984, 1985, 1986

Reissued 1989

Reprinted 1990

Associated companies in Auckland, Delhi, Dublin, Gaborone,
Hamburg, Harare, Hong Kong, Johannesburg, Kuala Lumpur, Lagos,
Manzini, Melbourne, Mexico City, Nairobi, New York, Singapore and
Tokyo

ISBN 0 333 49815 1

Photoset by Rowland Phototypesetting Limited
Bury St Edmunds, Suffolk

Printed by Cox & Wyman Ltd, Reading

CONTENTS

BIOGRAPHICAL NOTE

Fay Sharman, Brian Chadwick and Klaus Boehm have dined together for many years. The establishment of The Knife and Cleaver Press put the dinners onto a proper business footing, and this is how they came to collaborate in compiling *The A–Z Gastronomique*, first published as *The Taste of France*.

After graduating from Oxford and several years in academic publishing, Fay Sharman is now a free-lance writer and an editor for the Royal Horticultural Society. Brian Chadwick, ex-Irish Guards, developed a taste for French food and wine while travelling in France as a member of the Philharmonia Orchestra. He is now the proprietor of a distinguished restaurant, The Knife and Cleaver, in the Bedfordshire village of Houghton Conquest, and also of Bedford Fine Wines Ltd. Klaus Boehm is a consultant editor and reference book publisher. At Cambridge he rapidly became and has since remained, an expert on the consumption of food and wine. Fay Sharman, Brian Chadwick and Klaus Boehm have also written *The Taste of Italy*.

Bryan Reading, who designed and illustrated the Dictionary, is a free-lance artist and cartoonist. His work appears regularly in the British press.

INTRODUCTION

The A–Z Gastronomique is a dictionary of French words and French terms connected with food. It has been designed to cover everything you might encounter on a menu in any French restaurant. We have included wines and spirits since they are essential to the enjoyment of French cuisine; however, since there are already many excellent works devoted to this subject, our treatment of it is rather more rudimentary.

The principles on which the Dictionary works are quite simple.

(a) The entries are arranged in strict alphabetical order. Phrases beginning 'à la' are given under the main entry heading ignoring the preposition; for example, to look up 'à la flamande', see **(À LA) FLAMANDE** under 'F'.

(b) Words in the text which appear in *italics* have their own entries.

(c) 'Lit.' indicates the literary, as opposed to culinary, meaning of a word.

(d) A regional name in parentheses immediately following an entry heading has its own entry elsewhere in the Dictionary.

(e) There are maps of the regions and of the main wine-growing areas on the inside of the front and back covers.

(f) A 'reverse' index, from English to French, has been added at the back of the book. This enables you to look up an English word and find the French translation. It is confined to basic words and it does not include words that are exactly the same in both languages, such as courgette and orange.

We invite our readers to write to us with details of any words or phrases we have overlooked, for inclusion in further editions.

Bon appétit!

PICTIONARY

À   See *à la*.

ABADÈCHE ROUGE   Type of sea bass (*bar*).

ABATIS   Giblets, of fowl.

ABATS   Offal – kidneys, liver, heart etc.

ABBAYE DE LA MEILLERAYE/DU MONT-DES-CATS   See *Meilleraye de Bretagne* and *Mont-des-Cats*.

ABEGNADES/ABIGNADES   (Gascogne) Goose tripe and blood on fried bread with lemon.

ABLETTE   Small freshwater fish, bleak, used especially in *fritures*.

ABONDANCE   Lit.: 'abundance' (Savoie). Firm, smooth, round cheese, made from cow's milk of the Abondance breed around the town of Abondance; also known as *Tomme d'Abondance*; see also *Vacherin*.
     Diluted wine.

ABRICOT   Apricot. *Oreillons d'abricots*: halved apricots. *Abricots Colbert*: poached, filled with rice and deep-fried; *à la diable*: poached, glazed, on macaroons. See also *pêche*.

ABRICOTINE   Apricot and brandy liqueur.

ABSINTHE   Wormwood, aromatic plant, used to flavour *vermouth*, and formerly for the potent drink of the same name, now banned in France.

ABUSSEAU   Type of sea smelt.

AC   See *appellation (d'origine) contrôlée*.

ACACIA   Acacia tree, with yellow blossoms which may be made into fritters or a liqueur.

ACAJOU   Lit.: 'mahogany'. *Noix d'acajou*: name for cashew nut (*anacarde*).

ACANTHE   Acanthus, plant whose leaves can be eaten in salads.

ACARNE   Name for sea bream (*pagre*).

ACAVE   Variety of snail.

ACELINE   Freshwater fish similar to perch.

ACHARD   Spicy vegetable or fruit pickle.

ACHE (DES MARAIS)   Wild celery.

ACIDULÉ(-E)   Acid, acidulated.

ACTINIE   Name for sea anemone (*tomate de mer*).

ACUCU   (Corse) Local name for grey mullet (*mulet*).

ADDITION   Bill, at the end of a meal.

ADÈLE   *Consommé Adèle*: clear soup with peas, carrots and chicken *quenelles*.

ADELINE   *Salade Adeline*: salsify, tomato and cucumber salad.

ADMIRABLE   Lit.: 'admirable'. Variety of table grape.

ADOBO DE PATASSOUN   (Provence) Jerusalem artichoke stew with wine, tomatoes and bacon.

ADOUR   River in *Pays basque*; see *alose*.

AEGLÉ   Ugli fruit, cross between grapefruit and tangerine.

AFFINÉ(-E)   Refined. Sometimes used to describe cheeses.

(À L')AFRICAINE   African-style. Garnish of mushrooms, aubergines, tomatoes and potatoes. See also *charlotte*.

(À L')AGATHOISE   In the style of Agde in *Languedoc*. See *seiche*.

AGEN   Capital of the Lot-et-Garonne department and of *Agenais*; see also *pruneau*.

AGENAIS   Region equivalent to the department of Lot-et-Garonne, S of *Périgord*.

(À L')AGENAISE   In the style of *Agenais*. *Oeufs à l'agenaise*: eggs fried in goose fat, with onions and aubergines.

AGLY   See *Côtes d'Agly*.

AGNEAU   Lamb. See *carré*, *côtelette*, *épaule*, *gigot*, *noisette*, *selle*, for the major cuts. *Agneau de lait*: baby, milk-fed lamb, also known as *agnelet*. *Agneau pascal*: spring lamb. (*Agneau de*) *pré-salé*: lamb pastured in salt meadows, particularly on the Atlantic coast, which gives it a special flavour.

AGNELET   See *agneau*.

AGNÈS SOREL Mistress of Charles VII. Garnish of chicken *mousse*, mushrooms and ox tongue. *Crème Agnès Sorel*: cream of chicken soup with mushrooms and ox tongue.

AGON Small fish similar to sardine.

AGOURSI Ridged, Russian cucumber, usually salted and sliced as a first course.

AGULIA/AGULIO (Provence) Local names for two fish – *aiguillat* and *aiguille*.

AIGLE DE MER Lit.: 'sea eagle' (Bretagne). Local name for skate (*raie*).

AIGLEFIN Haddock, also known as *aigrefin*, *anon*, *églefin*, *égrefin*, *morue noire* and (*morue*) *Saint-Pierre*, and as *haddock* when smoked.

AIGLON See *pêche*.

AIGO (Provence) Garlic soup poured over slices of bread. *Aigo bouido*: garlic soup with oil and egg, perhaps cubes of fried bread, traditionally served to newly-weds and on Christmas Eve; also known as *boulido* and *bullido*. *Aigo à la ménagère*: onion, leek, garlic and tomato soup with poached eggs. *Aigo sa(o)u*: fish and garlic soup similar to *bouillabaisse*, but without the *rascasse* and with potatoes; also known as *bouillabaisse borgue/blanche*.

AIGRE Sour, bitter.

AIGRE DE CÈDRE Variety of citron (*cédrat*).

(Á L')AIGRE-DOUX (DOUCE) Sweet-sour, bitter-sweet.

AIGREFIN Name for haddock (*aiglefin*).

AIGRETTE Lit.: 'crest'. Fritter, usually savoury and cheesy.

AIGROSSADE (Provence) Chick peas and vegetables with *aïoli*.

AIGUEBELLE Green or yellow liqueur, made near *Valence*.

AIGUILLAT Spur dog, type of small shark or dogfish; also known as *chien de mer* and *agulia*.

AIGUILLE Lit.: 'needle'. Garfish, striking beaked sea fish with green bones and a delicious flavour; also known as *orphie*, *aiguillette*, *bécassine de mer* and *agulio*.

AIGUILLETTE Long thin slice cut from the breast, of poultry or game. See also *aiguille* and *pièce de boeuf*.

(L')AIGUILLON   Bay at the mouth of the Sèvre Niortaise in *Vendée*; see also *huître* and *moule*.

AIL (pl. AULX)   Garlic. *Gousse d'ail*: clove of garlic. *Rôti à l'ail*: garlic toast. *Soupe à l'ail* (S France): garlic soup with egg yolks poured on slices of bread.

AILE   Wing, of poultry, game birds.

ALLERON   Wing tip, of poultry, game. Fin, of fish.

AILLADA   (Gascogne) Spicy garlic and oil sauce, served with snails.

AÏLLADE   (S France) Mayonnaise-type sauce of pounded garlic, herbs, tomatoes and oil, similar to *aïoli*; sometimes added to stews, roasts etc. *Aïllade albigeoise*: version of *aïoli*: *à la toulousaine*: *aïoli* with walnuts.

AILLÉ(-E)   Flavoured with garlic. *Aillée*: green part of garlic, used in *Poitou*.

AILLOLI   See *aïoli*.

AILLONS   See *Vacherin*.

AÏOLI   (S France) Garlic-flavoured mayonnaise, sometimes with breadcrumbs added, or cooked seaweed and *Pernod*; also known as *ailloli* and *beurre de Provence*. Essential accompaniment to *bourride*, and often served with fish, snails (a traditional Christmas Eve supper) or salad; the old spelling was 'ayoli/ail-y-oli'–lit.: 'garlic and oil'. *Aïoli garni*: salt cod with *aïoli* and vegetables, eaten especially on Fridays. *Grand aïoli*: meat with *aïoli*. *Aïoli à la grecque*: *vinaigrette* with garlic and nuts, served with fish.

AIR   Lit.: 'air'. *Pommes* (*de terre*) *en l'air*: potato puffs; or see also *pommes*.

AIRELLE   Name for different berries, including cranberry (*airelle rouge*), whortleberry and bilberry. Also a spirit made from berries, especially in *Alsace*.

AISY   See *Candré d'Aisy*.

AIX-EN-PROVENCE   Town in *Provence*; see *Coteaux d'Aix-en-Provence*.

(Á L')AIXOISE   In the style of *Aix-en-Provence*; or of Aix-les-Bains, in *Savoie*; see also *noix*.

AJACCIO   Capital of *Corse*; *AC* wine region around the city.

À LA (À L', AU pl. AUX)   To, at, on etc. With (e.g. *aux haricots verts*: with French beans). See also *commande*.

Short for *à la mode*: in the style (e.g. *à la flamande*: Flemish-style).

ALAPEDO   Name for limpet (*patelle*).

ALBARELLE   Type of fungus which grows on trees.

ALBERGE   (Touraine) Local name for peach (*pêche*).

ALBERT   *Sauce Albert*: creamy horseradish sauce, named after Prince Albert by Queen Victoria's chef. See also *sole*.

ALBERTINE   *Sauce Albertine*: white wine sauce with mushrooms and truffles, for poached fish.

ALBI   Capital of the Tarn department in *Languedoc*.

(À L')ALBIGEOISE   In the style of *Albi*. Garnish of stuffed tomatoes, ham and potato croquettes. *Soupe/potée albigeoise*: meat soup with sausage, preserved goose, vegetables and garlic. See also *aïllade*, *caneton*, *côtelette* and *épaule*.

ALBIGNAC   Town in *Limousin*. *Salade d'Albignac*: truffle salad with crayfish, chicken, celeriac, hard-boiled eggs, lettuce etc.

(À LA D')ALBUFÉRA   Elaborate chicken dish with truffles, cockscombs etc, named after one of Napoleon's generals, created Duc d'Albuféra (in Spain). *Sauce Albuféra*: rich white sauce with pimento butter. See also *caneton*.

ALCAZAR   See *gâteau*.

ALCOOL   Alcohol. *Alcool blanc*: see *eau-de-vie*.

ALÉNOIS(-E)   Probable corruption of *Orléanais*, region once known for watercress. *Soupe (au cresson) alénois*: watercress soup. See also *cresson*.

ALENÇON   Capital of the Orne department in *Normandie*.

(À L')ALÉSIENNE   In the style of Alès in *Languedoc*. See *tripes*.

ALEVIN   Name for young fish (*fretin*).

ALEXANDRA   See *pêche* and *poulet*.

(À L')ALGÉRIENNE   Algerian-style. Garnish of sweet potato croquettes and tomatoes; or tomato sauce with red peppers.

ALGUE (ROUGE)   Dulse, type of seaweed sometimes cooked like spinach. See also *crème*.

ALICOT/ALICUIT   (SW France) Lit.: 'wings cooked'. Giblets and wings especially of goose or duck, stewed with *cèpes* and chestnuts; also known as *alycot* and *alycuit*.

ALIFRANCIU   (Corse) Local name for grey mullet (*mulet*).

ALIGOT   (Auvergne, Rouergue) Fresh uncured cheese, basis for *Cantal* cheese and similar to Italian Mozzarella; made in mountain dairies, also known as *Tomme d'Aligot/ Fraîche*. The name perhaps derives from dialect 'alicoter' – to cut.
    Puréed potatoes with *Aligot* cheese and often garlic, also made into flat cakes and fried.

ALIGOTÉ   Variety of grape used in *Bourgogne*, giving fresh clean ordinary wines, the best grown in Bouzeron (*AC*).

ALIMENTAIRE   To do with nutrition, food.

ALIMENTATION(S)   Nutrition, food. Food shop, grocery.

ALISE/ALISIER   Service berry/service tree, similar to rowan and *sorbier*. Also a spirit made from service berries, especially in *Alsace*.

ALISSON   (S France) Local name for sea urchin (*oursin*).

ALKÉKENGE   Strawberry tomato, sweet-sour fruit used in desserts and confectionery; also known as *coqueret*.

ALLACHE   Type of large sardine.

ALL GRENAT   See *bouillade*.

ALLELUIA   (Languedoc) Small cake.

(À L')ALLEMANDE   German-style. Garnish of noodles and mashed potatoes. Roasted with cream or sour cream sauce, of hare and venison. *Sauce allemande*: rich white sauce, originally so named to distinguish it from *sauce espagnole*, and perhaps because of its blond colour; also known as *sauce parisienne*. *Salade allemande*: apple, potato, gherkin, herring and onion salad. See also *bifteck* and *cerise*.

ALLUES   See *Tomme de Chèvre*.

ALLUMETTE   Lit.: 'match'. Small strip of puff pastry, sweet or savoury. *Pommes (de terre) allumettes*: matchstick chips.

ALLYMES   See *tâtre*.

ALMA   See *poire*.

ALOSE

Shad, migratory sea fish which comes up rivers in spring, similar to herring but larger, with bony, tasty flesh; also known as *finte*. Found in the *Gironde* where it is often grilled over vine shoots or stuffed with sorrel, and in the *Loire*, where it may be served with *beurre blanc*. *Alose à l'Adour*: stuffed with sorrel and baked on ham; *à l'avignonnaise*: braised with sorrel and lemon; *Claudine*: slices baked with mushrooms, white wine and cream; *à la mode de Cocherel*: stuffed, wrapped in bacon, grilled, with potatoes, artichokes and onions; *à la dacquoise*: in white wine sauce with onions, grapes and ham. Freshwater shad, found in deep lakes.

ALOUETTE   Lark, also known as *mauviette*; often made into *pâté*. *Alouette sans tête*: see *paupiette*.

ALOUETTE DE MER   Sandpiper, summer snipe, prepared like woodcock; also known as *bécasseau*, *chevalier*, *guignette* and *maubèche*.

ALOXE-CORTON   Important commune (*AC*) of *Côte de Beaune*, *Bourgogne*, producing mainly red wine, for which its most famous *grand cru* vineyard is *Le Corton*, and some white, including the *grand cru Corton-Charlemagne* (both overlap with neighbouring *Pernand-Vergelesses*); neighbouring *Ladoix-Serrigny* uses the name *Aloxe-Corton* for its best wines.

ALOYAU   Sirloin, of beef, large joint including the *contre-filet* and rump.

ALPHÉE   Type of large prawn, similar to *langouste*.

ALPHONSE LA VALLÉE   Variety of black table grape.

ALSACE

Province of NE France, comprising the departments of Bas-Rhin and Haut-Rhin.
   The wines of *Alsace* are almost exclusively white and are unique in France in that, under the *Appellation Contrôlée* regulations, they are known by the names of grape varieties rather than of vineyard areas. The grapes are *Chasselas*, *Sylvaner*, *Riesling*, *Gewürztraminer*, *Pinot Blanc*, *Muscat* and *Pinot Gris* or *Tokay d'Alsace*; *Pinot Noir* is used for some light red or rosé wines. Wines from a mixture of grape varieties are called *Edelzwicker*, and a sparkling white wine is sold as *Crémant d'Alsace* (*AC*). Although vineyard names are rarely seen, a new classification of *grand cru* has recently been introduced for some of the best (e.g. the Kaefferkopf from Ammerschwihr and the Sporen from Riquewihr).

(À L')ALSACIENNE   In the style of *Alsace*. With *choucroute*, ham, sausage, potatoes, *foie gras* – any or all. Of chicken, fish, cooked in local wine, often *Riesling*. *Soupe à* *l'alsacienne*: *choucroute* soup with potato dumplings. See also *boudin*, *escargot*, *saucisson* and *tarte*.

ALTIER   See *Pélardon des Cévennes*.

ALYCOT/ALYCUIT   See *alicot*.

AMANDE   Almond. Kernel, of fruit. See also *sausson*.

AMANDE DE MER   Dog-cockle, small shellfish.

AMANDIN(-E)   With almonds, almond-flavoured.

AMANITE   Family of fungi including *coucoumelle* and *oronge*.

AMBASSADEUR   Lit.: 'ambassador'. *Potage ambassadeur*: puréed pea soup with sorrel, lettuce and rice.
     Brand of aperitif, wine-based, flavoured with quinine, gentian, orange and herbs.

AMBERT   See *Brique de Forez* and *Fourme d'Ambert*.

AMBOISE   Town in *Touraine*, known for *rillettes*.

AMBRETTE   Variety of pear.

AMÉLÉON   (Normandie) Type of cider.

AMENLOU   (Languedoc) Almond pastry.

AMER (AMÈRE)   Bitter.

(À L')AMÉRICAINE   American-style. *Homard à l'américaine*: lobster sautéed in oil with white wine, brandy, garlic, shallots and tomatoes; also known as *homard à l'armoricaine*. *Sauce américaine*: lobster sauce. The origin of *homard à l'américaine* is controversial, some claiming that it was invented by the chef Pierre Fraisse, a native of *Languedoc* who spent a few years in America, others maintaining that it belongs to the legendary Armorica (*Bretagne*).
     With bacon and tomatoes. *Oeufs à l'américaine frits*: fried eggs and bacon with grilled tomatoes. *Salade américaine*: celeriac, celery or cucumber salad, with tomatoes and hard-boiled eggs. See also *bifteck*, *faisan*, *haricot blanc* and *madrilène*.

AMER PICON   See *Picon*.

AMIENS   Capital of the Somme department and of *Picardie*.

(À L')AMIRAL   Lit.: 'admiral's style'. Garnish for large fish like turbot, including mussels, oysters, crayfish tails, truffles etc. *Oeufs amiral*: scrambled eggs with lobster. *Sauce amiral*: anchovy sauce with herbs.

AMMOCÈTE   Fish similar to lamprey.

AMOU   (Gascogne) Farm-made sheep's milk cheese with strong flavour, named after the nearest town.

AMOURETTES   Spinal bone marrow (*moelle*), usually of calves.

AMPLOVO   (S France) Local name for anchovy (*anchois*).

AMUSE-GUEULE   Lit.: 'amuse-mouth'. Appetizer, small snack, sometimes served with aperitifs.

ANACARDE   Cashew nut, also known as *cajou* and *noix d'acajou*.

ANANAS   Pineapple. *Ananas à la martiniquaise*: hot, with coffee and rum; *royale*: filled with fresh fruit soaked in *kirsch*.

ANCENIS   See *Coteaux d'Ancenis*.

ANCHOÏADE/ANCHOYADE   (Provence, Corse) Anchovy, oil and garlic paste, sometimes with figs added, served with raw vegetables or spread on toast.

ANCHOÏO   See *anchois*.

ANCHOIS   Anchovy, usually filleted and preserved, but often used fresh in *Provence*; also known as *anchoïo* and *amplovo*. *Anchois à la silésienne*: cold with herring roes and potato and apple salad; *à la suédoise*: cold with apple and beetroot salad and hard-boiled eggs.

ANCHOIS DE NORVÈGE   Name for sprat (*esprot*).

ANCHOYADE   See *anchoïade*.

(À L')ANCIENNE (MODE)   In the style of the 'old school', now a fairly meaningless label sometimes describing braised beef, *quenelles*, *blanquettes* and *fricassées*. Formerly it meant an elaborate garnish, for chicken, veal, fish, eggs. See also *croûte-au-pot*.

(À L')ANDALOUSE   Andalusian-style. With tomatoes (e.g. *potage andalouse*), plus, as a garnish, rice and sweet peppers, perhaps aubergines and sausages.

ANDOUILLE   Type of sausage, generally pork and made from a pig's large intestine filled with strips of chitterling and stomach; sold ready cooked, usually served cold as a first course. Among the best known are those of *Cambrai*: mainly of veal tripe; *Guéméné*: large, with concentric circles; *Jargeau*: of shoulder and breast of pork, sometimes spiced; *Troyes*: of pork tripe in strips; and *Vire*: large, lightly smoked, with marbling and black skin.

ANDOUILLETTE   Type of pork sausage, made like *andouille* but using the small intestine of a pig; sold ready-cooked, usually grilled and served hot with strong mustard and vegetables. Different varieties – including those of *Arras*, *Caen*, *Cambrai*, *Troyes* and *Vouvray* – are mainly distinguished by the spices used. *Andouillette à la ficelle*: stuffed with tripe cut into long strips; *au Saint-Véran*: cooked in *Saint-Véran* wine; *vouvri(ll)on*: *Vouvray* sausage cooked in *Vouvray* wine.

ANDUZE   See *Pélardon des Cévennes*.

ANÉMONE DE MER   Sea anemone, also known as *ortie de mer*, *pastegue* and *rastègne*.

ANESBREDLAS   (Alsace) Aniseed-flavoured macaroon.

ANETH   Dill, the herb.

ANFOUNSOU   (Nice) Local name for grouper (*mérou*).

ANGE   Lit.: 'angel'. *Anges à cheval*: angels on horseback – grilled oysters wrapped in bacon. See also *cheveux d'ange*.

ANGE (DE MER)   Angel fish, angel shark, similar to dogfish; also known as *angelot* and *squeru*.

ANGÉLIQUE   Angelica, plant whose candied stem is used in cakes and creams; also an ingredient in liqueurs (e.g. *Bénédictine*) and basis for *sève d'angélique*.

ANGELOT   Name for angel fish (*ange*).
      Old name for *Normandie* cheeses, especially *Pont-l'Evêque*.

ANGERS   Capital of the Maine-et-Loire department and of *Anjou*.

(À L')ANGEVINE   In the style of *Anjou*. With *Anjou* wine. See also *anguille*, *fricassée* and *rillettes*.
      Variety of table grape.

(À L')ANGLAISE   English-style. Applies to many typically English dishes – *crème anglaise*: light egg custard; *oeufs frits à l'anglaise*: fried eggs finished in the oven; *foie de veau à l'anglaise*: grilled calf's liver with bacon; *bonbon anglais*:

fruit drop. Plainly poached or boiled in water, or steamed, usually of fish or vegetables, especially potatoes; see also *morue* and *tête*. Dipped in egg and breadcrumbs and fried, of fish. See also *assiette* and *crabe*.

ANGLET   (Charentes) Ring-shaped cake.

ANGLOIS   (Champagne) Plum tart.

ANGOULÊME   Capital of the Charente department and of *Angoumois*. See also *pâté* and *tripes*.

ANGOUMOIS   Province corresponding to the Charente department, in *Charentes*.

(À L')ANGOUMOISE   In the style of *Angoumois*. See *faisan* and *veau*.

ANGUILLE   Eel, usually caught in fresh water, although it is spawned and dies at sea (as opposed to conger or sea eel – *congre*). *Anguille à la mode d'Arleux*: cooked with shallots and sorrel; *à la Beaucaire*: stuffed, braised with wine, brandy, mushrooms and onions; *Durand*: stuffed, poached in white wine; *à la ploërmelaise*: marinated, cooked over charcoal; *aux pruneaux* (Bretagne): sliced, cooked with white wine, onions and prunes; *à la romaine*: sliced, fried, with peas, lettuce and white wine sauce; *Suffren*: sliced, poached with white wine, tomatoes and anchovies; *à la d'Ussel*: jellied; *au vert/à la flamande*: cold, with herbs and white wine. *Roulade d'anguille à l'angevine*: stuffed, wrapped in bacon, tied in a ring, cooked in *Anjou* wine with cream and crayfish sauce. *Terrine d'anguille à la martégale*: baked whole with leeks, garlic, white wine and black olives, a traditional Christmas Eve dish.

ANGUILLE DE MER   Name for conger eel (*congre*).

ANGUILLETTES   (Pays basque) Tiny eels.

ANGURIES   (Bugey) Stewed water melon, served as a starter.

ANIAU   (Bretagne) Local name for mackerel (*maquereau*).

ANIMELLES   Testicles, often fried in batter or poached and served with *vinaigrette*; also known as *rognons blancs*, and as *criadillas* in *Languedoc*.

ANIS (VERT)   Anise, the plant, aniseed, used in confectionery and liqueurs.
　　　　Small aniseed sweet.
　　　　Aniseed-flavoured aperitif, usually taken with water (e.g. *Pernod*).

ANISBROD   (Alsace) Aniseed-flavoured macaroon.

ANISÉ(-E)   Flavoured with aniseed or caraway.

ANISETTE   Aniseed-flavoured liqueur, made with aniseed or coriander and fennel.

ANJOU   Province roughly equivalent to the Maine-et-Loire department.
          Important wine-growing region producing large quantities of wine sold as *Anjou Rosé* or *Rosé d'Anjou*, *Anjou Gamay*, *Anjou Mousseux* etc (all *AC*), as well as many wines under their own *AC* (e.g. *Coteaux du Layon*, *Saumur*).

ANNA   *Pommes* (*de terre*) *Anna*: potatoes cut into thin rounds and baked in layers with butter; invented for Anna Deslions, 19th-century courtesan.

ANNECY   Capital of the Haute-Savoie department in *Savoie*.

ANNETTE   *Pommes* (*de terre*) *Annette*: as *pommes Anna*, except that the potatoes are cut into strips.

ANNOT   (Provence) Mild sheep or goat's milk cheese, made on farms; also known as *Tomme d'Annot*, an invented name.

ANON   (Bretagne) Local name for haddock (*aiglefin*).

ANONE   Custard apple, tropical fruit, often made into fritters, or sliced and steeped in wine. A variety is known as *corossol*.

ANTAN   See *pain*.

(À L')ANTIBOISE   In the style of Antibes in *Provence*. *Oeufs à l'antiboise*: baked eggs with tiny fried fish, cheese and garlic. See also *sardine* and *tomate*.

ANTILLES   French West Indies.

(À L')ANTILLAISE   In the style of *Antilles*. Often with rum.

(À L')ANVERSOISE   In the style of Antwerp (Anvers) in Belgium. Garnish of hop shoots in cream. See also *cornet*.

AOC   See *appellation* (*d'origine*) *contrôlée*.

APÉRITIF   Lit.: 'appetizing'. Aperitif, drink taken before a meal to stimulate the appetite (e.g. *vermouth*, *pastis*, *anis*, *Dubonnet*, *Suze*).

APÉRO   Short for *apéritif*.

APHIE   Onos, rockling, Mediterranean fish.

APOGON   Name for red mullet (*rouget*).

APPELLATION (D'ORIGINE) CONTRÔLÉE French system of quality control, often shortened to *AC/AOC*, applied in particular to wine and cheese, and to a range of other products, including butter (*beurre des Charentes/des Charentes et du Poitou*), poultry (*poulet de Bresse*), walnuts (*noix de Grenoble*). It gives specific legal definition to the product, regulating the place of origin and also the breed/variety and methods of manufacture/production. See also *eau minérale*, *fromage* and *vin*.

APPELLATION RÉGLEMENTÉE   See *Calvados*.

APPÉTIT   Appetite. You may be wished 'bon appétit' before a meal.
   Name for chives (*ciboulette*).

APRON   Small fish similar to perch.

AQUITAINE   See *Guyenne*.

ARACHIDE   Groundnut.

ARACK   Arrack, usually distilled from fermented rice; also known as *raki*.

ARAGNO/ARAIGNÉE   (S France) Local name for type of weever (*vive*).

ARAIGNÉE DE MER   Lit.: 'sea spider'. Spider crab, also known as *esquinadoun* and *squinado*. *Araignée de mer à la libourdine*: stuffed with coral, egg, wild mint, sweet pepper and lemon.

ARAPÈDE   Name for limpet (*patelle*).

ARAVIS   See *Persillé des Aravis* and *Chevrotin des Aravis*.

ARBENNE   Snow partridge, found in mountains.

ARBOIS   Town in *Jura* making *AC* wines – red, white and rosé, a small amount of *vin jaune*, and the sparkling *Arbois Mousseux*.

ARBOUSE   Arbutus berry, fruit of the strawberry tree, used for jams and jellies. *Crème d'arbouse*: sweet arbutus berry liqueur, made especially in *Corse*.

ARCACHON   Bay on the coast of *Bordelais*; see also *huître*.

ARCANETTE   (Lorraine) Local name for type of wild duck.

ARC-EN-CIEL   Lit.: 'rainbow'. See *truite*.

ARCHE DE NOÉ   Noah's Ark, small shellfish.

(À L')ARCHIDUC   Lit.: 'archduke's style'. With paprika and cream, usually of chicken and eggs.

ARDENNES   Department, and region, in *Champagne*.

(À L')ARDENNAISE   In the style of *Ardennes*. With juniper berries, especially of small game birds and pork. *Pommes (de terre) à l'ardennaise*: potatoes stuffed with eggs, ham, cheese and mushrooms; or fried in slices as a flat cake with juniper berries. *Soupe à l'ardennaise*: chicory, leek and potato soup. See also *endive*.

ARDI-GASNA   (Pays basque) Firm yellow sheep's milk cheese, strong in flavour, made on mountain farms; dialect for 'local cheese'.

ARÊCHES   See *Grataron d'Arêches*.

ARÊTE   Fishbone.

ARGENTEUIL   Town in *Ile-de-France*, known for asparagus. With asparagus, especially *crème Argenteuil*: cream of asparagus soup.

ARGENTINE   Argentine, sea fish with silvery scales, similar to sardine.

ARIÈGE   Department in Pyrenees, equivalent to *Foix*, and river.

(À L')ARIÉGEOISE   In the style of *Ariège*. With cabbage, salt pork and potatoes (e.g. *soupe ariégeoise*). With kidney beans. See also *poitrine* and *poulet*.

(À L')ARLEQUINE   Lit.: 'harlequin-style'. Arrangement of multi-coloured food; originally a motley assortment of food given by restaurants to the poor.

ARLES   Town in *Provence*, known for *saucisson*.

(À L')ARLÉSIENNE   In the style of *Arles*. With tomatoes, and onions, aubergines, potatoes, rice or olives. *Salade arlésienne*: potato and artichoke salad with tomatoes, olives and anchovies. *Soupe arlésienne*: chick pea and spinach soup with pasta and cheese. See also *becfigue*, *escargot*, *sole* and *Tomme de Camargue*.

ARLEUX   Town in *Flandre*. See *anguille*.

ARMAGNAC   Region equivalent to the Gers department, in *Gascogne*.
   The second great brandy of France, produced in the departments of *Gers* and *Landes* (*Gascogne*) and Lot-et-Garonne (*Agenais*). The vineyard area is divided into

Haut-Armagnac, *Ténarèze* and *Bas-Armagnac*. *Armagnac* sold under these three names, or simply as *Armagnac*, must be at least one year old; if it bears *VO*, *VSOP* or *Réserve* on the label, it must be at least four years old; *Hors d'Age* indicates that it is a blend of spirits ten years old or more.

(À L')ARMÉNIENNE   Armenian-style. *Salade arménienne*: sweet pepper and celery salad with mushrooms, bacon and garlic. See also *aubergine*.

ARMENONVILLE   *Paris* restaurant. *Oeufs Armenonville*: poached eggs on toast with sherry-flavoured white sauce. See also *glace*.

ARMILLAIRE   Family of fungi, with one variety especially prized around *Nice*.

(À L')ARMORICAINE   In the style of Armorica, i.e. *Bretagne*. See *américaine* and *moule*.
Oyster cultivated in *Bretagne*; see also *huître*.

ARMOTTE   (Gascogne) Maize flour cooked in goose fat; eaten hot in place of bread, or cold, perhaps with sugar.

AROMATES   Seasoning. *Sauce aromates*: white sauce with herbs.

AROMATIQUE   Aromatic.

AROME/ARÔME   Aroma, fragrance.

Aromes: very strong cheese mixture. *Aromes au gène de marc* (Lyonnais): goat's or cow's milk cheese steeped in *marc*. *Aromes de Lyon*: cheese soaked in new white wine, sometimes wrapped in vine leaves.

(À L')ARPAJONNAISE   In the style of Arpajon in *Ile-de-France*, known for haricot beans. With haricot beans.

ARPENTEUR   Lit.: 'land surveyor'. Name for plover (*pluvier*).

ARQUEBUSE   Herb liqueur, especially from *Lyonnais*.

(À L')ARRAGEOISE   In the style of *Arras*.

ARRAS   Capital of the Pas-de-Calais department and of *Artois*. See also *andouillette*.

ARROCHE   Orache, similar to spinach; also known as *bonne-dame*.

(À LA D')ARTAGNAN   Probably after *Dumas'* fictional hero. Garnish of *cèpes*, stuffed tomatoes and potato croquettes. *Consommé d'Artagnan*: clear beef and game soup with peas.

(À L')ARTÉSIENNE In the style of *Artois*. Cooked with beer. See also *lapin*.

ARTICHAUT   Globe/leaf, artichoke; two common varieties are the large round green *camus* from *Bretagne*, and the long violet type from *Provence*. *Foin d'artichaut*: choke of artichoke. *Fond d'artichaut*: artichoke bottom. *Artichauts à la barigoule* (Provence): stuffed with mushrooms, ham, onion and garlic, cooked in oil, wine and water; *à la bretonne*: chopped, simmered in oil and butter, with onions and cider; *à la cannoise*: cooked in white wine with tomatoes, onions and ham; *Cavour*: browned in butter and cheese, served with hard-boiled eggs and anchovy essence; *à la diable*: with fried eggs in the middle and vinegar and butter poured over; *favorite*: stuffed with asparagus, coated with cheese sauce, browned; *à la juive*: stuffed with herbs and fried; *Ninette*: cold with shrimps; *à la poivrade*: small and young, eaten raw with peppery *vinaigrette*; *à la provençale*: young, cooked in oil with herbs and garlic; *à la royale*: stuffed with brains, eggs, cheese and herbs, finished in the oven; *Stanley*: cooked with ham, onions, white wine and cream.

ARTICHAUT D'ESPAGNE Name for custard marrow (*pâtisson*).

ARTICHAUT D'HIVER/DU CANADA Name for Jerusalem artichoke (*topinambour*).

ARTOIS Northern province equivalent to the Pas-de-Calais department. *Potage d'Artois*: haricot bean and vegetable soup.

ARVÈZE Yellow gentian aperitif made in *Auvergne*.

ASCO See *Niolo*.

ASPERGE(S)   Asparagus. *Pointe d'asperges*: asparagus tip. White, as opposed to green, asparagus is particularly esteemed in N France; wild asparagus (*asperges sauvages*) is also found, especially in *Provence*. *Asperges à la flamande*: with sauce of hard-boiled egg yolks and melted butter; *à la Fontenelle*: dipped in melted butter and soft-boiled eggs; *à la sibérienne*: cold, on ice, with mayonnaise.

ASPERGILLE (N France) Local name for small snail.

ASPIC Aspic, jelly. Cold dish set in aspic.

ASSAISONNEMENT Condiment, seasoning, dressing.

ASSIETTE Plate, dish, both literally and figuratively. *Assiette anglaise*: plate of cold meats with jelly, cress and gherkins, usually served at lunch. *Assiettes assorties*: mixed dishes for a first course. *Assiette de fruits de mer*: platter of mixed seafood and shellfish, cooked and raw. *Assiette volante*: selection of several items of food on one plate.

ASSORTI(-E) Assorted, mixed.

ASTRODERME Vividly coloured fish common in the Mediterranean and used in *bouillabaisse*; also known in *Nice* as *feï d'Amérique*.

ATHÉRINE Sandsmelt, small common sea fish, usually deep fried; also known as *prêtre*, and *cabassoun*, *faux éperlan*, *joël*, *piètre*, *sauclet* and *siouclet*.

ATTELET Small metal skewer; originally a kind of decorative hatpin threaded with truffles, cockscombs etc as a garnish for grand dishes.

ATTEREAU Metal skewer on which different ingredients are threaded. Food cooked in such a way, either savoury or sweet, first coated in a sauce, rolled in breadcrumbs and (unlike *brochettes*) deep-fried.

ATTIGNOLE (Normandie) Baked meat ball, with jelly.

AU Masculine of *à la*.

AUBANCE See *Coteaux de l'Aubance*.

AUBAZINE Aromatic liqueur from Aubazine in *Limousin*.

AUBÉPINE Hawthorn, whose berries are sometimes made into jam.

AUBERGE Inn.

AUBERGINE Aubergine, eggplant, also known as *melongène*. *Aubergines à l'arménienne*: stuffed with lamb and baked; *à l'égyptienne*: stuffed, baked with tomatoes; *en gigot* (Roussillon): larded with bacon and slices of garlic, baked; *Imam Bayeldi*: stewed in oil with tomatoes, onions and spices, eaten cold; *des papes*: see *papeton*; *à la roussillonnaise*: stuffed with hard-boiled eggs, ham and herbs, baked; *à la serbe*: stuffed with mutton, rice and onions, baked with tomato sauce; *à la turque*: baked with onions and tomatoes.

AUBOURG Name for dace (*dard*).

AUCH Capital of *Gers*.

(À L')AUCHOISE/(À L')AUSCITAINE In the style of *Auch*.

AUDE Department of *Languedoc*, producing large quantities of wine (*Vin de Table*, *Vin de Pays* and *VDQS*), and containing *Corbières*, *Fitou*, part of *Minervois*, and *Limoux*.

AUGE   Region in *Normandie*, also known as *Pays de Vallée d'Auge*. See also *Calvados* and *Pavé de Moyaux*.

AULUS   See *Bethmale*.

AULX   Plural of *ail*: garlic.

AUMONIÈRE   Lit.: 'purse'. *Oeufs frits en aumonière*: fried eggs with fried bread, cheese and ham in a pancake.

AUNIS   Province forming part of the Charente-Maritime department, in *Charentes*. See also *Caillebotte d'Aunis*.

(À L')AUNISIENNE   In the style of *Aunis*.

AURILLAC   Capital of *Cantal*.

AURIN   (S France) Local name for grey mullet (*mulet*).

AURIOL/AURIOU (Provence) Local name for mackerel (*maquereau*).

AURIQUETTE   (Lorraine) Milk bread.

AURORE   Lit.: 'dawn', implying a red colour. *Consommé aurore*: clear soup with tomato and chicken. *Sauce aurore*: white sauce with tomato purée. See also *nymphes* and *pêche*.
                  (Normandie) Double cream cheese.

(À L')AUSCITAINE   See *auchoise*.

AUTOMNE   Autumn.

(À L')AUTRICHIENNE Austrian-style. With paprika, and sometimes onion, fennel and sour cream.

AUTUN   See *Charolais*.

(À L')AUVERGNATE   In the style of *Auvergne*. *Oeufs auvergnate*: poached eggs with cabbage and sausages. *Potée/soupe à l'auvergnate*: salt pork and cabbage soup, often with other vegetables and meats. See also *cèpe*, *perdrix* and *queue de boeuf*.

AUVERGNE   Province centred on the departments of Puy-de-Dôme and *Cantal*, merging indistinctly with *Languedoc* in the E and *Bourbonnais* in the N. See also *Bleu d'Auvergne*, *Côtes d'Auvergne* and *Tomme d'Auvergne*.

AUX   Plural of *à la/au*.

AUXERRE   Capital of the Yonne department in *Bourgogne*.

AUXEY-DURESSES Commune of *Côte de Beaune*, *Bourgogne*, producing mostly red wine (*AC*).

AVEC   With.

AVELINE   Filbert, variety of hazelnut.

AVESNES   Town in *Flandre*. See *Boulette d'Avesnes*.

(À L')AVESNOISE   In the style of *Avesnes*. See *carpe*.

AVEYRON   Department equivalent to *Rouergue*, and river.

(À L')AVEYRONNAISE   In the style of *Aveyron*. *Soupe/potée à l'aveyronnaise*: cabbage and salt pork soup with haricot beans, preserved goose etc, poured over slices of bread.

AVIGNON   Capital of *Vaucluse* and of *Comtat Venaissin*. See *alose* and *daube*.

AVOCAT   Lit.: 'lawyer'. Avocado pear. *Avocat Fermont*: hot, filled with poached egg and *béarnaise* sauce.

AVOCETTE   Small bird similar to wild duck, found especially in *Poitou*.

AVOINE   Oats.

AXONGE   Pork lard.

AZEROLE   Neapolitan medlar, whose berries may be used for jam.

AZIMINU   (Corse) Fish soup similar to *bouillabaisse*.

AZYME   Unleavened, as in *pain azyme*.

BABA   (Rum) baba, spongey yeast cake steeped in rum or *kirsch*; said to have been discovered by Stanislas Lesczinski when he dipped a *kougelhopf* in rum, named after Ali Baba of the 1001 Nights.

BABEURRE   Buttermilk, sometimes made into soup.

BACILE   Name for samphire (*Christ-marine*).

BACKENOFF/BAECKAOFFA/BAECKEOFFE/BECKENOFFE   (Alsace) Stew of beef, mutton and pork, first marinated in local wine, with potatoes and onions; originally cooked in the baker's oven.

BADASCO   (Provence) Local name for *rascasse*.

BADÈCHE   Type of sea bass (*bar*).

BADIANE   Star anise, stronger than aniseed (*anis*) but used in the same way.

BADOCHE   Name for *stockfish*.

BADOIT   Brand of sparkling mineral water from Saint Galmier in *Lyonnais*.

BADRÉE   (Berry) Apple and pear preserve.

BAECKAOFFA/BAECKEOFFE   See *backenoff*.

BAGRATION   Russian general who fought Napoleon and died at the battle of Borodino. *Potage Bagration*: cream soup with macaroni and grated cheese. *Salade Bagration*: substantial salad in the shape of a dome.

BAGUETTE   Lit.: 'stick'. Long thin white loaf.

BAGUETTE LAONNAISE   (Ile-de-France, Champagne) Rectangular very strong cheese, produced in the *Laon* region. *Demi-baguette Laonnaise* is a smaller version.

BAGUETTE DE TAMBOUR   Lit.: 'drumstick'. Drumstick mushroom, common in wooded sandy soil, often used in salads.

BAIE   Berry, of fruit. *Baie de ronce*: name for blackberry (*mûre*).

BAIGNÉ(-E)   Bathed in.

BAIGNETON   (Poitou) Light pastry.

BAISER   Lit.: 'to kiss' (also used in a more vulgar sense). Two small meringues joined with cream.

BAJAINA   (Provence) Local name for small snail.

BAJOUE   Cheek, of pig.

BALANE   Acorn barnacle, small shellfish.

BALAOU   Type of garfish (*aiguille*); also known as *gastadelo*.

BALISTE   Triggerfish, brightly-coloured Mediterranean fish; also known as *cochon de mer*.

BALLON   Lit.: 'ball'. Boned and rolled into a ball-shape (e.g. *épaule de mouton en ballon*).

BALLOT(T)INE   Type of loaf or galantine, of meat, poultry, sometimes game or fish, boned, stuffed and rolled into a bundle, usually served hot.

BALLOTTE   (Corse) Boiled chestnuts with fennel.

BALVET   *Potage Balvet*: puréed pea soup with other vegetables; also known as *potage jubilé*.

(À LA)BAMBOCHE   Lit.: 'living it up'. *See morue*.

BAMBELLE   Freshwater fish like carp.

BAMBOU   Bamboo, whose shoots are used in salads.

BANARUT   (Provence) Local name for small snail.

BANADRY   Liqueur made from bananas.

BANANE   Banana. *Bananes baronnet*: with *kirsch* and cream; *Beauharnais*: cooked with rum and sugar, served with cream and crushed macaroons.

BANDOL   Village in *Provence* growing fine red, white and rosé wines (*AC*).

BANON   (Provence) Small round cheese, of sheep's, goat's or cow's milk, wrapped in chestnut leaves; named after the market town. *Banon au Pèbre d'Ai*: see *Poivre d'Ane*.

(À LA) BANQUIÈRE   Lit.: 'banker's style'. Garnish of *quenelles*, mushrooms, truffles and larks, with madeira sauce.

BANYULS/BANYULS GRAND CRU   Strong sweet red wines (*AC*) from the *Grenache* grape, made around the town of Banyuls-sur-Mer in *Roussillon*.

BAR   Sea bass, white-fleshed, flavoursome and free of bone; also known as *loup (de mer)*, *perche de mer*, *loubine*, *loupassou* and *louvine*.
    Bar, café.

BARAQUET   (Languedoc) Local name for haricot bean.

BARAQUILLE   Triangular stuffed pastry, served hot as a starter.

BARATTÉ(-E)   Churned.

BARBADINE   Passion fruit, also known as *fruit de Passion*.

BARBARIN   Name for red mullet (*rouget*).

BARBARINE   Type of vegetable marrow.

BARBE-À-PAPA   Lit.: 'papa's beard'. Candyfloss.

BARBEAU   Barbel, common freshwater fish, with little taste, many bones and barbels around the mouth.

BARBE-DE-BOUC   Lit.: 'goat's beard'. Wild variety of salsify (*salsifis*).

BARBE DE CAPUCIN   Lit.: 'friar's beard'. Variety of wild chicory (*chicorée*).

BARBE DE CHÊNE   Lit.: 'beard of oak'. Name of type of fungus (*clavaire*).

BARBERON   (S France) Local name of salsify (*salsifis*).

BARBERY   (Champagne) Soft cheese cured in ashes, made around the village of Barbery, near *Troyes*; also known as *Fromage de Troyes* and *Troyen Cendré*.

BARBEZIEUX   Town in *Charentes* known for poultry.

BARBILLON   Small barbel (*barbeau*).

BARBOTEUR   Lit.: 'paddler'. Name for duck (*canard*).

BARBOUILLADE   (Provence) Artichokes with broad beans; also aubergine stew.

(EN) BARBOUILLE   Lit.: 'smeared'. See *poulet*.

BARBUE   Brill, flat sea fish, lesser cousin of turbot; also known as *turbot lisse*, *rhum*, *roun* and *ro(u)mbou*. *Barbue Brancas*: sliced, baked with vegetables and tomato sauce; *chérubin*: baked with tomato sauce, sweet peppers and truffles, served with *hollandaise* sauce; *portaise*: poached, with cream sauce and scallops. *Filets de barbue à la toulonnaise*: fillets fried in oil, with tomato and garlic sauce and aubergines.

BARDATTE   (Bretagne) Cabbage stuffed with hare, cooked in white wine, served with chestnuts and roast quail.

(À LA) BAREUZAI   (Bourgogne) Wine-based preparation for meat; corruption of 'bas rouges' – red stockings, of the grape-treaders, made red from the juice.

BARGE   Godwit, marsh bird, cooked like woodcock.

BARGENCOTE   Variety of small fig from *Provence*.

BARIGOULE/BERIGUOLO/BOURIGOULE/BRIGOULE   Type of fungus similar to *mousseron*. See also *artichaut*.

(À LA) BARISIENNE   In the style of *Bar-le-Duc*.

BAR-LE-DUC   Capital of the Meuse department in *Lorraine*, known for jams.

BARNACHE   Name for limpet (*patelle*).

BARON   Large joint comprising the two legs and saddle, usually of lamb or mutton.

BARON BRISSE   19th-century cookery writer. See *rouget*.

BARONNET   Lit.: 'baronet'. See *banane*.

BARQUETTE   Small boat-shaped pastry.

BARSAC   Commune of *Sauternes*, *Bordeaux*, whose sweet white wines (*AC*) may be sold as *Barsac* or *Sauternes*; its best known châteaux are Coutet and Climens.

BARTAVELLE   Rock partridge, common in the Alps; also red partridge.

BAS(-SE)   Low.

BAS-ARMAGNAC   See *Armagnac*.

BASELLE   Indian spinach; used like ordinary spinach.

BASILIC   Sweet basil, the herb.

BASILLAC   See *Bleu de Basillac*.

BAS-MÉDOC   See *Médoc*.

(À LA) BASQUAISE   In the style of *Pays basque*. With tomatoes, peppers, rice etc (e.g. *consommé basquaise*). Garnish of *cèpes*, *Bayonne* ham and potatoes. *Pommes* (*de terre*) *basquaise*: baked potatoes stuffed with tomatoes, sweet peppers, ham and garlic. See also *piment*.

BASQUE   Basque, of *Pays basque*. The Basque language. See also *gâteau* and *Pays basque*.

BASSE   Feminine of *bas*: low.

BASSE VENAISON   Lit.: 'low venison'. Meat of hare, rabbit.

BASSIN   Lit.: 'basin'. Name for limpet (*patelle*).

BASTARDEAU   (Berry) Local name for bustard (*outarde*).

BASTELLE   (Corse) Vegetable pastry.

BA-TA-CLAN   Rich almond and rum pastry.

BÂTARDE   Lit.: 'female bastard'. Vienna roll. *Sauce bâtarde*: thick butter sauce.

BÂTARD-MONTRACHET   *Grand cru* (*AC*) vineyard shared between the communes of *Chassagne-Montrachet* and *Puligny-Montrachet* in *Côte de Beaune*, *Bourgogne*.

BATAVIA   Short for *laitue Batavia*.

(À LA) BATELIÈRE   Lit.: 'boatman's style'. Garnish for fish of mushrooms, onions, fried eggs and crayfish; also pastry boats filled with seafood in white sauce.

BÂTON(NET)   Lit.: 'stick'. Small French loaf. Stick-shaped biscuit or pastry. *Soupe au bâton* (Provence): soup traditionally stirred with a branch of bay.

BATTU(-E)   Beaten, whipped up, of eggs etc. See also *gâteau*.

BAUDROIE   Name for monkfish (*lotte*).

(LES) BAUGES   See *Chevrette des Bauges*, *Tomme de Savoie* and *Vacherin*.

BAUME   Balm, mint-type herb.

(LES) BAUX-DE-PROVENCE   See *Coteaux des Baux-de-Provence*.

BAVAROIS   Bavarian. Cold dessert of thick egg custard and whipped cream set in a mould, variously flavoured, often served with fruit; also known as *crème bavaroise* and originally as *fromage bavarois*.
    Savoury mould/loaf, especially of shellfish.

BAVECCA   Name for (freshwater) blenny (*blennie cagnette*).

BAVETTE   Skirt, of beef.

BAVEUSE   Lit.: 'runny'. Blenny, small sea fish.

(À LA) BAYONNAISE   In the style of *Bayonne*. *Oeufs frits à la bayonnaise*: fried eggs with *Bayonne* ham. See also *côte*, *jambon*, *poularde* and *riz*.

BAYONNE   Town in *Pays basque*, famous for ham; see *jambon*.

BÉARN   Province covering two thirds of the Pyrénées-Atlantiques department.
    Red, white and rosé wine, made in *Béarn*, known as *Vin du Béarn* (*AC*).

(À LA) BÉARNAISE   In the style of *Béarn*. See *cèpe*, *daube*, *palombe* and *poule*.
    With *sauce béarnaise*: thick sauce of egg yolks, vinegar, shallots, tarragon and white wine with butter; created at *Saint-Germain* around 1830, usually served with steaks (e.g. *entrecôte béarnaise*), sometimes with lamb.

BÉATILLES   Poultry offal.

BÉATRIX   Garnish of carrots, mushrooms, potatoes and artichokes.

BEAU (BELLE) Beautiful.

(À LA) BEAUCAIRE Château-town in *Provence* once famous for its fair. See *anguille*, *carré* and *pastissoun*.

BEAUCE Region in *Orléanais*.

(À LA) BEAUCERONNE In the style of *Beauce*. *Omelette beauceronne*: omelette with bacon, sorrel and potatoes. See also *culotte*, *gâteau* and *pâté*.

BEAUFORT (Savoie) Large round cheese (*AOC*), with smooth ivory interior, rich and fruity; made in small dairies in the Beaufort mountains, also known as *Gruyère de Beaufort*. See also *Tomme de Chèvre*.

BEAUGÉ Popular singer in *Bordelais* in the 1920's. See *rognon*.

(À LA) BEAUGENCY Garnish of poached eggs, bone marrow, artichokes and *béarnaise* sauce.

BEAUHARNAIS Family which became prominent after Napoleon's marriage to Josephine Beauharnais. Garnish of stuffed mushrooms and artichokes. *Sauce Beauharnais: béarnaise* sauce with green tarragon butter. See also *banane*.

BEAUJOLAIS Region at the southern tip of *Bourgogne*, bordering *Lyonnais*, famous for its light red wines from the *Gamay* grape. The general *Beaujolais AC* covers a large area of about 60 communes; *Beaujolais supérieur* has a higher degree of alcohol than basic *Beaujolais*; and about half the communes, all in the N, have the right to the higher *AC Beaujolais-Villages*. The finest wines come from the *Beaujolais crus* – nine villages, each with their own *AC* – *Moulin-à-Vent*, *Juliénas*, *Morgon*, *Chénas*, *Fleurie*, *Saint-Amour*, *Chiroubles*, *Brouilly* and *Côte de Brouilly*. Some white and rosé wines are also made.

BEAULIEU See *poulet*.

BEAUMES-DE-VENISE Town in *Vaucluse*, and its fortified sweet wines (*AC*) from the *Muscat* grape.

BEAUMONT (Savoie) Mild cheese, made around the town of Beaumont.

BEAUNE Historic town in *Bourgogne*, centre for the wine trade and commune (*AC*) growing mainly red wines. Although it contains no *grands crus*, Beaune has 34 *premier cru* vineyards; also the home of the *Hospices de Beaune*, endowed with some of the best vineyards of the *Côte de Beaune*.

BEAUVAIS Capital of the Oise department in *Ile-de-France*.

(À LA) BEAUVAISIENNE   In the style of *Beauvais*. See *truite*.

BEAUVILLIERS   Founder of the first luxury restaurant in Paris in 1872. Cream cake with almonds and *kirsch*.

BÉCASSE   Woodcock, considered to be the finest winged game; gourmets insist that it should be cooked undrawn, with only the gizzard removed, while the choicest bit is supposed to be the trail (intestines), chopped up with bacon or *foie gras*, flavoured with brandy and spices, spread on fried bread. *Bécasse à la Diane*: cold, roasted, stuffed with the trail and truffles; *à la fine Champagne*: roasted, cut up, and served in a sauce of the best *Cognac*, chopped intestines and its own blood; *à la Riche*: roasted, served on fried bread with brandy, *foie gras* and butter sauce.

BÉCASSEAU   Young woodcock; name for sandpiper (*alouette de mer*).

BÉCASSE DE MER   Trumpet fish, large sea fish, also known as *voilier porte-glaive*.
Name for red mullet (*rouget*), from the fact that, like woodcock, it may be cooked ungutted.

BÉCASSIN   Great snipe; also known as *cul-blanc* (white-tail) because of its white marking.

BÉCASSINE   Snipe; the finest part of the bird is supposed to be the brain.

BÉCASSINE DE MER   Name for garfish (*aiguille*).

BÉCASSINE LA SOURDE   Lit.: 'snipe the deaf'. Jack snipe, smaller type of snipe, often silent when flushed.

BECFIGUE/BECFIN/BEC-FIN   Figpecker, tiny bird found particularly in S France, usually grilled on skewers; also known as *gobemouche*. *Becfigues à l'arlésienne*: baked in a bread loaf with mushrooms; *à la landaise*: wrapped in vine leaves and bacon, grilled on skewers, served with *Armagnac* and grapes.

BÉCHAMEL White sauce made with flour, butter and milk, one of the 'mother' sauces and the basis for others (e.g. *Mornay* and *Soubise*). Possibly invented by the Marquis de Béchameil in Louis XIV's reign.

BECKENOFFE See *backenoff*.

BEC-POINTU Lit.: 'sharp beak'. Name for white skate (*raie blanche*).

BEDEU (Provence) Local name for tripe (*tripes*).

BEDJAR (Charentes) Local name for type of clam (*mye*).

BEGUINETTE Garden warbler, similar to *becfigue*, found in N France.

BEIGNE(T) Fritter, sweet or savoury.

BELLE Feminine of *beau*: beautiful. Beauty. Used to describe varieties of fruit and vegetables – *Belle-Alliance*, *Belle-Angevine* (see also *poire*), *Belle-de-Berry*, *Belle-et-Bonne* (pear); *Belle-Chevreuse*, *Belle-Garde* (peach); *Belle de Juillet*: variety of potato; *Belle de Soissons*: white haricot bean.

BELLE AURORE Lit.: 'beautiful dawn'. See *poularde*.

BELLE BRESSANE (Bresse) Smooth, creamy blue cheese, round with hole in centre, factory-made; similar to *Bleu de Bresse*.

(À LA) BELLE-DIJONNAISE With blackcurrants, for which *Dijon* is well known. Fruit with blackcurrant ice and purée and *crème de cassis*.

BELLEGARDE Village in *Gard*, making white wine (*AC*) from the *Clairette* grape.

BELLE-HÉLÈNE Garnish of asparagus croquettes, truffles, mushrooms etc. See also *poire*.

BELLE-ÎLE Island off *Bretagne*. See *congre*.

BELLET Area near *Nice*, making fine red, white and rosé wines (*AC*) in small quantities.

(À LA) BELLEVILLAISE In the style of Belleville-sur-Saône in *Lyonnais*. *Oeufs à la bellevillaise*: baked eggs with onions and sausage.

BELLEVILLE See *Tomme de Savoie*.

BELLE VUE Lit.: 'beautiful view'. Elaborately displayed dish, often served cold in jelly (e.g. *saumon en belle vue*).

BELLEY   Capital of *Bugey*, and birthplace of *Brillat-Savarin*. See also *Tomme de Chèvre*.

(À LA) BELLIFONTAINE   In the style of *Fontainebleau*.

BELLONE   Variety of large fig from *Provence*.

BELON   Oyster from *Bretagne*; see also *huître*.

BELUGA   See *caviar*.

BELUGO   Name for red sea bream (*dorade*).

BELVAL   (Picardie) Mild firm cheese with shiny rind, made at the Abbey of Belval; also known as *Trappiste de Belval*.

BÉNARI   (Languedoc) Local name for variety of *ortolan*.

BÉNÉDICT   *Oeufs Bénédict*: poached eggs with *hollandaise* sauce and ham.

BÉNÉDICTIN   Cake flavoured with *Bénédictine*.

BÉNÉDICTINE   Lit.: 'Benedictine' (monk). Liqueur invented by a Benedictine monk in the 16th century, distilled at Fécamp in *Normandie*; also known as *liqueur de Fécamp*.
   Garnish, for fish or eggs, of pounded cod with garlic, cream and perhaps truffles, covered with cream sauce. See also *morue*.

(À LA) BÉNÉVENT   See *noisette*. *Talleyrand* was Prince de Bénévent.

BENOÎTE   Herb bennet, used as a salad green.

(À LA) BENOÎTON   With onion and red wine sauce, of fish.

BERAWECKA/BIREWECK   (Alsace) Bread roll with dried fruit, *kirsch* and spices.

BERCY   The Quai de Bercy, area of wine warehouses in *Paris*. With red or white wine, shallots and bone marrow, as in *beurre/sauce Bercy*. *Oeufs Bercy*: fried eggs with sausage and tomato sauce. *Vin de Bercy*: plonk, cheap wine, the implication being that the wines which come out of Bercy are not always the same as when they went in.

BERDANEL   Name for type of fungus (*russule*).

BERGAMOTE   Bergamot, variety of orange. Variety of pear.

BERGER   Lit.: 'shepherd.' *Soupe du berger* (Béarn): onion soup with cheese, tomatoes, leeks and garlic.
   Brand of *pastis*.

(À LA) BERGÈRE Lit.: 'shepherdess's style.' Meat or poultry baked with ham, onions, mushrooms and straw potatoes.

BERGERAC Major town in *Périgord*, producing red, white and rosé wines (*AC*), using the same grape varieties as in *Bordeaux*.

BERGERETTE *Salade bergerette*: rice, hard-boiled egg and chive salad.

BERGUES (Flandre) Small round cheese cured in beer, with sharp taste; made around the town of Bergues. See also *hareng de Bergues*.

BERIGOULO Name for type of fungus (*barigoule*).

BERLINGOT Boiled sweet, usually peppermint-flavoured.

BERLINGUETO (Provence) Chopped spinach with hard-boiled eggs.

BERLO Type of watercress from *Vaucluse*.

BERNACH/BERNACLE Name for limpet (*patelle*).

BERNARD-L'(H)ERMITE Lit.: 'Bernard the hermit.' Hermit crab, which takes over the shells of other creatures; also known as *pagure*.

BERNICHE/BERNICLE/BERNIQUE Name for limpet (*patelle*).

BERNY Garnish of potato croquettes, chestnut tartlets and pepper sauce, for game. *Pommes (de terre) Berny*: potato and truffle croquettes.

(À LA) BERRICHONNE In the style of *Berry*. Garnish of cabbage rolls, onions, chestnuts and bacon. Cooked in blood, of meat. *Pommes (de terre) berrichonne*: potatoes browned and cooked in stock with bacon and onions, or with black pudding. See also *flan*, *princesse*, *rognon*, *terrine* and *Valençay*.

BERRY Province equivalent to the departments of Cher and Indre.

BERTON (Savoie) Cheese *fondue* with garlic and wine.

BESANÇON   Capital of the Doubs department in *Franche-Comté*.

BESI   Variety of pear.

BESUGO   (Pays basque) Sea bream (*dorade*) with garlic and peppers.

BETHMALE   (Foix) Hard strong cheese, made by farms and dairies in the Bethmale valley and environs; also known as *Aulus*, *Castillon*, *Cier de Luchon*, *Ercé*, *Ousted* and *Saint-Lizier*.

BÉTHUNE   Town in *Artois*. See *fromage*.

BETTE   Spinach beet, similar to Swiss chard (*blette*).

BETTERAVE   Beetroot, thought to have been introduced to France by Napoleon. *Betteraves à la provençale*: beetroot, potato and hard-boiled egg salad with anchovy dressing.

BEUCHELLE À LA TOURANGELLE   Veal sweetbreads and kidneys with morels and truffles in cream sauce; invented by the chef to Emperor Franz Josef of Austria, and based on a Viennese dish 'Beuschell'.

BEUDA   (Languedoc) Local name for clam (*palourde*).

BEUGNON   (Berry, Orleánais) Sweet, ring-shaped fritter.

BEURRE   Butter. *Beurre demi-sel*: slightly salted; *doux*: unsalted, the commonest. Fine butter is produced in many parts of France, and there is an *AC beurre des Charentes (et du Poitou)*.

Savoury butter, in which a flavouring is beaten into butter, then chilled, often served as a slice on top of meat, especially steaks and chops, or fish. *Beurre Bercy*: with white wine, bone marrow and shallot; *maître d'hôtel*: with parsley; *marchand de vin*: with shallot and red wine; *de Montpellier*: with herbs, anchovies, capers, gherkins and eggs; *de ravigote*: with herbs and shallot; *rouge*: red, with shellfish, and see also below; *vert*: green, with herbs.

Butter sauce, served hot. *Beurre blanc* (Nantais, Anjou, Touraine): the famous 'white butter', reduction of shallots and vinegar or *Muscadet* wine, whipped up with butter, served especially with fish like pike and shad, supposedly invented to counteract their dryness; *breton*: herb butter; *meunière*: brown butter (*beurre noisette*) with lemon juice and parsley; *noir*: butter heated until almost black, with vinegar added, served especially with skate and brains; *noisette*: butter heated to light brown nut colour; *rouge*: made like *beurre blanc* but with red wine.

Butter-type paste or sauce. *Beurre de Gascogne*: pork lard mixed with garlic, served with lentils or vegetables. *Beurre de Provence*: name for *aïoli*. See also *petit beurre*.

BEURRÉ   Variety of pear.

BEURRÉE   Slice of buttered bread.

BEURSAUDES   (Nivernais, Morvan) Fried and baked pieces of pork, kept in earthenware jars and eaten warm; also known as *gri(ll)audes*. See also *galette*.

BÉZUQUE   (Provence) Local name for type of sea bream (*pageau*).

(À LA) BIARROTTE   In the style of Biarritz in *Pays basque*. Garnish of *cèpes* and potato cakes. *Soupe de poissons à la biarrotte*: soup of mixed fish, goose fat, sorrel and lettuce. See also *poulet*.

BIBBELSKÄSE   (Alsace) Home-made mixture of fresh cheese flavoured with horseradish and herbs.

BICHE   Doe, hind, of deer. (Vivarais) Mutton tripe and potatoes in layers, cooked in the baker's oven.

BIENVENUES-BÂTARD-MONTRACHET   See *Puligny-Montrachet*.

BIÈRE   Beer. *Bière blonde/brune*: pale/brown ale. *Bière bouteille/pression*: bottled/draft beer. *Bière limonade*: shandy, also known as *panaché*. *Soupe à la bière* (N France): chicken soup with beer and onions. See also *saucisse*.

BIFTE(A)CK   Steak, of beef or perhaps horse, fried or grilled (but treat with caution). *Bifteck à cheval*: fried or grilled steak with fried eggs on top.
                 Minced beef. *Bifteck à l'américaine*: name for *steak tartare*; *haché/à la hambourgeoise*: hamburger, also known as *steak à l'allemande*; *poitevin*: with sorrel and bone marrow; *à la russe*: see *bitok*.

BIGARADE   Bitter orange. *Sauce bigarade*: orange sauce, for wild duck or game.

BIGARREAU   Variety of cherry.

BIGNON   (Bourbonnais) Sweet fritter.

BIGORNEAU   Winkle, also known as *biou*, *brelin*, *escargot/limaçon de mer*, *guignette*, *littorine*, *vigneau*, *vignot* and *vignette*.

BIGORRE   Region corresponding to the Hautes-Pyrénées department, E of *Béarn*.

BIGOUDEN   Region in *Bretagne*.

(À LA) BIGOUDENN   In the style of *Bigouden*. *Pommes (de terre) à la bigoudenn*: baked, sliced, unpeeled potatoes. See also *chotenn* and *ragoût*.

(À LA) BIGOURDANE   In the style of *Bigorre*.

BIGUENÉE   (Nantais, Vendée) Sliced ham wrapped in pancake and fried.

BIJANE   (Anjou) Cold soup of bread in sweetened red wine.

BILLY BY/BYE   *Potage Billy By*: cream of mussel soup. Perhaps invented at Maxim's in *Paris* for a customer known as Billy; or served at a farewell dinner for an American soldier in *Normandie*.

BIOU   Name for winkle (*bigorneau*).

BIREWECK   See *berawecka*.

BIS(-E)   Wholemeal, as in *pain bis*.

(À LA) BISCAÏENNE   In the style of the Bay of Biscay. Garnish of piped potatoes, lettuce and cauliflower. See also *morue*.

BISCOTIN   Sweet biscuit.

BISCOTTE   Rusk.

BISCUIT   Sponge cake, sponge mixture, lighter and drier than *génoise*; used as the basis for many cakes, also for *biscuit de Savoie*, and for *biscuit à la cuiller*: sponge finger. *Biscuit glacé*: ice-cream with sponge and fruit and/or liqueur. *Biscuit (sec)*: biscuit, cracker.

(À LA) BISONTINE   In the style of *Besançon*.

BISOTTE   Name for variety of fungus (*russule*).

BISQUE   Thick soup based on puréed seafood, often lobster, with white wine, tomato purée and cream; originally, game soup coloured red with crayfish. *Bisque aux légumes*: puréed lentil soup plus other vegetables, with paprika.

BISQUEBOUILLE   (Provence) Soup of freshwater and sea fish, with *anis* and garlic, thickened with eggs, cream and *aïoli*.

BISSALÉ   (Picardie) Buttered bread dough.

BISTORTO   (Foix) Ring-shaped *brioche* flavoured with saffron and aniseed; also known as *coco* and *coucou*.

BISTOUILLE   (Flandre) Coffee laced with spirit.

BISTRO(T)   Café, snack bar, small restaurant. The *bistro* came into fashion in Paris in the 1940s; various theories for its origin connect it with 'bistouiller' – to make bad mixtures; with 'bastringue' – dance hall; and with 'bystro' –

quick, supposedly shouted by hungry Russian soldiers as they made for the cafés on entering Paris in 1815.

(À LA) BITERROISE   In the style of Béziers in *Languedoc*.

BITOK   Minced meat or poultry cake, fried and served with sour cream, of Russian origin; also known as *bifteck à la russe* when of beef.

BLADE   (Provence) Local name for saddled bream (*oblade*).

BLAGNY   Village of the *Côte de Beaune*, *Bourgogne*, making red wine (*AC*); its white wine is generally sold as *Meursault-Blagny*.

(À LA) BLAISOISE/BLÉSOISE   In the style of *Blois*.

BLANC(-HE)   White. White wine. White, of egg. *Blanc (de volaille)*: white meat, of chicken. *Au blanc*: cooked to preserve whiteness or paleness (e.g. of brains, artichokes). See also *hareng* and *seiche*.

BLANC-CASSIS   See *Kir*.

BLANC DE BLANC(S)   Lit.: 'white of white'. White wine made from white grapes, but only significant applied to *Champagne* (normally made from a blend of red and white grapes).

BLANC-FUMÉ   See *Pouilly-Blanc-Fumé*.

BLANCHAILLE   Whitebait, invariably deep-fried.

BLANCHE   Feminine of *blanc*: white.

BLANCHE-NEIGE   Lit.: 'snow-white'. Cold chicken, fish etc, coated in a firm cream sauce.

BLANCHET   Name for small clam (*fausse palourde*).

BLANCHI(-E)   White, whitened.

BLANCHOTS   See *Chablis*.

BLANC-MANGER   Blancmange, correctly almond milk with gelatine chilled in a mould.

BLANQUET   Variety of pear.

BLANQUETTE   Stew of veal, lamb, chicken or seafood (previously simmered in stock, as opposed to sautéed for a *fricassée*), in white sauce made from cream and egg yolks.

BLANQUETTE DE LIMOUX   Sparkling white wine (*AC*), said to be the oldest in France, from around Limoux in *Aude*; not to be confused with *Vin de Blanquette*.
    Vin de Blanquette: still white wine from the same area.

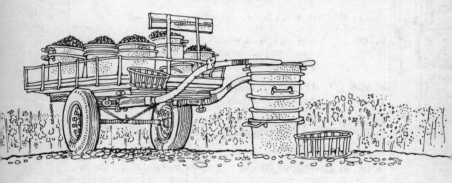

BLAVET   Name for type of fungus (*russule*).

BLAYE   See *Côtes de Blaye*.

BLÉ   Corn, wheat. *Blé noir*: buckwheat, also known as *sarrasin*. *Blé de Turquie*: maize, sweet corn, also known as *maïs*.

BLÉA   (Provence) Local name for chard (*blette*).

BLENNIE CAGNETTE   Blenny, scaleless freshwater fish; also known as *bavecca*, *chasseur* and *lièvre*.

(À LA) BLÉSOISE   See *blaisoise*.

BLÈTE   See *blette*.

BLETTE   Swiss chard, vegetable similar to spinach beet (*bette*), cultivated for its large leaves and especially the fleshy white ribs, which are sometimes known as *cardes/côtes de blette*; also known as *bette*, *bléa*, *blète*, *jointes*, *jottes* and *poirée à carde*.

BLEU(-E)   Blue. Term for steak cooked very rare.
    Au bleu: method of cooking trout especially, by plunging into boiling vinegar *court-bouillon* as soon as it is killed and gutted, resulting in a bluish tinge to the skin.
    Blue-veined cheese (see below); or cheese with a bluish rind.

BLEU D'AUVERGNE   (Auvergne) Uncooked unpressed blue-veined cheese (*AOC*) in the form of a large disk, with sharp smell and flavour; created by a 19th-century peasant.

BLEU DE BASILLAC   (Limousin) Blue sheep's milk cheese, also known as *Basillac*.

BLEU DE BRESSE   (Bresse) Factory-made blue cheese in the shape of a small cylinder, creamy and smooth with strong flavour; also known as *Bresse Bleu*, and *Grièges* after the town.

BLEU DES CAUSSES   (Rouergue) *AOC* cheese, large, cylindrical, lightly veined and supple, made from the milk of cows pastured on the chalk plateau (*Causses*), which gives it a distinctive flavour.

BLEU DE CORSE   (Corse) Blue sheep's milk cheese made in shepherds' huts, cured in caves; the only cheese to resemble *Roquefort*.

BLEU DE COSTAROS   See *Bleu de Loudes*.

BLEU DE GEX-HAUT-JURA   (Franche-Comté) Large round blue-veined cheese (*AOC*), best between May and October when the herbs in the milk give a pronounced taste; made in mountains of the Gex region, also known as *Gex* and *(Bleu de) Septmoncel*.

BLEU DE LAQUEUILLE   (Auvergne) Similar to *Bleu d'Auvergne*, made around Laqueuille.

BLEU DE LOUDES   (Languedoc) Firm round blue cheese, with little smell but savoury flavour; made in the *Velay* region, also known as *Bleu du Velay*, *Bleu de Costaros*, and *Fourme du Mézenc*.

BLEU DE SAINTE-FOY   (Savoie) Similar to *Bleu de Tignes*, made around Sainte-Foy.

BLEU DE SASSENAGE/DE SEPTMONCEL   See *Sassenage* and *Bleu de Gex-Haut-Jura*.

BLEU DE THIÉZAC   (Auvergne) Similar to *Bleu d'Auvergne*, made around Thiézac.

BLEU DE TIGNES   (Savoie) Small round blue-veined cheese, smooth and even, with strong flavour; made by dairies and farms around Tignes, also known as *Persillé de Tignes* and *Tignard*.

BLEU DU QUERCY   (Quercy) Similar to *Bleu d'Auvergne*.

BLEU DU VELAY   See *Bleu de Loudes*.

BLINI   Small thick Russian pancake.

BLOIS   Capital of the Loir-et-Cher department in *Orléanais*.

BLOND(-E)   Fair, blond; light-coloured, pale.
Blonde: pale ale.

BOEUF   Beef. See *aloyau, bifteack chateaubriand, contre-filet, côte, culotte, entrecôte, filet, gîte à la noix, pièce de boeuf, queue de boeuf, rumsteak, steak, tournedos*, for major cuts. *Boeuf à la bourguignonne/boeuf bourguignon*: cooked in red wine with bacon, small onions and mushrooms, the classic dish of *Bourgogne*, also adopted by *Paris*, often just *bourguignon*; *à la ficelle*: tied with string, roasted, then dropped by the string into broth; *à la gardiane* (Camargue): marinated, then stewed with onions, tomatoes, garlic, olives and red wine; *au gros sel*: boiled, with vegetables and sea salt; *miroton*: reheated slices with onions, mustard and broth; *à la mode*: simmered in wine with vegetables and herbs, served hot, or cold in jelly.
  Star-gazer, common Mediterranean fish; also known as *rat*, and *miou* and *muou* in *Provence*.

BOGARAVELLE   Type of a sea bream.

BOGUE   Boops, brightly coloured Mediterranean fish.

(À LA) BOHÉMIENNE   Lit.: 'Bohemian-', 'gypsy-style'. Garnish of rice, tomatoes, onions, sweet peppers and paprika. *Pommes (de terre) bohémienne*: baked potatoes filled with sausage. See also *boumiane* and *faisan*.

BOIS   Wood. *Au bois de chêne*: smoked over oak wood.

BOISSON   Drink. *Boisson sucré*: soft drink.

BOÎTELLE   Poached in white wine with mushrooms, of fish.

BOIVIN   See *poulet*.

BOLES/BOULES DE PICOULAT   (Roussillon) Small meat balls.

BOLET   Boletus, large family of fungi, fleshy and usually very good to eat; also known as *cèpe*. Main varieties also known as *cèpe de Bordeaux/d'été/noir, champignon polonais* and *tête de nègre*.

BOMBE (GLACÉE)   Ice cream of two different flavours, originally made in a spherical mould. *Bombe cardinal*: raspberry filled with vanilla; *favorite*: chestnut filled with apricot; *Monte-Carlo*: vanilla filled with strawberry.

BON(-NE)   Good.

BONBEL   Brand name for *Saint-Paulin* cheese.

BONBON   Sweet, candy. *Bonbon acidulé*: acid drop; *anglais*: fruit drop; *fourré*: soft-centred sweet.

BON-CHRÉTIEN   Lit.: 'good Christian'. Variety of pear, first planted by Saint François de Paule in *Touraine*.

BONDARD   (Normandie) Soft, creamy cheese made by farms, with strong smell and fruity flavour; shaped like the bung ('bonde') of a barrel.

BONDAROY AU FOIN   (Orléanais) Small tangy cheese covered with wisps of hay (*foin*) in which it is cured, made by farms and small dairies around Bondaroy and Pithiviers; also known as *Pithiviers au Foin*.

BONDON (DE NEUFCHÂTEL)   See *Neufchâtel*.

BON-HENRI   Wild spinach; also known in English as 'good King Henry'.

BONITE   Bonito; small oily fish similar to tuna, often sold in steaks; also known as *pelamide*.

BONITOU   (S France) Local name for frigate mackerel (*melva*).

BONNE   Feminine of *bon*: good.

BONNE-DAME   Lit.: 'good lady'. Name for orache (*arroche*).

BONNE-FEMME   Lit.: 'good woman', 'wife'. Baked with potatoes, onions, mushrooms and bacon, of chicken. Poached in white wine with onions and mushrooms, in a potato border, of fish, especially sole. *Oeufs bonne-femme*: baked eggs with mushrooms. *Potage/soupe bonne-femme*: potato and leek soup, sometimes plus carrots. See also *crêpe*, *haricot vert* and *pomme*.

BONNES MARES   *Grand cru* vineyard of *Côte de Nuits*, *Bourgogne*, divided between the communes of *Chambolle-Musigny* and *Morey-Saint-Denis*, producing fine red wine (*AC*).

BONNEVILLE   See *Pavé de Moyaux*.

BONNEZEAUX   Sweet white wine (*AC*) made in *Anjou*.

BONVALET   Cake almost identical to *Beauvilliers*.

Potage Bonvalet: turnip, potato, leek and haricot bean soup.

BORDEAUX   Capital of *Gironde* and of *Bordelais*.

The most important area of France for the production of fine wine. The finest reds are from *Médoc*, *Graves*, *Saint-Emilion* and *Pomerol*; the finest whites are the great dessert wines of *Sauternes* and *Barsac*; some magnificent dry whites are also made in *Graves*. *Appellation Contrôlée* works as follows: most of the production is simply *AC Bordeaux*; then comes *Bordeaux supérieur*, indicating a higher degree of alcohol; next, the name of a defined district (e.g. *Graves*, *Saint-Emilion*); finally the name of an individual commune or

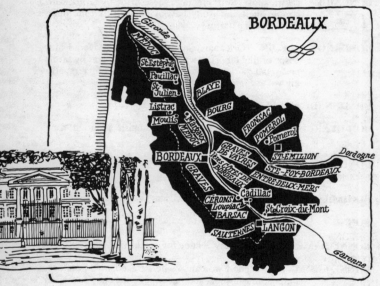

village, like *Margaux*, *Pauillac* or *Saint-Estèphe*. This is the highest *AC*. The greatest wines such as Château Latour or Château Lafite-Rothschild are simply *AC Pauillac*, along with other wines produced in the commune of *Pauillac* (and unlike the finest wines of *Bourgogne* have no *AC* of their own). However, the top quality wines of *Médoc* were separately classified in 1855, divided into 5 classes or *crus*: at the top the *premiers crus* – Lafite-Rothschild, Latour, Château Margaux, Mouton-Rothschild and Haut-Brion (in fact in the *Graves*), followed by 14 *deuxièmes crus*, 15 *troisièmes crus*, 10 *quatrièmes crus* and 18 *cinquièmes crus*; all carry the term *cru classé* on their labels. Under these ranks of the very finest red wines are other classifications of *cru bourgeois*, *bourgeois supérieur*, *grand bourgeois*, *bourgeois exceptionnel*, all wines of excellent quality. The wines of *Saint-Emilion* are also classified into 12 *premiers grands crus* and about 70 *grands crus*.

BORDELAIS   Area around *Bordeaux*, roughly the same as *Gironde*.

(À LA) BORDELAISE   In the style of *Bordelais* or *Bordeaux*. With *sauce bordelaise*: sauce of shallots, red or white wine, butter, tarragon and sometimes bone marrow (e.g. *entrecôte à la bordelaise*). Of fish and shellfish, cooked in wine with vegetables and herbs; see also *homard*, *huître*, *lamproie* and *morue*. Or simply cooked in wine (e.g. *pêches à la bordelaise*). Garnished with *cèpes* sautéed in oil with shallots and parsley (*cèpes à la bordelaise*) and potatoes. With finely diced vegetables and sometimes ham. Garnish of artichokes and potatoes, for poultry. *Pommes* (*de terre*) *bordelaise*: potatoes cooked in butter with garlic.

BORDET VERT   Name for type of fungus (*russule*).

BORDURE   Border, ring (e.g. of potatoes).

BORGHÈSE   *Consommé Borghèse*: clear chicken soup with asparagus tips and chicken breast.

BORIS   See *esturgeon*.

BORTSCH   Beetroot soup with cream, of Russian origin.

BOSSONS (MACÉRÉS)   (Languedoc) Home-made mixture of goat's milk cheese steeped in oil, white wine and *marc*.

BOSTON   See *filet*.

BOTT(E)REAU   (Nantais, Charentes) Sweet fritter.

BOUC   Name for goat (*chèvre*).
    (Charentes) Local name for shrimp (*crevette*).

BOUCHÉ(-E)   Bottled, stoppered, of wines and ciders, as opposed to straight from the barrel. See also *cidre*.

BOUCHÉE   Lit.: 'mouthful'. *Bouchée* (*à la reine*): small light pastry or *vol-au-vent* filled with savoury mixture, often chicken; created for Marie Leszcinska, gourmet queen of Louis XV. *Bouchées* (*au chocolat*): chocolates.

(À LA) BOUCHÈRE   Lit.: 'butcher's style'. *Consommé à la bouchère*: clear beef broth with cabbage and bone marrow on toast. *Salade bouchère*: cold boiled beef with tomatoes, potatoes and hard-boiled eggs.

BOUCHERIE Butcher's shop. *Boucherie chevaline*: horsemeat butcher.

BOUCHON Cork, of a bottle.
(Lyonnais) Small eating house specializing in sausage meals and wine.

BOUCHOT Wooden post on which mussels are cultivated; see *moule*.

BOUCOT Name for prawn (*crevette*).

BOUDIN Type of large fat sausage or savoury pudding, of two kinds. *Boudin noir*: black/blood pudding, made of pig's blood and suet wrapped in an intestine, usually grilled. *Boudin blanc*: white pudding, sort of large *quenelle*, of white pork meat, poultry or game, and fat, eggs, cream, but no blood. Among well-known types are *boudin blanc havrais*, *boudin de Brest*, *boudin de Saint-Romain*, *boudin de Strasbourg/alsacien*. *Boudin de langue*: see *zungenwurst*.

(À LA) BOUDINE See *saucisse*.

BOUDY Variety of apple.

BOUFFI Type of kippered herring (*hareng*).

BOUGNETTE (Languedoc) Pork sausage, eaten hot or cold.

BOUGON (Poitou) Small smooth goat's milk cheese with nutty flavour, made around Bougon.

BOUGRAS (Périgord) Cabbage, leek, onion and potato soup, using stock in which a black pudding has cooked; also known as *soupe à l'eau de boudin*.

(LES) BOURGROUS See *Chablis*.

BOUGUETTE (Auvergne) Sweet pancake.

BOUILLABAISSE (S France especially) Celebrated fish soup of *Provence*, found under different forms and names along the Mediterranean coast. Authentically, it should contain *rascasse*, conger eel and gurnard, plus many other fish (e.g. monkfish, John Dory, whiting, weever, *galinette*, red mullet, sea bass), often mussels, crab and *langouste*, with onion, tomato, saffron, garlic, herbs, orange peel, perhaps white wine or *Cognac*, and water and olive oil, boiled rapidly to amalgamate; served poured on slices of bread.
Bouillabaisse à la parisienne: northern version using more readily available fish. *Bouillabaisse borgne*: 'one-eyed' *bouillabaisse*, containing no fish but a mixed vegetable soup made on the same lines. See also *aigo* and *épinards*.

BOUILLADE (Roussillon) Sweet pepper, garlic and wine sauce, for snails, and for fish (where it becomes *bouillinade*); also known as *all grenat*.

BOUILLANT(-E) Boiling, hot.
Small pastry puff filled with chicken, served hot.

(LA) BOUILLE (Normandie) Soft creamy cheese, strong smelling and with fruity flavour; made around La Bouille, a version of *Monsieur-Fromage*.

BOUILLETURE/BOUILLITURE (W France) Freshwater fish stew, often of eels, with red wine, shallots, prunes and garlic.

BOUILLI(-E) Boiled. Boiled beef (*boeuf bouilli*) from a dish of boiled beef and broth (*pot-au-feu*), as opposed to the broth (*bouillon*).
Bouillie: gruel, porridge.

BOUILLINADA/BOUILLINADE (Roussillon) Fish stew, with potatoes, onions, garlic, peppers, oil and water; Catalan version of *bouillabaisse*.

BOUILLITURE See *bouilleture*.

BOUILLON Stock, broth, especially from a *pot-au-feu*; soup. *Bouillon de boeuf aux quenelles de moelle* (Alsace): broth from a *pot-au-feu* with bone marrow *quenelles*. *Bouillon de noce* (Périgord): soup of beef, calf's foot, stuffed chicken, vegetables, pasta. See also *court-bouillon*.

BOULAIGOU (Limousin) Thick pancake.

BOULANGERIE Bakery, baker's shop.

(À LA) BOULANGÈRE   Lit.: 'baker's style'. Braised or baked with onions and potatoes, of lamb, chicken, fish like cod; from the practice of bringing casseroles to the baker's oven for cooking. *Oeufs durs boulangère*: hot bread rolls filled with hard-boiled eggs and onion sauce.

BOULAUD   (Orléanais) Pastry cake with fruit.

BOULAY   Town in Lorraine. See *grenouille*.

BOULBON   Variety of apricot grown in *Provence*.

BOULE DE LILLE   See *Mimolette*.

BOULE DE NEIGE   Lit.: 'snowball'. Little round sponge cake or ice cream covered in whipped cream.
Name for variety of fungus (*psalliote*).

BOULE DES MOINES   See *Boulette de La Pierre-Qui-Vire*.

BOULES DE PICAULAT   See *boles de picoulat*.

BOULETTE   Small ball of food; meat ball; croquette. *Boulette de semoule*: semolina and potato croquette. See also below.

BOULETTE D'AVESNES   (Flandre) Soft herb-flavoured cheese with red rind, often pear-shaped, very strong smelling and tasting; made in the Avesnes region.

BOULETTE DE CAMBRAI   (Picardie) Fresh white mild herb-flavoured cheese; made in homes and farms around Cambrai.

BOULETTE DE LA PIERRE-QUI-VIRE   (Bourgogne) Fresh round herb-flavoured cheese, made at the Abbey of La Pierre-Qui-Vire; also known as *Boule des Moines*.

BOULIDO   See *aigo bouido*.

BOULONNAIS   Region between Boulogne and Calais on the *Picardie* coast.

(À LA) BOULONNAISE   In the style of *Boulonnais* or Boulogne. See *grondin* and *maquereau*.

BOULOT   Lit.: 'plump.' See *rabotte*.

BOUMIANE/BOUMIANO   (Provence) Dialect for *bohémienne*: gypsy; aubergine and tomato stew with anchovies.

BOUQUET   Lit.: 'bouquet, of flowers'. Name for prawn (*crevette*) and see also *crevette*.
Crowning piece, of decorative preparation.
Bouquet; nose, of wine.

BOUQUET GARNI   Bunch of herbs, to flavour soups, stews etc.

(À LA) BOUQUETIÈRE   Lit.: 'flower-seller's style'. Garnish of mixed vegetables in bouquets.

BOUQUETTE AUX POMMES DE TERRE   (Bourbonnais)   Small fried potato cake.

BOURBONNAIS   Province usually equated with the Allier department, although the southern cantons are sometimes assigned to *Auvergne*. See also *Chevrotin du Bourbonnais*.

(À LA) BOURBONNAISE   In the style of *Bourbonnais*. See *choufleur*, *pâté* and *tarte*.

BOURCETTE   Name for lamb's lettuce (*mâche*).

BOURDAINE   (Anjou, Maine) Apple dumpling with plum jam.

BOURDALOUE   Hot poached fruit with vanilla custard, crushed macaroons, apricot and *kirsch* sauce (e.g. *abricots Bourdaloue*). See also *tarte*. The rue Bourdaloue in *Paris* was known for *pâtisserie*, but the dish may have been named after a 17th-century preacher.

BOURDELOT   (Normandie) Whole apple pastry.

BOURG   See *Côtes de Bourg*.

BOURG-EN-BRESSE   Capital of the Ain department and of *Bresse*.

(À LA) BOURGEOISE   Lit.: 'bourgeois, middle-class, style'. *Cuisine bourgeoise*: good family cooking. With carrots, onions and bacon, usually of braised meat or poultry. See also *Bordeaux*.
   In the style of *Bourg-en-Bresse*.

BOURGES   Capital of the Cher department in *Berry*.

BOURGOGNE   Burgundy, province covering the departments of *Côte-d'Or*, Saône-et-Loire, Nièvre, Yonne and parts of Ain, *Rhône* and *Loire*.
   The name of Burgundy conjures up some of the finest wines in the world, and the vineyard area stretches from *Auxerre* in the N almost to *Lyon*, embracing 5 regions – *Chablis*; *Côte-d'Or*; *Côte chalonnaise* and *Mercurey*; *Mâconnais*; and *Beaujolais*. Wines entitled to *appellation contrôlée* fall broadly into four categories: first, wines within the regional *AC Bourgogne/Bourgogne Grand Ordinaire*; next, village or commune wines (e.g. *Nuits-Saint-Georges*, *Gevrey-Chambertin*, *Beaune*); then, wines of the second-rank vineyards of a commune, known as *premiers crus* (but not in the same sense as in

Bordeaux), where the name of the commune must also be present (e.g. *Nuits-Saint-Georges*-Les Porets, *Beaune*-Clos du Roi); finally, wines of the finest vineyards of the commune, known as *grands crus* or *têtes de cuvée*, where the name stands alone with its own *AC*, not that of the parish (e.g. *Le Montrachet*, *Le Chambertin*, *Bonnes Mares*, *La Romanée*).

See also *gros*.

BOURGOGNE-IRANCY   Red and rosé wines (*AC*) made in the village of Irancy, near *Chablis*.

BOURGUEIL   Area in *Touraine* which, together with neighbouring *Saint-Nicholas-de-Bourgueil*, produces red and rosé wines (*AC*).

(À LA) BOURGUIGNONNE   In the style of *Bourgogne*. With red wine sauce, mushrooms, small onions and sometimes bacon (e.g. *boeuf bourguignonne*). *Oeufs en bourguignonne*: poached eggs in wine sauce. *Potée bourguignonne*: cabbage and salt pork soup with sausage, vegetables etc, poured over slices of bread. *Omelette bourguignonne*: pig's blood omelette. See also *escargot*, *fondue*, *glace* and *matelote*.

BOURIGOULE   Name for type of fungus (*barigoule*).

BOURRACHE   Borage, herb, used in salads, drinks etc.

BOURRE-CHRÊTIEN   Lit.: 'Christian padding'. See *truffiat*.

BOURRIDE   (S France) Fish stew with *aïoli*, poured on slices of bread.

BOURRIOLE   (Auvergne) Sweet or savoury pancake.

BOURSADAS   (Limousin) Boiled chestnuts.

BOURSAULT   See *Lucullus*.

BOURSE-À-BERGER/BOURSE-À-PASTEUR/BOURSETTE   Lit.: 'shepherd's purse'. Name for lamb's lettuce (*mâche*).

BOURSIN   (Ile-de-France, Normandie) Factory-made, soft, round, creamy cheese, usually flavoured with herbs or garlic.

BOURSOTTO   (Nice) Small pastry stuffed with vegetables, rice, anchovies and Parmesan cheese.

BOUTARGUE   (Provence) Paste of dried salted pressed mullet or tuna roe; also known as *poutargue* and *caviare blanc*.

BOUTEILLE   Bottle. See also *mise*.

Burgundy and Beaujolais · Bordeaux · Champagne · Alsace · Languedoc-Roussillon · Loire · Vin de Table · Côtes du Rhone · Provence

BOUTIFARE/BOUTIFARON (Roussillon) Black pudding of bacon and herbs.

BOUTON-DE-CULOTTE Lit.: 'breeches button'. (Bourgogne) *Mâconnais* cheese aged until hard and very sharp.

BOUZIGUE Variety of large mussel cultivated at Bouzigues in *Languedoc*, often eaten raw with vinegar and shallots.

BOUZY Village in *Champagne* making still red wine.

(À LA) BRABANÇONNE In the style of Brabant (Belgian province). With Brussels sprouts. With chicory or hop shoots.

BRACQ/BROCKEL/BROQ (Lorraine) Fresh, home-made curd cheese.

BRAGANCE Braganza, in Portugal. Garnish of stuffed tomatoes and croquette potatoes. *Oeufs Bragance*: poached eggs on fried tomatoes with *béarnaise* sauce.

BRAISE Charcoal. *Sur la braise/les braises*: cooked on embers.

BRAISÉ(-E) Braised, originally with heat above and below in glowing embers (*braises*); see also *carbonnade*.

BRAISIN Variety of haricot bean from *Poitou*.

BRAMAFAM *Salade Bramafam*: artichoke stuffed with raw mushrooms, scampi and walnuts.

BRANCAS Garnish of *Anna* potatoes and braised lettuce. See also *barbue*.

BRANDADE (DE MORUE) (Languedoc) Creamed salt cod with olive oil, milk or cream, sometimes truffles, served warm; originally from *Nîmes*.
　　　Brandade de thon (Bretagne): tinned tuna fish mixed with haricot beans.

BRANCHE   Lit.: 'branch'. *En branche*: whole, of vegetables (e.g. asparagus, spinach).

BRAOU/BROU BOUFFAT   (Roussillon) Rice and cabbage soup.

BRASSADEAU/BRASSADO   (Vivarais) Small pastry ring, also known as *cordillon*.

BRASSERIE   Brewery, beer shop.
Café-restaurant serving wide range of food and drink and often open from breakfast to early morning.

BRAY   Region in *Normandie*. See *Carré de Bray*, *Coeur de Bray*.

BRAYAUDE   (Auvergne, Bourbonnais) *Omelette brayaude*: omelette with bacon, cream, potatoes and cheese. *Pommes (de terre) brayaude*: baked potatoes. See also *gigot*.

BREBIS   Ewe. Short for *fromage de brebis*: sheep's milk cheese. *Brebis d'Oléron*: see *Jonchée*.

BREBIS-PYRÉNÉES   (Pays basque) *AOC* cheese, firm, cylindrical, with a yellow to grey rind, white and smooth inside, and rich flavour.

BRÉCHET   Breastbone, of poultry.

BRÉGEAUDE/BRÉJAUDA/BRÉJAUDE   (Limousin) Cabbage and bacon soup; from 'bréjou' – pork rind.

BRÉHAN   Garnish of artichokes, cauliflower, puréed broad beans and *hollandaise* sauce.

BRÉJAUDA/BRÉJAUDE   See *brégeaude*.

BRELIN   (Normandie) Local name for winkle (*bigorneau*).

BRÈME   Freshwater bream, similar to carp.

BRÈME DE MER   Ray's bream, type of sea bream; also known as *castagnole*.

BRÈME DE ROCHERS   Name for black bream (*griset*).

BRÉMONT   *Potage Brémont* (Mâconnais): milk and walnut soup.

BRESAOLA   Dried salt beef, served in thin slices; of Italian origin.

BRÉSI   (Franche-Comté) Beef or veal, smoked, salted and dried, served in thin slices.

BRESOLLES   Slices of veal, or perhaps beef or mutton, baked with shallots and white wine; apparently created for the Marquis de Brézolles on a battlefield of the Seven Years' War. See also *brézolle*.

BRESSAN   (Bresse) Soft small goat's milk cheese, mild to fruity, made on farms; also known as *Petit Bressan*.

(À LA) BRESSANE   In the style of *Bresse*. *Potage bressane*: pumpkin soup with cubes of fried bread. *Sauce bressane*: brown sauce with madeira, chicken livers and orange juice, for poultry. See also *Belle Bressane*, *chapon*, *grenouille* and *marmite*.

BRESSE   Region occupying about half the Ain department, loosely included with *Bourgogne* and bordering *Lyonnais*. See also *Bleu de Bresse*, *chapon* and *poulet*.

BRESSUIRE   Town in *Poitou* known for poultry.

BREST   Town in *Bretagne*. See *boudin*, *huître* and *Paris-Brest*.

(À LA) BRESTOISE   In the style of *Brest*. See *daurade* and *morue*. *Brestois*: solid sponge cake flavoured with almonds and orange liqueur.

BRETAGNE   Brittany, province covering the departments of Ille-et-Vilaine, Côtes-du-Nord, Finistère, *Morbihan* and Loire-Atlantique.

(À LA) BRETONNE   In the style of *Bretagne*. With white haricot beans, especially of lamb. Of fish or poultry, with *sauce bretonne*: white wine and cream sauce. See also *artichaut*, *beurre*, *coquille Saint-Jacques*, *gâteau*, and *haricot blanc*.

BRETONNEAU   (Normandie) Local name for *turbot*.

BRETZEL   (Alsace) Pretzel biscuit.

(À LA) BRÉVAL   See *turbot*.

BRÉZOLLE   Slice, thick *escalope*, of veal. See also *bresolles*.

BRIAND   19th-century politician and gourmet. See *chevreuil*.

BRICQUEBEC   (Normandie) Mild firm cheese made at the Abbey of Bricquebec; also known as *Trappiste de Bricquebec*, and *Providence* (brand name).

BRIE   Province E of *Paris*, capital *Meaux*, partly in *Ile-de-France*, partly in *Champagne*.
    The famous cheese, in fact several cheeses, made mainly in *Brie*; see below.

BRIE (LAITIER)   Cheese made by factories in *Brie* and other parts of France and abroad; this, together with the versions from *Coulommiers* and *Meaux* (see below) is *Brie* as we know it – large, flat, round, with a downy white rind, pale yellow inside, faint mushroomy smell and full flavour.

BRIE DE COULOMMIERS   (Ile-de-France) Smaller version of *Brie* (*Laitier*), enriched with cream, usually factory-made around Coulommiers; also known as *Brie Petit Moule*.

BRIE DE MEAUX (FERMIER)   (Ile-de-France) *AOC* cheese made on farms, matured for 5–6 weeks, with more bouquet than the commercial *Brie*; the 'true' Brie, dubbed 'King of cheeses' by *Talleyrand*.

BRIE DE MELUN (AFFINÉ)   (Ile-de-France) *AOC* cheese made in small traditional dairies around Melun, ripened for 7 weeks, with a stronger smell than *Brie de Meaux* and pronounced flavour; perhaps the ancestor of modern *Brie*.

BRIE DE MELUN FRAIS   (Ile-de-France) Soft white mild cheese made from fresh salted curds. *Brie de Melun Bleu* is sprinkled with charcoal.

BRIE DE MONTEREAU   (Ile-de-France) Cheese similar to *Brie de Melun* (*Affiné*), made around Ville-Saint-Jacques and Montereau; also known as *Ville-Saint-Jacques*.

BRIE PETIT MOULE   See *Brie de Coulommiers*.

BRIÉ   See *pain*.

BRIGNE   (Provence) Sweet fritter.

BRIGNOLE   Type of prune, after the town of Brignoles in *Provence*; also known as *pruneau fleuri*.

BRIGOULE   Name for type of fungus (*barigoule*).

BRILLAT-SAVARIN   Gastronome, ambassador and philosopher (1755–1826), born in *Belley*; his name is associated with *foie gras*, truffles etc. *Consommé Brillat-Savarin*: clear soup with strips of chicken, lettuce, herbs and tapioca. See also *caille*, *escalope*, *fondue*, poire and *savarin*.

   (Normandie) Mild creamy cheese with high fat content, invented in 1930s, now made all over France; similar to other triple-cream cheeses (e.g. *Excelsior*, *Magnum*, *Délice de Saint-Cyr*, *Boursin*).

BRILLOLI/BRILLULI/BRIOLI   (Corse) Chestnut flour porridge, often sweet with milk or cream.

BRIMBELLE   Spirit flavoured with bilberries; also known as *myrtille*.

BRIMONT   See *esturgeon*.

BRINDAMOUR   (Corse) Soft, herb-flavoured cheese, of goat's or sheep's milk or a mixture; also known as *Fleur du Maquis*.

BRINDINELLE/BRINDINETTE (Flandre) Macaroon.

BRIOCHE Rich bun, made from yeast dough with eggs and butter; eaten for breakfast, or sometimes filled with savoury cream sauce for *hors d'oeuvre*. *Brioche* dough is used for breads, cakes, and for enclosing other ingredients (e.g. *saucisson en brioche*, Lyonnais: sausage in *brioche* dough with truffled *pâté de foie gras*). *Brioche en couronne*: ring-shaped *brioche*. *Brioche tressée/tordée* (Lorraine): twisted ring-shaped *brioche* (lit.: 'plaited/twisted').

BRIOCHÉ(-E) Like a *brioche*. See also *pain*.

(À LA) BRIOCHAINE In the style of *Saint-Brieuc*.

BRIOCHIN Type of fruit *brioche*.

BRIOLI See *brilloli*.

BRIONNE Name for *chayote*.

BRIQUE DU FOREZ (Auvergne) Small brick-shaped (*brique*) goat's milk cheese, with nutty flavour; made by farms in the Ambert and Monts du Forez region; also known as *Cabrion du Forez* and *Chevreton d'Ambert*.

BRISCAT (Gascogne) *Garbure* with maize.

BRISCO/BRISE-GOÛT/BRISEGO Lit.: 'break-taste'. (Savoie) Strong soft cheese, made by mountain farms.

(À LA) BRISSAC See *ortolan*.

BRISTOL Garnish of rice croquettes, flageolet beans and potatoes.

BROCCANA (Limousin) Veal and pork *pâté*.

BROCCIO/BROCCIU (Corse) Fresh mild sheep's milk cheese, made on farms, sometimes salted; similar to *Brousse*, the name derived in the same way.

BROCHE Spit. *À la broche*: roasted on the spit.

BROCHET Pike, large freshwater fish with tiny bones and dry flesh, esteemed in France, often made into *quenelles*. *Brochet au beurre blanc* (Anjou, Nantais): poached, with 'white butter'; *à l'orléanaise*: baked, with vinegar and shallot sauce; *rôti à la mode de Bugey*: stuffed, spit-roasted, with crayfish tails, truffles and cream sauce; *à la vésulienne*: roasted with shallots and mushrooms.

BROCHET DE MER Barracuda, large sea fish; also known as *spet*.

BROCHETON Small pike. *Brocheton à la martinière*: marinated, grilled, with walnuts and mayonnaise; *à la Valvins*: larded with anchovy, roasted, with mustard sauce.

BROCHETTE Skewer. Food grilled or fried on a skewer (e.g. *brochettes de veau*). *Brochettes jurassienne*: of cheese wrapped in ham, fried in oil; *du Puy*: of ham, sweetbreads and morels.

BROCKEL See *bracq*.

BROCOLI Broccoli, also known as *choux brocolis*.

BROCQ See *bracq*.

BROSME Name for torsk (*loquette*).

BROU BOUFFAT See *braou bouffat*.

BROU DE NOIX Lit.: 'walnut husk'. Walnut liqueur.

BROUFADO (Provence) Stew of marinated beef and onions, with vinegar, capers and anchovies.

BROUILLADE Scrambled eggs. *Brouillade aux truffes* (Périgord): scrambled eggs with truffles.
Mixture (e.g. *brouillade d'aubergines* (Provence): stewed aubergines with tomatoes).

BROUILLÉ(-E) Scrambled, of eggs. Mixed.

BROUILLY See *Beaujolais*.

BROUSSE (Provence) Fresh, unsalted sheep's or goat's milk cheese, made by farms, mild, white and creamy, often served with fruit; so called because the cheese is stirred ('broussé' in dialect). Varieties include *Brousse du Rove* and *Brousse de la Vésubie*.

BROUTARD Name for young goat (*chevreau*).

BROUTES/BROUTONS (Béarn) Boiled cabbage and sometimes leeks with oil and vinegar.

BROUTIGNAN Variety of olive from *Provence*.

BROUTONS See *broutes*.

(LA) BROYE/BROYO (Béarn) From 'broyé' – pounded. Maize flour and milk porridge, savoury or sweet, often made into fritters; also known as *gaudines* and *yerbilhou*.

BRUANT Bunting, water bird.

BRUGNON Nectarine, also known as *nectarine*.

BRÛLE(-E)   Burnt, flamed. Roasted, of coffee. See also *crème*.

BRÛLOT   Flamed brandy.

BRUN(-E)   Brown. *Sauce brune*: name for *sauce espagnole*.
Brune: dark brown beer.

BRUNOISE   Mixture of finely chopped, cubed or shredded ingredients, for soups, stuffings, garnishes etc; usually of
vegetables, especially as a basis for *consommé brunoise*.

BRUT(-E)   Lit.: 'raw', 'crude'. Unsweetened, very dry, especially of
Champagne.

(À LA) BRUXELLOISE   In the style of Brussels. Garnish of Brussels
sprouts and chicory. *Potage bruxelloise*: Brussels sprout
soup.

BUCARDE   Name for cockle (*coque*).

BUCCIN   Whelk, small shellfish; also known as *pilot canteux*.

BÛCHE   Lit.: 'log'. Rolled up sponge cake, Swiss roll. *Bûche de
Noël*: Christmas log, often of puréed chestnuts and
chocolate.

(À LA) BÛCHERONNE   Lit.: 'woodcutter's style'. *Soupe à la bûcheronne*: vegetable and haricot bean soup.

BUDICU   (Corse) Local name for monkfish (*lotte*).

BUFFET   As in English, buffet meal.
Refreshment room, particularly *buffet* (*de gare*):
station buffet, often consisting of a large bar and quality
restaurant.

(À LA) BUFFETIÈRE   In the style of the buffet.

BUGEY   Region, capital *Belley*, covering roughly half the Ain
department, S of *Franche-Comté*. See also *rissole*.
Red, white and rosé wines (*VDQS*), some sparkling,
made in *Bugey*.

(À LA MODE) BUGISTE   In the style of *Bugey*. See *brochet*.

BUGNE   (Lyonnais, Bourgogne) Sweet pastry fritter. *Lyon* is the
capital of *bugnes*.

BUISSON   Lit.: 'bush'. *En buisson*: food, usually fish or shellfish,
piled up in a dish.

BULLIDO   See *aigo bouido*.

BUNYETE   (Roussillon) Sweet fritter.

BURUTE   (Champagne) Black pudding, used in soups.

BUSSY   *Pommes (de terre) Bussy: dauphine* potatoes with truffles and parsley.

BUVETTE   Small bar; refreshment room; counter selling drinks and snacks.

BUZET   See *Côtes de Buzet*.

BYRON   *Pommes (de terre) Byron*: potato cake covered with cream and cheese, browned. *Sauce Byron*: red wine sauce with truffles.

BYRRH   Aperitif based on fortified red wine and quinine.

CABARDÈS   Area near *Carcasonne*, producing red and rosé wines (*VDQS*).

CABASSOL(LES) (Languedoc) Boiled lamb's tripe, head and trotters, with ham and vegetables.

CABASSOUN   (Provence) Local name for sandsmelt (*athérine*).

CABÉCOU   (Périgord, Rouergue) Small, round, soft cheese, of goat's or sheep's milk, made on farms; dialect for 'little goat'. Versions include *Cabécou d'Entraygues*, and *(Cabécou de) Livernon*, also known as *(Cabécou de) Rocamadour*.

CABERNET   Variety of red grape, of two main types: *Cabernet Franc*, grown in the *Loire* and also *Bordeaux*; and *Cabernet Sauvignon* (not to be confused with *Sauvignon*), main constituent of the finest red wines of *Bordeaux*.

CABESSAL/CHABESSAL   Folded ring of cloth once worn on the head to carry a pail of water. See *lièvre*.

CABILLAUD/CABLIAUD   Fresh cod (as opposed to *morue*: salt cod), also known as *gade. Cabillaud à la lyonnaise*: cooked in vinegar; *quimperoise*: with hard-boiled eggs.

CABIROS   (Corse) Local name for young goat (*chevreau*).

CABLIAUD   Name for cod (*cabillaud*).

CABOT   Name for chub (*chevaine*).

CABOUSSAT   (Quercy) Wine soup.

CABRI   Name for young goat (*chevreau*).

CABRICHIU   See *Chabichou*.

CABRION DU FOREZ/DE MÂCON See *Brique du Forez* and *Mâconnais*.

CACAO   Cocoa (powder). *Crème de cacao*: cocoa-flavoured liqueur.

CACAHOUETTE/CACAHUÈTE   Peanut.

CACCAVELLI   (Corse) Cheese and lemon cake.

CACHAT   (Provence) Fresh, salted sheep's milk cheese, made on farms around *Mont Ventoux*; also known as *Tomme de Mont Ventoux*.

CACHIR   Kosher.

CADILLAC   Area in *Bordeaux*, making mainly sweet white wines (*AC*).

(À LA) CADURCIENNE   In the style of *Cahors*. See *tripes*.

CAEN   Capital of *Calvados*. See *andouillette*, *demoiselle* and *tripes*.

CAFÉ   Coffee (-flavoured). *Un café*: a small black coffee (*café noir*). *Café au lait*: large coffee with hot milk. *Café crème*: small black coffee with cream or cold milk. *Café brûlot*: coffee flamed with brandy and spices; *à la chaussette*: dripped into a jug; *complet*: continental breakfast; *express*: espresso coffee; *filtre*: filter coffee; *gallois* (lit.: 'Welsh') coffee; *glacé*: iced coffee (*glace au café*: coffee ice cream); *liégeois*: iced coffee poured over ice cream with whipped cream; *noisette* (Bourgogne): black coffee with cream and *kirsch*. *Faux café*: decaffeinated coffee. In a shop – *café en grains*: coffee beans; *moulu*: ground coffee; *en poudre*: instant coffee.
Café, bar.

CAGOUILLE   (Charentes, Poitou) Local name for small snail.
The people of *Charentes*, reputedly slow, or nicknamed 'cagouillards'.

(LOU) CAGARAULAT   See *escargot*.

CAHORS   Capital of the Lot department in *Quercy*.
Red wine made in Cahors (*AC*).

CAÏEU (D'ISIGNY)   Giant variety of mussel which grows naturally at *Isigny*.

CAILLADA DE VOUILLOS/CAILLADE   See *Tomme de Brach*.

CAILLE   Quail, small bird, usually bred for the table; in the past often prepared with truffles (*à la gourmande*, *à la Lamballe*, *Saint-Mars*, *à la Talleyrand*), and *foie gras* as well (*Brillat-Savarin*, *à la Stanislas*). *Cailles à la dauphinoise*: wrapped in vine leaves and pork fat, roasted, with peas; *aux raisins*: roasted with white grapes; *à la romaine*: casseroled with peas, onions and ham. See *roi de cailles*.

CAILLE D'AMÉRIQUE   Bob-white, American quail, also known as *colin loui*.

CAILLÉ   Curds, of milk, sometimes served with fritters.

CAILLEBOTTE   Curds. (Charentes, Poitou) Fresh, soft, white curd cheese, of cow's, goat's or sheep's milk, mild and creamy, often in a rush basket, made by farms and homes; also known as *Pigouille* when moulded.

CAILLETEAU   Young quail.

CAILLETOT   (Normandie) Local name for *turbot*.

CAILLETTE/CAYETTE   (S France) Baked pork and vegetable faggot, served hot or cold; also known as *gaillette* and *gayette*. *Caillette varoise*: baked liver and belly of pork.

CAION   (Savoie) Local name for pig, pork.

CAIRANNE   See *Côtes-du-Rhône-Villages*.

CAISSE(ETTE)   Lit.: 'small box'. *En caisse*: cooked in a papercase. See also *cassolette*.
(Champagne) Meringue.

CAJASSE   (Périgord) Sweet pastry.

CAJASSOUS   See *Chabichou*.

CAJOU   Name for cashew nut (*anacarde*).

CAKE   Fruit cake.

CALADON   (Languedoc) Dry almond cake.

(À LA) CALAISIENNE   In the style of Calais in *Picardie*. See *hareng*.

CALAMAR/CALMAR/CALMARET   Squid, inkfish; also known as *encornet*, *claougeou*, *taouten(n)*, *tautenne* and *chipirons*.

CALAPPE   Box crab, type of small crab; also known as *coq de mer*.

CALISSO(U)N/CANISSOUN   (S France) Marzipan sweet, also known as *galichon* and *galichou*.

CALMAR/CALMARET   See *calamar*.

CALVA   Short for *Calvados* (the drink).

CALVADOS   Department and region in *Normandie*.

Cider brandy, produced throughout *Normandie* and named after the region of origin (e.g. *Calvados* du Cotentin, *Calvados du Calvados*). The best comes from *Auge*, with the *AC Calvados du Pays d'Auge*; others carry the lesser *Appellation Réglementée Calvados* on the label. Cheaper, less refined, apple brandy must be called *eau-de-vie de cidre*, not *Calvados*. Indications of age are 3 stars: at least 1 year in wooden casks; *Vieux/Réserve*: 2 years; *VO/Vieille Réserve*: 3 years; *VSOP*: 4 years; *Extra/Napoléon/Hors d'Age*: 5 years or more. A glass of *Calva* in the middle of a meal is known as 'un trou normand', said to make a hole ('trou') for more food.

(À LA) CALVAISE   In the style of Calvi in *Corse*. See *homard*.

CALVILLE   Variety of apple, originally from the town of that name in *Normandie*.

CAMARD   Name for type of gurnard (*grondin*).

(À LA) CAMARGUAISE   In the style of *Camargue*. With all or any of wine, brandy, tomatoes, garlic, herbs, orange peel, black olives. See also *moule*.

CAMARGUE   Wild region of salt marshes in the *Rhône* delta, *Provence*; famous for horses and bulls, much of it now devoted to the cultivation of rice, and also vines. See also *gardiane* and *Tomme de Camargue*.

CAMBACÉRÈS   Napoleon's arch-chancellor, who died from overeating. Elaborate garnish of truffles, frog's legs, mussels etc, for large fish like turbot. *Crème Cambacérès*: cream of pigeon, chicken and crayfish soup with *quenelles*.

CAMBAJOU   (Languedoc) Salted pork hock.

CAMBO-LES-BAINS   Town in *Pays basque*. See *tournedos*.

CAMBRAI   Town in the Nord department, usually considered part of *Picardie*. See also *andouille*, *andouillette* and *Boulette de Cambrai*.

(À LA) CAMBRAISIENNE   In the style of *Cambrai*. See *tripes*.

CAMEMBERT   (Normandie) The well-known cheese, small and circular with mild creamy flavour, said to have been perfected around 1790 by a farmer's wife; named after a village in *Auge*. *Camembert de Normandie*: *AOC* version, farm-made from unpasteurized milk in the 5 departments of *Normandie* and sold in wooden boxes. *Camembert Fermier*: farm-made but rare, best in summer, more fruity than the commercial version. *Camembert Pasteurisé*: mass-produced cheese using pasteurized milk, made throughout France and abroad. *Demi-Camembert*: half Camembert.

CAMOMILLE   Camomile, used in herb teas and *vermouth*.

CAMPAGNARDE/(DU) CAMPAGNE   Countrified. *Omelette campagnarde*: layered omelette enclosing rounds of fried sausage. See *foie*, *jambon*, *pain*, *pâté*, *saucisson*, *terrine*.

CAMPÉNÉAC   (Bretagne) Semi-soft yellow pressed cheese, made at the Abbey of Campénéac; also known as *Trappiste de Campénéac*.

CAMUS (DE BRETAGNE)   Lit.: 'pug-nosed'. Variety of globe artichoke, large and green.

CANAPÉ   Cocktail snack. Piece of bread with titbit on it.
(Boulonnais) Local name for hake (*colin*).

CANARD   Duck. See also *caneton*, the usual menu description. Main breeds are *canard nantais*: *Nantes* duck, the most common, bred around Challans in *Vendée*, correctly called *canard challandais*; *canard rouennais*: *Rouen* duck, raised around Yvetot in *Normandie*, a special breed killed by smothering to retain the blood and give a distinct flavour; *Duclair*: variety of *Rouen* duck, bred around the town of that name; *canard de Barbarie/d'Inde*: Barbary duck, raised mainly in S France; *mulard*: cross between *Rouen* and Barbary duck, bred for *foie gras* and *confits*, mainly in central and S France.

CANARDEAU   Duckling.

CANARD SAUVAGE   Wild duck, mallard, also known as *colvert*. *Canard sauvage à la navarraise*: stewed with sweet peppers and white wine; *à la tyrolienne*: stuffed with apples, spit-roasted, with vinegar and redcurrant sauce.

CANARD SIFFLEUR   Lit.: 'duck whistler'. Widgeon, type of wild duck.

CANARON   Name for grey gurnard (*grondin gris*).

(À LA) CANCALAISE   In the style of Cancale in *Bretagne*.
With oysters, often shrimps, cream and white wine sauce.
Oyster from Cancale.

CANCOILLOTTE   (Franche-Comté) Mixture of ripe *Metton* cheese, butter, garlic and white wine.

CANDI   Candy.

CANEPETIÈRE   Field duck, little bustard.

CANETON   Duckling; the usual menu description for duck. *Caneton à la l'albigeoise*: stewed with bacon and herbs, served on fried bread with apples or redcurrant jelly; *d'Albuféra*: roasted with ham, served with mushrooms and madeira sauce; *au Muscadet* (Bretagne): roasted, with *Muscadet*, shallot and cream sauce; *à la rouennaise*: Rouen duck stuffed with its liver, lightly roasted, the carcase pressed for blood to thicken the sauce; (*rouennais*) *à la presse*: version of *à la rouennaise*; *Saint-Martin* (Touraine): boned, stuffed with pork, cooked in *marc* or wine, served cold in jelly; *à la solognote*: stuffed, roasted, with onion and tomato sauce; *à la suédoise*: marinated in brine, poached with vegetables; *Tour d'Argent*: version of *à la rouennaise*; *en vessie* (Touraine): cooked in a pig's bladder with walnuts.

CANETTE   Female duckling.

CANISSOUN   See *calisson*.

CANISTRELLI   (Corse) Aniseed-flavoured nut cakes.

CANNEBERGE   Cranberry, small red fruit often made into jelly; also known as *airelle rouge*, *coussinet* and *groseille de cheval*.

CANNELLE   Cinnamon, spice. See also *tarte*.

CANNELON   Savoury puff pastry cone.

(À LA) CANNOISE   In the style of Cannes in *Nice*. See *artichaut* and *trucca*.

CANOLES   (Limousin) Small dry cakes.

CANON FRONSAC   See *Côtes de Fronsac*.

(À LA) CANOTIÈRE   Lit.: 'boatman's style'. Poached in white wine, of freshwater fish. See also *matelote*.

CANTAL   Department in *Auvergne*.

Large cylindrical uncooked cheese (*AOC*), firm and yellow, with faint smell and nutty flavour; made by mountain farms and dairies in *Cantal*, also known as *Fourme de Cantal* (not to be confused with *Tomme de Cantal*).

(À LA) CANTALIENNE   In the style of *Cantal*. With sauce/covering of *Cantal* cheese.

CANTALET/CANTALON (Auvergne) Smaller version of *Cantal* cheese; also known as *Fourme de Rochefort*.

CANTALOU(P) Cantaloupe melon.

CANTAREU (Nice) Small snails in tomato sauce.

CANTHARE/CANTHÈRE Name for black bream (*griset*).

CAP CORSE Wine-based aperitif made in *Corse*.

CAPEL(AN)/CAPELIN/CAPLIN Poor cod, small bony sea fish; also known as *fico*.

(EN) CAPILOTADE Lit.: 'in bits', 'crumbs'. Cold poultry, unless otherwise specified, in sauce. *Capilotade de morue* (Provence): salt cod with capers and wine.

CAPITAINE Lit.: 'captain'. Sea fish resembling carp.

CAPLIN Name for poor cod (*capelan*).

CAPOCCHIO (Corse) Local name for grey mullet (*mulet*).

CAPOUM Name for *rascasse*.

CAPOUNS (Nice) Baked cabbage or Swiss chard (*blette*), stuffed with sausage, rice and cheese.

CÂPRES Capers, pickled flowerbuds of caper plant; also known as *tapéno*.

CAPRETTU (Corse) Name for goat (*chèvre*).

CAPRICE See *sole*.

CAPRICE DES DIEUX Lit.: 'whim of the gods'. (Champagne) Factory-made, pasteurized, creamy cheese, shaped like small oval loaf; brand name.

CAPUCIN(E) Lit.: 'Capuchin monk or nun'. Nasturtium, whose peppery leaves and flowers are used in salads. *Consommé capucine*: clear chicken soup with lettuce and spinach strips. See also *civet*.

CAQHUSE (Picardie) Pork braised with onions.

CAQUELON Small earthenware dish, used especially for cheese.

CARAFE Carafe, decanter.

CARAGAOU/CARAGUOLO (Provence, Languedoc) Local name for small snail.

CARAMBOT   Tiny shrimp (*crevette*).

CARAMEL   Caramel; burnt sugar. Fudge or toffee sweet. See also *crème*.

CARAMOTE   Large prawn; also known as *crevette royale* and *grosse crevette*.

CARAQUE   Lit.: 'galleon'. Chocolate sponge cake.

CARBONNADE(S)   Lit.: 'glowing coals' ('charbons ardents'), implying not just grilling over charcoal, but braising in the fire (see also *braise*). *Carbonnade(s)* (*de boeuf à la*) *flamande*: beef and onions braised with herbs and beer. *Carbonnade nîmoise*: lamb or mutton baked with potatoes, bacon and garlic. *Carbonnades de porc*: thin slices of pork grilled over charcoal, or perhaps fried.

CARCASSE   Carcase. *Soupe de carcasses d'oies* (Périgord): goose carcase soup.

CARCASSONNE   Capital of *Aude*.

(À LA) CARCASSONNAISE   In the style of *Carcassonne*. See also *chapon* and *pot-au-feu*.

CARDAMINE   Name for cress (*cressonnette*).

CARDAMOME   Cardamom, the spice.

CARDE   Name for rib of chard (*blette*).

CARDEAU   (NW France) Local name for *sardine*.

(À LA) CARDINAL   Lit.: 'cardinal's style'. Pink or red in colour, after the colour of the cardinal's robes, perhaps specifically Cardinal *Mazarin*. *Sauce cardinal*: lobster sauce with truffles and diced lobster, for fish. *Homard cardinal*: lobster with *sauce cardinal* in the half shell, browned. See also *sole*.
   Coloured red in some other way (e.g. with cochineal, *crème de cassis* or raspberry purée).
   Variety of black table grape.
   Aperitif of *crème de cassis* mixed with red wine.

CARDINE   Name for megrim (*limandelle*).

CARDON   Cardoon, like coarse celery and related to thistle ('chardon'). *Cardons à la moelle* (Lyonnais): baked with bone marrow; *de Noël* (Provence): in white sauce, a Christmas speciality.

CARÊME   Marie-Antoine Carême (1784–1833), founder of classic

French cookery; his name is associated with truffles, *foie gras*, cockscombs etc.

Lent, once a period of fasting.

CARGOLADE   (Languedoc, Roussillon) Snails stewed in wine, or cooked over charcoal.

CARI   Curry (powder).

CARIGNAN   Garnish of *foie gras*, asparagus, eggs and *Anna* potatoes.

CARIGNANE   Grape variety used in wines of S France.

CARMES   See *eau*.

CAROLINE   Small savoury pastry.

(À LA) CAROLOMACÉRIENNE   In the style of *Charleville-Mézières*.

CAROTTE   Carrot. Two names are associated with carrots – *Crécy*, as in *potage Crécy*: carrot soup; and *Vichy*, as in *carottes Vichy*: glazed carrots, cooked in water (properly *Vichy* water) with butter and sugar, sprinkled with parsley. *Carottes en cheveux d'ange*: carrot jam.

CAROUBE   Carob bean.

CARPE   Carp, freshwater fish of ponds and rivers, sometimes reaching enormous size. *Carpe à l'alsacienne*: stuffed, cooked in white wine, with *choucroute* and boiled potatoes; *à l'avesnoise*: stuffed with the roes, poached in wine, with cream and crayfish tails; *à la bière*: braised in beer, with soft roes; *à la Chambord*: larded, braised, with *quenelles*, soft roes, truffles etc and red wine sauce; *à la juive*: served cold in white wine and onion sauce; *à la Neuvic*: stuffed with *foie gras* and truffles, baked in white wine; *à la polonaise*: stuffed, poached in red wine with vinegar and almonds.

CARPEAU/CARPILLON   Young carp; also freshwater mullet.

CARPION   Variety of trout.

CARRAGHEEN   Red seaweed, used in drinks, soups, jellies etc.

CARRAT   Variety of sweet pepper from *Provence*.

CARRÉ   Lit.: 'square'. Rack, best end of neck, of lamb usually, but also pork and veal. *Carré d'agneau Beaucaire*: (lamb) baked with artichokes and tomatoes; *Marly*: baked with *mange-tout* peas; *Mireille*: baked with potatoes and artichokes; *à la toscane*: baked between potato layers.

Square-shaped cheese; see below.

CARRÉ DE BONNEVILLE   See *Pavé de Moyaux*.

CARRÉ DE BRAY   (Normandie) Small, soft, white cheese packed on straw, with salty taste; made by dairies in *Bray*.

CARRÉ DE L'EST   (Champagne, Lorraine) White, creamy cheese similar to *Camembert* but softer in texture and taste.

CARRÉ DE LILLIE   (Flandre) Dark spice bread.

CARRELET   Plaice, also known as *plie* (*franche*).

CARRINGUE   Name for horse mackerel (*saurel*).

CARTE   Menu. *À la carte*: menu which gives you the freedom to pick and choose, with each item separately priced, as opposed to (and probably more expensive than) *menu*: fixed price meal.
    Carte des vins: wine list.

CARTHAGÈNE   Grape juice and *marc* aperitif, from *Vivarais*.

CARVI   Caraway, the spice; also known as *cumin* (*des prés*).

(À LA) CASCAMÈCHE   Possibly a corruption of *escabèche*. See *goujon*.

CASERETTE   Fresh cheese drained in a straw basket (*caserette*).

CASSADE/CASSATE(S)   Ice cream of two different flavours, with crystallized fruit; from Italian 'cassata'.

CASSE   Earthenware pot. *Casse rennais*: calf's head, feet and stomach with white wine, baked in a *casse*.

CASSÉ(-E)   Cracked, broken.

CASSE-CROÛTE   Lit.: 'break-crust'. Snack (bar).

CASSE-MUSE(AU)   Lit.: 'jaw-breaker'. Rock cake.

CASSEMUSE   (Touraine) Cream cheese *brioche*.

CASSE-NOIX   Lit.: 'nutcracker'. Name for hawfinch (*gros-bec*).

CASSEROLE Saucepan (rarely casserole dish).

CASSERON (Charentes) Local name for cuttlefish (*seiche*). *Casserons en matelote*: stewed with red wine and garlic.

CASSETTE Lit.: 'casket'. See *gigot*.

CASSIS Blackcurrant. Short for *crème de cassis*: blackcurrant liqueur, speciality of *Dijon*. Not to be confused with *Cassis*, coastal town in *Provence*, known for its dry white and red wines (*AC*).

CASSISSINE (Bourgogne) Blackcurrant stuffing. Small blackcurrant sweet.

CASSOLETTE Small portion of food, for *hors d'oeuvre* or dessert, served in a dish of the same name; also known as *caissette*.

CASSONADE Soft brown sugar.

CASSOULET (Languedoc) Stew, essentially of haricot beans and different meats – pork, sausage and preserved goose – cooked at length in a 'cassole' (earthenware pot), with garlic and herbs. Originally from *Toulouse*, with different versions including mutton, salt pork, partridge, fresh goose or preserved duck.

CASTAGNACI (Corse) Thick chestnut fritters.

CASTAGNE ARRUSTITE (Corse) Roast chestnuts.

CASTAGNOLE (S France) Local name for Ray's bream (*brème de mer*).

(À LA) CASTELROUSSINE In the style of *Châteauroux*.

CASTIGLIONE Garnish of mushrooms filled with rice and ham, plus aubergines and bone marrow.

(À LA) CASTILLANE Castilian-style. Garnish of potato nests filled with tomato and fried onions.

CASTILLON See *Bethmale* and *Côtes de Castillon*.

CATA (S France) Local name for dogfish (*roussette*).

(À LA) CATALANE Catalan-style, in the style of *Roussillon*. With tomatoes, garlic, onions and perhaps peppers, aubergines, rice or chick peas. With Seville oranges, especially in a sauce with garlic. *Soupe catalane*: onion, ham and tomato soup; or fish soup. See also *moule*, *perdrix*, *pistache* and *pois*.

CATIGAU/CATIGOT D'ANGUILLES (Camargue) Eel stew with red wine, garlic and tomatoes.

(À LA) CAUCASIENNE Caucasian-style. See *noix de veau*.

(À LA) CAUCHOISE In the style of *Caux*. With cream, *Calvados* and apples, especially of veal. *Salade cauchoise*: potato, celery, ham and cream salad; also known as *salade normande*.

CAUDEBEC Town in *Normandie*. See *saumon*.

CAUDIÈRE/CAUDRÉE (N France) Seafish soup.

(À LA) CAUSALADE *Oeufs à la causalade* (Foix): fried eggs and bacon.

(LES) CAUSSES See *Bleu des Causses*.

CAUX Region in *Normandie*.

CAVAILLON Town in *Provence*, known for melons and asparagus.

CAVALLO Name for mackerel (*maquereau*).

CAVE Cellar, wine cellar. See also *mise*.

CAVIAR(E) Caviar, sturgeon roe; mainly of Russian origin, but also produced in *Bordelais* from sturgeon caught in the *Gironde*. The main types are *beluga*: largest grained and most expensive; *oscietre*: with large grains; *sevruga*: smaller grained; *caviar pressé*: made from damaged eggs, salted and pressed.

Caviar blanc: name for mullet roe (*boutargue*).

Caviar niçois: paste of pounded anchovies, olives, herbs and oil. *Caviar de saumon*: salmon roe.

CAVOUR   Italian statesman and ally of Napoleon III. Garnish of pasta. See also *artichaut* and *queue de boeuf*.

CAYENNE   See *poivre*.

CAYETTE   See *caillette*.

CÉDRAT   Citron, large sour citrus fruit grown in *Provence* and *Corse*, used in confectionery and liqueurs.

CÉDRATINE   Citron liqueur, a speciality of *Corse*.

CELAN   Name for *sardine*.

CÉLERI   Celery; also short for *céleri-rave*.

CÉLERI-RAVE   Celeriac, type of celery cultivated for the root.

Céleri(-rave) rémoulade: shredded, raw, in spicy mayonnaise; *à la sicilienne*: in salad with artichokes, apples and tomatoes.

CÉLESTINE   Chef to Napoleon III and native of *Vivarais*. *Consommé Céléstine*: clear soup with noodles. *Omelette Céléstine*: sweet omelette with apricot jam. See also *poulet*.

CENDRE   Ash. *Aux cendres/sous la cendre*: cooked on ashes, but often meaning wrapped in pastry and baked, especially of small birds and truffles.

CENDRÉ   Cheese ripened in ashes, often from wine-growing areas; see below.

CENDRÉ D'AISY   (Bourgogne) Firm cheese with strong smell and fruity flavour, cured in ashes and *marc*; made around Aisy-sur-Armançon, also known as *Aisy Cendré*.

CENDRÉ DE CHAMPAGNE (DES RICEYS)/DES ARDENNES   See *Riceys* and *Rocroi*.

CENDRILLON   Cinderella. Baked in ashes (e.g. *pommes Cendrillon*). Of small birds, flattened and grilled, often with truffle sauce. See also *tournedos*.

CÉPAGE   General term for vine variety (e.g. *Cabernet*, *Gamay*).

CÈPE   Name for boletus (*bolet*). *Cèpes à l'auvergnate*: browned in the oven with oil, garlic and parsley; *à la mode béarnaise*: grilled with garlic, breadcrumbs and parsley; *à la bordelaise*: sautéed in oil with shallots or garlic and parsley; *à la landaise*: cooked in goose fat with ham and shallots, flamed with *Armagnac*, plus tomatoes and white wine; *à la périgourdine*: with bacon, herbs and grape juice; *à la viande* (Gascogne): grilled with ham and garlic.

CÉPOLE ROUGEÂTRE   Thin pink Mediterranean fish.

CERDAGNE   Region in *Roussillon*.

CERF   Red deer.

CERFEUIL   Chervil, herb.
Cerfeuil bulbeux: turnip-rooted chervil, vegetable.

CERISE   Cherry; *Montmorency* indicates their presence (e.g. *canard Montmorency*). *Cerises à l'aigre-doux/à l'allemande*: sweet-sour, as an *hors d'oeuvre* or with cold meats; *jubilé*: poached, flamed with *kirsch*.

CERNEAU   Green, unripe walnut. *Cerneaux aux verjus* (Touraine): marinated in acid grape juice, as a first course.

CERNIER   Type of sea bass (*bar*).

CÉRONS   Small area between *Graves* and *Barsac*, *Bordeaux*, making semi-sweet white wine (*AC*).

CERVELAS   Saveloy; smooth pork sausage originally made with brains (*cervelles*), large and lightly smoked; usually poached, eaten hot or cold. Those of *Paris*, *Lyon*, *Nancy* and *Strasbourg* are well known. *Cervelas en brioche* (Lyonnais): baked in *brioche* dough.
Cervelas de poisson (Champagne): pike loaf.

CERVELLE(S)   Brains, usually of calf. *Cervelles à la génoise*: fried with tomatoes and cheese; *royale*: puréed, mixed with egg yolks and cream; *de porc en matelote*: pig's brains stewed with vegetables.

CERVELLE DE CANUT   Lit.: 'silk-weaver's brain'. (Lyonnais) Home-made mixture of fermented curds, vinegar, white wine, oil and garlic; also known as *Claqueret Lyonnais*.

CÉSAR   Julius Caesar, apparently responsible for the dish with his name; see *poulet*.

CÉTEAU   (Charentes, Poitou) Local name for small sole (*solette*).

CÉVENNES   Mountainous region of *Languedoc*. *Salade des Cévennes*: potato, walnut and celery salad. See also *Rogeret des Cévennes*.

(À LA) CÉVENOLE   In the style of *Cévennes*. With chestnuts or mushrooms. See also *côtelette*.

CHABESSAL   See *cabessal*.

CHABI/CHABICHOU   (Poitou) Small, cone-shaped, goat's milk cheese, with strong smell and flavour, made by farms and dairies; also known as *Cabrichiu*, *Cajassous*, *Chaunay*, *Civray* and *Cujassou*.

CHABLIS   The most famous of dry white wines, and the most imitated. The small town of Chablis (*AC*) in N *Bourgogne* has seven *grand cru* (*AC*) *vineyards* – *Vaudésir*, *Les Preuses*, *Les Clos*, *Grenouilles*, *Bougros*, *Valmur* and *Blanchots* – and several *premiers crus*. Outside the central vineyards *Petit Chablis* (*AC*), a lighter wine, is grown. The grape variety is *Chardonnay*.

(À LA) CHABLISIENNE   In the style of *Chablis*. With *Chablis* wine. See also *escargot*.

CHABOISSEAU   Sea scorpion, fish related to *rascasse*.

CHABOT   Common name for various Mediterranean fish, including gurnard (*grondin*), goby (*gobie*), and *rascasse*; also name for chub (*chevaine*).

CHABRIS   Brand of *Valençay* cheese.

CHABROL   See below.

CHABROT   (SW, central France) Finishing touch to *garbure* – red or white wine poured into the last of the soup after the bread and vegetables have been eaten, and the mixture then drunk; also known as *chabrol* and *goudale*.

CHACHA   (Provence) Local name for thrush (*grive*).

CHACHLIK   Cubes of marinated lamb grilled on a skewer; the Russian shashlik.

CHAI   Wine and spirit cellar, especially in *Bordelais*. See also *maître de chai*.

(LA) CHAISE-DIEU   See *Galette de la Chaise-Dieu*.

CHALLANDAIS(-E)   Of Challans, in *Vendée*, known for table ducks; see also *canard*.

(À LA) CHALONNAISE   In the style of Chalon-sur-Saône in *Bourgogne*. Garnish of cockscombs and kidneys, mushrooms and truffles in white sauce, for poultry and sweetbreads. See also *Côte Chalonnaise*.

CHÂLONS-SUR-MARNE   Capital of the *Marne* department in *Champagne*.

(À LA) CHALUTIÈRE   Lit.: 'trawler's style'. *Salade chalutière*: (Boulonnais): herring, potato and mustard salad.

CHAMBARAND (Dauphiné) Small creamy mild cheese, made at the Abbey of Chambarand; also known as *Trappiste de Chambarand*.

CHAMBERTIN/CHAMBERTIN-CLOS DE BÈZE Two famous *grand cru* (*AC*) vineyards of the commune of *Gevrey-Chambertin* (considered together since *Clos de Bèze* may call itself *Chambertin*), producing some of the finest red wines of *Côte de Nuits*, *Bourgogne*; *Chambertin*, originally 'Champ de Bertin' (Bertin's field) was Napoleon's favourite wine. The village of *Gevrey* and seven other vineyards hyphenate their names with the magic of *Chambertin*; see *Gevrey-Chambertin*.

CHAMBÉRY Capital of *Savoie*.
One of the best and driest *vermouths* (*AC*), with a herby aroma, made around *Chambéry*.

CHAMBOLLE-MUSIGNY Commune (*AC*) of *Côte de Nuits*, *Bourgogne*, producing fine red wines, and a small quantity of white; it contains the *grand cru* (*AC*) vineyard *Les Musigny*, and part of *Bonnes Mares*.

(À LA) CHAMBORD See *carpe* for the dish probably created at the château of Chambord in *Orléanais*.

CHAMBOURCY Well-known brand of cream cheese, fresh and mild.

CHAMOIS Chamois, rare wild mountain antelope from the Alps and Pyrenees (where it is known as *isard*).

CHAMONIX Town in *Savoie*. *Pommes (de terre) Chamonix*: *dauphine* potatoes with cheese.

CHAMOURE (Bourgogne) Marrow flan.

CHAMPAGNE Province covering the departments of *Marne*, *Ardennes*, Aube and Haute-Marne. See also *Cognac* and *Riceys*.

The wine-growing regions of the province, the Montagne de Reims, Côte des Blancs and Vallée de la Marne, produce the most famous and most expensive sparkling wine in the world. Red and white grapes go into its composition – *Pinot Noir*, *Pinot Meunier* and *Chardonnay*, although the wine is almost always white, since the juice is not allowed to lie on the skins long enough to extract any pigment. The juice is fermented to make wine in the normal way and is then bottled with the addition of a small amount of sugar, which induces a second fermentation in the bottle; carbon dioxide gas is produced which is absorbed into the wine and results in the sparkle when the bottle is finally opened (this, in essence, is the *méthode champenoise*). Before being finally sealed, a mixture of sugar and old wine, known as the 'dosage', is added to the bottle, determining the degree of sweetness. *Champagne* is sold under the name of its maker, either a small grower (*récoltant-manipulant*), a co-operative, or one of the great *Champagne* houses (e.g. Moët et Chandon, Bollinger, Krug, Pol Roger, Louis Roederer, Veuve Cliquot; some of them known as *grandes marques*). Vintage *Champagne* is made in the best years, and there is also pink *Champagne*; *blanc de blancs*, made from white grapes only; and *Crémant*, with less sparkle.

(À LA) CHAMPENOISE In the style of *Champagne*. See *Coteaux champenois* and *quartier*.

CHAMPIGNON Mushroom. *Champignon de couche*: white cultivated mushroom, of the *psalliote* family. *Champignon de Paris*: cultivated button mushroom; the *Paris* area was a centre for mushroom farms in the 19th century.

General term for edible fungi. *Champignon de pin* (Provence): type of *cèpe* found in pine woods in autumn. *Champignon à la bague*: name for parasol mushroom (*coulemelle*, lit.: 'with the ring'). *Champignon polonais*: name of variety of boletus (*bolet*). (*Champignon*) *rose des champs/des prés*: name for wild variety of *psalliote*.

CHAMPIGNY Small puff pastry filled with apricot jam. See also *Saumur-Champigny*.

CHAMPOLÉON (Dauphiné) Hard cheese made from skimmed milk.

CHAMPOREAU Black coffee fortified with spirit.

CHAMPVALLON See *côtelette*.

CHANCIAU See *sanciau*.

(À LA) CHANOINESSE   Lit.: 'in the style of the canoness'. Garnish of carrots in cream with truffles.

CHANTECLAIR   See *poularde*.

CHANTERELLE   Yellow, trumpet-shaped fungus with fragrant flavour, found especially in wet summers, often bottled in oil; also known as *girolle*, *gyrole* and *petit gris*.

CHANTILLY   (*Crème*) *Chantilly*: stiffly whipped cream, sweetened and flavoured with vanilla or liqueur; sometimes served on its own with puréed fruit. *Sauce Chantilly*: mayonnaise, *béchamel* or *hollandaise* sauce with whipped cream; also known as *sauce mousseline/vierge*. Probably created by the chef to the *Condé* family at Chantilly in *Ile-de-France*.

CHAOURCE   (Champagne) Small cylindrical cheese (*AOC*), white, soft and creamy, with fruity flavour; made by dairies around Chaource.

CHAPEAU CHINOIS   Lit.: 'Chinese hat'. Name for limpet (*patelle*).

CHAPELLE-CHAMBERTIN   See *Gevrey-Chambertin*.

CHAPELURE   Breadcrumbs.

CHAPON   Capon, castrated cock; in practice interchangeable with *poularde* and *poulet*. *Chapon de Bresse gros sel*: *Bresse* capon with sliced truffles under the skin, surrounded in rock salt and baked; *à la carcassonnaise*: stuffed and spit-roasted.
　　　Piece of bread rubbed with garlic, oil, sometimes vinegar, used especially in *salade au chapon*.
　　　Name for *rascasse*.

CHARBON   Coal, charcoal. *Au charbon de bois*: grilled over charcoal.

CHARBONNÉ(-E)   Description for goat's milk cheeses dusted with charcoal to turn them blue.

CHARBONNIER   Lit.: 'to do with coal'. Name for coal fish (*lieu noir*). Also name for variety of fungus (*russule*).

CHARCUTERIE   Prepared and cooked pork – hams, sausages, *boudins*, *pâtés*, brawns, knuckles etc. Shop selling such products, run by a *charcutier* (from '*cuiseur de chair*' – cooker of meat), in practice usually like a delicatessen and including other meat products and made-up dishes (e.g. pies, *quiches*, pizzas, salads).

(À LA) CHARCUTIÈRE   Lit.: 'in the style of the *charcutier*'. *Sauce charcutière*: piquant sauce of white wine, vinegar,

shallots, mustard and gherkins, for pork. With *char-cuterie*. See also *haricot blanc*.

CHARDONNAY Variety of white grape, also known, incorrectly, as *Pinot Chardonnay*: used to make *Chablis* and the fine white wines of *Côte de Beaune*, and essential to *Champagne*.

(À LA) CHARENTAISE In the style of *Charentes*. See *homard*, *huître*, *lavagnon*, *mulet* and *rognon*.
　　Charentais: Charentais melon, originally from *Charentes*.

CHARENTES Region covering the departments of Charente and Charente-Maritime, the same area as the provinces of *Angoumois*, *Aunis* and *Saintonge*. See also *beurre*.

CHARGOUÈRE/CHERGOUÈRE (Bourbonnais) Plum or prune pastry.

CHARIOT Trolley, of *hors d'oeuvres* or desserts.

CHARLEROI See *côtelette*.

CHARLEVILLE-MÉZIÈRES Capital of *Ardennes*.

CHARLOTTE Hot fruit pudding, usually of apples, baked in a mould lined with buttered bread; known in France and England in the 18th century.

Cold custard cream (*bavarois*) or *mousse* in a mould lined with sponge fingers; invented by *Carême* when chef to Czar Alexander I, originally called *charlotte parisienne*, later *charlotte russe*. *Charlotte africaine*: with chocolate *mousse*; *aux cheveux d'ange*: with grated carrots and cream; *mexicaine*: with coffee and chocolate *mousse*.

Charlotte des Adhemars (Dauphiné): chocolate and *kirsch* cake.

CHARMES-CHAMBERTIN See *Gevrey-Chambertin*.

CHAROL(L)AIS Region in *Bourgogne*.

Breed of cattle with distinctive pale coats, considered excellent beef, originally from *Charollais*.

Dry goat's milk cheese; farm-made in *Charollais*, also known as *Autun*.

(À LA) CHAROL(L)AISE In the style of *Charolais*. Garnish of puréed turnips and cauliflower. See also *queue de boeuf*.

(À LA) CHARTRAINE/CHARTRES (In the style of) Chartres, capital of the Eure-et-Loir department in *Orléanais*. Garnish of potatoes with tarragon; or braised lettuce and stuffed mushrooms; or turnips and puréed peas and potatoes. *Oeufs à la Chartres*: poached eggs with tarragon. See also *pâté*.

CHARTREUSE Lit.: 'Carthusian'. Liqueur made by Carthusian monks in the Massif de la Chartreuse (where the Carthusian order was founded in the 11th century) in *Dauphiné*; a secret recipe, but brandy-based with herbs and plants, in 2 colours – green, the strongest, and yellow.

Of game birds, occasionally meat and large fish, braised with cabbage, bacon, sausage etc and served, often elaborately, turned out of a mould with vegetables (e.g. *faisan à la/en chartreuse*).

Chartreuse au citron: lemon jelly with grapes and cream. *Chartreuse de sardines* (Pays basque): sardines baked with spinach, garlic and sweet peppers.

CHASSAGNE-MONTRACHET Commune (*AC*) of *Côte de Beaune*, *Bourgogne*, known for fine white wines, also growing excellent reds; it contains the *grand cru* (*AC*) vineyard *Criots-Bâtard-Montrachet*, and part of the prestigious *Le Montrachet* and *Bâtard-Montrachet*.

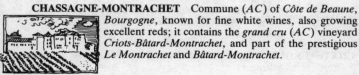

CHASSELAS Variety of white table grape, originally named after a village in *Bourgogne*. Used for second-class wines in *Alsace*, *Savoie* and *Nivernais*.

CHASSEUR Lit.: 'huntsman'. Garnish of mushrooms stuffed with onion purée. *Sauce chasseur*: white wine, mushroom and tomato sauce, sometimes mixed with brown sauce (e.g. *poulet chasseur*). *Consommé chasseur*: clear game soup with port and mushrooms.

(Savoie) Local name for blenny (*blennie cagnette*).

CHÂTAIGNE   Chestnut, also known as *marron*.

CHÂTAIGNE D'EAU   Water chestnut, plant with chestnut-flavoured fruit; also known as *macre*.

CHÂTAIGNE DE MER   (S France) Local name for sea urchin (*oursin*).

CHÂTEAU   Lit.: 'castle'. In wine terms, wine-growing estate; there are literally thousands of wines sold under *château* names.

   Pommes (*de terre*) *château*: potatoes in strips or olive shapes cooked in butter; garnish for grilled *chateabriand* steak. See also *entrecôte*.

CHATEAUBRIAND/CHÂTEAUBRIANT   Thickest part of the fillet of beef, usually for two people; often grilled, garnished with *pommes château*, and served with *sauce chateaubriand*: white wine, shallot and herb sauce. The name perhaps alluded to a book by Chateaubriand, or was created by his chef, or may have originated in the town of Châteaubriant in *Bretagne*.

   (Normandie) Triple cream cheese; brand name.

CHÂTEAU-CHALON   Town in *Franche-Comté* (not a château), celebrated for its *vin jaune* (*AC*).

CHÂTEAU GRILLET   Vineyard (*AC*) in the *Rhône* valley, making rare, expensive, white wine from the *Viognier* grape.

CHÂTEAUMEILLANT   Small area in Berry, making red and rosé wines (*VDQS*).

CHÂTEAUNEUF-DU-PAPE   Lit.: 'new castle of the Pope'. Village in *Vaucluse*, so named from its 14th-century castle built for the Popes of *Avignon*; they too were responsible for the original vineyards, which now produce the most famous red wine (*AC*) of the *Rhône*, as well as a small amount of fine white wine.

CHÂTEAUROUX   Capital of the Indre department in *Berry*. See also *Valençay*.

(À LA) CHÂTELAINE   Lit.: 'in the style of the lady of the manor'. Garnish of artichoke hearts filled with chestnut purée, plus braised lettuce, potato balls, sometimes creamed onions.

CHÂTILLON-EN-DIOIS   Area in *Dauphiné*, making red, white and rosé wines (*AC*).

CHATOUILLARD   *Pommes* (*de terre frites*) *chatouillard*: fried ribbon potatoes. 'Chatouiller' means to tickle.

CHAUCETIER   See *Coulandon*.

CHAUCHAT   Of fish, poached in white wine and surrounded with potatoes.

CHAUD(-E)   Warm, hot. Heat.

CHAUDÉ   (Lorraine) Large plum tart.

CHAUDEU   (Nice) Orange-flavoured tart.

CHAUD-FROID   Lit.: 'hot-cold'. Poultry or game served cold in thick white sauce, glazed with jelly.

CHAUDRÉE   (Charentes, Poitou) Conger eel and white fish stew with potatoes, garlic and white wine; originally cooked in a *chaudron*.

CHAUDRON   Cauldron, kettle.

CHAUDRONNÉE   Kettleful.

CHAUME   Area of *Anjou*, producing sweet white wines (*AC*).

CHAUMONT   Capital of the Haute-Marne department in *Champagne*. Small spicy cheese made around *Chaumont*.

CHAUNAY   See *Chabichou*.

(À LA) CHAURIENNE   In the style of Castlenaudary in *Languedoc*.

CHAUSSETTE   Lit.: 'sock'. See *café*.

CHAUSSON   Puff pastry turnover with sweet or savoury filling.

CHAVANNE   Name for chub (*chevaine*).

CHAVIGNOL(-SANCERRE)   (Berry) Small, flat, round, goat's milk cheese, with mild nutty flavour, made by farms around Chavignol and *Sancerre*; often known wrongly as *Crottin*.

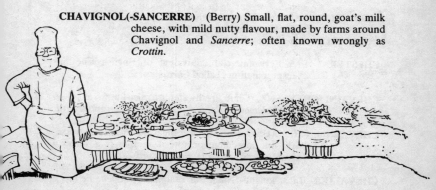

CHAYOT(T)E   Chayote, type of gourd (sometimes translated as custard marrow, although others give this name to *patisson*); also known as *brionne*. *Chayotes à la créole*: stewed with onion, garlic and tomato, plus rice.

CHEDDAR   See *Chester*.

CHEF   Chef, short for *chef de cuisine*: head of the kitchen. A dish described as *du chef* should be a speciality of the restaurant.

CHEILLY-LES-MARANGES   Commune of *Côte de Beaune*, *Bourgogne*, making red and white wines (*AC*), the red usually sold as *Côte de Beaune-Villages*.

CHEMISE   Lit.: 'shirt'. Term used for an ingredient or dish in some kind of wrapping, either its natural one, or pastry, pancake batter, spinach leaves, ice cream etc. *Négresse en chemise*: chocolate *mousse* or ice cream covered with ice cream or cream. *Pommes (de terre) en chemise*: jacket potatoes. *Saucisses en chemise*: sausages in pastry.

CHEMITRÉ   (Lorraine) Waffle.

CHÉNAS   See *Beaujolais*.

CHENIN BLANC   Variety of white grape, important in the *Loire*; also known as *Pineau de la Loire*.

CHERBOURG   Port in *Normandie*. See also *demoiselle*.

(À LA) CHERBOURGEOISE   In the style of *Cherbourg*. See *pied* and *vras*.

CHERGOUÈRE   See *chargouère*.

CHERRY   Cherry brandy.

CHÉRUBIN   Lit.: 'cherub'. See *barbue*.

CHERVILLE   See *chevreuil*.

CHESTER   French commercial equivalent of English Cheshire cheese; sometimes called *Cheddar*.

CHEVAINE/CHEVESNE   Chub, freshwater fish; also known as *cabot*, *chabot*, *chavanne*, *dobule*, *meunier*, *rotisson* and *testard*.

CHEVAL (pl. CHEVAUX)   Horse; horse meat. *À cheval*: on horseback, one ingredient on top of another (e.g. *anges à cheval*, *bifteck à cheval*). See also *groseille*.

CHEVALIER   Lit.: 'knight'. Name for sandpiper (*alouette de mer*);

also for wader (*échassier*). Name for variety of fungus (*tricholome*). See also *omble-chevalier*.

(À LA) CHEVALIÈRE   Lit.: 'knightly style'. See *poularde*.

CHEVALIER-MONTRACHET   See *Puligny-Montrachet*.

CHEVALIN(-E)   Of horses (e.g. *boucherie chevaline*).

CHEVERNY   Small commune in *Orléanais*, making light white wines (*VDQS*).

CHEVESNE   Name for chub (*chevaine*).

CHEVEUX D'ANGE   Lit.: 'angel's hair'. Vermicelli, thin pasta, as used in *consommé cheveux d'ange*.
   Grated carrot; see *carotte* and *charlotte*.

CHÈVRE   Goat. Short for *fromage de chèvre*: goat's milk cheese. *Chèvre à la Feuille*: see *Mothe-Saint-Héray*. *Chèvre Long*: see *Sainte-Maure*. See also *Tomme de Chèvre*.
   Name for *rascasse*.

CHEVREAU   Young goat, kid, eaten particularly in *Charentes*, *Poitou*, S France and *Corse*; also known as *broutard*, *cabiros*, *cabri* and *tetard*.

CHEVRET   See *Tomme de Chèvre*.

CHEVRETON D'AMBERT (DE VIVEROLS)/DE MÂCON   See *Brique du Forez* and *Mâconnais*.

CHEVRETTE   (Charentes) Local name for shrimp (*crevette*). See also *serran*.

CHEVRETTE DES BAUGES   (Savoie) Small mild goat's milk cheese, made by mountain dairies in Les Bauges.

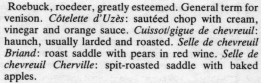

CHEVREUIL   Roebuck, roedeer, greatly esteemed. General term for venison. *Côtelette d'Uzès*: sautéed chop with cream, vinegar and orange sauce. *Cuissot/gigue de chevreuil*: haunch, usually larded and roasted. *Selle de chevreuil Briand*: roast saddle with pears in red wine. *Selle de chevreuil Cherville*: spit-roasted saddle with baked apples.
   En chevreuil: cooked like venison. *Gigot de mouton en chevreuil*: leg of mutton larded with bacon, marinated and roasted. And/or with *sauce chevreuil*: game sauce with red wine and sometimes redcurrant jelly.

CHEVREUSE   Garnish of artichokes, truffles and mushrooms; probably after the 17th-century Duc de Chevreuse.

CHEVRIER   Type of green haricot bean, from Arpajon in *Ile-de-France*; named after its 'inventor'.

CHEVRINE DE LENTA   (Savoie) Firm, fresh, goat's milk cheese, with nutty to sharp flavour, made in dairies in Haute-Maurienne; also known as *Tomme Maurienne*.

CHEVROTIN DES ARAVIS   (Savoie) Firm, mild, goat's milk cheese; made in dairies in the Massif des Aravis.

CHEVROTIN DU BOURBONNAIS   (Bourbonnais)   Cone-shaped goat's milk cheese, eaten fresh or semi-dry, creamy to strong in taste; farm-made, also known as (*Chevrotin de*) *Conne* and *Chevrotin de Moulins/de Souvigny*.

CHEVRU   (Ile-de-France) Soft, round cheese with fruity flavour, similar to *Brie*, made by traditional factories; originally from the village of Chevru.

CHEZ NOUS   At our place. *La tarte de chez-nous*: our own special home-made flan.

CHICHI FRÉGI   (Provence) Small round sweet fritter.

CHICON   Name sometimes given to chicory (*endive*); also to cos lettuce (*laitue romaine*).

CHICORÉE (FRISÉE)   Curly endive – in English, called chicory in the USA – salad green like a frizzy lettuce. (But English chicory, American endive, the tightly furled white vegetable, is *endive belge/witloof*.) *Chicorée* can also be applied to Batavian endive or escarole, properly *scarole*. *Moelle de chicorée*: stumps of curly endive, also known as *gourilos*.
    Chicorée sauvage: wild chicory, including the varieties *barbe de capucin* and *pain de sucre*. *Chicorée à café*: chicory (root), used as an addition to or substitute for coffee.

CHIEN (DE MER)   Lit.: '(sea) dog'. General name for dogfish (*aiguillat, roussette*); also for types of shark, sometimes eaten as steaks (*émissole, milandre, requin marteau, taupe*).
    (Provence) Local name for scad (*saurel*).

CHIFFONNADE   Preparation of vegetables, especially sorrel or lettuce, cut into thin strips or ribbons, often added to clear soups; from 'chiffon'-rag. Sometimes means a green pea soup.

(À LA) CHILIENNE   Chilean-style. *Consommé à la chilienne*: clear chicken soup with rice and sweet peppers.

CHIMAY   *Oeufs Chimay*: eggs with white sauce. Named after the dancer, Clara Ward, who appeared at the Folies Bergère as the Princess Caraman-Chimay.

CHINCHARD   Name for scad (*saurel*).

CHINE/CHINOIS(-E)   China/Chinese. *Chinois*: small candied orange.

CHINON   Town in *Touraine*, growing red, white, rosé wines (*AC*).

(À LA) CHINONAISE   In the style of *Chinon*. Garnish of potatoes and cabbage stuffed with sausage. See also *lamproie*.

CHIP   *Pommes* (*de terre*) *chip*(*s*): hot or cold potato crisps.

CHIPIRONS   (Pays basque) Local name for squid (*calamar*). *Chipirons à l'encre*: stuffed and stewed with tomatoes in their own ink.

CHIPOLATA   Chipolata sausage. Garnish of chipolatas, onions, bacon and chestnuts.

CHIRLAT   (Pays basque) Local name for clam (*palourde*).

CHIROUBLES   See *Beaujolais*.

CHIVRY   With white wine, shallot, tarragon and chervil, as in *beurre/sauce Chivry*.

CHOCART   (Bretagne) Apple pastry.

CHOCH'CREUPÉ   (Lorraine) Sweet fritter.

CHOCOLAT   Chocolate. *Un chocolat*: a cup of hot chocolate, a common alternative to coffee at breakfast. In a shop – *chocolat à croquer*: plain chocolate; *au lait*: milk chocolate; *de ménage/à cuire*: cooking chocolate; *en poudre*: drinking chocolate.

CHOISY   Garnish of braised lettuce and potatoes. *Crème Choisy*: lettuce cream soup.

CHOIX   Choice, selection (e.g. *omelette aux choix*). Choice, fine.

CHOLANDE AUX POMMES   (Lorraine) Apple tart.

CHOPE   Beer mug. Glass of beer.

CHOQUART   (Bretagne) Cinnamon and apple pastry.

CHOREY-LES-BEAUNE   Minor commune (*AC*) of *Côte de Beaune*, *Bourgogne*, most of its wine sold as *Côte de Beaune-Villages*.

CHORIZO   (Pays basque) Highly seasoned sausage, of Spanish origin.

CHORLATTE   (Bourgogne) Stuffed baked cabbage dumplings in pastry.

CHORON   Chef at the *Voisin* restaurant. Garnish of artichoke hearts filled with peas or asparagus, and potato balls. *Sauce Choron*: *béarnaise* sauce with tomato purée.

CHOTENN BIGOUDENN   Pig's head with garlic, roasted in the baker's oven.

CHOU (pl. CHOUX)   Cabbage. Types include *chou cabus*: white cabbage; *chou frisé*: kale; *chou de mai*: spring (lit.: 'May') cabbage; *chou pommée*: firm round cabbage; *chou vert*: green cabbage; see also below. *Chou à la poitevine*: cooked with pork and goose; *farci à la limousine*: rolled, stuffed with bacon and chestnuts; *farci à la vivaraise*: stuffed, braised with sausages, tomatoes and sweet peppers. See also *lapin*.

Choux bun, puff, looking like a small cabbage (hence the name), made of *choux* pastry. *Pâte à chou*: light puff pastry used for *éclairs*, *profiteroles* etc, and savoury dishes; invented by *Carême*.

CHOU CARAÏBE   Caribbean cabbage, grown in S France.

CHOUCROUTE   (Alsace, Champagne) Pickled, fermented white cabbage, like the German 'Sauerkraut', processed commercially and sold throughout France; eaten cold or hot, usually cooked in pork or goose fat with onion, juniper berries, white wine or *kirsch*. *Choucroute garni*: with any or all of sausages, bacon, pork, fresh or smoked goose, potatoes. *Choucroute royale*: with *Champagne*.

CHOU DE CHINE   Chinese cabbage/leaf, resembling coarse cos lettuce.

CHOU DE MER/CHOU MARIN   Sea kale, whose long thick leaf stalks are eaten; also known as *chou marin* and *crambe*.

CHOUÉE   (Angoumois, Poitou, Anjou) Boiled, buttered cabbage, sometimes with boiled potatoes.

CHOU-FLEUR   Cauliflower; *Dubarry* indicates its presence. *Chou-fleur à la bourbonnaise*: with vinegar, shallot and cream sauce; *pimprenelle*: cold, cooked in mustard and cream sauce, as a first course; *à la polonaise*: fried, sprinkled with hard-boiled eggs, parsley and breadcrumbs.

CHOU MARIN   Name for sea kale (*chou de mer*).

CHOU-NAVET   Swede, also known as *rutabaga*.

CHOU-RAVE   Kohlrabi, delicately-flavoured, with round swollen stem.

CHOU ROUGE   Red cabbage. *Chou rouge à la flamande*: stewed with vinegar, apples and sugar; *landais*: stewed with red wine, sausages, onions, apples and sweet peppers;

à la lilloise: cooked in butter with onion and spices; *à la limousine*: stewed with pork fat and chestnuts; *à la d'Orléans*: stewed with red wine, apples and spices; *à la Valenciennes*: stewed with bacon and apples.

CHOUX   Plural of *chou*.

CHOUX BROCOLIS   Broccoli; also known as *brocoli*.

CHOUX DE BRUXELLES   Brussels sprouts. *Brabançonne/bruxelloise* signifies their presence.

CHRAU   (S France) Local name for umbrine (*ombrine*).

CHRIST-MARINE   Samphire, type of vegetable; also known as *bacile*, *criste-marine*, *fenouil marin*, *herbe de Saint-Pierre* and *perce-pierre*.

CHUSCLAN   See *Côtes du Rhône-Villages*.

CIBOULE   Spring onion.

CIBOULETTE   Chives, the herb; also known as *appétit*, *cives* and *civette*.

CICERELLE   Name for sand eel (*équille*).

CIDRE   Cider, traditional drink of W France, and used in local cooking, particularly in *Normandie*. *Cidre bouché*: sparkling cider.

CIER DE LUCHON   See *Bethmale*.

CIGALE   Lit.: 'cicada'. Flat lobster, which makes a cricket-like chirp; also known as *marieta*.

CIGARE   Lit.: 'cigar'. Name for grey mullet (*mulet*).

CIGARETTE (RUSSE)   Thin round cigarette-shaped biscuit.

CILLETTE   (Normandie) Local name for queen scallop (*pétoncle*).

CIMEREAU   (Bretagne) Cake eaten with butter.

CIMIER   Haunch, of venison.

(À LA) CINGALAISE   Singhalese-style. With curried sauce.

CIRITA   (Corse) Local name for grey mullet (*mulet*).

CITRON   Lemon; not to be confused with *limon*: lime (also known as *citron vert*), nor with *cédrat*: citron. *Citron pressé*: fresh lemon juice, served as a drink with sugar.

CITRONNADE   Lemon squash.

CITRONNELLE   Lemon liqueur.

CITRONNÉ(-E)   Lemon-flavoured.

CITROUILLAT   (Berry) Pumpkin pie.

CITROUILLE   Pumpkin; also known as *potiron*. *Soupe à la citrouille*: puréed pumpkin soup.

CIVELLES   (Bretagne, Nantais) Tiny eels, usually deep-fried.

CIVES   Name for chives (*ciboulette*).

CIVET   Rich stew of hare or venison, with wine, bacon, vegetables, and the sauce thickened with the blood of the animal; perhaps derived from *cives*, originally used to flavour the dish. *Civet de lièvre de Capucin* (Bourgogne): hare marinated and stewed with wine, *marc*, shallots and herbs; *Diane de Châteaumorand* (Bresse): stewed hare with red wine, onions and mushrooms; *landais*: hare stewed in red wine with ham, tomatoes and cèpes; *à la lyonnaise*: stewed hare with chestnuts.
   Civet de langouste (Languedoc): *langouste* stewed with white wine, onions, tomatoes and garlic. *Civet de pêcheur* (Bretagne): shellfish (*ormeaux*) with red wine, onions and bacon. *Civet de tripes d'oie au vinaigre* (Gascogne): goose tripe stewed in vinegar with shallots and garlic, the sauce thickened with blood. *Civet d'écureuil* (Languedoc): squirrel with red wine and orange peel. *Civet de marmotte* (Dauphiné): of mountain squirrel.

CIVETTE   Name for chives (*ciboulette*).

CIVRAY   See *Chabichou*.

CLAFOUTI(S) (AUX CERISES)   (Limousin, Berry especially) Batter cake with black cherries; traditionally given to grape harvesters.

CLAIRE   Oyster park in *Marennes*, sometimes used to describe the oyster itself; see also *huître*.

CLAIRET   Lit.: 'light'. Very light style of red wine, made in *Bordeaux*, *Bourgogne* and elsewhere.

CLAIRETTE   Variety of white grape grown in S France. See also below.
   Name for lamb's lettuce (*mâche*).

CLAIRETTE DE BELLEGARDE   Dry white wine (*AC*) from *Gard*.

CLAIRETTE DE DIE   Sparkling white wine (*AC*), made partly from the *Clairette* grape at Die in *Dauphiné*.

CLAIRETTE DU LANGUEDOC   Dry white wine (*AC*) from *Hérault*.

CLAM Name for clam (*palourde*).

CLAMART Area in *Ile-de-France* known (like *Saint-Germain*) for peas. With peas. Formal garnish of artichoke hearts or pastry cases filled with peas, and potato balls.

(À LA) CLAMECYÇOISE In style of Clamecy in *Bourgogne*. See *cul*.

CLAOUGEOU (Provence) Local name for squid (*calamar*).

CLAPOTONS *Salade de clapotons*: salad of boiled sheep's trotters, served with mayonnaise.

CLAQUEBITOU (Bourgogne) Fresh, herb-flavoured goat's milk cheese.

CLAQUERET LYONNAIS See *Cervelle de Canut*.

CLARENCE With curried cream sauce.

CLAUDINE See *alose*.

CLAVAIRE Family of fungi of various colours, rather tough; some varieties also known as *barbe de chêne* and *mainotte*.

CLAVELADO (Provence) Local name for ray (*raie bouclée*).

CLÉMENTINE Clementine, small citrus fruit.

CLÉOPÂTRE Cleopatra. See *truite*.

(À LA) CLERMONT With cabbage rolls and salt pork; or with chestnuts and onions.

CLERMONT-FERRAND Capital of the Puy-de-Dôme department in *Auvergne*.

CLIMAT Lit.: 'climate'. Individual field in a vineyard, especially in *Bourgogne*.

CLITOPILE Type of fungus similar to *chanterelle*, firm and good to eat; also known as *mousseron d'automne* and *oreille de meunier*.

CLOCHARD See *Reinette*.

CLOCHE Dome-shaped cover, of silver or glass, for serving (e.g. *champignons sous cloche*).

CLOS Lit.: 'enclosure'. Orchard of apple trees. Vineyard, originally walled, especially in *Bourgogne*. (*Les*) *Clos*: see *Chablis*.

CLOS DE BÈZE See *Chambertin*.

CLOS DE LA ROCHE/DE TART   See *Morey-Saint-Denis*.

CLOS DES LAMBRAYS   See *Morey-Saint-Denis*.

CLOS DE VOUGEOT   See *Vougeot*.

CLOS SAINT-DENIS   See *Morey-Saint-Denis*.

CLOU DE GIROFLE   Clove, the spice.

CLOUTÉ(-E)   Studded.

CLOVISSE   Small type of clam.
(Provence) Local name for clam, carpet-shell (*palourde*).

COCHEREL   Village in *Normandie*. See *alose*.

COCHERELLE   Name for parasol mushroom (*coulemelle*).

COCHON   Pig. *Cochon de lait Saint-Fortunat*: roast sucking pig stuffed with its liver, barley, herbs, sausages, chestnuts.

COCHON DE MER   Triggerfish (*baliste*).

COCHONNADE/COCHONNAILLE   Pork products. *Assiette de cochonnaille*: selection of cold pork, ham etc. *Cochonnailles lyonnaises*: boiled pig's head, ribs, trotters and rind with vegetables and sausage, served with hot potato salad and onion sauce.

COCKTAIL   Cocktail (party). Mixture. Can mean tiny, miniature.

COCO   Coconut, also known as *noix de coco*. See also *lait*.
(Provence) Local name for haricot bean.

COCON   Lit.: 'cocoon'. Name for variety of fungus (*oronge*).

COCOTTE   Casserole (e.g. *poulet en cocotte*: pot-roasted, casseroled chicken).
Small round dish, especially for *oeufs en cocotte*: eggs lightly cooked; served in *cocotte* dishes, often with cream.

CODONAT   (Provence) Local name for quince (*coing*).

COEUR   Heart, core. *Coeur de boeuf/de veau*: ox/calf's heart (but see also below). *Coeur de filet*: best cut of fillet, of beef.
Heart-shaped, especially of cheese; see also below.
Coeur à la crème: small cream cheese, often homemade, drained in a heart-shaped mould and served with cream, sugar or fruit.

COEUR D'ARRAS   (Artois) Version of *Quart Maroilles* or *Rollot* cheese, made around *Arras*.
Spice bread, from *Arras*.

COEUR DE BOEUF   Heart-shaped shellfish.

COEUR DE BRAY   (Normandie) Firm, white cheese, with fruity flavour, made in *Bray*.

COEUR DE PALMIER   Palm heart, tinned palm tree shoots; usually served cold with *vinaigrette* as a first course.

COFFRE   Lit.: 'chest'. Body, of lobster.

COGNAC    Town in *Charentes* which has given its name to the world's most famous brandy, distilled from white wine grown in a strictly defined area, with the *AC Cognac*. The vineyards cover most of the departments of Charente and Charente-Maritime and some of the offshore islands, but it is around *Cognac* itself that the finest brandy is produced. The recognized areas of excellence present a rough pattern of circles radiating from *Cognac*, with *Grande Champagne*, the very best, at the centre, surrounded in descending order by *Petite Champagne* and Borderies, Fins Bois (all considered first-class vineyards), Bons Bois and Bois Ordinaires. Most of the spirit goes to the famous *Cognac* houses (e.g. Courvoisier, Hennessy, Martell) for maturation and selling. The words *Grande/Petite Champagne* mean high quality brandy from those vineyards, while *Fine Champagne* denotes brandy from either *Champagne* area or a mixture of the two. Indications of age are 3 stars: under 4½ years old; *VS/VO/VSOP*: at least 4½ years old; *Extra/Napoléon/XO/Grande Réserve*: at least 5½ years old, although part of the blend may be much older.

COGNE   (Languedoc) Dry, pepper cake.

COIFFE   See *crépine*.

COING   Quince, like small tart apple, used in confectionery, especially for *cotignac*; also known as *codonat*. Also fruit brandy made from quinces.

COINTREAU   Colourless orange-flavoured liqueur, made at *Angers* by the firm of Cointreau.

COIREAU   (Charentes) Maize cake.

(À LA) COLBERT   Chief minister of Louis XIV. Dipped in egg and breadcrumbs and fried, usually of fish. *Beurre/sauce Colbert*: butter/sauce based on meat glaze and tarragon. *Consommé Colbert*: clear chicken soup with vegetables and poached egg. See also *abricot*.

COLIMAÇON   Name for snail.

COLIN   Hake, also known as *saumon blanc*, *merlu(che)*, *merlan*, and *canapé*. *Colin à la granvillaise*: marinated, fried, with shrimps; *à la grenobloise*: cooked with butter, capers and lemon.

    Colin (jaune/noir): name for pollack/coalfish (*lieu jaune/noir*).

COLIN LOUI   American quail, also known as *caille d'Amérique*.

COLINEAU/COLINOT   Codling, also known as *merluchon*.

COLLERETTE   Lit.: 'collaret'. *Pommes (de terre frites) en collerette*: finely sliced fried potatoes, also known as *en liards*.

COLLET/COLLIER   Collar, neck. Scrag, of mutton.

COLLIOURE   Port in *Roussillon*. *Sauce Collioure*: anchovy-flavoured mayonnaise.
    Robust red wine (*AC*) made in small quantities around *Collioure*.

COLMAR   Capital of the Haut-Rhin department in *Alsace*.

(À LA) COLMARIENNE   In the style of *Colmar*. See *grenouille*.

COLOMBE   Dove.

COLOMBIÈRE   (Savoie) Variety of *Reblochon*, made on farms around the Col de la Colombière.

COLOMBINE   Savoury croquette with outer layer of semolina and Parmesan cheese.

COLONEL   Lit.: 'colonel'. See *Livarot*.

COLVERT   Lit.: 'green neck'. Name for wild duck (*canard sauvage*).

COLZA   Colza. See *huile*.

COMBOVIN   See *Tomme de Chèvre*.

COMMANDE Order. *À la commande*: cooked in the way you ask. *Sur commande*: cooked to order.

COMMANDER To order (a meal).

COMMODORE Lit.: 'commodore'. Garnish of crayfish, mussels and fish *quenelles*, for fish.

COMMUN(-E) Common, usual.

COMMUNARD (Bourgogne) *Crème de cassis* with red wine.

COMMUNE Commune, parish. In wine-growing terms, village containing several vineyards.

COMPIÈGNE Town in *Ile-de-France* known (like *Soissons*) for white haricot beans (e.g. *potage Compiègne*).

COMPLET (COMPLÈTE) Complete, whole. Full. See also *café* and *pain*.

COMPOSÉ(-E) Compound. See also *salade*.

COMPOTE Compote, stewed fruit, usually served cold.
Slow-cooked stew of pigeon, partridge etc.

COMPOTIER Fruit bowl, dish.

COMPRIS(-E) Included. See also *couvert*.

(À LA) COMTADINE In the style of *Comtat Venaissin*.

COMTAT VENAISSIN Region approximating to *Vaucluse*, a former papal state.

COMTÉ County. Also short for *Franche-Comté*.
Large round cheese (*AOC*), cooked, ripened 3–4 months, with slightly holey interior and fruity flavour; also known as *Gruyère de Comté*, made in *Franche-Comté*.

COMTÉ DE FOIX See *Foix*.

COMTÉ DE NICE See *Nice*.

COMTESSE Lit.: 'countess'. *Crème contesse*: cream of asparagus soup.

(À LA) COMTOISE In the style of *Franche-Comté*.

(À LA) CONCARNOISE In the style of Concarneau in *Bretagne*. See *thon*.

CONCASSÉ(-E) Crushed, ground. Of tomatoes, skinned, deseeded and coarsely chopped, used as a garnish or in salads.

CONCOMBRE   Cucumber; *Doria* signifies their presence. *Concombres à la dijonnaise*: stewed with oil, vinegar and mustard, as a first course.

CONCORDE   Lit.: 'concord'. Garnish of peas, carrots and mashed potatoes.

CONDÉ   Important noble family residing at *Chantilly*; 'Le Grand Condé', cousin of Louis XIV, had as his chef Vatel, who committed suicide when there was not enough food for a royal feast. With red haricot beans (e.g. *potage Condé*). See also *sole*.
　　　Fruit and creamed rice (e.g. *poires Condé*).
　　　Pastry with almond icing.

CONDRIEU   Commune on the *Rhône*, making a small quantity of high quality dry white wine (*AC*). See also *grillade* and *Rigotte de Condrieu*.

CONFÉRENCE   Conference pear.

CONFIDOU(S)   (Rouergue) Beef stewed in red wine with tomatoes, garlic, onions.

CONFISERIE   Confectionery, sweets. Confectioner's shop.

CONFIT(-E)   Preserved. Candied, crystallized, especially of fruit.
　　　(SW France) Preserved meat, especially goose (*confit d'oie*), duck and pork, occasionally turkey and chicken, salted, cooked and preserved in its own fat in stoneware pots.

CONFITURE   Jam, fruit preserve. *Confiture d'oranges*: orange marmalade.

CONFRÉRIE DES CHEVALIERS DU TASTEVIN   See *tastevin*.

CONGRE   Conger eel, sea eel (as opposed to *anguille*); also known as *anguille de mer* and *fiéla*. *Congre à la mode de Belle-Ile*: sliced, cooked in butter with potatoes; *à la dinardaise*: cooked in cider with onions; *au lait* (SW France): baked with milk, onions and potatoes.

CONNE   See *Chevrotin du Bourbonnais*.

CONQUE   See *coque*.

CONSEILLÉ(-E)   Advised, recommended.

CONSERVE   Preserve, conserve. Tinned.

CONSOMMATIONS   Drinks, snacks, ordered in a café.

CONSOMMÉ   Clear soup, usually of beef, game or poultry and garnished with vegetables, herbs, pasta etc. *Consommé en gelée*: cold jellied clear soup. For the many different types, see under their distinguishing names (e.g. *consommé Céléstine*: see *Céléstine*).

CONTAR (Provence) Local name for small snail.

CONTI Important noble family. With lentils and bacon (e.g. *potage Conti*).

CONTRE-FILET Part of the sirloin, of beef; also known as *faux-filet*.

CONTREX Brand of still mineral water from the spa at Contrexéville in *Lorraine*.

CONVERSATION Lit.: 'conversation'. Iced puff pastry tarts with almond filling.

COPEAU Lit.: 'wood shaving'. Shaving of chocolate, to decorate a cake. Small cake.
　　Pommes (*de terre*) *frites copeaux*: fried ribbon potatoes.

COPPA (Corse) Smoked pork in a large sausage.

COPRIN/(À CHEVELURE) Shaggy ink cap (lit.: 'with hair'), type of fungus.

COQ Cock, cockerel, in practice interchangeable with *poularde* and *poulet*. *Coq au Riesling* (Alsace): with *Riesling* wine and cream; *au vin*: flamed in brandy, stewed in red wine, with button onions and mushrooms; *au vin jaune* (Franche-Comté): stewed in the yellow wine of *Arbois*, with cream and morels.
　　Ship's cook.

COQ DE BRUYÈRE Lit.: 'cock of heath'. Wood grouse, capercaillie, now rare; also black grouse.

COQ DE MER Name for box crab (*calappe*).

COQUE Shell. *Oeufs à la coque*: soft-boiled eggs, eaten in the shell. See also *perdreau*.
　　Cockle; also known as *bucarde*, *hénon* and *sourdon*.
　　(Quercy) Citron- and angelica-flavoured *brioche*, traditionally made at Easter; also known as *conque*.

COQUE RAYÉE Lit.: 'striped shell'. (Bretagne) Local name for clam (*palourde*).

COQUELET Cockerel. *Coquelet à la vesulienne*: stuffed with its liver and bacon, baked in pastry.

COQUELICOT Name for poppy (*pavot*).

COQUELIN   See *sole*.

COQUERET   Name for strawberry tomato (*alkékenge*).

COQUIBUS   See *lapin*.

COQUILLAGES   General term for shellfish.

COQUILLE   Shell. Scallop shell or shell-shaped dish containing various ingredients, often in cream sauce with breadcrumbs and grated cheese, browned.

COQUILLE SAINT-JACQUES   Scallop, shellfish with white flesh and orange coral; also known as *peigne*, *pélerine* (lit.: 'pilgrim'), and *godfiche*. The scallop shell was the badge of pilgrims to the shrine of Saint James (Saint Jacques) in Spain. *Coquilles Saint-Jacques à la bretonne*: baked with butter and breadcrumbs; *havraise*: sautéed with shallots plus prawns, white wine, cream sauce; *landaise*: sautéed with pine nuts, served with parsley and vinegar; *à la nantaise*: with white wine sauce, mushrooms, mussels.

COQUILLETTES   Pasta shells.

CORAIL   Coral, of lobster.

CORB(EAU)   Mediterranean fish like small sea bass; also known as *cotère*, *poisson juif* and *peï coua*.
   Corbeau: crow, raven; apparently eaten in *Normandie*.

CORBEILLE (DE FRUITS)   Basket (of fruit).

CORBIÈRES (SUPÉRIEURES)   Red, white and rosé wines (*AC*), produced in *Aude*.

(À LA) CORBIGEOISE   In the style of Corbigny in *Nivernais*. *Potage corbigeois*: beef broth with chervil and egg yolks, poured on slices of toast. See also *grenadin*.

CORDE   (Touraine) Sweet pastry.

CORDILLON   (Vivarais) Small pastry ring, also known as *brassadeau*.

CORDON BLEU/ROUGE   Lit.: 'blue/red ribbon'. See *escalope* and *tournedos*. The *cordon bleu* was originally awarded to female chefs.

CORDONNIERO   (Nice) Local name for *rascasse*

CORIANDRE   Coriander, the spice.

CORIPHÈNE   Dolphin fish (no relation to dolphin); also known as *dorade*.

CORNAS   Commune of the *Rhône*, making vigorous red wine (*AC*).

CORNE   Lit.: 'horn'. (Périgord) Variety of walnut (*noix*). (Nantais) Type of *brioche*.

CORNEL/CORNOUILLE   Name for Cornelian cherry.

CORNET   Cornet. Thin slice of ham, tongue etc, rolled into a cornet and stuffed. *Cornet de jambon/d'York*: of ham, also known as *filet d'Anvers*.
Cornet-shaped pastry. (Auvergne) Cream horn. *Cornet de glace*: ice cream cornet.
Horn shell, small shellfish; also known as *escargot de mer*.

CORNETTE   Variety of scarole (*scarole*).

CORNICE   (Bretagne) Sweet pastry like a *croissant*.

CORNICHON   Gherkin.

CORNICHON DE MER   Name for type of seaweed (*passe-pierres*).

CORNIOTTE   (Bourgogne) Triangular cream cheese pastry.

CORNOUILLE   See *cornel*.

COROSSOL   Variety of custard apple (*anone*).

CORPS   See *Tomme de Chèvre*.

CORRÈZE   Department in *Limousin*.

(À LA) CORRÉZIENNE   In the style of *Corrèze*. See *galette*.

(À LA) CORSAIRE   Lit.: 'corsair-style'. The chicken recipe from *Saint-Malo* probably used spices brought back by local sailors; see *poulet*.

CORSE   Corsica, French Mediterranean island, divided into the departments Corse du Sud and Haute-Corse. See also *Bleu de Corse*.
Red, white and rosé wines made in Corse, known as *Vin de Corse* (*AC*), with the added names of Patrimonio, Coteaux de Cap Corse, Calvi, (Coteaux d') Ajaccio, Figari-Porto-Vecchio and Sartène.

(À LA) CORSOISE   In the style of *Corse*. See *anchoiade* and *jambon*.

CORTON/CORTON-CHARLEMAGNE   See *Aloxe-Corton*.

COSSE   Pod, of peas, beans.

COSTARDS   See *Bleu de Costaros*.

COSTIÈRES DU GARD   Large wine-growing area in *Gard* (*AC*).

CÔTE   Rib. *Côte de boeuf*: rib of beef, also known as *train de côtes*. Rib of a vegetable, particularly chard (*blette*).
Chop, especially *côte de porc/veau*: of pork/veal, usually sautéed (as in the following examples), or grilled. *Côtes de porc à la bayonnaise*: with herbs, *cèpes* and potatoes; *Pilleverjus*: with onions, cabbage, cream and potatoes; *à la vosgienne*: with onions, plums, vinegar and white wine. *Côtes de veau Custine*: with tomato sauce; *à la Dreux*: stuffed with tongue and truffles, with madeira sauce; *Foyot*: baked with cheese; *à la gironnaise*: with cream, mustard and gherkin sauce; *Pauline*: with wine sauce, covered with cheese and browned.
Coast, shore. See also below.

CÔTE/COTEAU (pl. CÔTES/COTEAUX)   Hillside, slope. In wine terms, hillside vineyards; see below.

COTEAUX CHAMPENOIS   Still wines (*AC*) produced in *Champagne*.

COTEAUX D'AIX-EN-PROVENCE   Area around *Aix*, growing red, white and rosé wines (*AC*).

COTEAUX D'ANCENIS   Area in *Nantais*, producing red, white and rosé wines (*VDQS*).

COTEAUX DE LA LOIRE   Region in *Anjou*, making white wine (*AC*).

COTEAUX DE L'AUBANCE   Area around the river Aubance, tributary of the *Loire*, producing white wine (*AC*), mostly semi-sweet.

COTEAUX DES BAUX-DE-PROVENCE   Area around Les Baux-de-Provence in *Vaucluse*, producing red, white and rosé wines (*VDQS*).

COTEAUX DE PIERREVERT   Group of wine-growing villages in *Provence* (*VDQS*).

COTEAUX DE SAUMUR   Area to the south-west of the town of *Saumur*, producing red and white wines (*AC*).

COTEAUX DU GIENNOIS/CÔTES DU GIEN Region in *Orléanais*, making red, white and rosé wines (*VDQS*).

COTEAUX DU LANGUEDOC Large *AC* area in Hérault and Gard making red and rosé wines; several sub-areas, e.g. La Clape and Mejanelle, are entitled to hyphenate their names with that of the main appellation.

COTEAUX DU LAYON Vineyards around the river Layon, producing the richest white wines (*AC*) of *Anjou*.

COTEAUX DU LOIR Area around the river Loir, tributary of the *Loire*, producing red, white and rosé wines (*AC*).

COTEAUX DU LYONNAIS Red, white and rosé wines (*AC*), made around *Lyon*; also known as *Vins du Lyonnais*.

COTEAUX DU TRICASTIN Region of the *Rhône*, making red, white and rosé wines (*AC*).

COTEAUX VAROIS Red, white and rosé wines grown in the *Var*, inland from Toulon.

COTEAUX DU VENDÔMOIS White and light red wine (*VDQS*) grown around Vendôme, north of *Tours*.

CÔTE CHALONNAISE Area W of Chalon-sur-Saône in *Bourgogne*, making good quality red and white wines, and including the communes of *Mercurey*, *Rully*, *Givry* and *Montagny*.

CÔTE DE BEAUNE Southern section of *Côte-d'Or*, containing some of the grandest names of *Bourgogne* (e.g. *Meursault*, *Pommard*). A small amount of red and white wine grown throughout the region is sold under the general *AC Côte de Beaune*, while red wine blended from the produce of several minor villages comes under the *AC Côte de Beaune-Villages*; there are also the *Hautes Côtes de Beaune*, an area of hills to the W, making red and white wines (*AC*).

CÔTE DE BEAUNE-VILLAGES See above.

CÔTE DE BROUILLY See *Beaujolais*.

CÔTE DE NUITS N section of *Côte d'Or*, known for some of the greatest red wines of *Bourgogne* (e.g. *Chambertin*, *Corton*). Wines, mainly red, produced by minor communes throughout the area are sold as *Côte de Nuits-Villages* or *Vins Fins de la Côte de Nuits* (both *AC*), and red and white wines come from the area of hills known as the *Hautes Côtes de Nuits* (*AC*).

CÔTE DE NUITS-VILLAGES See above.

CÔTE D'OR Lit.: 'golden hillside'. Department, capital *Dijon*, and wine-growing region, at the heart of *Bourgogne*, which takes its name from the range of low hills W of the Saône river, stretching from *Dijon* to Chagny; embracing *Côte de Nuits* and *Côte de Beaune*.

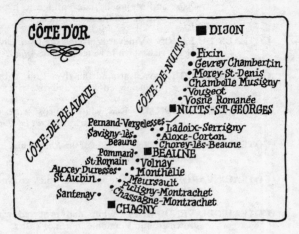

CÔTELETTE Cutlet, especially of lamb and mutton, as in the following examples. *Côtelettes d'agneau/de mouton à l'albigeoise*: sautéed with *cèpes*, white wine and tomato sauce; *Champvallon*: baked with potato and onion layers; *Charleroi*: coated with cheese and onion mixture, sautéed; *à la cévenole*: braised with chestnuts, onions, bacon and sausages; *mousquetaire*: baked with cream, mushrooms and artichokes; *Nelson*: baked with creamed onions and madeira sauce; *Périnette*; sautéed with courgettes, tomatoes and sweet peppers; *persane*: as *Périnette*, with aubergines instead of courgettes; *à la turque*: sautéed, with rice, tomato and garlic sauce.

'False' cutlet, slice or savoury mixture shaped like a cutlet, usually fried. *Côtelette parisienne*: see *tendron*. *Côtelette de volaille*: see *suprême*.

COTÈRE Name for *corb*.

CÔTE ROANNAISE Area round Roanne in *Lyonnais*, making red and rosé wines (*VDQS*).

CÔTE RÔTIE Steeply terraced area on the *Rhône*, producing fine red wine (*AC*).

CÔTES D'AGLY Fortified sweet wine (*AC*) from *Roussillon*.

CÔTES D'AUVERGNE Red, white and rosé wines (*VDQS*) grown around *Clermont-Ferrand*; village names (e.g. Chanturgue) may be added to the title.

CÔTES DE BLAYE   Most northerly of the *Bordeaux* vineyards, growing red and white wines (*AC*).

CÔTES DE BORDEAUX-SAINT-MACAIRE   Area of *Bordeaux* producing sweet white wine (*AC*). See also *Premières Côtes de Bordeaux*.

CÔTES DE BOURG   Area of *Bordeaux*, making red wines (*AC*).

CÔTES DE BRULMOIS   Area of the South-west, near to Agen, producing *VDQS* wines.

CÔTES DE BUZET   Region SE of *Bordeaux*, producing *Bordeaux*-style wines (*AC*).

CÔTES DE CABARDÈS ET DE L'ORBIEL   Area, near to *Carcassonne*, producing red and rosé wines.

CÔTES DE CASTILLON   District near *Saint-Emilion*, *Bordeaux*, making red wine (*AC*).

CÔTES DE DURAS   Area SE of *Bordeaux*, making *Bordeaux*-style wines (*AC*).

CÔTES DE FRANCS   Area east of *Bordeaux* producing red and white wines (*AC*).

CÔTES DE FRONSAC/CANON FRONSAC   Area of *Bordeaux*, producing mainly red wines (*AC*).

CÔTES DE LA MALAPÈRE   Area, near to *Carcassonne*, known for its red wines (*VDQS*).

CÔTES DE PROVENCE   Region mainly in *Var*, known chiefly for dry rosé wine, also making white and red (*AC*).

CÔTES DE ST MONT   Red wines (*VDQS*), grown in South-west, north of *Pau*.

CÔTES DE TOUL   Red, white and rosé wines (*VDQS*) grown in *Lorraine*.

CÔTES DE VENTOUX   Area on the slopes of *Mont Ventoux*, in *Vaucluse*, producing light, mainly red wines (*AC*).

CÔTES DU FOREZ   Red and rosé wines (*VDQS*), grown on the *Auvergne-Lyonnais* borders.

CÔTES DU FRONTONNAIS   Area in *Languedoc*, N of *Toulouse*, known particularly for red wine but also making white and rosé (*AC*).

CÔTES DU GIEN   See *Coteaux du Giennois*.

CÔTES DU JURA   Red, white, rosé, sparkling wines, *vin jaunes* and *vins de paille*, produced in the west of *Franche-Comté* (*AC*).

CÔTES DU LUBERON   Area in *Vaucluse*, making red, white and rosé wines (*AC*).

CÔTES DU MARMANDAIS   Red, white and rosé wines (*VDQS*) grown S of *Périgord*.

CÔTES-DU-RHÔNE   See *Rhône*.

CÔTES-DU-RHÔNE VILLAGES   Red, white and rosé wines (*AC*) made by 17 designated communes in the *Rhône* area, which may add their individual names to the label. These include (Vaucluse) *Cairanne*, *Rasteau*, *Roaix*, *Sublet*, *Séguret*, *Vacquéyras*, *Valréas* and *Visan*; (Gard) *Chusclan* and *Laudun*; and (Dauphiné) *Vinsobres*.

CÔTES DU ROUSSILLON (-VILLAGES)   Red, white and rosé wines (*AC*), produced in *Roussillon*.

CÔTES DU VIVARAIS   Red, white and rosé wines (*VDQS*) grown in *Vivarais*, to the west of the *Rhône*; those which reach 11° of alcohol may add the village name to the title.

COTIGNAC   Quince paste, cut into squares and eaten as a sweet, made especially in *Orléanais*; also known as *pâte de coings*.

COTRIADE   (Bretagne) Stew of white fish with mussels, onions, potatoes, herbs and cream.

COU   Neck. *Cou d'oie farci* (Périgord): neck of goose stuffed with sausage, duck liver or *foie gras*, chopped truffles and cooked in its own fat; eaten hot or cold with walnut oil salad, sometimes added to *garbure* or *cassoulet*.

COUCOU   See *bistorto*.

COUCOUMELLE (GRISE)   Fungus of *amanite* family with grey cap, mild scent and flavour; also known as *grisette*.
  Coucoumelle blanche: name for variety of *oronge*.

COUCHE   Layer, bed. See also *champignon*.

COUDENAT/COUDENOU   (SW France) Large pork sausage eaten hot in thick slices.

COUDES   Lit.: 'elbows'. Elbow-shaped pasta.

COUENNES (DE PORC)   Pork rinds, used in stews.

COUHÉ-VÉRAC   (Poitou) Goat's milk cheese with nutty flavour, wrapped in chestnut or plane tree leaves, made on farms around Couhé-Vérac.

COUKEBOOTRAM   See *kokeboterom*.

COULANDON (Bourbonnais) Soft fresh cheese, also known as *Chaucetier*.

COULÉE DE SERRANT See *Savennières*.

COULEMELLE/COURMELLE Parasol mushroom, large fungus of *lépiote* family with delicate flavour; also known as *champignon à la bague*, *cocherelle* and *grisotte*.

COULIBIAC Hot pastry filled with salmon, or sometimes chicken, of Russian origin; also spelt *koulibiak*.

COULIS Thick sauce or purée (e.g. *coulis de tomates*).

COULOMMIERS (Ile-de-France) Creamy white cheese, similar to *Brie de Coulommiers* but smaller; made by farms and factories around Coulommiers and elsewhere. *Demi-Coulommiers*: smaller version.
    Coulommiers Frais: soft fresh cream cheese.

COUP Lit.: 'blow'. *Coup de Jarnac*: meringue sponge cake with jam and *Cognac*.

COUPE Dish, glass. Ice cream served in a *coupe* with fruit soaked in liqueur. *Coupe Jacques*: lemon and strawberry ice cream, with fruit steeped in *kirsch*.

COUQUE (Flandre) Small sweet *brioche*. Gingerbread. From the Dutch 'kock' – cake or something baked.

COURCHEVEL See *Tomme de Chèvre*.

COURGE General name for gourd (e.g. pumpkin, squash and especially vegetable marrow).

COURGETTE Courgette, baby marrow, zucchini. *Courgettes à la mentonnaise*: baked, stuffed with spinach, cheese and garlic; *à la niçoise*: sliced, fried with tomatoes and garlic.

COURLIEU/COURLIS Curlew, the bird, sometimes eaten in *Corse*.

COURMELLE Name for parasol mushroom (*coulemelle*).

COURONNE Lit.: 'crown', 'ring'. Ring-shaped loaf. *Couronne de côtelettes rôties*: crown roast of lamb. *Brioche en couronne*: ring-shaped *brioche*.

COURQUIGNOISE (Artois) *Soupe courquignoise*: fish soup with mussels, leeks, shallots, herbs and white wine, sprinkled with cheese.

COURRAYE (Normandie) Black pudding made with offal.

COURT-BOUILLON Aromatic broth of vegetables, herbs and white wine or vinegar, mainly for poaching fish and seafood.

COURT(-E)   Lit.: 'short'. *Soupe courte* (Provence): mutton cutlets with onions, garlic, tomatoes and pasta.

COUSCOUS   Semolina steamed over lamb or chicken and vegetable stew, usually with hot pimento sauce; of North African origin. Crushed semolina grain.

COUSINA(T)   (Vivarais, Auvergne) Chestnut soup with milk, prunes or apples, and slices of bread.
       (Pays basque) *Bayonne* ham stewed with artichokes, broad beans, carrots and tomatoes.

COUSINÈTE/COUSINETTE   (Béarn, Pays basque) Vegetable soup of spinach, sorrel and chicory.

COUSSINET   Lit.: 'cushion'. Name for cranberry (*canneberge*).

COUTEAU   Knife.

COUTEAU COURBE   Lit.: 'curved knife'. Razor shell, type of long clam, like a cut-throat razor; also known as *rasoir*.

COUVERT   Cover charge. *Couvert gratuit*: no cover charge. *Couvert, vin et service compris*: price includes cover charge, wine and service.
       Place, table setting.

COUVERTURE   Lit.: 'cover'. Fine-grade pure chocolate.

CRABE   Crab. *Crabe froide à l'anglaise*: dressed crab. *Crabes à la malouine*: cold, shelled, with herb mayonnaise and hard-boiled eggs. See also *araignée, bernard l'hermite, calappe, ériphie, étrille* and *tourteau* for other types.
       Crabe enragé/vert: small shore crab (lit.: 'enraged/green') used in soups, a fierce fighter when caught; also known as *favouille* in S France.

CRAINQUEBILLE   *Pomme (de terre) crainquebille*: whole potatoes cooked in stock with onions and tomatoes.

CRAMBE/CRAMBÉ   Name for sea kale (*chou de mer*).

CRAMIQUE   (Flandre) Raisin bun or loaf.

CRAPAUD   Lit.: 'toad'. Name for *rascasse*.

(À LA) CRAPAUDINE   Spatchcocked, of birds – split down the middle, flattened (like a toad), and grilled; often served with *sauce diable*.

CRAPIAU   (Bourgogne) Fritter, often with herbs. See also *sanciau*.

CRAQUELIN   Cracker, biscuit. (Artois) Oval *brioche*.
       (Bretagne) Light pastry, sometimes stuffed with apple.

CRAQUELOT See *hareng*.

CRATERELLE Type of fungus black when damp, horn-shaped and tough, but with a good flavour, in season August-September; also known as *corne d'abondance* and *trompette/des morts*.

CRÉA(T) (Bordelais, Charentes) Local name for sturgeon (*esturgeon*). *Créat mariné*: sliced and marinated, with the gut, in white wine and herbs, then stewed.

CRECHENTE (Nice) Raisin *brioche*.

(À LA) CRÉCY Indicates the presence of carrots, especially *potage/purée Crécy*; probably after the town of Crécy in *Ile-de-France*, known for carrots.

CRÉMANT Lit.: 'creaming'. Applied to *Champagne*, less sparkling than normal. Of other wines, fully sparkling, the same as *mousseux* but suggesting superior quality (e.g. *Crémant d'Alsace*, *Crémant de Bourgogne*, *Crémant de Loire*).

CRÈME Cream, in various senses. Cream – from the cow. *Crème Chantilly*: stiffly whipped cream, sweetened and flavoured with vanilla or liqueur. *Crème fleurette*: light cream, similar to whipping cream. *Crème fouettée*: whipped cream. *Crème fraîche*: slightly soured cream. *À la crème*: in a cream sauce, with cream.

Custard. *Crème anglaise*: light egg custard. *Crème pâtissière*: confectioner's custard, for pastries and cakes.

Baked custard, cooked 'cream', usually made in a mould (*crème moulée*), and served for dessert, either cold in the same dish or turned out. *Crème bavaroise*: see *bavarois*. *Crème brûlée*: rich cream-based custard with topping of brown sugar which is burnt under the grill to form a hard coating. *Crème caramel*: vanilla-flavoured custard surrounded with soft caramel; also known as *flan*. *Crème renversée*: cream caramel turned out of its mould (lit.: 'reversed'). *Crème des algues* (Bretagne): sweetened milk thickened with seaweed. *Crème glacée*: name for ice cream (*glace*). *Crème d'Homère* (Languedoc): rich cream caramel with sweet wine and honey.

(*Potage*) *crème*: cream soup, usually based on *béchamel* sauce and finished with fresh cream. For the various cream soups, see under their distinguishing names (e.g. *crème Argenteuil*: see *Argenteuil*).

Sweetened liqueur in which the named flavour is predominant (e.g. *crème de menthe*: mint; *crème de cassis*: blackcurrant). See under their distinguishing names for other examples.

Reduced to a cream, cream-like. *Crème de riz*: rice flour, ground rice. *Crème au beurre*: butter cream, of butter, eggs and sugar, for filling and icing cakes.

Processed, of cheese (e.g. *crème de Gruyère*: processed *Gruyère*).

CRÉMET (Nantais, Anjou) Small, fresh, unsalted cream cheese, pure white and with mild creamy flavour; often home-made, eaten as dessert with fruit, jam or sugar and cream.

CRÉNILABRE Corkwing, type of wrasse (*vieille*); also known as *lucrèce*.

(À LA) CRÉOLE Creole-style. With rice, sweet peppers and tom-atoes, for savoury dishes. With rice, often orange-flavoured, for sweet dishes. See also *chayote* and *riz*.

CRÉPAZE Pancake layered with ham and cream, sprinkled with cheese.

CRÊPE Large thin pancake, sweet or savoury, made of wheat flour (as opposed to *galette*). *Crêpe bonne-femme*: flavoured with orange peel and *Calvados*, stuffed with apple; *dentelle* (Bretagne): very thin pancake (lit.: 'lace'); *landaise*: filled with sausage, ham and *cèpes*; *Suzette*: flamed with orange liqueur, in orange butter sauce; *vonnassienne*: potato.

CRÉPIAU (Bourgogne) Local name for pancake.

CRÉPINE (DE PORC) Pig's membrane, used to wrap sausages, liver, chopped meat etc; also known as *coiffe*.

CRÉPINETTE Small flat sausage, usually grilled or fried; in *Bordelais* and *Charentes* traditionally accompanied by oysters.

CRÉPY Dry white wine made from the Chasselas grape in Haut-Savoie, near to Swiss border; has a natural ten-dency to sparkle.

CRESPÈRE/CRESPEU *Omelette crespeu* (Provence): omelette with bacon and potatoes; or flat omelette layered with chopped tomatoes and sweet peppers.

CRESPET (Béarn) Sweet fritter.

CRESSON (ALÉNOIS, DE FONTAINE)/CRESSONIER (CRESSON-IÈRE) (With) watercress.

CRESSONNETTE Cress; also known as *cardamine* and *cresson amer/ des prés*.

CREST See *Tomme de Chèvre*.

CRÊTE (DE COQ) Cockscomb, used in formal garnishes, often with cock's kidneys.

CRETONS (Béarn) Crackling, obtained from rendered fat.

CREUSE   Department equivalent to *Marche*, and river.
Feminine of *creux*. Flat oyster; see also *huître*.

(À LA) CREUSOISE   In the style of *Creuse*. See also *Guéret*.

CREUX (CREUSE)   Hollow, concave.

CREVETTE   Shrimp, prawn. *Crevette grise*: shrimp, also known as
bouc, chevrette and *sauterelle*. *Crevette rose*: prawn, also
known as *boucot, bouquet* and *crevuche*. *Crevettes bouquet*: prawns with lemon and salt. *Crevette nordique*:
northern prawn, found in deep waters especially around
Norway. *Crevette rose du large*: large pink prawn, found
in deep water; also known as *gamba*. *Crevette rouge*:
large red prawn, good to eat. *Crevette royale/grosse
crevette*: name for *caramote*.

CREVUCHE   See above.

CRÉZANCY-SANCERRE   (Berry) Small white mild goat's milk
cheese; made on farms around Crézancy and *Sancerre*.

CRIADILLAS   (Languedoc) Local name for bull's testicles (*animelles*);
speciality of *Nîmes*, available after a local bullfight.

CRIOTS-BÂTARD-MONTRACHET   See *Chassagne-Montrachet*.

CRIQUE(TTE)   (Auvergne) Potato pancake with garlic.

CRISPÉ   (Périgord) Fried bread dumplings.

CRISTE-MARINE   Name for samphire (*christ-marine*).

CRISTILLE   Liqueur from *Auvergne*.

CROISSANT   Lit.: 'crescent'. Crescent-shaped light yeast pastry, for
breakfast.

CROMESQUI   Small ball of food dipped in batter and fried; of Russian
origin.

CROQUANT(-E)   Crisp, crunchy. Almond *petit four*. (Auvergne,
Limousin) Honey biscuit.

(À LA) CROQUE AU SEL   Eaten raw, seasoned with salt (e.g.
artichauts).

CROQUEMBOUCHE   Lit.: 'crisp-in-mouth'. Elaborate tall cone of
choux puffs filled with cream or custard, coated with
caramel, traditional at weddings.
(Bordelais) Cream-filled *choux* bun.

CROQUE-MADAME   Toasted cheese sandwich filled with ham and
fried egg.

CROQUE-MONSIEUR   Toasted cheese sandwich filled with ham.

CROQUET   Crisp almond biscuit.
Type of croquette, usually made of noodle paste.

CROQUETTE   Small cylinder of food, egg-and-breadcrumbed and deep-fried; either savoury, of potatoes or other vegetables, rice, pasta, cheese, meat, poultry, fish etc, or sweet, usually of fruit. Small cake or sweet.
Croquette reinequet (Dauphiné): pancake stuffed with ham, chicken and mushrooms.

CROQUIGNOLE   Small crisp biscuit.

CROSNE DU JAPON   Chinese artichoke, similar to Jerusalem artichoke; first cultivated in France at Crosne in *Ile-de-France*.

CROTTIN (DE CHAVIGNOL)   (Berry) *AOC* cheese (lit.: 'dung'), of goat's milk, small, dry with sharp smell and taste, becoming more pronounced in autumn, best between March and November; made by farms and dairies around Chavignol. The name is also given incorrectly to *Chavignol-(-Sancerre)*.

CROUPION   Parson's nose, of poultry.

CROUSTADE   Deep shell, made of pastry, bread, potato, rice or semolina, and filled, usually savoury. *Croustade jurassien*: cheese pastry.

CROUSTADINE   Shallow case of puff pastry, in various shapes.

CROUSTILLANT(-E)   Crisp, crunchy.

CROUSTILLE   Very thinly sliced fried potato.

CROÛTE   Lit.: 'crust'. Slice of bread, hollowed out for filling or as an open sandwich. Pastry case. *Croûtes aux abricots*: baked pudding of bread and apricots. *Coûte landaise*: fried bread with *foie gras* and cheese sauce. *Croûte rouge*: Edam cheese. *Croûte savoyarde*: ham on a layer of puff pastry with cheese sauce, grilled. See also *pâté*.

CROÛTE-AU-POT   Clear soup with vegetables from a dish of boiled beef and broth (*pot-au-feu*); also known as *consommé à l'ancienne*.

CROÛTON   Small cube or other shape of fried bread, used in soups, stews, salads or as a garnish.

CROZES-HERMITAGE   Red and white wines (*AC*) grown around the hill of Hermitage on the *Rhône*.

CRU Lit.: 'growth', in the usual translation. In wine terms, vineyard of special quality, often officially classified *cru classé*. See also *Alsace, Beaujolais, Bordeaux* and *Bourgogne*.

 Cru(-e): raw, uncooked (e.g. *jambon cru*).

CRUCHADES (SW France) Maize meal porridge, made into fritters or pancakes.

CRUDITÉS Selection of raw vegetables, as a first course with cold sauces, dips and mayonnaises.

CRUSPECT (Landes) Sweet fritter.

CRUSTACÉS Crustaceans (i.e. crabs, lobsters, shrimps etc).

CUBAT Chef to Czar Alexander II. See *sole*.

CUDASPRU (Corse) Local name for scad (*saurel*).

CUILLER/CUILLÈRE Spoon, spoonful.

CUIRE To cook.

CUISINE Cooking; kitchen. See also *nouvelle cuisine*.

CUISINE MINCEUR See *nouvelle cuisine*.

CUISSE Lit.: 'thigh'. *Cuisse de poulet*: chicken drumstick. *Cuisses de grenouilles*: frogs' legs.

CUISSEAU Leg, of veal.

CUISSON Cooking. Cooking liquid (e.g. stock).

CUISSOT Haunch, of venison (*chevreuil*), wild boar (*marcassin*); also known as *gigue*.

CUIT(-E) Cooked. See also *steak*.

CUJASSOU See *Chabichou*.

CUL Lit.: 'bottom'. Chump end, of veal, also known as *quasi*. *Cul de veau clamecyçoise*: boiled with vegetables, eaten cold.

CUL-BLANC Lit.: 'white tail'. Wheatear, small bird cooked like lark. Also name for great snipe (*bécassin*).

CULOTTE (DE BOEUF) Rump, of beef. *Culotte de boeuf à la beauceronne*: braised with potatoes, onions and bacon.

CULTIVATEUR Lit.: 'farmer's style'. With vegetables (e.g. *potage cultivateur*), and sometimes bacon.

CULTIVÉ(-E)   Cultivated.

CUMIN   Caraway seed or cumin, the spice.

CURAÇAO   Orange-flavoured liqueur, Dutch in origin but also made in N France.

CURÉ   Lit.: 'priest'. *Omelette du curé*: omelette with soft roes and tuna fish. See also *Nantais*.

CURCUMA   Turmeric, the spice.

CURNONSKY   Pseudonym of Maurice-Edmond Sailland (1872–1956), author of *La France gastronomique* in 32 volumes. See also *tournedos*.

CUSSY   Steward of Napoleon's household. Garnish of mushrooms, chestnuts, cock's kidneys and truffles.

(À LA) CUSTINE   See *côte*.

CUVÉE   Lit.: 'contents of a vat' ('cuve'). Special selection or blend, of wines (e.g. *cuvée exceptionnelle/personelle/privée*). In *Champagne*, *vin/tête de cuvée* is highest quality wine made from the first pressing of the grapes. In *Bourgogne*, *tête de cuvée* denotes the best vineyards of a commune (the same as *grand cru*); elsewhere, it is less specific, although still with the assertion of quality.

D'   See *de*.

(À LA) DACQUOISE   In the style of Dax in *Landes*. See *alose*.

DAIL   Piddock, large shellfish.

DAIM   Fallow deer.

DAINE   (S France) Local name for umbrine (*ombrine*).

DALAYRAC   *Consommé Dalayrac*: clear chicken soup with strips of chicken, mushroom and truffle.

DAME-BLANCHE   Lit.: 'white lady'. See *pêche*.

(À LA) DANOISE   Danish-style. *Consommé danoise*: clear wild duck soup, with mushrooms and game *quenelles*. See also *saumon*.

DANS   In.

DARBLAY   *Potage Darblay*: creamy potato soup with vegetable strips.

DARD   Dace, freshwater fish; also known as *aubourg*, *gravelet* and *vandoise*.

DARIOLE Small bucket-shaped pastry, or custard baked in a dariole mould, sweet or savoury; originally perhaps 'doriole' – golden, from the colour of the pastry.

DARNE Steak, thick slice, from large fish, especially salmon.

DARPHIN *Pommes (de terre) Darphin*: grated potatoes cooked as a flat cake.

DARTOIS Perhaps referring to *Artois*, or to the Comte D'Artois, brother of Louis XVI, or to Dartois, a 19th-century vaudeville writer. Garnish of carrots, turnips, celery and potatoes. Sweet or savoury pastry puff.

DÂTRÉE DE CHOUX (Anjou) Cabbage, potatoes and *beurre blanc*.

DATTE Date, the fruit.

DATTE DE MER Small shellfish similar to mussel.

DATTIER Date palm. Variety of table grape.

DAUBE Meat, poultry, game or fish braised in wine and stock with vegetables, herbs etc, technically in a 'daubière' (earthenware pot), sometimes served cold. Used without qualification, *daube* means beef in red wine, as in *daube du Béarn/à la béarnaise*: with ham and tomatoes: *provençale*: with mushrooms, tomatoes, black olives etc. However, *daube à l'avignonnaise*, made with mutton or lamb, is an exception. *Daube de macreuse* (Charentes): wild duck with red wine and *Cognac*. *Daube de muscardins* (Provence): small cuttlefish with their own ink, red wine, garlic and tomatoes.

(À LA) DAUMONT Lit.: 'with four horses and two postilions', after the Duc d'Aumont. Garnish for large fish of *quenelles*, soft roes, mushrooms and crayfish tails. *Sauce Daumont*: *hollandaise* sauce with oysters, truffles and mushrooms. *Consommé Daumont*: clear beef soup with strips of ox palate and mushroom, and rice.

DAUPHIN Lit.: 'Dauphin', eldest son of the French king. (Flandre) Soft smooth, herb-flavoured cheese, with strong smell; said to be named after Louis XIV's son.

DAUPHINE Lit.: 'female Dauphin'. Elaborate preparation of large fish, with crayfish, truffles etc. *Pommes (de terre) dauphine*: deep-fried croquettes of puréed potato mixed with *choux* paste.

DAUPHINÉ Province equivalent to the departments of Drôme, Isère and Hautes-Alpes.

(À LA) DAUPHINOISE   In the style of *Dauphiné*. *Soupe dauphinoise*: vegetable soup with milk. See also *caille*, *gratin*, *poulet* and *poularde*.

DAURADE (ROYALE)   Gilt-head bream, regarded as the best of the sea bream family; also known as *dorade*, *palmata* and *saouqueno*. *Daurade du pecheur* (Bretagne): with red wine and *Calvados*; *à la brestoise*: with shallots, shrimps and mussels.

DAUSSADE   (Picardie) Dish of onions, lettuce, cream and vinegar.

DE (D', DE LA, DU, pl. **DES)**   Of, from (the). Some, any, etc.

(À LA) DEAUVILLAISE   In the style of Deauville in *Normandie*. Poached with onions and cream, of sole particularly.

DÉFARDE/DEFFARDE   (Dauphiné) Stew of lamb's tripe and trotters.

DÉGLACÉ(-E)   Deglazed, of a sauce.

DÉGORGÉ(-E)   Cleaned. Food soaked in water or sprinkled with salt before cooking, to remove bitterness, impurities etc. Of *Champagne*, with sediment removed before final corking.

DÉGRAISSÉ(-E)   With fat removed.

DÉGUSTATION   Tasting, sampling, savouring (e.g. of wine, cheese, oysters).

DÉJAZET   See *sole*.

DÉJEUNER   Lunch. *Petit déjeuner*: breakfast.

DE LA   See *de*.

DÉLICE   Delight, deliciousness. Flowery menu description, often dessert or ice cream. *Délice aux amandes*: chocolate ice cream with chocolate sauce and almonds.

DÉLICE DE SAINT-CYR   (Ile-de-France) Soft mild creamy cheese, made in factories around Saint-Cyr-sur-Morin; also known as *Grand Vatel*.

DEMI(-E)   Half. *Un demi*: a 25 cl. glass of beer.
 Used to describe various cheeses which are smaller versions of their parents: *Demi-Baguette Laonnaise*; *Demi-Camembert*; *Demi-Coulommiers*; *Demi-Pont-L'Evêque*; and *Demi-Reblochon*, also known as *Reblochonnet*.

(À LA) DEMI-DEUIL   Lit.: 'half mourning'. See *poularde*.

DEMIDOFF   Russian prince of the Second Empire. Poultry baked with artichokes, carrots, turnips, truffles, etc and rich madeira sauce.

DEMI-ÉTUVÉ   Lit.: 'half-stewed'. See *Edam* and *Gouda*.

DEMI-GLACE   Lit.: 'half glaze'. Rich brown sauce, sometimes flavoured with madeira or sherry to glaze the food, based on meat stock.

DEMI-LIVAROT   See *Petit Lisieux*.

DEMI-SEC   Lit.: 'half dry'. Sweet, of *Champagne*.

DEMI-SEL   Lightly salted (e.g. of butter); see also *hareng* and *jambon*.
  Small square soft fresh cream cheese, originally from *Normandie*, now made all over France.
  (Charentes) Slightly salted sardine.

DEMI-TASSE   Small cup, especially of black coffee.

DEMOISELLE   Lit.: 'young lady'. Name for type of wrasse (*vieille*).
  Demoiselles (Gascogne): grilled bits of duck carcase.
  Demoiselle de Caen/Cherbourg: name for scampi (*langoustine*).

DENTÉ   Dentex, large member of sea bream family.

DENTS-DE-LION   Lit.: 'lion's teeth'. Name for dandelion (*pissenlit*).

DÉPARTEMENT   Department, major administrative division in France; the country is divided into 95 departments.

(À LA) DERBY   Elaborate preparation for poultry, with rice, truffles, *foie gras* etc.

DERVAL   Formal garnish of artichokes.

DES   See *de*.

DÉS   Dice. *En dés*: diced, of vegetables, ham etc.

DESSERT   Dessert, in France the course following cheese. *Grand dessert*: unlimited choice from perhaps 20 desserts.

DEUIL   Lit.: 'mourning'. See *poularde*.

DÉZIZE LES MARANGES   Minor commune of *Côte de Beaune*, *Bourgogne*, whose wines (*AC*) are generally blended and sold as *Côte de Beaune-Villages*.

(À LA) DIABLE   Lit.: 'devil's style'. Devilled, usually of poultry or game birds, split, flattened and grilled, with *sauce diable*; 'hot' wine and vinegar sauce. *Oeufs à la diable*: fried eggs with mustard and vinegar. See also *abricot* and *artichaut*.

Earthenware pot for cooking potatoes and chestnuts without liquid (e.g. *pommes de terre en diable*).

DIABLE DE MER   Lit.: 'sea devil'. Name for monkfish (*lotte*). Also name for *rascasse*.

DIABLOTIN   Lit.: 'imp'. Toasted cheese with cayenne pepper, served with soup.
Chocolate sweet.

(À LA) DIANE   In the style of Diane. *Sauce Diane*: highly peppered cream sauce, for venison; supposed to be after Diane de Poitiers, mistress of Henri II. See also *glace*.

DIANE DE CHÂTEAUMORAND   17th-century beauty who divorced her husband for his brother, and then neglected him for the company of her greyhounds. See *civet*.

DIE   See *Clairette de Die*.

(À LA) DIEPPOISE   In the style of Dieppe in *Normandie*. Of fish, especially sole, poached in white wine with mussels and shrimps, plus mushrooms and cream sauce. See also *hareng* and *marmite*.

DIEULEFIT   See *Picodon de Dieulefit*.

DIGESTIF   Drink, usually spirit or liqueur, taken after the meal to aid digestion.

DIGNE   Capital of the Alpes-de-Haute-Provence department (formerly Basses-Alpes) in *Provence*.

DIGOIN   Town in *Bourgogne*. *Sauce Digoin*: wine sauce with cream.

DIJON   Capital of *Côte-d'Or*, and of *Bourgogne*. Mustard and *crème de cassis* are two of its famous products.

(À LA) DIJONNAISE   In the style of *Dijon*. With mustard sauce (e.g. *gras-double à la dijonnaise*). With blackcurrants or *crème de cassis*. See also *belle-dijonnaise* and *escargot*.

(À LA) DINARDAISE   In the style of Dinard in *Bretagne*. See *congre* and *morue*.

DINDE   Turkey hen.

DINDON   Turkey (cock); usually called *dinde/dindonneau* on menu.

DINDONNEAU Young turkey.

DÎNER Dinner, evening meal. To dine.

DIOT (Savoie) Vegetable and pork sausage, preserved in oil and cooked in white wine.

(À LA) DIPLOMATE Lit.: 'diplomat's style'. Formal garnish of calf's sweetbreads, cockscombs and kidneys, mushrooms and madeira sauce. *Sauce diplomate*: rich lobster and truffle sauce, for fish, especially *sole*; also known as *sauce Riche*.
Cold moulded pudding of sponge, custard and crystallized fruit.

DIVERS(-E) Different, varied.

DOBULE Name for chub (*chevaine*).

DOCTEUR JULES GUYOT Variety of table pear.

DODINE Preparation of poultry, especially duck, or meat, boned, stuffed and braised; similar to *ballotine*.

DODINETTE Smaller version of *dodine*.

DOMAINE Estate. In wine-growing terms, especially in *Bourgogne*, collection of vineyards under one ownership (e.g. *Domaine de la Romanée-Conti*).

DOMINIQUE See *sole*.

DONZELLE Lit.: 'young miss'. Name for rainbow wrasse (*girelle*).

DORADE Red sea bream, less good than the related *daurade*; also known as *belugo*, *fausse daurade*, *gros yeux* and *rousseau*.
Name, confusingly, for gilt-head bream (*daurade*). Also name for dolphin fish (*coriphène*).
Dorade grise: name for black bream (*griset*).

DORDOGNE Department equivalent to *Périgord*; also river.

DORÉ(-E) Gilded, golden. *Dorée*: name for John Dory (*Saint-Pierre*).

DORIA With cucumber (e.g. *sole Doria*: fried sole with stewed cucumber balls).

DORMEUR Lit.: 'sleeper'. Name for large crab (*tourteau*).

DORNECY (Nivernais) Farm-made goat's milk cheese, dry and strong, made around Dornecy.

DORURE Lit.: 'gilt', 'gilding'. Gilded pastry dish.

(À LA) DOUAISIENNE In the style of Douai in *Flandre*. See *ramequin*.

DOUARNENEZ Sardine port in *Bretagne*. *Soupe de Douarnenez*: sardine and potato soup.

DOUBLE Lit.: 'double'. *Consommé double*: strong clear soup with sherry or madeira.
Cut of meat including both hind legs, usually of lamb.

DOUBLE-CRÈME Cream cheese.

DOUCE Feminine of *doux*.

DOUCETTE Name for lamb's lettuce (*mâche*).

DOUILLON (Normandie) Whole pear wrapped in pastry; perhaps from *douillette* – priest's overcoat.

DOUX (DOUCE) Sweet. Very sweet, of *Champagne*. Soft. Mild. Fresh, of water. See also *beurre*, *pain* and *vin*.

DOYENNÉ DU COMICE Variety of table pear, often considered the finest; first shown at the *Angers* agricultural show ('comice') in 1849.

(À LA) DRACÉNOISE In the style of *Draguignan*.

DRACHÉE/DRAÎCHE Cake with melted butter.

DRAGÉE Sugared almond, traditionally given at christenings; possibly invented in the 13th century at Verdun in *Lorraine*.
(Auvergne) Preserved plum.

DRAGENA (S France) Name for type of weever (*vive*).

DRAGUIGNAN Capital of *Var*.

DRAÎCHE See *drachée*.

DRAINE Missel thrush.

(À LA) DREUX In the style of Dreux in *Orléanais*. See *côte* and *Feuille de Dreux*.

(À LA) DUBARRY Comtesse du Barry, mistress of Louis XV. Garnish of cauliflower, often with cheese sauce.

(À LA) DUBLEY Garnish of potato nests and mushrooms.

DUBOIS Urbain Dubois, 19th-century chef and writer. *Oeufs (Urbain) Dubois*: scrambled eggs with lobster. See also *sole*.

DUBONNET   Brand of wine-based aperitif, bitter-sweet and red; there is also a dry light version.

DU   See *de*.

DUC   Lit.: 'duke'. See *grand/petit duc*.

(À LA) DUCHAMBAIS/DUCHAMBET   Gourmet priest of the Ancien Régime. See *lièvre*.

(À LA) DUCHESSE   Lit.: 'duchess-style'. *Pommes (de terre) duchesse*: puréed potatoes mixed with egg yolks, moulded into various shapes and baked. Small glazed savoury pastry puff. *Petit four* with nuts and chocolate. Variety of pear.

DUCLAIR   Town in *Normandie* known for duck; see also *canard*.

DUCS   Lit.: 'dukes'. (Bourgogne) Brand name for small, cylindrical curd cheese.

DUGLÉRÉ   Chef at one of the first *Paris* restaurants in the 18th century. See *sole*.

DUMAS   Alexandre Dumas, 19th-century author and gourmet. See *entrecôte*.

(À LA) DUNOISE   In the style of Châteaudun in *Orléanais*. See *gâteau* and *palais de boeuf*.

DUR(-E)   Hard. *Oeufs durs*: hard-boiled eggs.

DURAND   19th-century chef and native of *Provence*. See *anguille*.

DURAS   See *Côtes de Duras*.

DUROC   Garnish of new potatoes browned in butter; probably dedicated to the 19th-century Marshal Duroc.

(À LA) DUSE   Garnish of French beans, tomatoes and potatoes. See also *sole*.

DUXELLES   Chopped mushrooms and shallots cooked in butter, as a basis for sauces etc; probably created by *La Varenne*, chef to the 17th-century Marquis d'Uxelles.

EAU (pl. EAUX)   Water. *Eau douce*: fresh water; *minérale*: mineral (see below); *potable*: drinking; *de robinet*: tap; *de Seltz*: soda.

Liqueur. *Eau* (*de mélisse*) *des Carmes*: lemon balm liqueur. *Eau de noix*: walnut liqueur.

EAU-DE-VIE   Lit.: 'water of life'. Brandy, distilled wine, unless qualified as some other kind of spirit (but see also *fine*). *Eau-de-vie de cidre*: cider brandy, less refined than *Calvados*. *Eaux-de-vie de fruits*: colourless fruit spirits (e.g. *kirsch, quetsch, mirabelle, poire Williams, framboise*), also known as *alcools blancs*, a speciality of *Alsace*. *Eau-de-vie de marc*: see *marc*. Cognac, Armagnac and Calvados are *AC*, and there are many of the lesser rank, Eau-de-Vie Reglementée.

EAU MINÉRALE   Mineral water. There are over 1000 registered springs in France, classified by the Ministry of Public Health as *eau minérale naturelle*, *eau de source* and *eau de table* (roughly equivalent to the wine terms *AC*, *VDQS* and *vin du pays*); for *eaux minérales naturelles*, about 50 in number, the strict requirements include constant supervision, proven therapeutic qualities and that they be pure and unadulterated. Among best known brands of mineral water are *Badoit, Contrex, Evian, Perrier, Vichy, Vittel* and *Volvic*.

(À LA) ÉBROÏCIENNE   In the style of *Evreux*.

ÉCAILLE D'HUITRE   Oyster shell.

ÉCARLATE   Lit.: 'scarlet'. *À l'écarlate*: pickled, salted, of meat (e.g. tongue).

ÉCHALOTE   Shallot, onion-type vegetable, as used in *Bordelais*.

ÉCHASSIER   Wader, small bird found especially in *Landes*.

ÉCHAUDÉ(-E)   Lit.: 'scalded'. (Provence) *Brioche*. (Auvergne) Poached, browned, pastry square.

(LES) ÉCHEZEAUX   Group title for 11 *grand cru* (*AC*) red wine vineyards of *Côte de Nuits, Bourgogne*. See also *Grands Echezeaux*.

ÉCHINE/ÉCHINÉE   Lit.: 'spine'. Chine, loin, especially of pork, also known as *épinée*.

(EN) ÉCHIQUIER   Lit.: 'chessboard'. In a chequered pattern.

ÉCHIRÉ   Commune in *Poitou* famous for butter.

(À L')ÉCHIRLÈTE   *Pommes* (*de terre*) *à l'échirlète* (Périgord): potatoes cooked in pork or goose fat with garlic.

ÉCHOURGNAC (Périgord) Small, round, holey cheese with yellow rind and mild flavour, made at the Abbey of Echourgnac; also known as *Trappiste d'Echourgnac*.

ÉCLADE (DE MOULES) (Charentes) Mussels cooked over pine needles; also known as *fumée* and *terré* (*de moules*).

ÉCLAIR Lit.: 'flash'. Eclair, sausage-shaped *choux* pastry.

(À L')ÉCOLOCHE See *tarte*.

ÉCORCE Peel, of orange, lemon. Bark, of cinnamon.

(À L')ÉCOSSAISE Scottish-style. With mixed vegetables including French beans, and sometimes with pearl barley.

ÉCREVISSE Crayfish, kind of large freshwater prawn. *Nantua* indicates their presence in a dish. *Ecrevisses à la bordelaise*: sautéed, with vegetables, brandy and wine; *à la liégeoise*: poached with butter sauce; *à la vauclusienne*: cooked in white wine with herbs and tomatoes. See also *gratin*.

ÉCUREUIL Squirrel. See *civet*.

EDAM (FRANÇAIS) French equivalent of Dutch Edam cheese, supple and mild, shaped like a shiny red sphere or loaf; the first French *Edam* was made after the Netherlands had concluded a treaty with England against Louis XIV in 1670. *Edam* (*Demi-*)*Etuvé*: cured longer, with stronger smell and flavour.

ÉDELZWICKER White wine (*AC*) made in *Alsace* from a blend of grape varieties.

EFFILOCHÉ(-E) Lit.: 'frayed'. Sometimes used to describe vegetables.

ÉGLANTINE Wild rose, sometimes distilled in *Alsace*, and made into jam.

ÉGLEFIN/ÉGREFIN Name for haddock (*aiglefin*).
    Eglefin (*noir*): name for pollack or coalfish (*lieu jaune/noir*).

ÉGRUGEOIR (DE TABLE) Salt mill, grinder.

(À L')ÉGYPTIENNE Egyptian-style. See *aubergine*.

EIERKUCHAS/EIERKUCKAS (Alsace) Small, sweet or savoury pancake.

ÉLAN Elk, large deer.

ELEDONE Small curled octopus.

ELZEKARIA (Pays basque) Haricot bean and cabbage soup with garlic.

EMBEURRÉ(-E) Buttered. *Embeurrée de chou* (Poitou): boiled cabbage with butter.

EMBRUCCIATE See *imbrucciate*.

ÉMINCÉ Thin slice, sliver. Reheated thinly sliced meat, poultry or game, in sauce.

ÉMISSOLE Smooth hound, type of small shark; also known as *chien de mer*.

EMMENT(H)AL FRANÇAIS (Franche-Comté, Savoie) French version of Swiss Emmental, large, waxy, holey and yellow, mild to fruity in flavour.

EN In. To. At etc.

ENCHAUD (Périgord) Baked loin of pork and pig's trotters with garlic and truffles.

ENCORNET Name for squid (*calamar*).

ENCRE Lit.: 'ink'. Ink of squid, octopus.

ENDIVE Chicory, tightly furled pale green vegetable; also known as *endive belge* and (*endive*) *witloof* (see also *chicorée*). *Endives à l'ardennaise*: braised with pork and ham; *à la flamande*: cooked with butter.

ENTE Lit.: 'graft'. See *pruneau*.

ENTIER (ENTIÈRE) Whole. See also *lait* and *pain*.

ENTOLOME Type of fungus; also known as *mousseron gris*.

ENTRAMMES (Maine) Supple cheese with fruity flavour, made at the Abbey of Entrammes, the original site of the monastery of Port-du-Salut; *Entrammes* was called *Port-Salut* until this name was sold.

ENTRAYGUES Village in *Rouergue*, making a small amount of light wines (*VDQS*), known as *Vins d'Entraygues et du Fel*. See also *Cabécou d'Entraygues*.

ENTRECÔTE   Lit.: 'between the rib'. Rib steak, of beef, sometimes amplified to *entrecôte château*. *Entrecôte Dumas*: sautéed with bone marrow, wine and shallot sauce.

ENTRE CUISSE   Lit.: 'between thigh'. Second joint, thigh, of poultry and winged game.

ENTRE-DEUX-MERS   Lit.: 'between two seas'. Area between the Dordogne and Garonne rivers in *Bordeaux*, producing red, rosé and white wines, only the latter with *AC*.

ENTRÉE   Lit.: 'entry'. Technically the dish preceding the roast (e.g. fish, chicken, eggs), but in practice often the main course of a meal.

ENTREMETS   Lit.: 'between dishes'. Originally, a course following the roast, but now meaning dessert, served after cheese.

ÉPAULE   Shoulder, of lamb, mutton, veal, pork. *Epaule d'agneau à l'albigeoise*: shoulder of lamb boned, stuffed and roasted in goose fat with garlic and potatoes; *farcie landaise*: boned, stuffed with veal, pork, brandy etc and roasted.

ÉPEAUTRE   Spelt, chaffy wheat. *Soupe d'épeautre* (Provence): mutton soup with spelt.

ÉPERLAN   Smelt, small sea and river fish. See also *athérine*.

ÉPICE   Spice. See also *pain*.

ÉPICERIE   Groceries. Grocer's shop.

ÉPIGRAMME   Lit.: 'epigram'. Two cuts of lamb served together – slice of breast and cutlet – both dipped in egg and breadcrumbs, grilled or fried. Also lamb cutlets prepared in 2 different ways – one coated in egg and breadcrumbs, the other not – sautéed and served together.
   Epigramme de poulet (Lorraine): chicken in pastry with mushrooms.

ÉPINAL   Capital of *Vosges*.

ÉPINARDS   Spinach. *Epinards en bouillabaisse/à la marseillaise*: spinach soup with potatoes; oil, garlic, saffron, poured over sliced bread, served with poached eggs; *Mère-Louisette*: cooked with much butter, diced ham and fried bread; *à la Viroflay*: spinach balls in cheese sauce.

ÉPINE D'HIVER   Lit.: 'winter thorn'. Variety of pear.

ÉPINÉE   Chine, loin, especially of pork; also known as *échine*.

ÉPINE-VINETTE   Barberry, sometimes made into jam, especially in *Lorraine*.

ÉPINOCHE   Stickleback, small river fish.

ÉPOISSES   (Bourgogne) Small cylindrical cheese cured in *marc*, with spicy smell and flavour, sometimes kept in ashes or *marc*; made around Epoisses, also known as *Saligny*.

ÉQUILLE   Sand eel, also known as *cicerelle* and *lançon*.

ERBSENSUPPE   (Alsace) Jewish pea soup.

ERCÉ   See *Bethmale*.

ÉRIPHIE   Small furry crab; also known as *pélou* and *fiou pelan*.

ERVY-LE-CHÂTEL   (Champagne) Firm cheese with mushroomy smell and milky flavour; made by dairies and farms around Ervy-le-Chatel.

ESAU   Biblical figure who sold his birthright for a mess of potage. With lentils (e.g. *potage Esau*).

ESBAREICH   (Béarn) Mild sheep's milk cheese, shaped like a large round flattened loaf, made in mountain cottages; also known as *Oloron-Sainte-Marie* and *Tardets*.

ESCABÈCHE   Fried fish, usually sardines, marinated and served cold as a first course; of Spanish origin.

ESCALOPE   Thin slice, of meat, occasionally fish. Especially veal escalope, usually sautéed, as in the following examples; also grilled, when it is known as *paillarde*. *Escalope Brillat-Savarin*: flamed with brandy, plus mushroom and cream sauce; *cauchoise*: with cream, *Calvados* and apple (similar versions are called *escalope normande*/*Vallée d'Auge*); *cordon bleu*: stuffed with ham and cheese; *Holstein*: with fried eggs and anchovies; *à la savoyarde*: with cream and *vermouth* or mushroom sauce, sprinkled with cheese; *Sophie*: rolled round ham and hard-boiled egg; *à la viennoise*: egg-and-breadcrumbed and sautéed.

ESCARGOT   Snail. The two main types are *escargot de Bourgogne*/*de vigne*: vineyard snail, and *petit gris*: smaller variety. *Escargots mode de l'abbaye*: with onions and cream sauce; *à l'alsacienne*: stuffed with spiced butter and herbs, cooked in local wine; *à l'arlésienne*: in white sauce with herbs, or with white wine, ham, tomatoes etc; *à la bourguignonne*: stuffed with butter, parsley and garlic; *à la chablisienne*: stuffed with shallots, cooked in *Chablis* wine, with garlic butter and parsley; *à la dijonnaise*: with white wine, shallots, bone marrow and garlic butter; *lou cagaraulat* (Languedoc): with nuts, anchovies and tomatoes; *au Melon* (Bourgogne): with *Melon* wine; *à la narbonnaise*: with bacon, anchovies, nuts and white wine; *à la suçarelle* (Provence): with garlic, tomatoes, sausages and white wine, sucked out of the shells; *à la*

vigneronne (Bordelais especially): fried in walnut oil, with white wine, shallot and garlic sauce; *Villebernier*: with shallots, red wine and vinegar.

ESCARGOT ESCOURGOL   (Provence) Local name for small snail.

ESCARGOT DE MER   Name given to various small shellfish – winkle (*bigorneau*), horn shell (*cornet*) and murex (*rocher*).

ESCAROLE   Name for *scarole*.

ESCAUTON/ESCO(U)TON   (Gascogne) Cornmeal fritter.

ESCOFFIER   Georges-Auguste Escoffier (1846–1935), illustrious chef at the Savoy and Carlton in London, and author of many cookery books including *Ma Cuisine*.

ESCO(U)TON   See *escauton*.

ESCUEDELLA   (Roussillon) Boiled beef with eggs and pasta, and sometimes stuffed turkey.

ESPADON   Swordfish, with white firm flesh, often served as steaks.

(À L') ESPAGNOLE   Spanish-style. With tomatoes, peppers, onions and garlic (e.g. *omelette espagnole*). *Sauce espagnole*: classic brown sauce, made with vegetables, flour and meat stock; also known as *sauce brune*.

ESPROT   Sprat, small member of herring family; also known as *anchois de Norvège*, *harenguet* and *sprat*.

ESQUINADE/ESQUINADO(UN)   (Provence) Local name for spider crab (*araignée*). *Esquinado à l'huile*: puréed and served cold in the shell.

ESSENCE   Essence, extract. Concentrated stock.

EST   East. See *Carré de l'Est*.

ESTAING   Small area in *Rouergue*, producing red and white wines (*VDQS*), known as *Vins d'Estaing*.

ESTIVAL(-E)   Of summer.

ESTOCAFIC(ADA)   Name for *stockfish*.

ESTOFAT   See *estouffade*.

ESTOFICADO/ESTOFINADO   Name for *stockfish*.

ESTOMAC   Stomach, often of sheep.

ESTOUFFADE / ESTOUFFAT / ESTOUFFLET / ÉTOUFFAT (S, SW France) Meat, usually in one piece, stewed in a sealed pot (*à l'étouffé*) with wine, herbs and vegetables, sometimes haricot beans and pork; also known as *estofat*, often similar to *cassoulet*. *Estouffat de haricots blancs à l'occitane*: white haricot beans stewed with salt pork, garlic and tomatoes. *Etouffat de Noël* (Gascogne): beef lengthily braised with *Armagnac*, wine and shallots.

ESTRAGON Tarragon, the herb.

ESTRANGLE BELLE-MÈRE (Provence) Lit.: 'mother-in-law-strangle'. Local name for scad (*saurel*).

ESTURGEON Sturgeon, also known as *créat*. *Esturgeon à la Brimont*: fillets larded with anchovies and baked with vegetables and white wine. *Filets d'esturgeon Boris*: baked with mushrooms, cream, white wine and truffles.

ÉTÉ Summer.

(L')ÉTOILE Lit.: 'star'. Region (*AC*) in *Franche-Comté*, producing dry white and sparkling wines, and some *vin jaune* and *vin de paille*.

ÉTOFFÉ(-E) Stuffed; sometimes written *étouffé*.

ÉTOUFFAT See *estouffade*.

(À L') ÉTOUFFÉE Cooked in a sealed pot, at low heat, with little or no liquid, especially of peas. See also *estouffade*, *étoffé*, and *étuvé*.

ÉTRILLE Small crab, also known as (*crabe*) *nageur*.

ÉTUVÉ(-E) Stewed, braised steamed (e.g. potatoes). See also *étouffée*, and *Edam* and *Gouda*.

EUGÉNIE Empress Eugénie, wife of Napoleon III. *Velouté Eugénie*: cream of shrimp soup.

ÉVIAN Brand of still mineral water from the spa of the same name on Lake Geneva in *Savoie*.

ÉVREUX Capital of the Eure department in *Normandie*.

EXCELSIOR (Normandie) Small firm creamy cheese with mild flavour; invented around 1890.

EXOCET Name for flying fish (*poisson volant*).

EXPLORATEUR Lit.: 'explorer'. (Ile-de-France) Trade name for small firm creamy cheese, made by commercial dairies.

EXPRESS Espresso coffee.

EXTRA First-rate, extra-special, of cheese, wine etc. Very mature, of *Calvados* and *Cognac*.

EXTRA-SEC Lit.: 'extra dry'. Dry, of *Champagne*.

(À LA) FAÇON (DE) In the manner of.

FAGOT (Charentes) Lit. 'bundle'. Small meat ball.

FAÏNE Beechnut.

FAISAN Pheasant. *Faison à l'américaine*: split, grilled, with bacon, tomatoes and mushrooms; *à l'angoumoise*: stuffed with truffles, roasted; *à la bohémienne*: stuffed with *foie gras*, truffles and paprika, casseroled; *à la mode de Gascogne*: stuffed with chicken livers and truffles, braised; *à la languedocienne*: casseroled with ham, mushrooms, truffles, wine and brandy; *à la normande*: casseroled with cream, *Calvados* and apples (*à la cauchoise* is similar); *à la Sainte-Alliance*: stuffed with woodcock forcemeat, roasted, served on toast with bitter oranges. See also *chartreuse*.

FAISANDÉ(-E) High, gamey, well-hung.

FAISANDEAU Young pheasant.

FAISANE Hen pheasant.

FAISSELLE Basket or pot for draining cheese.

FALCULELLA (Corse) Cheese brioche.

FALLETTE (Rouergue) Breast of mutton stuffed with vegetables and bacon.

FALUE (Normandie) Sweet pancake.

FANCH(ONN)ETTE (Bordelais) Meringue.

FANES Tops, of carrots, turnips, radishes etc.

FANFRE Pilot fish, similar to mackerel; also *poisson pilote*.

FANTAISIE Lit.: 'fancy'. Synthetic, of jam etc. Of bread, sold by the piece not by weight.

FAON Fawn, young deer.

FAR (Bretagne) Buckwheat/wheat flour porridge, poached or baked, sweet or savoury and with many flavourings, including bacon, prunes and raisins. See also *farci*.

FARANDOLE *Provençal* folk dance. Flowery description for a composite dish of some kind.

FARCE   Stuffing, forcemeat.

FARCEMENT   See *farçon*.

FARCI(-E)   Stuffed. Short for *chou farci*: stuffed cabbage, usually with sausage or pork, cooked in stock. *Farci poitevin*: stuffed with vegetables, herbs, pork, bacon etc, cooked in stock and eaten hot or cold; also known as *far*. *Soupe au farci* (Auvergne): soup with stuffed cabbage.
    Farci niçois: stuffed courgettes, aubergines, tomatoes and onions stewed in oil.

FARCIDURE   (Limousin) Small vegetable dumplings, often served with cabbage soup.
    Large potato cake with eggs, onions and bacon.

FARÇON   (Auvergne, Rouergue) Large fried sausage and vegetable cake.
    (Savoie) Potatoes baked with milk, eggs, and sometimes bacon, raisins and prunes; also known as *farcement*.
    (Dauphiné) Large saveloy sausage.

FARÉE   (Charentes) Stuffed cabbage.

FARIGOULE(TTE)/FRIGOLET   (Provence) Local name for wild thyme (*serpolet*).

FARINE   Flour. *Farine d'avoine*: oatmeal. *Farine de froment*: wheat flour, also known as *farine de gruau*. *Farine de maïs*: maize flour. *Farine de sarrasin*: buckwheat flour, also known as *blé noir*. *Farine de seigle*: rye flour.

FARINETTE   (Auvergne) Omelette made with flour, or savoury pancake.

FASÉOLE   Kidney bean.

FASSUM   See *sou-fassum*.

FAUBONNE   *Potage Faubonne*: white haricot bean or split pea soup.

FAUDE   (Auvergne) Hot or cold dish of veal or mutton with various sauces.

FAUGÈRES   Red wine area north of Beziers in *Languedoc* (*AC*).

FAUSSE   Feminine of *faux*: false.

FAUSSE DAURADE   Name for red sea bream (*dorade*).

FAUSSE LIMANDE   Scaldfish, flat sea fish; also known as *sole maudite* and *petro*.

FAUSSE PALOURDE/PRAIRE   Small clam, also known as *blanchet* and *flie*.

FAUSSE SOLE   Type of flat fish, also known as *sole d'Ecosse*.

FAUVES   Wild animals, especially deer.

FAUX (FAUSSE)   False.

FAUX CAFÉ   Decaffeinated coffee.

FAUX ÉPERLAN   Name for sandsmelt (*athérine*).

FAUX-FILET   Part of sirloin, of beef; also known as *contre-filet*.

FAUX MOUSSERON   Scotsman's bonnet mushroom, fungus of the *marasme* family, with white flesh and pleasant taste; also known as *nymphe des montagnes*.

FAVEROLLE/FAVEROTTE/FAVIOLE   (S France) Local name for haricot bean. *Faverolle* (Lorraine): fritter.

(À LA) FAVORITE   Lit.: 'favourite-style'. Garnish of *foie gras* with truffles and asparagus tips. *Purée favorite*: puréed French beans. See also *artichaut* and *bombe*.

FAVOU(ILLE)   (S France) Local name for type of crab (*crabe enragé*).

FAYOL/FAYOT   Name for haricot bean.

(À LA) FÉCAMPOISE   In the style of Fécamp in *Normandie*. See *Bénédictine*, *hareng*, *moule* and *sole*.

FÈCHE   (Languedoc) Salted and dried pork liver with radishes.

FECHUN   (Franche-Comté) Stuffed cabbage.

FÉCULE   Starch. *Fécule de pommes de terre*: potato flour.

FEÏ D'AMÉRIQUE   (Nice) Local name for *astroderme*.

FENOUIL   Fennel; vegetable or herb with aniseed flavour.

FENOUILLET   Variety of pear with aniseed taste.

FENOUIL MARIN   Name for samphire (*bacile*).

FENOUILLETTE   Liqueur made from fennel seeds.

FENUGREC   Fenugreek, the herb.

FÉOUSE   (Lorraine) Local name for *quiche*.

FÉRA   Type of salmon found in lakes of *Savoie*, highly prized.

FERCHUSE   (Bourgogne) Heart, liver and lungs of pork cooked in red wine with onions and potatoes; corruption of *fressure*.

FERINANA   (Corse) Chestnut porridge with olive oil.

FERMÉ(-E)   Closed.

(À LA) FERMIÈRE   Lit.: 'in the style of the farmer's wife'. With mixed vegetables, especially meat braised with vegetables; chicken sautéed with vegetables plus ham; fish, baked on a bed of vegetables with white wine and cream. *Potage fermière*: vegetable soup with white beans.
　　Fermier: farm-made, of cheese, butter; free-range, of chickens.

FERMONT   See *avocat*.

FERRECAPIENNE   Fish soup, with one kind of fish.

(LA) FERTÉ-MACÉ   Town in *Normandie*. See *tripes*.

FERVAL   Garnish of artichokes and croquette potatoes.

FEU   Fire, heat.

FEUILLANTINE   Small light pastry.

FEUILLE   Leaf. *Feuilles de chêne rouge*: oak leaf lettuce, reddish with oak-like leaves. *Feuille de laurier*: bayleaf. *Feuille de pêche*: peach leaf, used in custards and home-made liqueurs. *Feuille de vigne*: vine leaf, sometimes wrapped round fish or game birds. Used to describe cheeses wrapped in leaves, of chestnut, plane tree or vine; see also *Feuille de Dreux*.

FEUILLE DE DREUX   (Orléanais) Small round cheese decorated with chestnut leaves, with fruity flavour; factory-made around Dreux, also known as *Dreux à la Feuille*.

FEUILLET   (Roussillon) Mixed eggs, tomatoes, olives and anchovies.

FEUILLETÉ(-E)   Made of puff pastry (*pâte feuilletée*). *Feuilletée*: puff pastry, often diamond- or crescent-shaped, filled with a mixture (e.g. *feuilletée de fruits de mer*: of seafood).

FEUILLETON   Lit.: 'serial'. Thinly sliced veal or pork, layered with stuffing, braised, served hot or cold.

FÈVE (DE/DU MARAIS)   Broad bean; grown especially in the *Marais*. *Fèves à la tourangelle*: in cream sauce with bacon.

FÉVEROLE   Field bean, smaller than broad bean.

FEVETTE   (Nice) Tiny early broad bean.

FIADONE/FIJADONE   (Corse) Cheese and orange flan.

FIATOLE   Mediterranean fish with delicate flesh; also known as *stromatée*, *lapuga* and *lippa*.

FICELLE   Lit.: 'string'. Very thin long loaf.
    Ficelle normande/picarde: pancake stuffed with cream or cheese and ham or mushrooms. See also *andouillette* and *boeuf*.

FICHU   Lit.: 'kerchief'. Wrapping for an ingredient (e.g. *glace en fichu de chocolat*: ice cream coated with chocolate).

FICO   (S France) Local name for poor cod (*capelan*).

FIEFS VENDÉENS   Red, white and rosé wines (*VDQS*) grown in an area to the South of Nantes.

FIÉLA   (S France) Local name for conger eel (*congre*).

FIGATELLI   (Corse) Pork liver and herb sausages.

FIGON   Type of small fig from *Provence*.

FIGOUN   (S France) Local name for meagre (*maigre*).

FIGUE   Fig, the fruit.

FIGUE-CAQUE   Name for persimmon (*kaki*).

FIGUE DE BARBARIE   Prickly pear, fruit of type of cactus, usually eaten raw.

FIGUE DE MER   Name for *violet*.

FIGUETTE   Fig wine.

FIJADONE   See *fiadone*.

FILET   Fillet, of meat. Especially beef, roasted whole (e.g. *filet de boeuf Régence*: on bed of vegetables with brandy); or cooked as individual steaks (e.g. *filet Boston*: fried, with oyster sauce). *Filet mignon*: small fillet steak, of beef.
    Fillet, of poultry (of chicken also known as *suprême*), or of game like hare.
    Fillet, of fish. See under various fish (e.g. *filet de sole*: see *sole*).

FILET D'ANVERS   See *cornet*.

FIN(-E)   Fine, high quality. Thin.

FINAGE   In wine terms, the same as *commune*, especially in *Bourgogne*.

(À LA) FINANCIÈRE   Lit.: 'financier's style'. Elaborate garnish of cockscombs and kidneys, *quenelles*, truffles etc.
    Financier (Orléanais): almond cake.

FIN-DE-SIÈCLE   Lit.: 'end of the century'. (Normandie) Small soft creamy cheese, the name refers to its time of invention; also known as *Parfait* and *Supreme*.

FINE   Feminine of *fin*: fine. Grape brandy, distilled wine (as opposed to *eau-de-vie* which can be otherwise derived); used on a label only when followed by the region of production (e.g. *Fine Bourgogne*, *Fine Marne*), except in the case of *Armagnac* or *Cognac*. Thus, *fine* alone usually means *Cognac* or *Armagnac*; and *fine maison*, the staple brandy of the house, is likely to be one of these two.

Fine Champagne: see *Cognac*.

FINE DE CLAIRE   Oyster raised in a special basin, usually in *Marennes*; see also *huître*.

FINES HERBES   Mixture of finely chopped herbs, usually parsley, chervil, chives and tarragon, used especially in omelettes.

FINTE   Name for shad (*alose*).

FIOU PELAN   (Provence) Local name for small crab (*ériphie*).

FIOUSE   (Lorraine) Cream, bacon and onion flan.

FISSURELLE   Small shellfish similar to limpet.

FISTULANE   Small shellfish; also known as *gastrochère*.

FISTULINE   Type of fungus, large, red and sourish; also known as *foie/langue de boeuf*.

FITOU   Area on the *Aude-Roussillon* borders, producing one of the best red wines (*AC*) of the south.

FIVEROLLE   See *frivolle*.

FIXE   Fixed, set (e.g. *prix fixe*: set price).

FIXIN   Village of *Côte de Nuits*, *Bourgogne*, making mainly red wines (*AC*).

FLADÈNE   (Corse) Vanilla-flavoured cheese tart.

FLAGEOLET   Lit.: 'flageolet'. Flageolet bean.

FLAGNARDE/FLAUGNARDE/FLOGNARDE   (Auvergne, Limousin) Sweet flan, or thick jam pancake.

(À LA) FLAMANDE   In the style of *Flandre*, Flemish-style. Garnish of braised cabbage, root vegetables, pork or sausage, for meat and poultry. With red cabbage (e.g. *épaule de mouton à la flamande*). With red wine, vinegar and onions. Of fish, poached in white wine with onions, mushrooms and perhaps mustard. With chicory, hop shoots or Brussels sprouts, the last, in for example *soupe à la flamande*. *Crème flamande*: cream of onion and potato soup. *Salade flamande*: chicory, potato, onion and herring salad. See also *anguille*, *asperges*, *carbonnade*, *chou*, *chou rouge*, *endive*, *lapin* and *petit pois*.

FLAMBÉ(-E)   Flamed, sprinkled with spirit and set alight. See also *flamme(r)kueche*.

FLAMERY   (Lorraine) Raisin and crystallized fruit cake.

FLAMICHE/FLAMIQUE   Lit.: 'Flemish'. (N France) Leek and cheese tart, with variations including pumpkin.

FLAMME(R)KUECHE   (Alsace) Bacon, cream and onion flan, sometimes with cheese; also known as *tarte flambée*.

FLAMRI   Moulded semolina pudding served with puréed raw red fruits, usually cold.

FLAMUSSE   (Bourgogne) Sweet omelette with fruit, usually apples. Cheese and egg flan.

FLAN   Open custard tart, sweet or savoury. *Flan de poireaux à la berrichonne*: leek, ham and cream tart.
Thick custard, or sometimes *crème caramel*.

FLANCHET   Flank, of beef; used in stews.

FLANDRE   Flanders, province equivalent to the Nord department. Name for flounder (*flet*).

FLAUGNARDE   See *flagnarde*.

(LA) FLÈCHE   Town in *Maine*, known for poultry.

FLET/FLÉTAN   Flounder, flat sea fish also found in rivers; also known as *flandre/flondre* (*de rivière/de picard*).

FLÉTAN   Halibut. See also *flet*.

FLEUR   Flower. Finest. *Fleur de Maquis*: see *Brindamour*.

FLEURETTE   See *crème*.

FLEURI(-E)   Flushed with red. See also *brignole*.

FLEURIE   See *Beaujolais*.

(À LA) FLEURISTE   Lit.: 'florist's style'. Garnish of stuffed tomatoes and potatoes.

FLEURON   Lit.: 'floret'. Puff pastry crescent, used as a garnish.

FLIE   Name for small clam (*fausse palourde*). Also name for limpet (*patelle*).

FLIP   (Normandie) Cider flamed with spirit.

FLOC DE GASCOGNE   Aperitif of fresh grape juice mixed with Armagnac.

FLOCON   Flake. *Flocons d'avoine*: oat flakes, porridge oats, used in soups. *Flocons de maïs*: cornflakes.

FLOGNARDE   See *flagnarde*.

FLON   (Lorraine) Local name for *quiche*.

FLONDRE   Name for flounder (*flet*).

FLÔNE   (Rouergue) Sheep's milk tart flavoured with orange blossom.

FLORÉAL   Eighth month in Republican calendar, 20 April–19 May. See *sole*.

(À LA) FLORENTINE   Florentine-style. Served on a spinach bed, usually covered with cheese sauce. Italian cooks under Catherine de *Médicis* are supposed to have introduced spinach to France.
          Biscuit of nuts, candied fruit and toffee, coated in chocolate.

FLORIAN   Garnish of braised lettuce, carrots, onions and potatoes.

FLOUTE   (Alsace) Potato dumpling.

FLÛTE   Long bread roll.
          Tall slender bottle, used especially for the wines of *Alsace*.

FOIE   Liver. *Foie de veau à l'anglaise*: grilled calf's liver with bacon; *compagnarde*: with mushrooms and herbs; *à l'étuvée*: braised with vegetables and brandy; *vénitienne*: baked with bacon, mushrooms and shallots..

FOIE-DE-BOEUF   Lit.: 'ox liver'. Name for type of fungus (*fistuline*).

FOIE GRAS   Lit.: 'fat liver'. Liver of goose or duck force-fed with maize, sometimes weighing up to 4 lb; considered a delicacy and produced mainly in SW France and *Alsace*. Cooked, either whole or in slices, served hot or cold; also made into *pâté de foie gras*, often *truffé* – with truffles, for which towns like *Strasbourg*, *Nancy*, *Toulouse* and *Périgueux* are famous. *Foie gras à la toulousaine*: studded with truffles, braised in white stock and wrapped in pastry.

FOIN Hay. Cheese is sometimes cured in hay, and ham was traditionally cooked in it. *Foin d'artichaut*: choke, of artichoke.

FOIRE TEILLOUSE Lit.: 'chestnut fair'. *Potage foire teillouse*: chestnut and vegetable soup, a speciality of Redon in *Bretagne*, famous for its fair.

FOIX County equivalent to *Ariège*; also capital of *Ariège*.

FOLLE Feminine of *fou*: silly. *Salade folle*: salad usually of French beans, *foie gras* and shellfish.

FOND Base, bottom. *Fond d'artichaut*: artichoke bottom.

FONDANT(-E) Lit.: 'melting'. Small croquette, of puréed vegetables, or of cream and cheese.
Fondant icing, for cakes and buns.

FONDS Stock.

FONDU(-E) Melted. Vegetables cooked gently and lengthily until melted to a pulp.
Processed, of cheese; see below.
(Marche) Cheese mixed with milk, flour etc, eaten hot or cold with potatoes; also known as *régal de Marchois*.

FONDU AU MARC (Savoie) Processed cheese with grape pip rind; also known as *Fondu au Raisin*.

FONDUE Cheese *fondue*: Gruyère cheese melted in white wine and flavoured with *kirsch*, in the version made popular by the Swiss; *fondue de Franche-Comté* adds eggs and leaves out the *kirsch*. *Brillat-Savarin*'s recipe for *fondue* is scrambled eggs with Gruyère. *Petites fondues à la bourguignonne*: fried squares of cheese.
Meat *fondue*, pieces of steak dipped into a dish of hot oil in the middle of the table; sometimes called *fondue bourguignonne*, although a Swiss invention.

FONTAINE Fountain.

FONTAINEBLEAU (Ile-de-France) Fresh unsalted creamy cheese, eaten for dessert with sugar or cream; factory-made around Fontainebleau.

FONTAL Smooth mild cheese, factory-made in E France; imitation of Italian Fontina.

FONTANGES Mlle de Fontanges, favourite of Louis XIV. *Crème Fontanges*: cream of pea soup with sorrel.

FONTENELLE Le Bovier de Fontenelle, author, for whom the dish was invented; see *asperges*.

FONTIMASSON   (Vendée) Cream fritter.

(À LA) FORESTIÈRE   Lit.: 'forester's style'. With mushrooms, bacon and potatoes, for meat and poultry.

FOREZ   Mountainous region on the *Auvergne-Lyonnais* borders. See also *Brique de Forez* and *Côtes du Forez*.

FORME   Lit.: 'shape'. See *fromage*.

FORT(-E)   Strong. See also *fromage*.

FOU (FOLLE)   Mad, silly.

FOUACE/FOUASSE/FOUGASSE   Name given to various cakes and pastries

FOUDJOU   (Languedoc) Strong mixture of fresh and matured goat's milk cheese with brandy and garlic, eaten with potatoes.

FOUÉE   (W France) Hearth cake; oil-seed cake.
(Bourgogne) Cream and bacon flan.

FOUETTÉ(-E)   Whipped, of cream. Whisked, of eggs.

FOUGASSE   (S France) Rich cake, See also *fouace*.

FOUGASSETTE   (Provence) Oval cake flavoured with orange blossom.

FOUGERU   (Ile-de-France) *Coulommiers*-type cheese, wrapped in ferns ('fougères').

FOULQUE   Coot, water bird, sometimes hunted, especially in *Berry* where it is known as *judelle*; often made into *pâté*.

FOUR   Oven. *Au four*: baked, roasted. *Pomme (de terre) au four*: baked jacket potato.

FOURCHETTE   Fork. Wishbone, of poultry.

FOURME   Lit.: 'shape' in dialect (like *forme* from which *fromage* is derived). Name given to family of cheeses from SW France; see below.

FOURME D'AMBERT   (Auvergne) Tall cylindrical cheese (*AOC*), uncooked, unpressed, ripened for two months, firm and blue-veined with fruity flavour; made by small farms in the Monts du *Forez*, also known as *Fourme de Montbrison*.

FOURME DE CANTAL/DE LAGUIOLE/DE MÉZENC/DE MONTBRISON   See *Cantal*, *Laguiole-Aubrac*, *Bleu de Loudes* and *Fourme d'Ambert*.

FOURME DE PIERRE-SUR-HAUTE (Auvergne) Cheese similar to *Fourme d'Ambert*; named after the highest peak of the Monts du *Forez*.

FOURME DE ROCHEFORT/DE SALERS See *Cantalon* and *Salers*.

FOURNITURES Lit.: 'supplies'. General term for salad greens and herbs.

FOURRÉ(-E) Stuffed. See also *bonbon*.

FOYOT Louis-Philippe's chef and owner of the Café Foyot in Paris. *Sauce Foyot*: *béarnaise* sauce with meat glaze; also known as *sauce valois*. See also *côte*.

FRAI Name for young fish (*fretin*).

FRAIS (FRAÎCHE) Cool. Fresh. Fresh, of cheese (i.e. not cured or aged). See also *crème*.

FRAISE Strawberry. *Fraises marquise*: soaked in *kirsch*, with whipped cream and strawberry *purée*; *Ritz*: with whipped cream mixed with strawberry and raspberry *purée*; *Romanoff*: soaked in orange juice and liqueur, covered with whipped cream; *Wilhelmine*: soaked in *kirsch* and orange juice, with whipped cream.
Fraises des bois: wild strawberries. Also a clear spirit made from (wild) strawberries, especially in *Alsace*.

FRAISE DE VEAU Calf's mesentry, membrane enclosing the intestines, usually fried after preliminary cooking.

FRAMBOISE Raspberry. Also a spirit made from raspberries, especially in *Alsace*.

(À LA) FRANÇAISE French-style. French. Garnish of potato nests filled with vegetables, plus braised lettuce and asparagus; also of spinach and *Anna* potatoes. See also *homard*, *merlan* and *petit pois*.

FRANCHE-COMTÉ Province based on the departments of *Jura*, Doubs and Haute-Saône; also known as *Jura*. See also *fondue*.

(À LA) FRANC-COMTOISE In the style of *Franche-Comté*. *Potée franc-comtoise*: pork, cabbage and potato soup with sausage. *Soupe à la franc-comtoise*: potato, turnip and milk soup. See also *gratin*.

FRANCILLON Dramatic heroine created by Alexandre *Dumas*. *Salade Francillon*: salad of mussels, potatoes marinated in *Chablis* wine, and truffles, with warm *vinaigrette*; also known as *salade japonaise*.

FRANÇOISE   See *suprême*.

FRANCOLIN   Francolin, bird like partridge.

FRANGIPANE   Frangipani, Italian nobleman at the court of Catherine de *Médicis*. Confectioner's custard with crushed macaroons, for cakes and pastries.
    Basic mixture of flour, eggs, butter and milk, for forcemeats.

FRANQUETTE   Variety of walnut (*noix*).

FRAPPÉ(-E)   Iced; chilled; surrounded by/served on crushed ice, of wine or fruit.

FRAPPO   (Languedoc) Stewed ox tripe.

(À LA) FRASCATI   *Paris* restaurant. Garnish of *foie gras*, large mushrooms filled with asparagus, and truffles.

FRÉCHURE   (Vivarais) Pig's lung stew; corruption of *fressure*, also known as *levadou*.

FREMGEYE   (Lorraine) Fresh cream cheese with salt and pepper, fermented in a crock; often spread on bread with chopped onions.

FRÉNETTE   Type of lemonade with ash leaves, traditional drink of *Picardie*.

FRENEUSE   Village in *Ile-de-France* known for turnips. *Potage Freneuse*: turnip and potato soup.

FRÉROTTES   (Franche-Comté) Potatoes with onions and lard.

FRESSURE   Pluck, fry (i.e. heart, liver and lungs), usually of pig or calf. *Fressure vendéenne*: pig's fry cooked with onions and bread, eaten cold.

FRETIN   Fry, young fish; also known as *alevin*, *frai* and *poissonnaille*.

FREUX   Rook, the bird.

FRIAND(-E)   Lit.: 'nice'. Small pastry, either savoury and often of meat, or sweet and often with almonds and elaborately decorated. *Friand sanflorain/de Saint-Flour*: small sausage wrapped in pastry or leaves.

FRIANDISE   Sweet, candy. *Petit four*.

FRICADELLE   Fried cake, ball, of minced meat, onions, bread or potatoes.

FRICANDEAU   Topside, of veal, also known as *noix* and *sous-noix*; usually larded with bacon and braised on a bed of chicory and sorrel. Also slice of large fish (e.g. tuna, sturgeon), especially cooked as above.

(Auvergne) Pork *pâté* cooked in a piece of salt pork or sheep's stomach; or braised meat balls of pork and pig's liver.

FRICASSÉE   Light stew, often chicken or veal, in cream sauce, first sautéed (which distinguishes it from a *blanquette*). *Fricassée de poulet à l'angevine*: chicken with onions, mushrooms, white *Anjou* wine and cream sauce; *de caion* (Savoie): pork with its own blood, cream and wine; *morvandelle*: of ox tripe, liver and blood.

Fricassée périgourdine: mixture of aromatic vegetables and sometimes bacon, browned in fat, added to soups and stews.

FRICASSIN   (Bourbonnais, Nivernais) Calf's/goat's mesentry (*fraise*) in cream sauce.

FRICAUDE   (Lyonnaise) Pig's offal stew.

FRIGOLET   See *farigoule*.

FRINAULT/FRINOT   (Orléanais) Small soft round cheese, lightly cured, with little smell and pronounced flavour; named after its inventor. *Frinault Cendré*: coated with ashes.

FRISÉ(-E)   Lit.: 'curly'. *Frisée*: short for *chicorée frisée* (curly endive).

FRIT(-E)   Fried. *Pommes (de terre) frites*: chips, French fries, often known as just *frites*.
Oeufs frits: deep-fried eggs.

FRITELLE   (Corse) Chestnut flour fritter, eaten with cheese.

FRITES   See *frit*.

FRITOT   Fritter, usually savoury (e.g. of chicken, sweetbreads, brains), with tomato sauce.

FRITTONS   (SW France) Leftovers from making preserved meats (*confits*) mixed with bits of pork or goose, cooked in fat.

FRITURE   Frying. Fried food, especially small fish fried and served with lemon (e.g. *friture de la Loire*). *Friture à l'italienne*: fry-up of various meats (e.g. calf's liver, brains, bone marrow, sheep's trotters); probably from the Italian 'fritto-misto'.

FRIVOL(L)E   Lit.: 'frivolous'. (Champagne) Fritter, also known as *fiverolle*.

FROID(-E)   Cold. Cool.

FROMAGE

Originally, moulded food of any kind, derived from *forme* – shape (see also *fourme*), whence 'formage' and then *fromage*; ice creams were called *fromages glacés*; *bavarois* was known as *fromage bavarois*; and the old usage survives in *fromage de porc/de tête*: brawn.

Cheese. France is the largest cheese producer in the world, after the USA, and has 24 cheeses with *AOC* (here indicated in the text under individual entries). The system of *Appellation d'Origine Contrôlée*, set up in 1955, gives legal protection and recognition based on the following criteria: that the cheese comes from a strictly defined region, and that it has certain qualities resulting from the interaction of the natural features of this region – climate, soil, vegetation – together with the breed of cattle, and the use of traditional methods in its manufacture.

Fromage blanc: fresh soft cream cheese, slightly salted; eaten with fruit, sugar, fresh cream, or salt and pepper; also used in cooking.

Fromage à la crème: cream cheese.

Fromage cult (Lorraine): fresh cream cheese, cooked, drained and fermented, finally melted with butter, egg yolks, milk and seasoning, served hot.

Fromage fondu: processed cheese.

Fromage fort: lit.: 'strong cheese'. Home-made preparation of cheese beaten to a paste, flavoured and fermented. *Fromage fort du Beaujolais*: with *marc*; *de Béthune*: with herbs; *du Mont Ventoux*: with herbs, sometimes vinegar or *marc*.

Fromage frais: medium-fat cheese with the consistency of yoghourt; served drained, mixed with sugar and egg white and eaten with fruit, or used instead of cream in the *nouvelle cuisine*.

Fromage en pot (Lorraine): fresh cheese fermented with fennel seeds.

Fromage à tartiner/pour tartine: cheese spread.

FROMAGÉ(E)   Moulded. With cheese. See also *fromaget*.

FROMAGE DE PORC/DE TÊTE   Brawn, head cheese, chopped pig's head in jelly. *Fromage d'Italie*: brawn made with pig's liver. See also *hure*.

FROMAGE DU CURÉ   See *Nantais*.

FROMAGET   (Charentes) Cheese cake; also spelt *fromagé*.

FROMENT   Wheat. Wheat flour.

FROMENTEAU   Variety of table grape.

FROMENTÉE   (Touraine) Wheat with boiled almond milk; like the old English frumenty.

FRONSAC   See *Côtes de Fronsac*.

FRONTIGAN   Town in *Hérault*, making sweet fortified wine (*AC*) from the *Muscat* grape.

FRONTONNAIS   See *Côtes du Frontonnais*.

FROTÉE   (Lorraine) Egg and bacon tart.

FRUIT   Fruit. *Fruits confits*: crystallized fruit. *Fruits rafraîchis*: fruit salad. See also *eau-de-vie*.

FRUIT DE LA PASSION   Passion fruit, also known as *barbadine*.

FRUITERIE   Fruit shop, greengrocers.

FRUITS DE MER   Seafood.

FUMÉ(-E)   Smoked, cured, of fish, meat.

FUMÉE (DE MOULES)   See *éclade*.

FUMET   Aroma. Bouquet, of wine. Strong stock, often of fish.

(À LA) FUXÉENNE   In the style of *Foix*.

GABRIELLE   See *suprême*.

GÂCHE   (W France) Sweet *brioche*.

GADE(LLE)   (W France) Local name for gooseberry (*groseille à maquereau*). Name for cod (*cabillaud*).

GAILLAC   Region near *Albi* in *Languedoc*, producing red, rosé and white wines (*AC*), some of the latter sparkling and semi-sparkling.

GAILLARDE   Lit.: 'lively'. See *gribiche*.

GAILLETTE   See *caillette*.

GAL   (S France) Local name for John Dory (*Saint-Pierre*).

GALABART   (S and SW France) Large black pudding.

GALANTINE   Cold jellied loaf, of poultry, meat or fish, bones, stuffed and pressed. *Galantine de porc*: type of brawn but with less jelly.
      Loaf shaped cheese of the *Edam* type, made commercially especially in N France.

GALATHÉE   Type of prawn.

GALETON/GALETOU   Coarse pancake. See also *tourton*.

GALETTE   Round flat cake, pastry, open tart, hearth cake, savoury or sweet. *Galette corrézienne*: chestnut and walnut tart; *aux griaudes/grillaudes* (Bourgogne): ring-shaped *brioche* filled with bits of bacon or pork fat (*griaudes*); *lyonnaise*: cake of puréed potatoes and onions; *des Rois*: traditional Twelfth Night cake.
      (Bretagne) Thick pancake, often of buckwheat flour (as opposed to *crêpe*, usually of wheat flour), sometimes described as *galette de sarrasin*; generally savoury.

GALETTE DE LA CHAISE-DIEU   (Auvergne) Small goat's milk cheese shaped like a thin flat disk or brick, with strong flavour; made by farms around the Abbey of La Chaise-Dieu.

GALICHON/GALICHOU   See *calisson*.

GALICIEN   Rich pistachio-flavoured cake.

GALIMAFRÉE   Lit.: 'gallimaufry', badly cooked stew. (Gascogne) Stew of fried chicken, or sometimes meat, in acid grape juice; an ancient recipe.
      Galimafrée à la Vauban (Morvan): roast shoulder of mutton stuffed with bacon, mushrooms and garlic, with spicy *vinaigrette*.

GALINETTE   Name for type of gurnard (*grondin*).

GALLREI   See *kaléréi*.

GALOPIAU/GALOPIN   (N France) Small thick pancake, made with bits of *brioche* or bread.

GAMAY   Variety of black grape, used especially in the making of *Beaujolais*.

GAMBA   Name for large prawn (*crevette rose du large*).

GANDOILLOT (Lorraine) Large pork sausage eaten with haricot beans.

GANGA   Pin-tailed grouse, found in S France.
               Ganga-cata: name for hazel grouse (*gélinotte*).

(À LA) GANNATOISE In the style of Gannat in *Bourbonnais*. See *poulet*.

GANSE   (Nice) Sweet fritter.

GANTOIS   (Flandre) Spicy pastry with greengage jam.

GAOFF'S   (Bretagne) Local name for buckwheat pancake.

GAOUTO-ROUSSO (S France) Local name for grey mullet (*mulet*).

GAP   Capital of the Haute-Alpes department in *Dauphiné*.

GAP(E)RON (Auvergne) Small soft garlic-flavoured cheese made by farms and dairies; derived from 'gape' – dialect for buttermilk.

GARBURE   (Gascogne, especially Béarn) Vegetable soup including cabbage, haricot and broad beans, garlic, herbs, sometimes chestnuts, with a piece of preserved goose, duck, ham, pork or turkey added and served separately; the liquid is poured over slices of bread and, to finish, the last of the soup swilled out with a glass of wine (*chabrot/goudale*). *Garbure* is made in an earthenware *toupin*; the name derives from 'gerbe' – sheaf or bundle (i.e. of vegetables).

GARCIAUX   (Bretagne) Small smoked eels, sautéed and eaten with cider.

GARD   Department of *Languedoc* (and river) making large quantities of wine (*VDQS* and *Vins de Pays*), and including *Costières du Gard* and *Clairette de Bellegarde (AC)*.

GARDE-ÉCUEIL Lit.: 'rock-guard'. Name for *rascasse*.

(À LA) GARDIANE In the style of a *gardian*, cowboy, herdsman of *Camargue*. See *boeuf*.

GARDON   Roach, freshwater fish.
               Gardon rouge: name for red-eye (*rotengle*).

GARENNE   Rabbit warren. See *lapin*.

GARGAMÉU   (Provence) Tomato omelette.

GARGOUILLAU   (Bourbonnais, Limousin) Pear cake.

GARNI(-E)   Garnished. On a menu often means served with vegetables and chips. See also *aïoli* and *choucroute*.

GARNITURE   Garnish. See under their distinguishing names for the most common garnishes (e.g. see under 'F' for *à la forestière*). *Servi(e) avec garniture*: served with vegetables.

GASCOGNE   Gascony, province covering *Landes* and *Armagnac* (*Gers*); sometimes loosely applied to the whole SW corner of France. See also *beurre* and *faisan*.

GASCONNADE   (Gascogne) Roast leg of lamb with anchovies and garlic.

(À LA) GASCONNE   In the style of *Gascogne*. *Omelette à la gasconne*: omelette with ham, garlic and parsley. See also *poitrine* and *pot-au-feu*.

GASTADELO   (Provence) Local name for type of garfish (*balaou*).

GASTRONOME   Gastronome, epicure. Garnish of chestnuts, truffles and cock's kidneys.

GAT   (S France) Local name for dogfish (*roussette*).

GÂTEAU   Sponge or pastry cake, open tart, *brioche* etc. *Gâteau Alcazar*: rich pastry cake with almond filling and apricot jam; *basque*: thick tart filled with custard, also known as *pastiza*; *battu/wattieu* (N France): *brioche*; *breton*: large crumbly cake, or apple tart, sometimes with cherries; *dunois*: almond and hazelnut cake, also known as *beauceron à la cendrée*; *au fromage* (Auvergne): curd cheese tart; *Opéra*: elaborate almond sponge cake with coffee and chocolate filling and icing; *parisien*: sponge cake covered with meringue; *Reine de Saba*: light chocolate and almond cake; *de Savoie*: light sponge cake; *toulousain*: almond cake flavoured with lemon and vanilla.

   Savoury cake, loaf, tart. *Gâteau au chou vert*: cabbage strips rolled up in pastry and baked; *de foies blonds de volaille* (Bugey): pounded chicken livers mixed with *foie gras*, eggs, cream, steamed and served with crayfish tail sauce; *à la poêle* (Béarn): thick pancake; *de veillées* (Lorraine): potato and bacon tart.

GÂTINAIS   Region in *Orléanais*, known for honey and saffron.

GATIS   (Languedoc) *Brioche* stuffed with *Roquefort* and *Cantal* cheese.

GATOULIN   (S France) Local name for dogfish (*roussette*).

GAUDES   (Bourgogne, Franche-Comté) Maize flour porridge with cream, served hot or cooled and sliced.

GAUDINES   See *broye*.

GAUFRE   Waffle.

GAUFRETTE   *Pommes* (*de terre*) *gaufrette*: lattice potato chips.

GAUTHIER   See *Pigeonneau*.

GAVARNIE   Valley in *Bigorre*. See *truite*.

GAVE   (Pays basque, Béarn) Local term for mountain stream. See *truite*.

GAYETTE   See *caillette*.

GAY LUSSAC   System for measuring alcohol content of wines and spirits as a percentage of volume; named after its inventor.

GAZEUX (GAZEUSE)   Fizzy, carbonated, of water etc.

GELÉE   Jelly.

GÉLINE   Name for chicken.

GÉLINOTTE   Hazel grouse, found in mountains; also known as *gangacata* and *poule des bois*.

GENDARME   Lit.: 'gendarme'. Name for salted and smoked herring (*hareng saur*).
   Gendarme (*suisse*): hard dry Swiss sausage.

GÉNÉPY   Herb-flavoured liqueur, made in *Grenoble*.

(À LA) GENEVOISE   In the style of Geneva. *Sauce genevoise*: sauce based on fish stock and red wine, chiefly for salmon and trout (formerly known as *sauce génoise*).

GENIÈVRE   Juniper berry. Gin, distilled from grain and flavoured with juniper berries.

GÉNISSE   Heifer, young cow.

(À LA) GÉNOISE   In the style of Genoa. With tomato sauce. See also *tomate*.
   Génoise: Genoa sponge cake, sponge mixture, used (like *biscuit*) as a basis for many cakes.

GENTIANE   Gentian, mountain flower used to flavour aperitifs and liqueurs. Also a liqueur or clear spirit made from gentians.

GENTILHOMME   Lit.: 'gentleman'. *Potage gentilhomme*: game and lentil soup.

GEORGETTE   *Pommes (de terre) Georgette*: potatoes stuffed with crayfish tails, served hot as a first course. *Potage Georgette*: (globe) artichoke soup.

GÉRARDMER   (Lorraine) Large mild white cheese, made by dairies in the Gérardmer region; also known as *(Gros) Lorraine*, connected with *Géromé* and *Munster*.

GERMINY   19th-century financier. *Potage Germiny*: sorrel soup with egg yolks and cream.

GERMON   Name for long-fin tuna (*thon blanc*).

GÉROMÉ   (Lorraine) Smooth round cheese with reddish rind, usually of pasteurized milk, smelly and spicy, sometimes eaten fresh or partly cured; made by dairies around Gérardmer in *Vosges*. Linked with *Gérardmer* and *Munster*, the name being dialect for *Gérardmer*. *Géromé Anisé*: flavoured with caraway seeds.

GERS   Department equivalent to *Armagnac*; also river.

(À LA) GERSOISE   In the style of *Gers*.

GERVAIS   Well-known brand of *Petit-Suisse* cheese, and the name of its first manufacturer.

GÉSIER   Gizzard, of poultry.

GEVREY-CHAMBERTIN   Important commune (*AC*) of *Côte de Nuits*, *Bourgogne*; it contains the famous *Chambertin* and *Clos de Bèze*, and seven other *grand cru* (*AC*) vineyards whose names, like *Gevrey*, are hyphenated with *Chambertin*: *Charmes*, *Chapelle*, *Griotte*, *Latricières*, *Mazis*, *Mazoyères* (usually sold as *Charmes-Chambertin*) and *Ruchottes*.

GEWÜRZTRAMINER   Variety of white grape grown in *Alsace*, making characteristically spicy wine; 'Gewürz' is German for spice.

GEX   See *Bleu de Gex-Haut-Jura*.

GIBASSIER   (Provence) Orange-flavoured yeast cake, traditionally eaten on Christmas Eve; also known as *pompe (de Noël)*.

GIBELOTTE   Stew, especially of rabbit. See also *lapin*.

GIBIER   Game. *Gibier d'eau*: wild water fowl.

GIEN   (Orléanais) Firm small cheese of goat's, cow's milk or a mixture, cured in plane tree leaves or ashes, with nutty flavour; made by farms around Gien. See *Côtes du Gien*.

(À LA) GIENNOISE   In the style of Gien in *Orléanais*. See *lapin*.

GIGONDAS   Commune of the *Rhône* in *Vaucluse*, making fine red and rosé wines (*AC*).

GIGORET/GIGORIT/GIGOURIT   (Poitou, Charentes, Morvan) Pig's head cooked in blood and red wine, with local variations; also known as *tantouillet*.

GIGOT   Hind leg, leg, of mutton; and of lamb, usually specified as *gigot d'agneau*. *Gigot brayaude* (Auvergne, Bourbonnais): stewed in white wine with bacon, onions, herbs, served with red haricot beans, braised cabbage and chestnuts; *à la bretonne*: roasted with white haricot beans; *pourri* (Rouergue): casseroled with whole unpeeled garlic cloves; *de sept heures*: braised (for seven hours) until so tender that it can be cut with a spoon, also called *gigot à la cuiller*; *de Sologne à l'eau*: boiled. *Gigot des grèves du Mont-Saint-Michel*: salt meadow (*pré-salé*) lamb. See also *chevreuil*.

False leg. *Gigot de mer* (Languedoc): monkfish with *ratatouille*, white wine and cream. See also *aubergine*.

GIGOUDAINE   (Bretagne) Buckwheat porridge.

GIGOURIT   See *gigoret*.

GIGUE   Haunch, of venison, wild boar; also known as *cuissot*.

GIMBLETTE   Ring-biscuit.

GINGEMBRE   Ginger, the spice.

GIRELLE   Rainbow wrasse, Mediterranean fish; also known as *donzelle*.

GIROFLE   Cloves, the spice.

GIROLLE   Name for type of fungus (*chanterelle*).

GIRONDE   Department equivalent to *Bordelais*, and estuary formed by the rivers Dordogne and Garonne.

(À LA) GIRONNAISE   In the style of Giron in *Bugey*. See *côte*.

GÎTE   Lodging. (Bordelais) Local name for type of shellfish (*phollade*).

GÎTE À LA NOIX   Silverside of beef, also known as *tendre de tranche*.

GIVRÉ(-E)   Frosted. See also *orange*.

GIVRY Commune of *Côte Chalonnaise*, *Bourgogne*, producing mainly red wines (*AC*).

GL See *Gay Lussac*.

GLAÇAGE Icing. Glaze.

GLACE Ice. Ice cream, also known as *crème glacée*. *Glace Armenonville*: coffee or vanilla ice cream with hot chocolate sauce; *bourguignonne*: ice cream with *crème de cassis*; *Diane*: chestnut *mousse* surrounded by vanilla ice cream, flavoured with *kirsch* and *maraschino*; *au café*: coffee ice cream; *Madeleine*: crystallized pineapple soaked in *kirsch*, mixed with vanilla ice cream and cream; *Plombières*: vanilla ice cream with crystallized fruit and *kirsch*, or almond ice cream with apricot jam. See also *bombe*.
Glaze, meat glaze. See also *demi-glace*.
Icing, for a cake.

GLACÉ(-E) Frozen; iced; ice-cold.
Glazed.
Iced, of cake.
Glacé, of fruit. See also *biscuit*, *bombe* and *jambon*.

GLAÇON Ice cube.

GLUI Lit.: 'straw'. See *sole*.

GNOCCHI Italian dumplings, made of *choux* paste, semolina or potatoes. *Gnocchi à la niçoise*: small poached potato dumplings; *à la parisienne*: *choux* dumplings with cheese; *à la romaine*: baked semolina dumplings with cheese.

GOBEMOUCHE (Languedoc) Lit.: 'gobble-fly'. Local name for fig-pecker (*becfigue*).

GOBIE Goby, tiny sea fish; also known as *chabot* and *goujon de mer*. See also *non(n)at*.

GODAILLE (Bretagne) Fisherman's portion of fish allocated after rest of catch sold. *Soupe godaille*: soup of different small fish with garlic, shallots and duck fat, poured on slices of stale bread.

GODARD   Garnish similar to *financière*.

GODE   Name for pout (*tacaud*).

GODFICHE   (Normandie) Local name for scallop (*coquille Saint-Jacques*).

GODIVEAU   Forcemeat containing veal, used especially for *quenelles*.

GOGUE   (Anjou) Small vegetable and pork sausage.

GOGUETTE   Highly spiced flat pork sausage.

GOLMOTTE   Name for variety of fungus (*oronge*).

GOMBOS/GOMBAUT   Okra, ladies' fingers, pods of tropical vegetable; often stewed with tomatoes.

GORENFLOT   Hero of a *Dumas* play. Garnish of red cabbage, sausage and potatoes.
Rich sweet pastry baked in hexagonal mould.

GORET   Young pig, no longer a sucking pig. See also *porcelet*.

GOUDA FRANÇAIS   French equivalent of Dutch Gouda cheese, with yellow rind, supple texture and mild flavour; made particularly in N France. *Gouda* (*Demi-*)-*Etuvé*: harder, stronger, sometimes with smooth shiny red rind.

GOUDALE   See *chabrot*.

GOUÈRE/GOUÉRON/GOUERRE   Various cakes or tarts. *Gouère/gouerre* (Bourbonnais): potato and cheese tart. *Gouère/gouéron* (Berry, Bourgogne): apple cake. *Gouéron* (Berry): goat's milk cheese cake. *Gouerre au cirage* (Bourbonnais): prune tart (lit.: 'blacking').

GOUFFÉ   19th-century chef and restaurant owner. Garnish of potato nests filled with mushrooms and asparagus.

GOUGELHO(P)F   See *kougelhopf*.

GOUGÈRE   (Bourgogne) Cheese-flavoured *choux* pastry in a ring, usually served cold.

GOUGNETTE/GOUGUETTE   (Quercy) Large fritter.

GOUGUENIOCHE   (Vendée) Small chicken pastry.

GOUGUETTE   See *gougnette*.

GOUJON/GOUJONETTE/GOUJONNIÈRE   Gudgeon, small freshwater fish. *Goujons à la cascamèche* (Nivernais): with shallots, garlic and vinegar; *en manchon*: the body dipped in a muff (*manchon*) of egg and breadcrumbs, leaving the head and tail free, deep-fried.

Strip of filleted fish, usually sole, floured or egg-and-breadcrumbed, and deep-fried.

GOUJON DE MER   Name for goby (*gobie*).

GOUJONETTE   Name for gudgeon (*goujon*).

GOUJONNIÈRE   Name for gudgeon (*goujon*). Also name for pope (*gremille*).

GOURILOS   Stumps of curly endive, also called *moelle de chicorée*.

GOURMET   Gourmet, connoisseur of food and wine; originally, a wine-taster's assistant.

GOURMAND(-E)   Fond of food. Gourmand, epicure. See also *caille*.

GOURMANDISE   Sweetmeat, dainty. Processed cheese flavoured with *kirsch*, covered in nuts.

GOURNAY (AFFINÉ)   (Normandie) Small round lightly cured cheese, packed on straw, with white downy rind and mild flavour, sometimes eaten fresh as *Gournay Frais*; made by dairies around Gournay in *Bray*, also known as *Malakoff* (brand name).

GOUSSE   Pod, shell, husk. *Gousse d'ail*: clove of garlic.

GOÛT   Taste.

GOÛTER   To taste. Afternoon tea; to take tea.

GOYAVE   Guava fruit, fruit of tropical tree, usually eaten raw.

GOYÈRE   (Flandre) *Maroilles* cheese tart.

GRAÇAY   (Berry) Goat's milk cheese dusted with charcoal, nutty in flavour, made by small dairies; invented name.

GRAILLONS   See *grattons*.

GRAIN   Berry. *Grain de raisin*: grape. *Grain de cassis*: blackcurrant. *Grains de café/café en grains*: coffee beans. *Poivre en grains*: whole peppercorns.

Grain. Short for *poulet de grain*.

GRAINE   Seed. *Graines de pavot*: poppy seeds.

GRAISSE   Fat; lard; dripping. *Graisse normande*: beef suet and pork fat cooked with vegetables and herbs, preserved in pots; used in local cooking, and also in *soupe à la graisse*:

vegetable and potato soup, with *graisse normande* and stale bread. *Graisse d'oie*: goose fat, essential ingredient of cookery in SW France. *Graisse de rognon*: suet.

GRAISSERONS   (Béarn) Fat and lean of pork cooked in fat, then pounded in a mortar and preserved; like large *rillettes*.

GRAMMONT   See *homard*.

GRAMOLATE   Type of water ice.

GRAND(-E)   Large; big; great.

GRAND AÏOLI   See *aïoli*.

GRAND AROME   See *rhum*.

(LE) GRAND-BORNAND   See *Persillé des Aravis*.

GRAND CRU   Lit.: 'great growth'. Wine term used to denote superior merit. See also *Bordeaux* and *Bourgogne*.

GRAND DESSERT   See *dessert*.

GRAND-DUC   Lit.: 'grand duke'. Garnish of asparagus, crayfish tails, truffles and cheese sauce.

GRANDE CHAMPAGNE   See *Cognac*.

GRANDE MARQUE   Lit.: 'great brand'. Term used especially by major *Champagne* houses.

GRANDE PALOURDE   Name for Venus shell (*verni*).

GRANDE RÉSERVE   Description for very mature *Cognac*.

GRANDEUR   Size. See also *selon*.

GRAND MARNIER   Orange-flavoured liqueur based on *Cognac*.

(À LA) GRAND'MÈRE   Lit.: 'grandmother's style'. With onions, mushrooms, bacon and potatoes. *Oeufs grand'mère*: scrambled eggs with cubes of fried bread. *Soupe à la grand'mère: vegetable soup with pasta and herbs.*

GRAND ORDINAIRE   Lit.: 'great ordinary'. General *appellation* for wines grown anywhere in *Bourgogne*.

GRAND ROUSSILLON   Sweet, fortified wines grown around Perpignan (*AC*).

GRANDS ÉCHEZEAUX   *Grand cru* (*AC*) red wine vineyard of *Côte de Nuits, Bourgogne*.

GRAND VATEL   See *Délice de Saint-Cyr*.

GRAND VENEUR Lit.: 'master of the king's hunt'. *Sauce grand-veneur*: red wine, redcurrant, cream and pepper sauce, for game and venison.

GRAND VIN Lit.: 'great wine'. Wine-label term claiming superior quality, used only by *AC* wines.

GRANITÉ Grainy water ice with ice crystals, sprinkled with sugar; from Italian 'granita'.

(À LA) GRANVILLAISE In the style of Granville in *Normandie*. See *colin*.

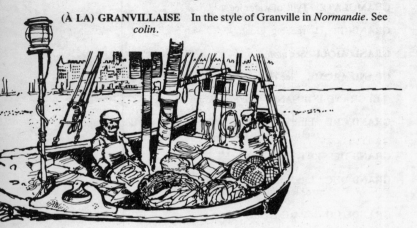

GRAPIAU (Bourbonnais, Berry, Bourgogne) Thick pancake, either savoury, often of potato, or sweet; also known as *sanciau*.

GRAPPA/GRAPPE Processed cheese covered with grape pips.

GRAS(-SE) Fat. Fatty. With meat (e.g. *soupe grasse*: meat soup), originally meat as the opposite of fasting – hence Mardi Gras: Shrove Tuesday. See also *tranche*.

GRAS-DOUBLE Ox tripe, technically 3 stomachs of ox (as opposed to *tripes*, all 4). *Gras-double à la lyonnaise*: sliced, fried, with onions, vinegar and parsley.

GRATARON D'ARÊCHES (Savoie) Round firm lightly cured goat's milk cheese, with pronounced tang; made in mountain dairies around Arêches, also known as (*Tommes d'*) *Arêches*.

GRATARON DE HAUTELUCE See *Hauteluce*.

GRATIN  Dish browned in the oven or under the grill, often sprinkled with breadcrumbs or cheese, to form a thin surface crust (e.g. *sole au gratin*). *Gratin dauphinois*: sliced potatoes baked with cream and browned on top –

the authentic version, although cheese and eggs are often added; also known as *pommes* (*de terre*) *à la dauphinoise*. *Gratin franc-comtois* is similar; *gratin savoyard* includes cheese and eggs, with beef stock. *Gratin languedocien*: baked aubergines, tomatoes and herbs. *Gratin de queues d'écrevisses à la Nantua*: crayfish tails in cream sauce and crayfish butter, browned.

GRATINÉ(-E)   Cooked *au gratin*. *Gratinée* (Lyonnais): clear soup with beaten egg, port (no onions), toasted cheese on top.
Short for *soupe à l'oignon gratinée*: onion soup poured over a slice of bread, grated cheese on top, browned.

GRATTE-CUL   Rose hip, sometimes made into jam.

GRATT(ER)ONS   (SW and central France) Small frizzled cubes of fat and lean of pork, sometimes pounded in a mortar, salted while hot and eaten cold, used in pies and *pâtés* or, in *Bordelais*, served with oysters; also known as *graillons*. See also *pompe*.

GRATUIT(-E)   Free, without charge.

GRAVELET   Name for dace (*dard*).

GRAVENCHE   Fish of salmon family, similar to *féra*, found in deep lakes in *Savoie* and much esteemed.

GRAVES   Large district (*AC*) of *Bordeaux*, producing great red wines (e.g. Château Haut-Brion, La Mission Haut-Brion), and whites both sweet and dry; the name comes from its sandy, stony soil.
A new *AC*, Graves Pessac-Léognan, was created in 1987 for that part of the region adjoining the city of *Bordeaux* which contains the finest vineyards.

GRAVES DE VAYRES   Area of gravel soil in *Bordeaux*, producing red and white wines (*AC*).

GRAVETTE   Especially flat type of oyster, from *Arcachon*; see *huître*.

(À LA) GRECQUE   Greek-style. Vegetables, stewed with oil and herbs, served hot or cold as a first course (e.g. *champignons à la grecque*). See also *aïoli* and *riz*.

GRÈLE   (Nivernais) Rye bread with grilled ham.

GRELETTE   Lit.: 'slender'. *Sauce grelette*: cold whipped cream sauce, for fish and salads; invented by the *nouvelle cuisine* chef, Roger Vergé.

GRELOT   Lit.: 'small round bell'. Variety of onion from S France.

GREMILLE   Pope, ruff, small freshwater fish; also known as (*perche*) *goujonnière*.

GRENACHE   Variety of red wine grape grown in the *Rhône* and *Midi* from Italian 'granaccio' – large seeds.

GRENADE   Pomegranate.

GRENADIER   Lit.: 'grenadier'. Sea fish of long, tapering shape.

GRENADIN   Small thick square of triangular slice, of veal (equivalent to *tournedos* of beef); also of other meat or poultry. *Grenadins de veau à la corbigeoise*: veal, larded with bacon, braised in white wine; *Laguipière*: sautéed, with madeira and truffle sauce, and artichokes filled with asparagus.

GRENADINE   Bright-red syrup, supposedly pomegranate juice, used as a sweetener in cocktails.

GRENOBLE   Capital of the Isère department in *Dauphiné*. See also *noix*.

(À LA) GRENOBLOISE   In the style of *Grenoble*. Fish, especially trout, hake, fried in butter, with capers and lemon. See also *poulet*.

GRENOUILLE   Frog, in culinary terms short for *cuisses de grenouille*: frog's legs (the only part that is eaten); also known as *nymphes*. *Grenouilles à la mode de Boulay*: baked with butter, shallots and parsley; *à la bressane*: with butter, cream and herb sauce; *à la colmarienne*: in cream sauce; *à la luçonnaise*: marinated in vinegar, fried with garlic; *à la provençale*: sautéed with parsley, garlic and lemon juice. *Soupe aux grenouilles* (Alsace): cream soup of frog's legs and white wine. See also *tourte*.

GRENOUILLES   See *Chablis*.

GRESSIN   Bread stick.

GRIAUDES   See *beursaudes*.

GRIBICHE   *Sauce gribiche*: cold *vinaigrette* with hard-boiled egg yolks, gherkins, capers, served with cold fish; also known as *sauce gaillarde*, perhaps originally from Brive-la-Gaillarde in *Limousin*.

GRIÈGES   See *Bleu de Bresse*.

GRIGNAN   Liqueur similar to *Chartreuse*, made in *Vaucluse*.

GRIGNAUDES   (Berry) Small fried cubes of pork. See also *pompe*.

GRIGNON   Piece of dry bread, or end crust of loaf; also known as *quignon*.

GRILLADE Grill, food which has been grilled. *Grillade au fenouil* (Provence): sea bass or red mullet grilled over fennel.
Toast, toasted sandwich.
Grillade des mariniers de Condrieu: layers of beef and onions braised with oil, vinegar, anchovies and garlic (probably derived like *carbonnade*).

GRILLAUDES See *beursaudes*.

GRILLÉ(-E) Grilled. Toasted, of bread.

GRILLETTES DE CANARD Tiny crisp bits of duck, grilled.

GRILLONS (Périgord) Leftover bits from cooking *confits* (preserves) of goose or pork.

GRIOTTE Variety of cherry, bitter and bright red.

GRIOTTE-CHAMBERTIN See *Gevrey-Chambertin*.

GRIS(-E) Grey. Light rosé colour, of wine. See also *petit gris*.

GRIS DE LILLE (Flandre) Slab-shaped cheese with sticky pinky-grey rind, cured in brine and sometimes beer, very strong-smelling and tasting; made by farms and dairies around *Lille*, derived from *Maroilles* cheese, and also known as *Puant Macéré* (lit.: 'stinking pickled'), *Gris Puant, Puant de Lille, Vielle Tête* and *Vieux*.

GRISET Black (sea) bream, also known as *brème (de rochers)*, *canthare, canthère, dorade grise* and *tanudo*.

GRISETTE Name for type of fungus (*coucoumelle*).

GRISOTTE Name for parasol mushroom (*coulemelle*).

GRIVE Thrush, often made into *pâté*. *Grives en croute à l'ardennaise*: stuffed with their livers, *foie gras*, truffles, juniper berries, braised and arranged in a large hot bread crust; *à la liégeoise*: casseroled with juniper berries and gin.

GROGNANT See *grondin*.

GRONDIN Gurnard, family of spiky scaly sea fish which make a grunting noise, some good to eat. Types include *grondin gris*: grey gurnard, the most common, also known as *grognant* (lit.: 'grunting'), *canaron, pinaou* and *trigle*; (*grondin*) *galinette*: tub gurnard, also known as *perlon, moelleux* and *tombe*; *grondin imbriago*: streaked gurnard, also known as *camard*; *grondin lyre*: piper; *grondin rouge*: red gurnard, also known confusingly as *rouget* (*-grondin*). *Grondin gris farci à la boulonnaise*: baked grey gurnard stuffed with pork and herbs, with cream sauce.

GROS(-SE)   Large; big. *Gros (de) Bourgogne*: name for vineyard snail (*escargot*).

GROS-BEC   Lit.: 'large beak'. Hawfinch, small bird; also known as *casse-noix* and *pinson royal*.

GROS-BLANQUET   Variety of pear.

GROSEILLE   Redcurrant. *Sirop de groseilles*: redcurrant syrup.
White currant.
Groseille à maquereau: gooseberry, from the gooseberry sauce which traditionally accompanies mackerel; also known as *groseille verte* and *gadelle*.
Groseille de cheval (Lorraine): local name for cranberry (*canneberge*).

GROS LORRAINE   See *Gérardmer*.

GROS MOLLET   Name for lumpfish (*lompe*).

GROS PAIN   Large crusty loaf.

GROS PLANT   Lit.: 'large plant'. Variety of white grape grown in the same region as *Muscadet*, around *Nantes*, producing crisp wine (*VDQS*).

GROSSE   Feminine of *gros*: large.

GROS SEL   Coarse rock, sea salt. See also *boeuf* and *chapon*.

GROSSE CREVETTE   Name for type of prawn (*caramote*).

GROSSE NOUNOU   Lit.: 'big nanny'. See *tête*.

GROSSE PALOURDE   Name for Venus shell (*verni*).

GROSSEUR   Size. See also *selon*.

GROS SUISSE   Larger version of *Petit Suisse*, also known as *Suisse*.

GROS VERT   Variety of white table grape.
Gros Vert de Laon: variety of globe artichoke.

GROS YEUX   Lit.: 'big eyes'. Name for red sea bream (*dorade*).

GROU   (Bretagne) Buckwheat flour fritter.

GROUIN D'ÂNE   Name for dandelion (*pissenlit*).

GROUSE   Name for grouse (*tétras*).

GRUAU   Corn, grain. *Gruau d'avoine*: groats, oatmeal. Short for *farine de gruau*: best wheat flour. See also *pain* and *saucisse*.

GRUILLOTTE DE PORC (Bourgogne) Pig's offal braised in red wine.

GRUYÈRE (Bourgogne, Franche-Comté, Savoie) Generic name for *Beaufort*, *Comté* and *Emmental* cheeses, all similar to Swiss *Gruyère*.

GRYPHÉE Name for Portuguese oyster (*portugaise*).

GUÉMÉNÉ Town in *Bretagne*, known for *andouille*.

GUENILLE Lit.: 'rag'. (Auvergne) Fritter.
(Limousin) *Pommes* (*de terre*) *à la guenille*: sautéed potatoes crushed in milk.

GUERBIGNY (Picardie) Invented name for *Rollet* cheese shaped like a heart.

GUÉRET Capital of *Creuse* and of *Marche*.
Small hard milk cheese, made by farms; also known as *Creusois*.

GUEYIN (Lorraine) *Trang'nat* cheese fermented in crocks.

GUIGNARD Dotterel, small rare game bird; also known as *pluvier guignard*.

GUIGNE Variety of cherry, used to make *guignolet*.

GUIGNETTE Name for sandpiper (*alouette de mer*).
(Charentes) Local name for winkle (*bigorneau*).

GUIGNOLET Cherry brandy made from *guignes*, a speciality of *Anjou*.

GUILLARET (Anjou) Substantial sweet pastry.

GUIMAUVE Marshmallow, wild plant; marshmallow sweets were once made from its roots – see *pâte*.

GUINCAMP Town in *Bretagne*. See *morue*.

GUITARE Lit.: 'guitar'. Guitar-shaped fish of skate family, also known as *violon*.

GULYAS Hungarian goulash; stew usually of beef, with paprika.

GUYENNE Province, capital *Bordeaux*, comprising *Bordelais*, *Périgord*, *Quercy* and *Agenais*; English corruption of the original name, *Aquitaine*.

GYMNÈTRE Long flat Mediterranean fish.

GYROLE Name for type of fungus (*chanterelle*).

HACHÉ(-E)   Chopped. Minced. *Sauce hachée*: tomato sauce with vinegar, capers, ham and mushrooms. See also *bifteck*.

HACHIS   Minced meat. Hash of chopped up leftovers in a sauce. *Hachis Parmentier*: shepherd's pie, sometimes served in potato jackets.
(Périgord) Mixed fried vegetables, for soups.

HACHUA   (Pays basque) *Bayonne* ham stewed with onions and peppers.

HADDOCK   Smoked haddock.

HAINAUT   Northern province, capital *Valenciennes*, usually considered part of *Flandre*.

HALBRAN   Young wild duck.

HALICOT DE MOUTON   Mutton stew with potatoes, turnips and onions; also known as *haricot de mouton* and may include haricot beans, although probably derived from the Old French *halicoter* or *harigoter* – to cut in small pieces.

(À LA) HAMBOURGEOISE   In the style of Hamburg. See *bifteck*.

HARENG   Herring. *Hareng blanc*: salt herring, also known as *hareng salé*.
   Hareng frais: fresh herring. *Harengs à la calaisienne*: stuffed with the roes and herbs, baked in paper-cases (also applicable to mackerel); *à la dieppoise*: cooked, served cold in marinade; *marinés à la fécampoise*: soused in vinegar and white wine, served cold with carrots, onions, lemon slices; *à la nantaise*: fried, with soft roe butter; *portière*: fried, with mustard, vinegar and brown butter; *Paramé*: baked in paper-cases; *à la quimperlaise*: grilled, with mustard sauce.
   Hareng fumé: smoked herring, usually served cold. *Harengs à la livonienne*: with potatoes and apples; *Lucas*: with mustard-flavoured mayonnaise; *à la russe*: with potatoes and *vinaigrette*.
   Hareng pec: freshly salted herring, barrelled without being smoked.
   Hareng roulé: rollmop–marinated, spiced herring, rolled round a gherkin, served with onions.
   Hareng salé: salt herring, also known as *hareng blanc*.
   Hareng saur: whole herring salted and smoked; also known as *gendarme* and *saur(et)*. Boulogne specializes in various types of salted and smoked herring – *craquelots* or *bouffis*: small herrings cured for only a few hours, sometimes over walnut leaves; *demi-sell/doux*: lightly smoked; *kippers*: larger herrings, lightly smoked and opened out.

HARENG BALTIQUE   Baltic herring, smaller type.

HARENG DE BERGUES/HARANGUET   (N France) Name for sprat (*esprot*). Also name for *sardine*.

HARICOT   Bean; see below. *Haricots panachés*: mixed French and flageolet beans (*haricots verts* and *flageolets*).

HARICOT BEURRE   Butter bean, large white dried bean; also known as *haricot jaune*.

HARICOT BLANC   Dried white haricot bean. *Haricots blancs à l'américaine*: with bacon and tomato sauce; *à la bretonne*: with onions, and perhaps shallots, garlic, tomatoes; *à la charcutière*: with ham, sausages and onions. See also *estouffade*.

HARICOT DE LIMA   Lima bean, type of dried bean.

HARICOT DE MER   Name for type of clam (*olive*).

HARICOT DE MOUTON   See *halicot de mouton*.

HARICOT D'ESPAGNE   Runner bean, also known as *haricot grimpant/rampant/à rame* (lit.: 'climbing', 'creeping', 'staked').

HARICOT JAUNE   Name for butter bean (*haricot beurre*).

HARICOT ROUGE   Red kidney bean.

HARICOT VERT   French bean, string bean. *Haricots verts à la bonne femme*: boiled, with butter and diced bacon.

HASE   Doe, of hare, rabbit.

HÂTELET   Small skewer.

HÂTELETTE/HÂTELLE   Food cooked on a small skewer (*hâtelet*).

HATEREAU   Small piece of food fried on a skewer, served in sauce as an *hors d'oeuvre*.
　　　Pork liver ball.

HAUT(-E)   High.

HAUT-ARMAGNAC   See *Armagnac*.

HAUT-BENAUGE   Area of *Entre-Deux-Mers, Bordeaux*, making white wine (*AC*).

HAUT-COMTAT   Red and rosé wines from the hills of Les Baronnies, N of *Vaucluse* (*VDQS*).

HAUTELUCE   (Savoie) Small tangy goat's milk cheese, made around Hauteluce; also known as *Grataron de Hauteluce*.

HAUTES CÔTES DE BEAUNE   See *Côte de Beaune*.

HAUTES CÔTES DE NUITS   See *Côte de Nuits*.

HAUT-MÉDOC   One of the most important districts (*AC*) of *Bordeaux*, in the southern half of *Médoc*. It grows some of the world's greatest red wines (e.g. Lafite, Latour, Mouton-Rothschild), and contains the important communes of *Listrac*, *Saint-Estèphe*, *Margaux*, *Moulis*, *Pauillac*, and *Saint-Julien*; a few white wines are also produced, but these may only be called *Bordeaux* (*AC*).

HAUT-POITOU   Wines (*VDQS*) grown in the Vienne department of *Poitou*, known as *Vins du Haut-Poitou*.

(À LA) HAVRAISE   In the style of Le Havre in *Normandie*. See *boudin*, *coquille Saint-Jacques*, *lapin* and *sardine*.

HELDER   The Café du Helder in 19th-century *Paris*. Garnish of potato balls and tomato-flavoured *béarnaise* sauce; also of artichokes and asparagus.

HÉLÈNE   See *poire*.

HÉLOÏSE   See *sole*.

HELVELLE   Family of fungi of various shapes, usually growing in woods, some with pleasant flavour; varieties also known as *oreille de chat/de Judas*.

HÉNON   (Picardie) Local name for cockle (*coque*).

HENRI DUVERNOIS   Writer and gourmet of the 1920s. See *homard*.

HENRI IV   Henri of Navarre, King of France and great hero of *Béarn*. Garnish of artichoke hearts filled with *béarnaise* sauce, plus fried potatoes and watercress (e.g. *tournedos Henri IV*). *Oeufs pochés Henri IV*: poached eggs with artichokes. See also *poule*.

HÉRAULT   Department of *Languedoc* (and river) making large quantities of wine (*VDQS*, *Vin de Pays* and *Vin de Table*), including many villages of the *Coteaux du Languedoc*; it also contains *Clairette du Languedoc* and the *Muscats* of *Frontignan*, *Mireval* and *Lunel*.

HERBE   Lit.: 'grass'. *Herbes aromatiques/potagères*: kitchen or pot herbs. *Herbe de Saint-Julien*: name for savory (*sarriette*). *Herbe de Saint-Pierre*: name for samphire (*christ-marine*). See also *fines herbes*.

HÈRE   Young stag.

HÉRISSON   Hedgehog.

HERMITAGE One of the finest *Rhône* vineyards, on a hill of the same name behind the village of Tain-L'Hermitage, producing red and white wines (*AC*). See also *poussin*, and *sole*.

(À LA) HIÉROISE/HYÉROISE In the style of Hyères in *Provence*. See *sardine*.

HIRONDELLE DE MER Lit.: 'sea swallow'. Name for flying fish (*poisson volant*).

HIVER Winter.

HOCCO Hocco, type of turkey from S America.

HOCHEPOT (À LA FLAMANDE) Soup of pig's ears and tails, breast of beef and mutton, salt pork, cabbage, other vegetables.

HOGUE VOSGIEN Round rye cake with plums.

(À LA) HOLLANDAISE Dutch-style. *Sauce hollandaise*: hot sauce of butter, egg yolks and lemon juice, usually with white wine and vinegar added, similar to *béarnaise* sauce. Method of preparing fish, poached, with boiled potatoes and melted butter, and perhaps *hollandaise* sauce.

HOLSTEIN See *escalope*.

HOMARD Lobster; often priced on the menu according to size (*selon grosseur – SG*). *Homard à l'américaine/armoricaine*: sautéed in oil, in white wine, brandy, garlic, shallot, tomato sauce, often with rice (see also *américaine*); *à la bordelaise*: flamed with brandy, with white wine and egg sauce; *à la calvaise*: with spicy tomato sauce; *cardinal*: see *cardinal*; *à la charentaise*: with sauce of cream and *Pineau des Charentes* or dry white *vermouth*; *à la française*: cooked in white wine and brandy; *Grammont*: cold, with lobster mousse and oysters; *Henri Duvernois*: with leeks, mushrooms, sherry, cream sauce, rice; *Lagardière*: cold in the shell with herb mayonnaise; *Newburg*: sautéed, with brandy, madeira, cream; *à la Palestine*: with curry sauce and rice; *à la parisienne/à la russe*: cold with mayonnaise; *Thermidor*: in the shell with wine sauce, browned.

HOMARDIN(-E) With lobster.

HOMÈRE　　Homer. See *crème*.

(À LA) HONGROISE　Hungarian-style. With paprika, onions, tomatoes, often in cream sauce.

HORRIBLE　　Lit.: 'horrible'. Name for John Dory (*Saint-Pierre*).

HORS D'AGE　Lit.: 'outside age'. Term for mature *Armagnac* and *Calvados*.

HORS D'OEUVRE　Lit.: 'outside the main work'. First course, starter.

HORTILLON(NAGE)　Market-garden bounded by canals, especially in *Picardie*. *Soupe des hortillons*: vegetable soup.

HOSPICES DE BEAUNE　See *Beaune*.

HÔTE　　Host. Landlord. Guest (confusingly). See *table d'hôte*.

HÔTEL　　Hotel. Large town mansion, public building. *Hôtel meublé*: lodging house. See also *maître d'hôte*.

(À LA) HÔTELIÈRE　Lit.: 'hotel(-keeper's) style'. With parsley butter (*beurre maître d'hôtel*) and mushrooms. See also *poulet*.

HÔTELLERIE　Hostelry, inn.

HÔTESSE　　Hostess. Landlady (but *hôte* is used for a female guest).

HOUBLON　　Hop. See *jet de houblon*.

HOUBLONNIER (HOUBLONNIÈRE)　Of hops, with hop shoots.

HOUX　　Holly, whose berries are roasted in *Corse* to make a drink. Also a clear holly spirit, a speciality of *Alsace*.

HOUX-FRÉLON　Name for butcher's broom (*petit-houx*).

(À LA) HUGUENOTE　Huguenot-style. *Oeufs pochés à l'huguenote*: poached eggs on fried bread with gravy and kidneys.

HUILE　　Oil. *Huile d'arachides*: groundnut oil. *Huile de colza*: rape seed oil. *Huile de noix*: walnut oil. *Huile d'oillette*: poppy-seed oil, also known as *huile blanche*. *Huile d'olive vierge*: top quality olive oil, from first pressing. *Huile de tournesol*: sunflower seed oil.

HUÎTRE　　Oyster; classified by size, from 00 the largest, to 6 the smallest. Among the most important centres of cultivation are *Marennes* and *Ile d'Oléron*, *Arcachon*, *l'Aiguillon*, *Ile de Ré*, *Morbihan*, *Belon* river, *Brest*, *Saint-Brieuc*, *Cancale*, *Mont-Saint-Michel*, *Saint-Vaast-la-Hougue*, *Thau*. There are 2 main types.

(*Huître*) *plate*: native European oyster, with a relatively flat, smooth, often round shell; now found in small quantities after disease early in the century. Major varieties are (*vertes de*) *Marennes*: naturally coloured green from algae in the basins, from *Marennes*, considered the finest; *Belons* and *Armoricaines*: with white flesh, from *Bretagne*; *gravettes d'Arcachon*: especially flat type, from *Arcachon*.

(*Huître*) *creuse*: introduced oyster, with a longer, thicker, rougher shell, about 90% of French production (this has replaced the similar Portuguese oyster – *Portugaise* or *gryphée*). Major varieties are (*fines de*) *claires*: usually from *Bretagne* and *Arcachon*, placed in the *claires* (parks) of *Marennes*; (*huîtres*) *speciales*: the largest; *huître de parc*: ordinary cultivated type. *Rapures*: large overgrown oysters, usually cooked rather than eaten raw.

Huîtres à la bordelaise: oysters with sausages; *farcies à la charentaise rapures*: opened over heat and stuffed with butter, herbs and garlic; *en écaille*: in the shell; *à la Monselet*: deep-fried on skewers.

HUÎTRIER (HUÎTRIÈRE) To do with oysters. Oyster catcher, small marsh bird.

HUPPEMEAU (Orléanais) Cheese similar to *Brie*, made around Huppemeau.

HURE (DE PORC) Potted pig's head in jelly; see also *fromage de porc/de tête*. *Hure blanche* (Alsace): jellied brawn; *à la parisienne*: minced pork or veal tongue in jelly; *rouge* (Alsace): jellied brawn of smoked pig's head; *de sanglier* (Lorraine): potted boar's head.

(À LA) HUSSARDE Lit.: 'hussar-style'. Garnish of stuffed potatoes, mushrooms with onion purée, aubergines and horseradish. *Sauce hussarde*: creamy white wine sauce.

HYDNE Family of fungi of different colours, often parasol-shaped; one variety also known as *pied de mouton blanc*.

HYDROMEL Mead, honey and water drink.

(À LA) HYÉROISE See *hiéroise*.

HYPOCRAS Red wine with sugar, cinnamon and cloves, speciality of *Franche-Comté* and *Lyonnais*.

HYSOPE Hyssop, the herb.

IGNAME   Yam, tropical root vegetable.

IGNY   (Champagne) Smooth mild cheese made at the Abbey of Igny; also known as *Trappiste d'Igny*.

ÎLE BARBE   Monastery near *Mont d'Or*. *Salade de l'Ile Barbe*: cold potatoes and peppers with ham, lobster, truffles and olives.

ÎLE-DE-FRANCE   Province centred on *Paris*, roughly covering most of the Oise, Seine-et-Oise, Seine-et-Marne and Aisne departments.

ÎLE DE RÉ   Island off *Charentes*. See also *huître*.

ÎLE D'OLÉRON   Island off *Charentes*. See also *huître*.

ÎLE FLOTTANTE   Lit.: 'floating island'. Sponge cake steeped in *kirsch*, layered with jam, raisins, almonds, covered with whipped cream and floating in vanilla custard; also poached whites of egg, caramelized and sprinkled with almonds, in vanilla custard (a version of *oeufs à la neige*).

ÎLE-SAINTE-MARGUERITE   Island off *Provence*, near Cannes. See *langouste*.

IMAM BAYELDI   Lit.: 'satiated Imam'. See *aubergine* for the dish in which the Imam over-indulged, causing his death.

IMBRUCCIATE   (Corse) Cheese tart, also known as *embrucciate*.

(À LA) IMPÉRATRICE   Lit.: 'empress-style'. See *poularde* for the dish created in honour of the Empress *Marie-Louise*, Napoleon's second wife. See *riz* for the dish which the Empress *Eugénie* reputedly inspired.

(À L')IMPÉRIALE   Lit.: 'imperial-style'. Elaborate garnish of truffles, cockscombs etc; also of crayfish, soft roes etc.

Plat impériale (Normandie): seafood platter with or without lobster.
Variety of plum.

INCHEVILLE   (Normandie) Type of *Neufchâtel* cheese, named after the town.

(À L')INDIENNE   Indian-style. With rice and curry-flavoured sauce. See also *riz*.

IRAGNO   (S France) Name for type of weever (*vive*).

IRANCY   See *Bourgogne-Irancy*.

IRATY   (Pays basque) Strong sheep's milk cheese, made in mountain homes around the Iraty forest. See also *Ossau-Iraty-Brebis-Pyrénées*.

IRIDÉE   Type of variegated seaweed.

(À L')IRLANDAISE   Irish-style. *Consommé à l'irlandaise*: mutton broth with pearl barley and vegetables.

IROULÉGUY   Small area in *Pays basque*, making red and rosé wines, and some white (*AC*).

ISARD/IZARD   Rare wild mountain antelope, *chamois*, found in the Pyrenees.

ISIDORE   See *sole*.

ISIGNY   Town in *Normandie*, major market for the fine butter of the same name, and for cream cheese; also known for its special type of mussel (*caïeu*). *Sauce Isigny*: butter and egg sauce.

(À L')ITALIENNE   Italian-style. With mushroom, pasta, or artichokes. *Sauce italienne*: brown sauce with white wine, onions, mushrooms and ham; or with tomato and mushroom sauce. *Salade italienne*: mixed vegetable salad with anchovies or salami, tomatoes, olives and capers, covered with mayonnaise, sometimes set in aspic; or pasta, ham and olives with mayonnaise. See also *friture*.

IVE   Herb-ivy, type of chive.

(À L')IVOIRE   Lit.: 'ivory-style'. Of poultry, poached in white stock, with mushrooms, *quenelles* and white sauce.

IVROGNE DE MER   Lit.: 'sea drunkard'. Small sea fish with red scales.

IZARD   See *isard*.

IZARRA   Liqueur made around *Bayonne*, yellow or green and similar to *Chartreuse*; from dialect for 'star'.

JACQUE   (Périgord) Apple pancake.

(À LA) JACQUES   See *coupe* and *sole*.

JAGUINS   *Soupe des Jaguins* (Bretagne): creamy mussel, potato and onion soup, poured on slices of bread.

JALOUSIE   Lit.: 'Venetian blind' (also 'jealousy'). Small flaky pastry cake with strips revealing fruit or jam.

JAMBE DE BOIS   Lit.: 'wooden leg'. *Potage à la jambe de bois* (Lyonnais): soup of leg of beef on the bone, plus other meats and vegetables.

JAMBLE   Name for limpet (*patelle*).

JAMBON   Ham. *Jambon de Bayonne*: Bayonne ham, mildly smoked and cured in wine mixture, made at Orthez in *Béarn*.

Jambon blanc/demi-sel/glacé/de Paris: cooking ham, unsmoked or lightly smoked, often sold boned and cooked.

Jambon de campagne/montagne/pays: country ham, made throughout France to local methods; usually salted and smoked, eaten raw (*jambon cru*) or used in cooking.

Jambon de Parme: Parma ham, from Italy, served raw in thin slices.

(*Jambon de*) *York*: York ham, usually applied to any ready-cooked ham.

Jambon à la bayonnaise: braised in madeira, with rice, tomatoes, mushrooms, sausages; *braisé à la lie de vin* (Bourgogne): braised in red wine and wine lees; *braisé nuitonne*: braised in *Nuits-Saint-Georges* wine; au *Chablis*: braised in *Chablis* wine; *à la corsoise*: raw, fried or baked with tomato and garlic sauce; *à la crème de Saulieu*: sliced, in cream and wine sauce with mushrooms, tomatoes, cheese; *au foin*: cooked in hay; *à la morvandelle*: braised in wine and served with piquant cream sauce, also known as *jambon à la crème*; *persillé* (Bourgogne): cold pressed ham layered with parsley and white wine jelly, a traditional Easter dish.

Leg of fresh pork. *Jambon de marcassin*: salted and smoked wild boar. *Jambon de poulet*: leg of chicken, often boned, stuffed and braised.

JAMBONNEAU   Small ham, often ready prepared from a *charcuterie*. *Jambonneau de volaille*: leg of chicken.

Fan mussel, large shellfish shaped like a leg of ham.

JAMBONNETTE   (Vivarais) Dried salt pork sausage in the shape of a ham.

(À LA) JAPONAISE   Japanese-style. With Chinese artichokes (*crosnes du Japon*). *Salade japonaise*: pineapple

tomato and orange salad with cream and lemon juice; see also *Francillon*.
>*Japonais*: little almond meringue.

(À LA) JARDINIÈRE Lit.: 'in the style of the gardener's wife'. With mixed vegetables, especially carrots and peas.

JARGEAU Town in *Orléanais*, known for *andouille*.

JARNAC Town in *Charentes*. See *coup*.

JARRET Shin, knuckle, of veal, beef.
>(S France) Local name for picarel (*mendole*).

JASEUR Waxwing, small bird.

JASNIÈRES Area of *Coteaux du Loir*, growing a small amount of white wine (*AC*).

JAU(D) (Bourgogne, Charentes) Local name for chicken (*poulet*).

JAUNE Yellow. *Jaune d'oeuf*: yolk of egg; also name for variety of fungus (*oronge*). See also *vin jaune*.

JEAN BART 17th-century pirate and hero of Dunkerque in *Flandre*; see *sole*.

JEAN-DORÉ (Boulonnais) Local name for John Dory (*Saint-Pierre*).

JEANNETTE See *suprême* for *Escoffier*'s dish, named after a ship trapped in ice at the South Pole.

JESSE Freshwater fish similar to carp.

JÉSU(S) Jesus. (Franche-Comté) Large smoked pork liver sausage, usually served hot. *Jésus de Morteau*: with a wooden pin at one end, smoked over juniper and fir wood.
>(Lyonnais) Small dried sausage.

JET DE HOUBLON Hop shoot, edible tip of the male flower (as opposed to the female cone used in brewing); cooked like asparagus, and served with butter, cream or sauce, as vegetable or garnish, especially in N France. *Omelette aux jets de houblon* (Alsace): omelette filled with hop shoots sautéed in butter.

JOËL Name for sandsmelt (*athérine*).

JOINTES (Charentes, Poitou) Local name for chard (*blette*).

JOINVILLE *Sauce Joinville*: rich cream sauce with shrimps, sometimes crayfish and truffles, for fish; probably named after one of Louis-Philippe's sons.
>Pastry cake with raspberry jam.

JONCHÉE (W France) Fresh unsalted sheep's or goat's milk cheese, white, soft, mild and creamy; made by farms and packed in a rush basket (*jonchée*) or in pots. *Jonchée Niortaise* (Poitou): of goat's milk, made around *Niort* and Parthenay; also known as *Parthenay*. *Jonchée d'Oléron* (Charentes): of sheep's milk, made on the *Ile d'Oléron*; also known as (*Brebis d'*)*Oléron*.

JOTTES (Charentes, Poitou) Local name for chard (*blette*).

JOUE Cheek (e.g. *joue de boeuf*: ox cheek).

JOUR Day.

JOUTE (Champagne) Cabbage with bacon and sausages.

JOYEUSES Testicles, especially of sheep.

JUBILÉ Lit.: 'jubilee'. See *Balvet* and *cerise*.

JUDELLE (Berry) Local name for coot (*foulque*).

JUDIC Garnish of braised lettuce, cock's kidneys, truffles, stuffed tomatoes, potatoes.

JUDRU (Bourgogne) Large dry pork sausage flavoured with *marc*.

JUIF (JUIVE) Jewish. See *artichaut*, *carpe*, *poisson* and *schaleth*.

JULIÉNAS See *Beaujolais*.

JULIENNE Matchstick strips, especially of vegetables (e.g. *consommé julienne*: clear soup with vegetable strips). Attributed to Jean Julien, 18th-century chef.
Name for ling (*lingue*).

JURA Name for *Franche-Comté*.
One of the three departments of *Franche-Comté*.
Range of mountains bordering *Franche-Comté* and extending into Switzerland. See also *Côtes de Jura*.

JURANÇON Small area (*AC*) in *Béarn*, producing unusual sweet or semi-sweet white wine, and also less interesting dry wine.

(À LA) JURASSIENNE In the style of *Jura* or *Franche-Comté*. *Omelette à la jurassienne*: omelette with bacon, onions and sorrel. See also *brochette* and *croustade*.

JUS Juice. *Jus d'orange*: orange juice.
Jus de viande: gravy.

(À LA) JUSSIÈRE Garnish of braised lettuce, onions, carrots, potatoes.

KAFFEEKRANTZ (Alsace) *Brioche* served with coffee.

KAKI Persimmon, sweet fruit resembling tomato; also known as *figue-caque*.

KALÉREI (Alsace) *Pâté* made of pig's ears, trotters and tail; also known as *gallrei*.

KARI Alternative spelling for *cari*: curry.

KATOFF See *poulet*.

KICHE Alternative spelling for *quiche*.

KIEV See *poulet*.

KIG HA FARS/KIK A'FARZ (Bretagne) Buckwheat dumpling with salt pork and cabbage.

KIG SAL ROSTEN (Bretagne) Rolled salt pork, first boiled then roasted.

KIPPER See *hareng*.

KIR Aperitif of *crème de cassis* mixed with dry white wine; also known as (*vin*) *blanc-cassis* and *rince cochon* (pig rinse), named after a mayor of *Dijon* and hero of the Resistance. *Kir royale*: made with *Champagne*.

KIRSCH Clear spirit distilled from small black wild cherries, particularly in *Alsace* and *Lorraine*.

KNACKWURST (Alsace) Small sausage.

KNEPF(L)E (Alsace) *Quenelle*. Fritter.

KNIPPERLÉ Variety of white grape grown in *Alsace*.

KOKEBOTEROM (Flandre) Raisin *brioche*, also known as *couke-bootram*. From the Dutch 'kock' – cake.

(À LA) KOSKERA See *merlu*.

KOUGELHO(P)F/KOUGLOF/KUGELHO(P)F (Alsace) Sweet *brioche* ring with raisins, currants and almonds, sometimes soaked in *kirsch*; also known as *gougelho(p)f*.

KOUIGN AMANN (Bretagne) Lit.: 'cake and butter' in dialect. Large rich yeast cake.

KOULIBIAK See *coulibiac*.

KRAMPOCH/KRAMPOEZ (Bretagne) Local name for pancake.

KUNPOD (Bretagne) Poached egg and raisin dumpling.

LABOUREUR Lit.: 'ploughman'. *Soupe du laboureur*: split pea and salt pork soup.

LABRE Name for wrasse (*vieille*). *Labre vert*: type of wrasse, also known as *limbert* and *tourdre*.

LAC Lake.

LACHE Small sea fish.

LACTAIRE Lactary, family of fungi with milky white juice; varieties also known as *vache* and *vachotte*.

LADOIX-SERRIGNY Village of *Côte de Beaune*, *Bourgogne*, producing red and white wines (*AC*); the name is rarely seen, as the best vineyards have the right to sell their wines as *Aloxe-Corton premier cru*.

LAGARDIÈRE See *homard*.

LAGNIEU See *Ramequin de Lagnieu*.

LAGOPÈDE Pyrenean partridge, ptarmigan.

LAGUIOLE(-AUBRAC) (Rouergue) Large round solid cheese (*AOC*), pressed, uncooked, matured for four months, with light smell and pronounced tang; made by mountain dairies in the Monts d'Aubrac and around Laguiole, also known as *Fourme de Laguiole*. See also *mariage*.

LAGUIPIÈRE One of Napoleon's chefs. *Sauce Laguipière*: fish and butter sauce. See also *grenadin*.

LAIT Milk. *Lait baratté* (Bretagne): churned milk, often eaten with pancakes. *Lait de coco*: coconut milk. *Lait entier*: full cream milk. *Lait de poule*: egg nog. *Lait ribot* (Bretagne): type of very liquid yoghourt. *Cochon/veau de lait*: sucking pig/calf. *Petit lait*: whey.

LAITAGE(S)   Dairy produce.

LAITANCE/LAITE   Soft roe, of fish, often carp, herring, mackerel. *Laitances en sabot*: in baked potatoes.

LAITERIE   Dairy.

LAITIAT   (Franche-Comté) Drink made from wild fruit steeped in whey.

LAITIER   Made of milk; to do with milk; dairy. Factory-made (as opposed to farm-produced), of cheese, butter (e.g. *Brie Laitier*).

LAITUE   Lettuce (so named for its milky juice). (*Laitue*) *Batavia*: large crinkly type, slightly bitter. *Laitue à couper*: cutting lettuce. *Laitue pommée/beurrée*: round hearted lettuce. (*Laitue*) *romaine*: cos lettuce; originally from the island of Kos, reaching France via Italy and the Papal court of *Avignon*.
   Laitue de chien: lit.: 'dog's lettuce'. Name for dandelion (*pissenlit*).

LAKMÉ   *Salade Lakmé*: sweet pepper, tomato and rice salad.

LALANDE DE POMEROL   Area of *Bordeaux*, next to the more famous *Pomerol*, making red wine (*AC*).

(À LA) LAMBALLE   *Potage Lamballe*: meat soup with tapioca and puréed peas. See also *caille*. Probably connected with the Princesse de Lamballe, friend of Marie-Antoinette.

LAMBIG   (Bretagne) Local name for *eau-de-vie de cidre*.

LAMIE   Name for type of shark (*taupe*).

LAMPRILLON   Small sea or river lamprey.

LAMPROIE   River lamprey, lampern.
   Lamproie (*marine*): (sea) lamprey, eel-like migratory fish usually caught in rivers; also known as *sept trous* and *sept yeux*, in reference to its seven small gills. *Lamproie à la bordelaise*: sliced, cooked with leeks, red wine and garlic, the sauce bound with the blood; *à la chinonaise*: fried in walnut oil; *à la solognote*: marinated in vinegar with pine kernels, cooked in butter with mushrooms, finally wrapped in pastry and baked in ashes – an old country recipe.

LAMPROYON   (Périgord) Type of eel, usually stewed.

LANÇON   Name for sand eel (*équille*).

(À LA) LANDAISE   In the style of *Landes*. With goose fat, garlic, pine kernels (e.g. *omelette landaise*) or *Armagnac*. *Pommes* (*de terre*) *landaise*: potatoes fried in goose fat, with ham and garlic. See also *becfigue*, *cèpe*, *chou rouge*, *civet*, *coquille Saint-Jacques*, *crêpe*, *croûte*, *épaule* and *ortolan*.

LANDES   Department and region in *Gascogne*.

LANGOUSTE   Spiny lobster, crawfish, prepared like lobster; see also *homard*. *Langouste en civet au Banyuls* (Roussillon): stewed in *Banyuls* wine with shallots, garlic, tomatoes and diced ham; *à la sétoise*: with brandy, tomato and garlic (perhaps original version of *américaine/armoricaine* method); *de l'Ile-Sainte-Marguerite*: cold with hot fried onions.

LANGOUSTINE   Dublin Bay prawn, scampi; also known as *demoiselle de Caen/de Cherbourg*.

LANGRES   (Champagne) Smooth strong cheese, made by dairies around Langres.

LANGUE   Tongue. *Langue à la Lucullus* (Flandre): smoked tongue and *foie gras*. *Langues d'oie* (Béarn): grilled goose tongues.

LANGUE D'AVOCAT   Lit.: 'lawyer's tongue'. (Bordelais) Local name for small sole (*solette*).

LANGUE-DE-BOEUF   Lit.: 'ox tongue'. Name for type of fungus (*fistuline*).

LANGUE DE CHAT   Lit.: 'cat's tongue'. Crisp dry biscuit, long and thin.

LANGUEDOC   Vast southern province covering the departments of Haute-Garonne, *Aude*, Tarn, *Hérault*, *Gard*, Lozère, *Ardèche* and most of Haute-Loire; sometimes thought to include *Roussillon* and *Rouergue* as well. See also *Clairette du Languedoc* and *Coteaux du Languedoc*.

(À LA) LANGUEDOCIENNE   In the style of *Languedoc*. With any or all of tomatoes, *cèpes*, aubergines, garlic. See also *faisan*.

LANGUETTE   (Languedoc) Small tongue.

LANGUIER   Smoked pig's tongue.

LAON   Capital of the Aisne department in *Ile-de-France*. See also *Baguette Laonnaise* and *Gros Vert*.

LAPEREAU   Young rabbit.

LAPIN   Rabbit. *Lapin de chou/de garenne*: domesticated/wild rabbit. *Lapin à l'artésienne*: stuffed with sheep's trotters, cooked in beer with onions, mushrooms, mustard and juniper; *Coquibus*: casseroled with onions, bacon, potatoes, white wine; *à la flamande*: marinated in red wine and vinegar, braised with onions and prunes; *en gibelotte*: stewed with mushrooms, onions, potatoes, white wine; *à la giennoise*: cooked in walnut oil with saffron; *à la havraise*: roast saddle wrapped in bacon with cream sauce; *à la solognote*: stuffed with bacon and breadcrumbs; *à la Valenciennes*: cooked in beer with prunes and raisins. *Râble de lapin à la moutarde* (Bourgogne): saddle roasted with mustard and cream sauce.

LAPUGA   (Nice) Local name for pomfret (*fiatole*).

LAQUEUILLE   See *Bleu de Laqueuille*.

LARD   Pork fat, bacon (not lard – *saindoux*). *Lard frais*: fresh pork fat, mainly used for lardoons. *Lard fumé*: cured, smoked pork, equivalent to bacon. *Lard gras/gros lard*: pure pork fat, without meat. *Lard maigre fumé*: lean bacon. *Lard de poitrine*: salted, sometimes smoked, pork belly, like streaky bacon. *Lard salé*: salt pork, used in stews; also known as *petit salé*.
   Lard nantais: pork chops baked on top of liver, lung etc of pork.
   Lard recet (Bretagne): paste of salt pork fat and shallots.

LARDON   Rasher, of bacon. Lardoon, strip of bacon or pork fat, threaded into meat, or added to soups and stews.

LARGE   Broad, wide; big.

LARRON D'ORS   Lit.: 'thief of Ors'. (Flandre) Brand name for a square or cross-shaped cheese with shiny rind, very smelly and strong, made around Ors on a small scale.

LARUNS   (Béarn) Large round loaf-shaped cheese of sheep's milk, mild, but becoming stronger with age; made in mountain cottages around Laruns.

LASAGNES   Lasagna.

LATAMA CASTAGNINA   (Corse) Cheese or vegetable tart.

LATOUR   Name for type of shark (*taupe*).

LATRICIÈRES-CHAMBERTIN   See *Gevrey-Chambertin*.

LAUDUN   See *Côtes-du-Rhône-Villages*.

LAURIER   Laurel tree. *Laurier-sauce*: bay tree. *Feuille de laurier*: bayleaf.

LAUTREC   See *perdreau*.

LAVAGNON   Tellin, small type of clam. *Lavagnons charentaise*: shelled and mixed with puréed onions, butter and parsley.

LAVAL   Capital of the Mayenne department in *Maine*.
    Firm smooth strong cheese, made at the Abbey of Laval; also known as *Trappiste de Laval*.

LAVALLIÈRE   Louise de La Vallière, a mistress of Louis XIV. Garnish of asparagus, artichokes, sweetbreads, crayfish and truffles.

LA VARENNE   Pierre-François de La Varenne, 17th-century chef and author, perhaps the inventor of *duxelles* (chopped mushrooms and shallots). *Sauce La Varenne*: mayonnaise with *duxelles* and herbs.

LAVARET   Salmon-type fish found in deep lakes, especially in *Savoie*, highly esteemed.

LAVILLEDIEU   Small area, north of Toulouse, producing light red wines sold as Vins de Lavilledieu (*VDQS*).

LAYON   See *Coteaux du Layon*.

LEBERKNEPFEN/LEBERKNOPFLEN   (Alsace) Calf's liver *quenelles*.

LÈCHE   Sliver, thin slice; from 'lécher' – to lick.

(À LA) LÉDONIENNE   In the style of *Lons-le-Saunier*.

LEGREST   (Bretagne) Local name for lobster (*homard*).

LÉGUMES   Vegetables.

LENTA   See *Chevrine de Lenta*.

LENTILLE   Lentil. *Lentilles blondes*: light brown, German, lentils. *Lentilles du Puy*: small green and grey lentils, from *Le Puy*. *Lentilles à la ponote*: with onion, garlic and tomato sauce.

LÉONTINE   *Potage Léontine*: leek, spinach, pea and lettuce soup.

LÉPIOTE   Family of fungi, usually white or reddish and mild, including *coulemelle*.

LETCHI/LITCHI   Lichee, sweet white oriental fruit.

LEVADOU   See *fréchure*.

LEVRAUT   Leveret, young hare.

LEVROUX   See *Valençay*.

LEVURE   Yeast.

(À LA) LEXOVIENNE   In the style of Lisieux in *Normandie*.

LÉZARD   Lit.: 'lizard'. Lizard fish, small type of sea eel.

LIAISON   Thickening, of a sauce; from 'lier' – to bind.

LIARD   Lit.: 'farthing'. *Pommes (de terre frites) en liards*: finely sliced fried potatoes, also known as *en collerette*.

(À LA) LIBOURDINE   See *araignée de mer*.

LICHE   Type of meagre (*maigre*).

LIE (DE VIN)   Lees, dregs, of wine. See also *jambon* and *Muscadet*.

LIÉ(-E)   Bound, thickened, of a sauce.

(À LA) LIÉGEOISE   In the style of Liège in Belgium. With juniper berries, sometimes gin, particularly of calf's liver, kidneys and thrushes. See also *café* and *écrevisse*.

LIERWECKE   (Alsace) Raisin bun.

LIEU   Lit.: 'place'. Name for two common fish of the cod family. *Lieu jaune*: pollack, also known as *colin* (*jaune*) and *églefin. Lieu noir*: coalfish, saithe, coley; also known as *charbonnier*, *colin* (*noir*), *églefin noir*, *merlan noir* and *merluche* (*noire*).

LIÈVRE   Hare. *Lièvre à la broche* (Bourbonnais): marinated, spit-roasted; *à la Duchambais/Duchambet* (Bourbonnais): simmered with cream, shallots, vinegar and pepper; *farci en c(h)abessal* (central France): boned, stuffed, tied into a ring, braised in red wine, the sauce thickened with the blood and liver; *à la périgourdine/à la royale*: boned, stuffed with *foie gras* and truffles, braised in red wine and brandy. *Râble de lièvre à la Piron* (Bourgogne): saddle marinated in *marc*, roasted, with grapes and peppery cream sauce. See also *civet*.

(Languedoc) Local name for blenny (*blennie cagnette*).

LIÈVRE DE MER   Name for lumpfish (*lompe*).

LIGNE   Fishing line. Caught with a line, of fish, as in *sole de ligne*.

LIGUEIL   (Touraine) Factory-made goat's milk cheese, quite strong; brand name.

(À LA) LIGURIENNE   In the style of Liguria, N Italy. Garnish of saffron rice and stuffed tomatoes.

LILLE   Capital of the Nord department and *Flandre*. See also *Gris de Lille* and *Mimolette Français*.

LILLET   Pale dry aperitif.

(À LA) LILLOISE   In the style of *Lille*. See *chou rouge*.

LIMACE/LIMAÇOU   (Provence) Local name for small snail.

LIMAÇON   General name for snail.

LIMAÇON DE MER   Name for winkle (*bigorneau*).

LIMANDE   Dab, flat sea fish. See also *fausse limande*.
                   Limande(*-sole*): lemon sole, also known as *sole limande*.

LIMANDELLE/LIMANDE SLOOP   Megrim, flat sea fish, also known as *cardine* and (*limande-*)*salope*.

LIMAOU   (Bordelais) Local name for small snail.

LIMASSADE   (Bordelais) *Vinaigrette* for serving with snails.

LIMAT   (Bordelais) Local name for small snail.

LIMBERT   (S France) Name for type of wrasse (*labre vert*).

LIMOGES   Capital of the Haute-Vienne department in *Limousin*.

LIMON   Lime (not lemon), also known (confusingly) as *citron vert*. See also *poisson*.

LIMONADE   Lemonade. Carbonated drink (e.g. *limonade à l'orange*: fizzy orange). See also *panaché*.

LIMOUSIN   Province corresponding to the departments of *Corrèze* and Haut-Vienne.

(À LA) LIMOUSINE   In the style of *Limousin*. With red cabbage and/or chestnuts. With *cèpes*. See also *chou, chou rouge* and *perdreau*.

LIMOUX   See *Blanquette de Limoux*.

LINGUE   Ling, long thin fish of cod family; also known as *julienne*. See also *mostèle*.

LIPPA   (Languedoc) Local name for pomfret (*fiatole*).

LIQUEUR   Liqueur, after-dinner drink. *Liqueur de Fécamp*: name for *Bénédictine*. *Liqueur de sapin*: fir tree liqueur, a speciality of *Franche-Comté*. *Vin de liqueur*: strong sweet wine (e.g. *Banyuls*, port).

LIQUOREUX (LIQUOREUSE)   Very sweet, especially of wine.

LIRAC   Area (*AC*) of the *Rhône*, making rosé wine similar to its neighbour *Tavel*, and some red wine.

LISETTO   Variety of melon from *Provence*.

LISIEUX   See *Petit Lisieux*.

LISSA   (S France) Local name for grey mullet (*mulet*).

LISTRAC   Commune of *Haut-Médoc*, *Bordeaux*, growing red wine (*AC*), and containing some fine châteaux (e.g. Fourcas-Dupré, Fourcas-Hosten, Fonréaud).

LIT   Bed (e.g. *sur lit d'épinards*: on a bed of spinach).

LITCHI   Name for lichee (*letchi*).

LITE   (Bretagne) Oatmeal porridge.

LITORNE   Fieldfare, small bird.

LITTORINE   Name for winkle (*bigorneau*).

LIVAROT   (Normandie) Flat round cheese (*AOC*), with orange rind, soft, slightly holey, strong-smelling and rich-tasting; made by farms and dairies, named after the market town. One of the ancient cheeses of *Normandie*, popularly known as *Colonel*, from the bands of grass, like service stripes, surrounding it. *Quart Livarot*: smaller version. See also *Petit Lisieux*.

LIVÈCHE   Lovage, the herb.

LIVERNON   See *Cabécou*.

(À LA) LIVONIENNE   In the style of Livonia in the Baltic. See *hareng* and *poulet*.

(À LA) LIVORNAISE   In the style of Livorno in Italy. Poached/baked fish with tomatoes, onions, perhaps truffles.

LIVRON   (Dauphiné) Factory-made strong goat's milk cheese; brand name, also known as *Tomme de Livron*.

LOCHE   Loach, barbed freshwater fish.
    (Touraine) Strong factory-made goat's milk cheese; trade name.

LOCHE DE MER   Name for rockling (*mostèle*).

(À LA) LOCHOISE   In the style of Loches in *Touraine*. *Sauce lochoise*: brandy, cream and onion sauce, for chicken.

LOIR   See *Coteaux du Loir*.

LOIRE   Department mostly in *Lyonnais*.
    The river *Loire*, rising on the *Auvergne-Languedoc* borders, and flowing N and W in a broad arc, to reach the sea at *Nantes*. Wines are grown all along the *Loire* and its surrounding region, often described as *Loire* wines, particularly those from the broad central stretch

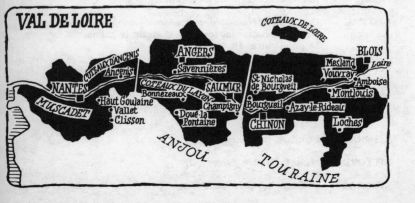

of château country (*Anjou*, *Touraine*, *Orléanais*). See also *Coteaux de la Loire*.

LO MIQUO   See *miquo*.

LOMPE   Lumpfish, valuable chiefly for lumpfish roe; also known as *gros mollet* and *lièvre de mer*.

LONGCHAMP   *Paris* racecourse. *Potage Longchamp*: puréed pea soup with shredded sorrel, chervil and thin pasta.

LONG(-UE)   Long.

LONGE   Top half of loin, of veal, pork, usually meaning the whole loin in one piece. *Longe de veau pontoise*: braised with carrots, onions and white wine.

LONGEOLE   (Savoie) Coarse sausage.

LONGUE   Feminine of *long*: long.

LONGUET   Lit.: 'longish'. Small long stick of dry bread.

LONGUEVILLE   Town in *Ile-de-France*. *Potage Longueville*: leek, pea and lettuce soup.

LONZO/LONZU   (Corse) Dried and salted raw ham.

LONS-LE-SAUNIER   Capital of *Jura* (department).

LOQUETTE   Torsk, obscure type of cod; also known as *brosme*.

LORETTE   Garnish of asparagus or peas, chicken croquettes and truffles. *Salad Lorette*: lamb's lettuce (*mâche*), celery and beetroot salad. *Pommes (de terre) Lorette*: cheese-flavoured *dauphine* potatoes in crescent shapes. Notre-Dame-de-Lorette in 19th-century *Paris* was the haunt of fallen women, known as *lorettes*.

LORGNETTE   Lit.: 'spyglass'. Rolled fillet of fish (e.g. *merlans en lorgnette*).

(À LA) LORIENTAISE   In the style of Lorient in *Bretagne*. See *palourde*.

LORMES   (Nivernais) Small firm strong goat's milk cheese; farm-made around Lormes.

LORRAINE   Province covering the departments of Meuse, *Moselle*, Meurthe-et-Moselle and *Vosges*. See also *Gérardmer*.
   (*À la*) *lorraine*: in the style of *Lorraine*. Garnish of red cabbage in red wine, potatoes and horseradish. *Oeufs à la lorraine*: baked eggs with bacon, cheese and cream. See also *quiche* and *tourte*.

LOTTE (DE MER)   Monkfish, angler fish, large, grotesque but good to eat; also known as *baudroie* and *diable de mer*, and *budicu* and *seyot*. *Lotte à la marseillaise*: baked with cheese, tomato and saffron.
   Lotte (*de rivière*): burbot, freshwater fish with drooping barbels, whose liver is considered a delicacy.
   Lotte des lacs: burbot, found in lakes, especially in *Savoie*, highly esteemed.

LOUBINE   Name for grey mullet (*mulet*). (Charentes) Local name for sea bass (*loup/bar*).

LOU CAGARAULAT   See *escargot*.

LOUDES   See *Bleu de Loudes*.

LOUISE   *Pommes de terre Louise* (Lyonnais): fried onion and potato cake.

LOUISE-BONNE   Variety of pear, named after a mysterious Dame Louise from *Poitou*.

LOUISIANE   Louisiana, in the USA. Garnish for chicken of sweetcorn, rice and bananas.

LOUKINKA/LOU-KENKA   (Pays basque) Small spiced garlic sausage, often eaten with oysters.

LOU MAGRET   See *magret*.

LOU MAJOURAN   See *majouran*.

LOUP (DE MER)/LOUPASSOU   Lit.: '(sea) wolf'. Name for sea bass (*bar*), especially in S France. *Loup grillé au fenouil* (Provence): grilled over fennel twigs, flamed with *Pernod*.

LOU PASTIS   See *pastis*.

LOUPIAC   Commune in *Bordeaux*, producing mainly sweet white wines (*AC*).

LOUP MARIN   Wolf fish, with flavoursome flesh.

LOURMARINE   Variety of almond, from Lourmarin in *Provence*.

LOU TRÉBUC   See *trébuc*.

LOUTRIP   (Pays basque, Béarn) Black pudding.

LOUVINE   (Pays basque) Local name for sea bass (*loup*).

LUBERON   See *Côtes de Luberon*.

LUCAS   *Paris* restaurant started by an Englishman in the 18th century. See *hareng*.

LUCHON   See *Bethmale*.

(À LA) LUÇONNAISE   In the style of Luçon in *Poitou*. See *grenouille*.

LUCRÈCE   (S France) Name for type of wrasse (*crénilabre*).

LUCULLUS   Roman general and gourmet. See *langue*.
(Ile-de-France, Normandie) Soft mild creamy cheese, factory-made; invented name, also known as *Boursault*.

LUIZET   Variety of apricot, originally from *Lyonnais*.

LUMA   (Charentes) Local name for small snail.

LUMBRINA   (Corse) Local name for umbrine (*ombrine*).

LUNEL   Small area in *Hérault*, making fortified sweet wine (*AC*) from the *Muscat* grape.

LUSIGNAN   (Poitou) Fresh creamy, mild goat's milk cheese; made by farms around Lusignan.

LUSSAC-SAINT-ÉMILION   Satellite region of *Saint-Emilion*, *Bordeaux*, growing red wines (*AC*).

LUTÈCE   Roman name for the Ile-de-la-Cité in *Paris*. See *sole*.

(À LA) LUZIENNE   In the style of Saint-Jean-de-Luz in *Pays basque*.

LYON   Capital of the *Rhône* department and *Lyonnais*. See also *arome*.

LYONNAIS   Region centred on *Lyon*, covering most of the *Rhône* and *Loire* and corners of the Isère and Ain departments. See also *Coteaux du Lyonnais*.

(À LA) LYONNAISE   In the style of *Lyonnais*. *Pommes* (*de terre*) *lyonnaise*: sautéed potatoes with onions. See also *cabillaud*, *cervelas*, *cochonnailles*, *Cervelle de Canut*, *civet*, *fromage*, *galette*, *gras-double*, *marron*, *rognons*, *saladier*, *saucisson* and *tripe*.

MACAIRE   *Pommes (de terre) Macaire*: baked flat cake or fried balls of puréed potato.

MACARON   Macaroon.

MACARONADE   (Provence) Macaroni with cheese and gravy, traditional accompaniment to *daube*.

MACARONI   Macaroni.

MACÉDOINE   Macedonia, created by Alexander the Great from a jumble of small states. Mixed vegetables. *Macédoine de fruits*: fruit salad.

MACÉRÉ(-E)   Macerated; pickled; steeped.

MÂCHE   Lamb's lettuce, corn salad, soft-leaved type of lettuce, both wild and cultivated; also known as *bourcette*, *boursette*, *bourse-à-berger/à-pasteur*, *clairette* and *doucette*.

MACIS   Mace, the spice.

MÂCON   Capital of the Saône-et-Loire department and of *Mâconnais*. Red, white and rosé wines (*AC*), sold as *Mâcon*, *Mâcon Supérieur* or *Mâcon Villages*. Several communes (e.g. Viré, Lugny, Burgy) may add their names to the main appellation.

MÂCONNAIS   Region of S *Bourgogne*, important wine-growing area.
   Small firm cone-shaped cheese, made of goat's, cow's milk or a mixture, eaten fresh when white and creamy, or aged until stronger; made by farms and dairies in Mâconnais, also known as *Cabrion/Chevreton de Mâcon* and *Rougeret*.

(À LA) MÂCONNAISE   In the style of *Mâconnais*. With *Mâcon* wine. Of fish, poached in *Mâcon* wine with onions and mushrooms.

MACRE   Name for water chestnut (*châtaigne d'eau*).

MACREUSE   Scoter duck, type of wild duck.
   Shoulder of beef.

MADELEINE   Small light shell-shaped sponge cake, originally from Commercy in *Lorraine*; dipped into a cup of tea, with great effect, in Proust's *A la Recherche du Temps Perdu*. See also *glace* and *poire*.
   Garnish of artichokes stuffed with puréed haricot beans.

MADÈRE   Madeira (fortified wine), used in classical sauces.

MADIRAN   Area of *Béarn* making strong red wine (*AC*).

(À LA) MADRILÈNE   In the style of Madrid. Tomato-flavoured. With tomatoes. *Consommé madrilène*: clear chicken soup with tomatoes, celery and peppers, served hot or cold; also known as *consommé à l'américaine*. See also *saucisse*.

MAGNUM   Bottle equivalent to two ordinary bottles, especially of *Champagne*.
 (Normandie) Rich soft triple-cream cheese, the same as *Brillat-Savarin* but eaten younger.

MAGRAVAN   Wine mixed with sugar and spirit, speciality of *Franche-Comté*.

(LOU) MAGRET/MAIGRET   (SW France) Fillet, breast, of fattened duck, grilled or fried and served rare.

MAIGRE   Lit.: 'thin'. Lean, of meat. Low-fat, of cheese. Meatless, fasting (the opposite of *gras*; e.g. *soupe maigre*: vegetable soup).
 Meagre, fish similar to large sea bass; also known as *sciène*, *peï rei* and *figoun*.

MAIGRET   See *magret*.

(À LA) MAILLOT   Garnish, especially for ham, of carrots, turnips, French beans, onions, peas and braised lettuce with madeira sauce; also known as *Porte-Maillot*.

MAINE   Province covering the departments of Mayenne and Sarthe.

MAINGAUX/MINGAUX/MINGOTS   (Bretagne) Whipped cream or cream cheese, similar to *crémet*, served with fruit.

MAINOTTE   Name for variety of fungus (*clavaire*).

(À LA) MAINTENON   Madame de Maintenon, mistress and finally wife of Louis XIV. Mixture of puréed onions and white sauce with mushrooms, sometimes truffles and tongue, as a garnish or filling. See also *pêche*.

MAIRE   Lit.: 'mayor'; also a *Paris* restaurant. *Pommes (de terre) Maire*: sliced potatoes with cream.

MAÏS   Maize, sweetcorn, made into porridge, bread and cakes; also known as *blé de Turquie*. See also *farine* and *flocon*.

MAISON   Lit.: 'house'. (*De la*) *maison*: of the house/restaurant, a speciality or home-made (e.g. *fine maison/pâté maison*).

MAÎTRE DE CHAI   Master of the wine and spirit cellar, especially in *Bordelais*. With wine sauce (e.g. *entrecôte maître de chai*).

MAÎTRE D'HÔTEL   Head waiter. With *beurre maître d'hôtel*: parsley butter (e.g. *entrecôte/pommes maître d'hôtel*).

(LOU) MAJOURAN   Orange-flavoured fortified wine, speciality of *Provence*.

MALAKOFF   (Franche-Comté) Almond pastry. See also *Gournay*.

MALARMAT   Armed gurnard, fish of the *grondin* family; also known as *peï furco*.

MALLETTE   (Boulonnais) Local name for red mullet (*rouget*).

(À LA) MALOUINE   In the style of *Saint-Malo*. *Potage malouin*: cream of cauliflower soup with onions and potatoes. See also *crabe*.

(À LA) MALTAISE   Maltese-style. With oranges or mandarins. *Sauce maltaise*: *hollandaise* sauce with blood orange juice.

MALVOISIE   Variety of grape, used to make Malmsey wine, similar to madeira.

MAMGOZ   (Bretagne) Baked apples with jam and butter; or potato and jam fritter.

MAMIROLLE   (Franche-Comté) Firm strong cheese with reddish rind, made at the dairying school of Mamirolle.

(À LA) MANCELLE   In the style of *Le Mans*.

MANCHON   Lit.: 'muff'. Small muff-shaped almond cake. See also *goujon*.
Beef steak.

MANDARINE   Mandarin orange. Also a liqueur made from mandarin oranges, especially around *Le Puy*.

MANGE-TOUT   Lit.: 'eat-all'. Sugar pea, also known as *pois princesse*, or young pod bean, where the pod is eaten as well as the seeds.

MANGOUSTAN   Mangosteen, tropical fruit, usually eaten raw.

MANGUE   Mango, orange-coloured tropical fruit.

MANICAMP   (Ile-de-France) Small firm strong cheese of the *Maroilles* type; after the village of Manicamp.

(À LA) MANIÈRE (DE)   (In the) style (of).

(À LA) MANOSQUINE   In the style of Manosque in *Provence*. *Omelette manosquine*: omelette with tomatoes and truffles.

MANOULS   (Rouergue) Lamb's tripe cooked with white wine, tomatoes, perhaps ham; also known as *trénels* and *tripes rouergates*.

MANQUÉ Lit.: 'failed'. Sponge cake.

(LE) MANS Capital of the Sarthe department in *Maine*. See also *rillette* and *Reinette*.

MANTE (DE MER) Lit.: '(sea) mantis'. Name for mantis shrimp (*squille*).

MANTEAU Lit.: 'coat'. (SW France) Piece of goose including the legs and wings.

(À LA) MANTOUE In the style of Mantua in Italy. See *truite*.

MAQUEREAU Mackerel, also known as *cavallo* and *auriol/auriou*. *Maquereaux à la boulonnaise*: poached, sliced, served hot or cold with mussels and butter sauce; *à la calaisienne*: see *hareng*; *à la facon de Quimper*: cold, poached, with egg, butter and herb sauce; *Rosalie*: fillets sautéed in walnut oil, with shallots, garlic and vinegar. *Filets de maquereaux au vin blanc*: fillets poached in white wine and served cold; common first course in N France, also available in tins.

MAQUIS Wild scrubland of *Corse*. See also *Brindamour*.

(À LA) MARAÎCHÈRE Lit.: 'market-gardener's style'. With mixed vegetables, often salsify, Brussels sprouts, potatoes, carrots, onions.

MARAIS Marsh. Market-garden.
Coastal area of *Vendée* and *Poitou*, which is both.

MARASME Family of fungus including *faux mousseron*, the only edible variety.

MARASQUIN Maraschino cherry. Also maraschino liqueur.

MARBRADE (SW France) Moulded pig's head in jelly.

MARBRÉ(-E) Lit.: 'marbled'. Striped sea-bream, also known as *morme*.

MARC Husks, skins, dregs, grounds. Short for *eau-de-vie de marc*: spirit distilled from grape residue (skins, pips, stalks etc) after wine-pressing, often very pungent (e.g. *Marc de Bourgogne*, *Marc de Champagne*).

MARCASSIN Young wild boar (as opposed to *sanglier*: mature boar). *Côtelettes de marcassin à la Saint-Hubert*: baked cutlets stuffed with mushrooms and juniper berries; *Saint-Marc*: braised cutlets with tongue, puréed chestnuts, cranberry sauce. *Cuissot de marcassin à la mode de Tours*: leg marinated in *Touraine* wine, braised with prunes. *Jambon de marcassin*: salted and smoked wild boar.

MARCELLIN   See *petit marcellin*.

MARCHAND DE VIN(S)   Wine-merchant. With butter/sauce based on red wine, meat stock and shallots (e.g. *entrecôte marchand de vin*).

MARCHE   County equivalent to *Creuse*, generally considered part of *Limousin*.

(À LA) MARCHOISE   In the style of *Marche*.

MARCILLAC   Area in *Rouergue*, growing red, white and rosé wines (*VDQS*), known as *Vins de Marcillac*.

(À LA) MARÉCHALE   Lit.: 'marshal's style'. Dipped in egg and breadcrumbs, fried in butter, sometimes garnished with asparagus tips and truffles, or peas and butter; applied to slices of meat and poultry, or fillets of fish.

MARÉE   Lit.: 'tide'. General term for fresh seafood.

MARENGO   Chicken (or veal) dish, supposedly improvised for Napoleon at the Battle of Marengo in 1800, or just named after that battle by a *Paris* restaurant; see *poulet*.

MARENNES   Town in *Charentes*, one of the most important regions for oyster cultivation; see also *huître*.
   Marenne: oyster from Marennes.

MARETTE   (Provence) Kind of bread to accompany *bouillabaisse*.

MARGAUX   Commune (*AC*) of *Haut-Médoc*, *Bordeaux*, containing Château Margaux, Château Palmer, Château Lascombes and many other renowned estates.

MARGUÉRY   Restaurant in 19th-century *Paris*. See *sole* and *tournedos*.

MARIAGE   Lit.: 'marriage'. *Soupe de mariage* (Provence): beef, mutton and chicken soup, with rice and saffron; (Rouergue) cheese soup, traditionally served in chamber pots after a wedding, also known as *soupe au Laguiole*.

MARIE-LOUISE   Napoleon's second wife, daughter of the Austrian Emperor. Garnish of artichokes, puréed onions, mushrooms and madeira sauce.

MARIETA   (S France) Local name for flat lobster (*cigale*).

MARIGNAN (Ile-de-France) Liqueur-flavoured cake with meringue and jam.

MARIN(-E) Of the sea, to do with the sea. Sailor.

MARINADE Mixture of wine, spices, herbs, vegetables, sometimes oil, in which food is steeped to season, tenderize, moisturize or preserve it.

MARINE Feminine of *marin*.

MARINÉ(-E) Marinated; cured; pickled; soused.

(À LA) MARINETTE See *thon*.

(À LA) MARINIÈRE/DES MARINIERS Lit.: 'boatman's style'. Of shellfish, especially mussels, cooked with shallots, white wine and herbs. Of fish, cooked in white wine, garnished with mussels. See also *grillade* and *matelote*.

MARINOUN (Languedoc) Huge pork sausage.

MARITCHU *Oeufs maritchu* (Pays basque): scrambled eggs with artichokes and tomato sauce.

MARIVAUX 18th-century writer. Garnish of potato nests filled with vegetables and French beans.

MARJOLAINE Marjoram, the herb.
Chocolate and nut sponge cake, layered with cream filling.

MARKNEPFEN/MARKNOEPPFLE (Alsace) Beef marrow *quenelles*, often in clear soup.

MARLY Marly-le-Roi in *Ile-de-France*, favourite spot for Louis XIV, and later for writers and artists. See *carré* and *perdreau*.

MARMANDAIS The *Marmande* area. See *Côtes du Marmandais*.

MARMANDE Variety of tomato, large, flat and ridged; originally from Marmande, South of *Périgord*.

MARMELADE Thick sweetened purée of fruit (not the same as English orange marmalade – *confiture d'oranges*). *En marmelade*: cooked to a mush.

MARMITE Tall stew pot, stock pot, used especially for *pot-au-feu*. Food cooked in a *marmite*. *Marmite bressane*: poached chicken. *Marmite dieppoise*: fish and shellfish stew with leeks, white wine and cream. Also soup tureen, soup bowl, for serving *consommé*. See also *petite marmite*.

MARMOTTE   Marmot, type of squirrel. See also *civet*.
Variety of cherry, originally from *Nivernais*.

MARNE   Department in *Champagne*, and river. See also *fine*.

(À LA) MAROCAINE   Moroccan-style. With saffron ice, courgettes and peppers.

MARO(I)LLES   (Flandre) *AOC* cheese, small, slab-shaped with supple creamy-coloured interior, strong smelling and tasting: made by farms and dairies, named after the monastery of Maroilles where it was invented in the 10th century. *Maroilles Mignon*, *Mignon Maroilles*, *Quart Maroilles*, *Sorbais*: smaller versions. See also *Puant*.

MAROUETTE   Type of rail, marsh bird, similar to quail.

MARQUE   Trademark. See also *grande marque*.

(À LA) MARQUISE   Lit.: 'marchioness's style'. Garnish of *foie gras*, truffles and cream sauce.
Pineapple and strawberry water ice. See also *fraise*.
Variety of winter pear.

MARQUISETTE   (Nivernais) Small chocolate log.

MARRON   Chestnut, also known as *châtaigne*. *Marron glacé*: candied chestnut. *Marrons à la lyonnaise*: chestnut cake. *Potage aux marrons* (Bretagne, Vivarais, Auvergne): chestnut soup with cream.

MARSANNAY-LA-CÔTE   Small town of *Côte de Nuits*, *Bourgogne*, known mainly for rosé wines (*AC*).

MARSANNE   Variety of white grape used in *Rhône* wines.

MARSEILLE   Capital of the Bouches-du-Rhône department in *Provence*. *Soupe de poissons de Marseille*: fish soup with leeks, tomatoes, herbs, pasta, sometimes grated cheese.

(À LA) MARSEILLAISE   In the style of *Marseille*. With tomatoes, garlic, onions, olives, anchovies etc. See also *épinards*, *lotte*, *moule* and *pilaf*.

(À LA) MARTÉGALE/MARTIGALE   In the style of Martigues in *Provence*. See *anguille* and *mulet*.

(À LA) MARTINIÈRE   See *brocheton*.

(À LA) MARTINIQUAISE   In the style of Martinique in West Indies. See *ananas*.

MARTIN-SEC/SIRE   Varieties of winter pear.

(À LA) MASCOTTE   Lit.: 'mascot-style'. Garnish of artichoke hearts, potatoes and truffles.
Coffee and hazelnut cake.

(À LA) MASSÉNA   One of Napoleon's generals. Garnish, for steaks especially, of artichokes filled with *béarnaise* sauce, and bone marrow.

MASILLON   Small almond tartlet; after a 17th-century preacher.

MASSEPAIN   Marzipan. Marzipan biscuit.

MATAFAN/MATAFAT/MATEFAIM   (Berry) Substantial pancake.

MATAHAMI   (Béarn) Baked salt pork layered with potatoes, onions, garlic.

MATEFAIM   See *matafan*.

MATELOTE   Stew of different freshwater fish, particularly eel, and carp, pike, perch or barbel, in red or white wine, with onions, mushrooms, sometimes crayfish tails and fried bread; from 'matelot' – sailor, and particularly associated with the *Loire* country – *Anjou*, *Touraine* and *Bourgogne*. *Matelote blanche*: with white wine; *à la bourguignonne*: with red wine and *marc*; *à la canotière*: of carp and eel with white wine; *à la marinière*: with white wine and brandy; *à la meunière*: with red wine and brandy; *à la tourangelle*: with salt pork and red wine.
Stew, of seafood, meat, poultry etc. *Matelote à la normande*: sole, conger eel and gurnard with cider, *Calvados* and cream. *Matelote de veau*: veal with red wine, onions and mushrooms. See also *casseron*, *cervelles* and *poulet*.

MATIAS   Flat savoury cake with onions, leeks and potatoes.

MATIGNON   Mixed vegetables cooked in butter, as a stuffing or garnish.

MATTONS   (Lorraine) Hard unmoulded cheese made from re-cooked whey; similar to *Metton*.

MATZNOPFLICH   (Alsace) Jewish ginger cake.

MAUBÈCHE   Name for sandpiper (*alouette de mer*).

MAURIENNE   See *Chevrine de Lenta*.

MAURY   Area on the *Roussillon-Aude* borders, producing mainly red fortified sweet wines (*AC*).

MAUVE   Mallow, plant whose leaves are sometimes eaten in salads or cooked as a vegetable.

MAUVIETTE   Lit.: 'softy'. Name for lark (*alouette*).

MAUVIS   Redwing, small bird.

MAYETTE   Variety of walnut (*noix*).

MAYONNAISE   Mayonnaise, cold sauce based on egg yolks and oil. Cold dish with mayonnaise. Perhaps invented during the siege of Port Mahon in Minorca in 1756; or derived from 'manier', to manipulate, or from 'moyeu', Old French for yolk of egg; or corruption of *bayonnaise*; or named after the Duc de Mayenne.

MAYORQUINA   (Roussillon) Tomato and cabbage soup.

MAZAGRAN   Tartlet lined with potatoes and variously filled. Goblet, for black coffee; coffee served cold in a glass.

MAZARIN   Cardinal-statesman under Louis XIV. Sponge cake filled with crystallized fruit.

MAZIS/MAZOYÈRES-CHAMBERTIN   See *Gevrey-Chambertin*.

MAZZERDU   (Corse) Local name for grey mullet (*mulet*).

MEAUX   Town in *Ile-de-France*. See *Brie de Meaux*.

MÉCHOUI   Barbecue, usually of lamb; of North African origin.

MÉDAILLON   Lit.: 'medallion'. Thin round or oval slice, of meat especially; also known as *mignonnette* and *noisette*, of lamb, and *tournedos*, of beef.

MÉDICIS   Garnish of artichokes, tomatoes and *béarnaise* sauce. Catherine de Médicis, of the Florentine banking family, was wife of Henri II.

MÉDOC   Area N of the city of *Bordeaux* on the left bank of the *Gironde*, divided into *Haut-Médoc* and *Bas-Médoc*, the former producing some of the finest red wines in the world. *AC Médoc* applies to red wines grown throughout the area.

MEGIN   See *tarte*.

(LA) MEILLERAYE DE BRETAGNE   Large smooth slab-shaped cheese, with strong flavour, made at the Abbey of La Meilleraye; also known as *Abbaye/Trappiste de La Meilleraye*.

MÉJANELS   (Provence) Thick vermicelli, used especially in *soupe au pistou*.

MÉLANGE   Mixture. Blend (e.g. of coffee).

MÉLASSE   Molasses; treacle.

(À LA) MELBA   Garnish of stuffed tomatoes and braised lettuce. See also *pêche* for *Escoffier*'s famous creation for the Australian soprano, Dame Nelly Melba, originally in the form of a swan, alluding to the opera *Lohengrin*. *Escoffier* also invented Melba toast to help her lose weight.

(À LA) MELDOISE   In the style of *Meaux*.

MÉLÉ-CASS   Drink of mixed *crème de cassis* and *marc*.

MELET   (Nice) Tiny sandsmelt, used like *poutine* and *nonnats*.

MÉLILOT   Melilot, the herb.

MÉLISSE   Lemon balm, herb. See also *eau*.

MELON   Melon. *Melon au porto*: chilled half, filled with port, as a first course; *rafraîchi en surprise*: chilled, filled with fruit and sprinkled with liqueur, also known as *melon à la parisienne*.
    Variety of white grape (more familiar as *Muscadet*), originally from *Bourgogne*. See also *escargot*.

MELON D'EAU   Lit.: 'water melon'; but in fact more like a Spanish melon (as opposed to *pastèque*: water melon).

MELONGÈNE   Name for *aubergine*.

MELSAT   Large white sausage (*boudin blanc*), eaten hot or cold.

MELUN   Capital of the Seine-et-Marne department in *Ile-de-France*. See also *Brie de Melun*.

MÉLUSINE   (Poitou) Small cake.

MELVA   Frigate mackerel, small type of tuna; also known as *bonitou*.

MÉNAGE   Housekeeping; household.

(À LA) MÉNAGÈRE   Lit.: 'housewife's style'. Garnish of braised lettuce, peas and potatoes. With vegetables, especially onions. *Potage ménagère*: vegetable soup with bacon, poured over bread. *Omelette à la ménagère*: omelette with pasta, or leftover beef and onions.

MENDE   Capital of the Lozère department in *Languedoc*.

MENDIANT   Lit.: 'mendicant friar'. See *quatre mendiants*.

MENDOLE (COMMUNE)   Picarel, type of sea bream; also known as *picarel*, and *jarret* and *varlet de ville*.

MENETOU-SALON   Area (*AC*) of *Berry*, known for crisp dry white wine from the *Sauvignon* grape, also producing some red and rosé.

MENGIN   See *tarte*.

MENON   (Provence) Roasted goat kid.

MENOUILLE   Salt pork baked with potatoes, beans and onions.

MENSONGE   Lit.: 'lie'. (Périgord) Fritter.

MENTCHNIKOFF   (Orléanais) Chocolate praline sweet; dedicated to a minister of Peter the Great.

MENTHE   Mint, spearmint, the herb. *Menthe poivrée anglaise*: peppermint. *A la menthe*: mint- or peppermint-flavoured. *Crème de menthe*: sweet peppermint-flavoured liqueur, green or white. See also *pouliot*.

(À LA) MENTONNAISE   In the style of Menton in *Provence*. Garnish of stuffed *courgettes*, artichokes and potatoes. Of fish, with tomatoes, olives and garlic.

MENU   Set menu, fixed price meal (as opposed to *carte*). In France, the full meal consists of: 1) *hors d'oeuvre* or soup; 2) *entrée* – fish, chicken or eggs; 3) main course, the *rôti* – meat, poultry or game; 4) vegetables or salad; 5) cheese, 6) *entremets* – dessert; 7) fruit.

MER   Sea.

MÉRANDE   (Lorraine) Farmworkers' snack of *Brocq* cheese.

MERCÉDÈS   Garnish of tomatoes, mushrooms, lettuce and potatoes.

MERCUREY   One of the largest vineyard areas (*AC*) of *Côte Chalonnaise*, *Bourgogne*, producing excellent red wine and a smaller quantity of white.

MÈRE   Lit.: 'mother'. See below.

MÈRE FILLOUX   One of the celebrated *mères*, or women restaurant owners, who brought renown to the cuisine of *Lyonnais* at the beginning of the century. See *poularde*.

MÈRE-LOUISETTE   See *épinards*.

MÈRE POULARD   Owner of the Hôtel Poulard in *Mont-Saint-Michel* in the early 1900s, who became famous for her *omelette de la Mère Poulard*: simple omelette, but impossible to imitate.

MERGUEZ   Spicy Arab sausage, grilled.

(À LA) MÉRIDIONALE   Southern-style, in the manner of the *Midi*.

MERINGUE   Meringue.

MERISE   Wild cherry.

MERLAN   Whiting. *Merlan en colère*: fried and arranged with the tail in the mouth (lit.: 'angry'); *à la française*: fried fillets with tomato sauce; *en raïto/en rayte*: in red wine sauce.
   Name for hake (*colin*), especially in S France. *Merlan noir*: name for coalfish (*lieu noir*).

MERLE   Blackbird; eaten especially in *Corse*, often roasted in sage leaves or made into *pâté*.
   Type of wrasse (*vieille*).

MERLOT   Variety of black grape, important in the red wines of *Bordeaux*.

MERLU(S)/MERLUCHE/MERLUZZA   Name for hake (*colin*), especially in S France. *Merluzza à la koskera* (Pays basque): baked with peas, asparagus, potatoes and garlic.
   Name for salt cold (*morue*).
   Merluche (*noire*): name for coalfish (*lieu noir*).

MERLUCHON   Name for codling (*colineau*).

MÉROU   Grouper, large sea fish; also known as *anfounsou*.

MERVEILLE   Lit.: 'marvel'. (Charentes, Périgord) Sweet fritter.

MÉSANGE   Tit, small bird, sometimes made into *pâté*.

MESCLOU   Mixture of plum and walnut liqueurs, speciality of *Périgord*.

MESCLUN   (Provence) Mixed green saladings, usually including cress, lettuce, lamb's lettuce (*mâche*), dandelion leaves, endive, chicory, fennel, chervil, all sown close together

and gathered young at the same time; originally consisting of wild plants and herbs, perhaps derived from Latin 'misculare' – to mix up.

(À LA) MESSINE   In the style of *Metz*. *Sauce messine*: herb and cream sauce, for fish like turbot. *Consommé à la messine*: clear meat broth with small sausages and cabbage rolls.

MESSIRE-JEAN   Variety of autumn pear.

MÉTHODE   Lit.: 'method'. (Pays basque) Preserved pork, often added to *garbure*.
Méthode champenoise: see *Champagne*.

METS   Prepared food, dish.

METTERNICH   19th-century Austrian chancellor and European statesman. See *selle*.

METTON   (Franche-Comté) Hard grainy cheese made from re-cooked whey, greenish, lumpy, with strong smell and dull taste, used in the preparation of *Cancoillotte*; dialect word.

MÉTURE   (Béarn) Dish of maize flour, eggs and *Bayonne* ham.

METZ   Capital of *Moselle*.

MEUILLE   (Charentes) Local name for grey mullet (*mulet*). *Meuilles à la charentaise*: poached with wine, tomatoes, garlic, covered with cheese, browned.

(À LA) MEUNIÈRE   Lit.: 'miller's wife style' (i.e. with floury hands). Of fish, coated with flour, fried in butter, served with *beurre meunière*: brown butter (*beurre noisette*) with lemon juice and parsley. See also *matelote* and *oreille*.
Meunier: name for chub (*chevaine*).

MEURETTE   (Bourgogne) Red wine sauce with onions, carrots, bacon, mushrooms; for freshwater fish (equivalent to *matelote*), poached eggs (*oeufs en meurette*), beef (which becomes *boeuf à la bourguignonne*), rabbit, brains etc.

MEURSAULT   One of the most important communes of *Côte de Beaune*, *Bourgogne*, producing white wines (*AC*); red wines from the commune are sold as *Volnay Santenots* (*AC*).

(À LA) MEXICAINE   Mexican-style. With mushrooms, tomatoes, peppers, often rice. See also *charlotte*.

MÉZENC   See *Bleu de Loudes*.

M'GIN   See *tarte*.

MIAS   See *millat*.

MIC   (Bretagne) Coffee laced with spirit.

MICHE   Large round loaf. *Miche beurée* (Bretagne): with sultanas and rum.
         Miche noire (Béarn): maize flour dumpling poached in water after a black pudding.

MI-CHÈVRE   Lit.: 'half-goat'. Description for cheeses containing at least 25% goat's milk.

MICHON   (Bretagne) Apple pancake.

MIDI   Midday. Lunchtime.
         South. Southern France.

MIDINETTE   Lit.: 'shop-girl', 'office girl' (who comes out at midday for lunch). *Salade midinette*: rice and pea salad; or chicken, apple, celery and cheese salad. *Consommé midinette*: clear chicken soup with poached eggs.

MIE   Crumb, soft part of the loaf. Bread without crusts. See also *pain*.

MIEL   Honey.

MIGISCA   (Corse) Smoked slice of goat.

MIGLIASSIS   (Corse) Chestnut flour cake.

MIGNARDISE   Dainty. *Petit four*.

MIGNON(-NE)   Dainty. See also *filet*.

MIGNON MAROILLES/MIGNONNET   Smaller version of *Maroilles* cheese.

MIGNONNETTE   Small round fillet, of lamb; also known as *noisette* and *médaillon*.
         Crushed black and white peppercorns, for steaks, etc.
         Small poultry or game *quenelle*.
         Pommes (*de terre frites*) *mignonnette*: crisp fried potato sticks.

MIGNOT   (Normandie) Fruity farm-made cheese in the shape of a thick disk, often eaten with sweet cider; named after a village.

MIGOURÉE   (Charentes) Fish stew with white wine, garlic and shallots.

MIJOT/MIOT   (Nivernais) Red wine and bread soup.

MIJOTÉ(-E)   Simmered.

MIKADO   Japanese Emperor. With a Japanese flavour. *Salade Mikado*: potato and shrimp salad with soya-flavoured mayonnaise, and chrysanthemum petals; also Chinese artichoke (*crosnes du Japon*) salad; also oyster salad with rice and sweet peppers.

(À LA) MILANAISE   In the style of Milan. Dipped in egg, breadcrumbs and cheese, fried, often served with spaghetti (e.g. *escalope de veau milanaise*). Garnish of macaroni with cheese, ham, mushrooms and tomato sauce. Of vegetables, browned with grated cheese and butter.
Milanais: sponge cake with apricot jam.

MILANDRE   Tope, type of small shark, sometimes eaten as steaks; also known as *chien de mer*.

MILCHSTREEVELE/MILCHSTRIWLE   (Alsace) Small dumplings poached in milk, finished with cheese, cream and butter.

MILCHEWECKE   (Alsace) Milk bread roll.

MILHAS/MILIASSE   See *millas*.

MILLA(RD)   See *millat*.

MILLAS   (S and SW France) Maize flour porridge, usually cooled, formed into flat cakes and fried, eaten like bread with soups and stews, or sprinkled with sugar for dessert; also known as *milhas* and *miliasse*, originally made with millet (hence the name).

MILLAS(SOU)   (W and central France) Sweet maize flour flan.

MILLAT   (central France) Cherry batter cake, similar to *clafoutis*; also known as *mias*, *milla*, *mill(i)ard* and *tuillard*.

MILLE-FEUILLE   Lit.: 'thousand leaf'. Thin layers of puff pastry sandwiched with cream, jam, etc. Also as a first course, filled with asparagus, salmon etc, served with rich sauce.

MILLES   (Périgord) Maize flour pastry.

MILLET   Millet.

MILLIA   (Périgord) Pumpkin maize flour flan.

MILLIARD   See *millat*.

MILLIAS(SOU)   (Bordelais) Small maize flour cake.

MILLIAT   (Bourgogne) Maize flour flan.

MILLIÈRE   (Anjou) Maize and rice porridge.

MILLOT   (Bourbonnais) Maize flour cake.

MIMOLETTE FRANÇAIS   (Flandre) Large firm oily cheese in the shape of an orange sphere, with fruity aroma and flavour, factory-made, especially in N France; imitation of Dutch Mimolette, also known as *Boule de Lille* and *Vieux Lille*.

MIMOSA   Mimosa, decorative plant with yellow blossom, which chopped hard-boiled egg yolk is supposed to resemble. *Salade mimosa*: lettuce and orange salad, sprinkled with hard-boiled egg yolk. *Potage mimosa*: clear soup garnished with green beans and hard-boiled egg.

MINARD   (Bretagne) Local name for octopus (*poulpe*).

MINCEUR   Slimness. See also *nouvelle cuisine*.

MINÉRAL(-E)   Mineral. See also *eau minérale*.

MINERVOIS   Region in *Hérault* and *Aude*, producing large quantities of sturdy red wine (*AC*).
   (*À la*) *minervoise*: in the style of *Minervois*. See *morue*.

MINGAUX/MINGOTS   See *maingaux*.

MINUTE   Lit.: 'minute'. Simply grilled or fried, with butter, lemon juice and parsley, especially of steak, sole.

MIOT   See *mijot*.

MIOU   (Provence) Local name for star-gazer (*boeuf*).

MIQUE   (Périgord, Limousin) Maize flour dumplings, served with soups, stews and cabbage dishes, or sliced and fried, or sprinkled with sugar.

(LO) MIQUO   (Vivarais) Cheese and potato dumplings.

(À LA) MIRABEAU   Politician before the Revolution. Garnish of anchovy fillets, tarragon, olives, anchovy butter, sometimes watercress and straw potatoes (e.g. *entrecôte Mirabeau*).

MIRABELLE   Small golden yellow plum. Also a clear spirit made from *mirabelle* plums, especially in *Alsace*.

MIRAMAR   See *sole*.

MIREILLE   *Pommes (de terre) Mireille*: sauté potatoes with artichokes and truffles. *Sauce Mireille*: *hollandaise* sauce with tomato purée and basil. See also *carré*, *morue* and *poularde*.

MIREPOIX   Diced carrots, onions, celery and ham stewed in butter, as a basis for sauces, braises etc; probably created by the chef to the Duc de Lévis-Mirepoix in the 18th century.

MIREVAL   Small area in *Hérault*, making sweet fortified wine (*AC*) from the *Muscat* grape.

MIRLITON   Lit.: 'pipe'. (Normandie) Small sweet tart, pastry puff. See also *tarte*.

MIROIR   Lit.: 'mirror'. *Oeufs au miroir*: fried or baked eggs, the whites forming a polished film over the yolks. See also *raie*.

MIROTON   See *boeuf*.

MISE/MIS EN BOUTEILLES   Bottled, of wine; from 'mettre' – to put. *Dans nos caves/à la proprieté*: in our cellars/at the property. *Dans la région de production/au château/au domaine*: in the region of production/at the estate, allowed only for *VDQS* and *AC* wines.

MISQUETTE   *Pommes (de terre) misquette* (Limousin): sautéed cubed potato with cream and egg yolks.

MISSIASOGA   (Corse) Goat's meat cured in the sun.

MISSISSA   (Corse) Grilled marinated pork.

MISSOUN   (Provence) Home-made sausage, often added to soups.

MISTRAL   Wind of *Provence* and *Rhône* valley; 19th-century poet and native of *Provence*. *Consommé Mistral*: beef broth with pasta, tomatoes, peas and cheese. *Omelette Mistral*: omelette with aubergines, tomatoes and herbs. See also *pêche*.

MITON(NÉE)   Lit.: 'simmered'. (Bretagne) Creamy onion soup.

MOCHE   (Vivarais) Pork sausage with cabbage, potatoes and prunes.

(À LA) MODE   In the manner, the full version of many *à la* phrases. See also *à la*.

(À LA) MODERNE   Lit.: 'in the modern style'. Garnish of braised cabbage and lettuce and mixed vegetables.

MOELLE   Bone marrow, rich soft pith from bones, usually of beef; used in sauces, stuffings, made into *quenelles* etc.
  Stump, stalk, of vegetables. *Moelle de chicorée*: stumps of curly endive, also known as *gourilos*.

MOELLEUX (MOELLEUSE)   Soft. (Boulonnais) Local name for tub gurnard (*grondin galinette*).

MOGETTE/MO(H)JETTE/MOUGETTE/MOUHJETTE   (Poitou) Variety of haricot bean from the *Marais*, supposed to resemble a nun (*mougette*) at prayer.

(À LA) MOISSONEUSE   Lit.: 'reaper's style'. Garnish of peas, lettuce, bacon and potatoes.

MOKA   Mocha, variety of coffee bean (originally from Moka in the Yemen). Coffee-flavoured.
  Crème de moka: sweet coffee-flavoured liqueur.
  Coffee sponge cake.

MOKATINE   Small coffee-flavoured cake.

MOLLE   Feminine of *mou*: soft.

MOLLET(-TE)   Soft. Soft-boiled. *Oeufs mollets*: soft-boiled eggs, shelled and used like poached eggs. See also *lompe*.

MONACO   Tiny independent principality on the Mediterranean coast; its cuisine has much in common with *Nice*.

MONBAZILLAC   Commune in *Périgord*, near *Bergerac*, making sweet white wine (*AC*), once considered to rival *Sauternes*.

(À LA) MONÉGASQUE   In the style of *Monaco*. *Salade monégasque*: salad of poached tiny fish (*nonats*) and tomatoes with rice. See also *tomate* and *tournedos*.

MONGETADO   (Languedoc) Stew of haricot beans (*mongetos*) and pork rinds.

MONGETO   (Languedoc) Local name for haricot bean.

MONOPOLE   Monopoly. Wine-label term indicating exclusive brand of the maker; or meaning that the whole vineyard belongs to the same proprietor.

(À LA) MONSELET   19th-century author and gastronome. Garnish of artichoke hearts, truffles and fried potatoes. See also *huître*.

MONSIEUR(-FROMAGE)   Lit.: 'Mr cheese'. (Normandie) Firm smelly fruity cheese with white rind dotted with red; made by small dairies, invented at the turn of the century by a farmer named Fromage.

MONTAGNE   Mountain.

MONTAGNE-SAINT-ÉMILION   Outlying part of *Saint-Emilion*, *Bordeaux*, producing red wines (*AC*).

MONTAGNY   Area of *Côte Chalonnaise*, *Bourgogne*, making good quality white wines (*AC*).

(À LA) MONTALBANAISE   In the style of *Montauban*.

MONTAUBAN   Capital of the Tarn-et-Garonne department in *Quercy*.

(À LA) MONTBARDOISE   In the style of Montbard in *Bourgogne*. See *truite*.

MONTBÉLIARD   Town in *Franche-Comté*, known for its caraway-flavoured sausage.

MONT-BLANC   Mont Blanc, in the Alps. Puréed chestnut dessert topped with whipped cream.

MONTBRISON   See *Fourme d'Ambert*.

MONT-BRY   Garnish of small spinach and cheese cakes, and *cèpes* in cream.

MONT-CENIS   Mountain in *Savoie*. See *Persillé du Mont-Cenis*.

MONT-DE-MARSAN   Capital of *Landes*.

MONT-DES-CATS   (Flandre) Strong round yellow cheese, made at the monastery on the hill of Mont-des-Cats; also known as *Abbaye du/Trappiste du Mont-des-Cats*.

MONT D'OR   Mountain in *Franche-Comté*. See *Vacherin*.

MONT-DORE   Mountain in *Auvergne*. *Pommes* (*de terre*) *Mont-Dore*: mashed potatoes with cheese, browned. See also *truite*.

MONTE-CRISTO   See *Montpensier*.

MONTEREAU   Town in *Ile-de-France*. See *Brie de Montereau*.

MONTESQUIEU   See *rouget*.

(À LA) MONTEYNARD   *Oeufs à la Monteynard*: soft-boiled eggs with rice and cheese, browned.

(À LA) MONTGLAS   Mixture of *foie gras*, tongue, truffles, mushrooms, madeira sauce, as a filling.

MONTGOLFIER   Of fish, stuffed and poached, with white sauce, mushrooms, truffles, lobster. The Montgolfier brothers were inventors of the hot-air balloon.

MONTHÉLIE   Commune of *Côte de Beaune*, *Bourgogne*, making mainly red wines (*AC*).

(À LA) MONTILIENNE   In the style of Montélimar in *Dauphiné*.

MONTLOUIS   Commune in *Touraine*, producing dry, semi-sweet and sweet wines (*AC*), similar to *Vouvray* across the *Loire*.

MONTMORENCY   Variety of cherry, named after the town in *Ile-de-France*. With cherries (e.g. *canard Montmorency*).
   Garnish of artichokes, asparagus, mixed vegetables and madeira sauce.

MONTOIRE   (Orléanais) Small cone-shaped goat's milk cheese, with fruity flavour; made by farms, also known as *Troo* and *Villiers-sur-Loir*.

(À LA) MONTOISE   In the style of *Mont-de-Marsan*.

MONTPELLIER   Capital of *Hérault*. See also *beurre*.

MONTPENSIER   Garnish of asparagus, artichokes, truffles and madeira sauce; dedicated to one of the noble Montpensier family.
   Sweet flan, also known as *Monte-Cristo*.

(LE) MONTRACHET   Small *grand cru* vineyard divided between the communes of *Chassagne-Montrachet* and *Puligny-Montrachet* in *Côte de Beaune*, *Bourgogne*, producing one of the finest dry white wines (*AC*) in the world.

(Bourgogne) Mild creamy goat's milk cheese, wrapped in chestnut or vine leaves, made by a small dairy; trade name chosen for the reflected glory of the great wine.

MONTRAVEL   Area of *Périgord*, producing white wines (*AC*), mainly semi-sweet.

MONTREUIL   Town in *Picardie*. Of fish, poached with white wine, shrimps and potato balls.
Suburb of *Paris*, once known for peaches. With peaches.
See also *poire*.

MONTROUGE   With mushrooms in cream.

MONT-SAINT-MICHEL   Dramatic rock, formerly the site of an abbey, on the *Normandie* coast. See *gigot* and *huître*.

MONTSÉGUR   (Foix) Large round cheese with blackish rind and bland flavour; made by commercial dairies, named after the nearest town.

MONT VENTOUX   Mountain dominating the *Vaucluse* plain and *Rhône* valley. See also *Cachat*, *Côtes de Ventoux* and *fromage fort*.

MOQUE   (N France) Dark spice buns, of Belgian origin.

MORBIER   (Franche-Comté) Large firm strong cheese with a black streak running through it; made by dairies around Morbier.

MORBIHAN   Department of *Bretagne*, taking its name from the Golfe du Morbihan. See also *huître*.

MORCEAU (pl. **MORCEAUX**)   Piece, morsel, bit.

MOREY-SAINT-DENIS Commune (*AC*) of *Côte de Nuits*, *Bourgogne*, containing the *grands crus Clos Saint-Denis*, *Clos de la Roche*, *Clos des Lambrays* and *Clos de Tart*, all red wine vineyards of great note, and part of *Bonnes Mares*.

MORGON See *Beaujolais*.

MORILLE Morel family of fungi of different colours, found in spring, particularly in mountains, highly esteemed; one variety also known as *morillon*.

MORILLON Black grape.
　　　　Name for variety of morel (*morille*).

MORME Name for striped sea bream (*marbré*).

MORNAY *Sauce Mornay*: white *béchamel* sauce with cheese; probably after an 18th-century chef, or perhaps dedicated to de Plessis Mornay, friend of *Henri IV*.

MORTADELLE Mortadella sausage, large sausage served thinly sliced as a first course; of Italian origin, also made in France.

MORTEAU Town in *Franche-Comté*, famous for its *Jésus* sausage.

MORTIER (Auvergne) Beef, ham and chicken soup.

MORUE Salt cod (as opposed to *cabillaud*: fresh cod, and slightly different from *stockfish*); also known as *merlu*. *Morue blanche*: dried and salted. *Morue noire*: dried slowly (and see also below). *Morue à l'anglaise*: poached, with boiled potatoes and hard-boiled eggs in a cream sauce; *à la bamboche*: fried fillets with mixed vegetables and cream; *à la bénédictine*: poached, mixed with mashed potatoes and milk, browned; *à la biscaïenne*: fried, with tomatoes, peppers, garlic; *à la bordelaise*: poached, with tomatoes, garlic, sweet peppers and white wine; *à la brestoise*: with leeks, onions and potatoes; *à la dinardaise*: pounded and mixed with puréed potatoes; *à la mode de Guincamp*: marinated, coated in pastry, fried; *Mireille*: fried fillets with spicy tomato sauce and rice; *à la minervoise*: with olives and anchovies; *à l'occitane*: baked with hard-boiled eggs, potatoes, tomatoes, olives etc; *à la niçoise*: stew with garlic, tomatoes, olives etc; *à la paimpolaise*: with potatoes, onion and cream sauce; *à la parisienne*: poached, with hard-boiled eggs, capers, parsley; *à la provençale*: baked with shallots and herbs; *à la turballoise*: with spinach and potatoes. See also *brandade*.
　　　　Morue borgne: lit.: 'low cod'. Name for pout (*tacaud*). *Morue noire/Saint-Pierre*: name for haddock (*aiglefin*).

MORVAN Region of *Bourgogne*. *Potage de Morvan*: cabbage, bacon and potato soup.

(À LA) MORVANDELLE   In the style of *Morvan*. See *fricassée* and *jambon*.

MOSAÏQUE   Lit.: 'mosaic'. Mixed dish, preparation (e.g. of vegetables).

(À LA) MOSCOVITE   Moscow-style. *Sauce moscovite*: spicy wine sauce with nuts and currants, for venison. *Salade moscovite*: elaborate version of *salade russe*.
Cold custard dessert, ice cream or fruit jelly, usually hexagonal in shape.

MOSELLE   Department and river in *Lorraine*.
Light red and rosé wines (*VDQS*), known as *Vins de Moselle*, made around *Metz*.

MOSTÈLE/MO(S)TELLE   Rockling, forkbeard, small sea fish; also known as *petite lingue and loche* (*de mer*).

MOTHAIS/(LA) MOTHE-SAINT-HÉRAY   (Poitou)   White goat's milk cheese with robust flavour, shaped as a flat disk, pyramid or log; made by the dairy of La Mothe-Saint-Héray, also known as *Chèvre à la Feuille*.

MOU   Lights (i.e. lungs).
Mou (*molle*): soft. Flat (e.g. of wine).

MOUCLADE   (Charentes) Mussels in creamy sauce with saffron and turmeric, plus white wine, and sometimes *Pineau des Charentes*.

MOUF(F)LON/MUFIONE/MUFOLI   (Corse) Wild sheep, now rare.

MOUGETTE   See *mogette*.

MOUGIN   See *tarte*.

MOUHJETTE   See *mogette*.

MOULE    Mussel, also known as *muscle* in *Provence*; cultivated in most coastal regions, usually on wooden posts or *bouchots* (a method first practised by an Irish sailor in the Baie de *l'Aiguillon* in the 13th century). *Moules* (*de*) *bouchot*(*s*): fine small type. *Bouzigues*: grown in the Bassin de *Thau*. *Moules barbues*: larger horse mussels. *Moules rouges*: tiny red-fleshed mussels from *Provence*. There are also natural wild mussels, including *caïeu d'Isigny*. *Moules à l'armoricaine*: with onions and tomatoes; *à la camarguaise*: in white wine, with lemon mayonnaise; *à la catalane*: with onions; *à la fécampoise*: in cider, with celeriac and mayonnaise; *à la marinière*: cooked with white wine, shallots and parsley; *à la marseillaise*: with shallots, parsley and oil; *nautile* (Provence): with tomatoes, onions, white wine and saffron; *à la niçoise*: with *pistou* (sauce); *à la normande*: with cream sauce; *à la rochelaise*: stuffed with herb butter and browned; *à la toulonnaise*: with rice. *Soupe de moules à la rochelaise*: mussel and fish soup with red wine, garlic, tomatoes and saffron.

Mould, in different shapes for custards, creams, charlottes, pastries etc.

MOULÉ(-E)   Moulded, shaped. See also *crème*.

MOULIN   Mill. *Moulin à poivre*: peppermill.

MOULIN-À-VENT   Lit.: 'windmill'. See *Beaujolais*.

MOULINS   Capital of the Allier department and of *Bourbonnais*. See also *Chevrotin du Bourbonnais*.

MOULIS   Commune (*AC*) of *Haut-Médoc*, *Bordeaux*, whose best known vineyard is Château Chasse-Spleen.

MOULU(-E)   Milled, ground (e.g. of coffee, pepper).

MOURÉ POUNTCHOU   (Provence) Local name for type of sea bream (*sar*).

MOURGETO   (Provence) Type of small snail.

MOURRE AGUT   (Nice) Local name for type of sea bream (*sar*).

MOURTAÏROL/MOURTAYROL   (Auvergne, Rouergue) Soup of beef, chicken, ham, vegetables and saffron, poured on slices of bread; also known as *tusset*.

(À LA) MOUSQUETAIRE   Lit.: 'musketeer's style'. *Sauce mousquetaire*: mayonnaise with shallots and meat glaze. See also *côtelette*.

MOUSSE   Lit.: 'froth', 'foam'. Bubbles (e.g. in *Champagne*). Mousse, savoury or sweet, usually cold (as opposed to hot *soufflé*).

MOUSSEAU   See *pain*.

MOUSSELINE   Lit.: 'muslin'. Small *mousse*, or light delicate preparation. *Mousseline de poisson*: made with puréed fish beaten with egg whites and cream, poached in a mould; served with sauce, or used as stuffing for large fish like turbot – popular in the *nouvelle cuisine*. *Sauce mousseline*: hollandaise sauce or mayonnaise lightened with whipped cream; also known as *sauce Chantilly*. *Pommes (de terre) mousseline*: puréed potatoes with milk and butter; also known as *mousse Parmentier*.

MOUSSERON(VRAI) St George's mushroom, small white or yellow, found in spring and autumn, highly esteemed. See also *faux mousseron*.

   Mousseron d'automne: name for type of fungus (*clitopile*). *Mousseron gris*: name for type of fungus (*entolome*).

MOUSSEUX(SE) Lit.: 'frothy'. Sparkling of wine (e.g. *Saumur Mousseux*). *Sauce mousseuse*: light sauce of butter and egg yolks with lemon juice.

MOUTARDE Mustard.

MOUTARDE DE CHINE Chinese/leaf mustard, with cabbage-like or curly leaves, used like spinach.

MOUTARDELLE Type of horseradish.

MOUTON Sheep. Mutton. See *carré*, *côtelette*, *épaule*, *gigot*, *noisette*, for major cuts.

MOYAUX See *Pavé de Moyaux*.

MUENSTER See *Munster*.

MUFIONE/MUFOLI (Corse) Local name for wild sheep (*mouflon*).

MUGE Name for grey mullet (*mulet*).

MUJOU LABRU/DE ROCO (S France) Local name for grey mullet (*mulet*).

MULARD Type of duck; see *canard*.

MULET Grey mullet, large common sea fish, good to eat if caught in clean water; also known as *cigare*, *loubine*, *muge* and *mulet/poisson sauteur*, and *acucu*, *alifranciu*, *aurin*, *capocchio*, *cirita*, *gaouto-rousso*, *lissa*, *mazzerdu*, *meuille*, *mujou labru/de roco* and *porqua*. *Boutargue* is made from the roe. *Mulet à la martégale*: baked with oil, tomatoes and onions.

MUNSTER/MÜNSTER/MUENSTER (GÉROMÉ) (Alsace) Large round supple cheese (*AOC*), with orange rind, matured for 3 to 6 weeks, with penetrating smell and spicy flavour; made both by farms (*Munster Fermier*) and commercially (*Munster Laitier*), an ancient monastic cheese named after the town of Munster. *Petit Munster*: smaller version. *Munster au Cumin*: flavoured with cumin or caraway seeds. *Munster-plate*: piece of *Munster* served with raw onions, caraway, bread and beer.

MUOU (Provence) Local name for star-gazer (*boeuf*).

MURAT   One of Napoleon's generals, later king of Naples. See *sole*.

MURÇON   (Languedoc) Sausage, eaten hot.

MUR-DE-BARREZ   (Rouergue) Goat's milk cheese ripened in walnut or blackcurrant leaves; made by farms around Mur-de-Barrez.

MÛRE   Mulberry. *Mûre* (*de ronce/sauvage*): blackberry; also known as *baie de ronce* and *mûron*. Also a clear spirit made from blackberries, especially in *Alsace*.

MURÈNE   Moray eel, carniverous sea fish sometimes used in *bouillabaisse*; prized by the Romans, who bred it specially, and satisfied its voracious appetite with wicked slaves.

MUREX   Name for murex (*rocher*).

MUROL   (Auvergne) Mild smooth cheese, in the shape of a flat disk with a hole, factory-made; invented at Murol, similar to *Saint-Nectaire*.

MÛRON   Name of blackberry (*mûre*).

MURSON   (Dauphiné) Caraway-flavoured sausage.

MUSARD   *Purée Musard*: puréed flageolet beans, often served with mutton.

MUSCADE   Nutmeg, the spice.

MUSCADELLE   Musk pear, with musky flavour.
Variety of white grape similar to *Muscat*, grown in *Bordeaux* and elsewhere.

MUSCADET   Dry white wine (*AC*) – and local name for the grape variety used – especially popular in *Bretagne* with seafood; produced in *Nantais* on both sides of the Sèvre Nantaise, tributary of the *Loire*. The best comes from the Sèvre-et-Maine area, labelled (*tirer*) *sur lie*: bottled straight from the lees without filtration, for maximum freshness.

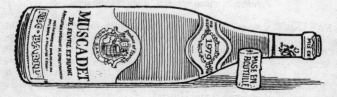

MUSCARDIN   (Provence) Local name for small cuttlefish (*sépiole*).

MUSCAT   Variety of table and wine grape with musky flavour, white or black.
   Wine made from *Muscat* grapes, with a characteristic raisin aroma, often heavy and sweet, as in the *vins doux naturels* of *Frontignan*, *Lunel* and *Beaumes-de-Venise*, although in *Alsace* producing elegant dry wine; also used in some sparkling wines (e.g. *Clairette De Die*).

MUSCLE   (Provence) Local name for mussel (*moule*).

MUSEAU   Muzzle, of ox or pig. *Museau de boeuf* is a common first course, sold ready-prepared and served sliced with shallot, parsley and *vinaigrette*.

MUSETTE   Lit.: 'bag'. *En musette*: boned, rolled into a ball and braised, usually of shoulder of mutton.

(LES) MUSIGNY   See *Chambolle-Musigny*.

MYE   Soft-shelled clam, eaten especially on the W coast; also known as *bedjar* and *vise en l'air*.

MYRTE   Myrtle, the spice; used in *Corse* to flavour a liqueur.

MYRTILLE   Bilberry. Whortleberry (both berries also known as *airelle*). Also a clear spirit made from bilberries, especially in *Alsace*; also known as *brimbelle*.

MYSTÈRE   Lit.: 'mystery'. Ice cream in meringue, coated with nuts.

(À LA) NAGE   Lit.: 'swimming'. Of lobster, *langouste*, crayfish, poached in aromatic liquid – white wine, shallots, herbs etc and usually cream.

NAGEOIRE   Fin, flipper. *Nageoire de tortue*: turtle flipper, usually braised in madeira.

NAGEUR   Lit.: 'swimmer'. Name for small crab (*étrille*).

(À LA) NANCÉIENNE   In the style of *Nancy*. *Omelette à la nancéienne*: omelette with black pudding.

NANCY   Capital of the Meurthe-et-Moselle department in *Lorraine*. See also *cervelas*, *foie gras* and *ursuline*.

NANTAIS   Area around *Nantes*, technically in *Bretagne*, but in culinary terms having much in common with neighbouring *Anjou*.
   Smooth yellow-rinded cheese with tangy flavour, made by small dairies around *Nantes*; invented by a 19th-century priest, also known as *Fromage du Curé*.
   Small almond biscuit.

(À LA) NANTAISE In the style of *Nantes* or *Nantais*. Garnish of turnips, peas and potatoes. *Sauce nantaise*: vinegar, shallot and gherkin sauce, for pork. *Potage nantais*: cream of potato soup. See also *canard, coquille Saint-Jacques, hareng, lard* and *rouget*.

NANTES Capital of the Loire-Atlantique department and of *Nantais* in *Bretagne*.

(À LA) NANTUA In the style of Nantua, town in *Bugey*, famous for its crayfish (*écrevisses*). With freshwater crayfish tails. *Sauce Nantua*: rich cream sauce with puréed crayfish, butter and truffles.

NAPOLÉON Napoleon. Term used to indicate age, of *Calvados* and *Cognac*.

(À LA) NAPOLITAINE Neapolitan-style. With spaghetti, cheese and tomato. See *tranche*. *Napolitain*: elaborate pastry and jam cake.

(À LA) NARBONNAISE In the style of Narbonne in *Languedoc*. With white haricot beans and aubergines. *Potage narbonnaise*: white haricot bean soup with rice and sorrel. See also *escargot*.

NATTE Lit.: 'plait'. Bread loaf in the shape of a plait.

NATURE/(AU) NATUREL Plain. In its natural state. *Café/thé nature*: coffee/tea without milk. *Vin nature*: still, as opposed to sparkling, wine. See also *eau minérale*.

NAUTILE Lit.: 'nautilus' (sea creature). See *moule*.

NAVARIN Mutton or lamb stew with potatoes and onions. *Navarin printanier*: with spring vegetables.

NAVARRE Province of *Pays basque*.

(À LA) NAVARRAISE In the style of *Navarre*. With sweet peppers, onions, and garlic. See also *canard sauvage*.

NAVET Turnip; also known as *rave*.

(À LA) NAZAIRIENNE In the style of Saint-Nazaire in *Bretagne*. See *poulet*.

NÉAC Town, north east of Libourne, *Bordeaux* making red wine (*AC*), usually sold as Lalande de Pomerol.

NECTARINE Nectarine; also known as *brugnon*.

NÈFLE Medlar, Mediterranean fruit.
 Nèfle du Japon: loquat, Japanese medlar, like tart small plum.

NÉGOCIANT   Merchant, dealer, especially in wines; man who buys from growers and blends, using his own name as guarantee of quality. *Négociant-éleveur*: dealer who also matures, brings up (*élever*) wines.

NÈGRE   Lit.: 'negro'. See below, and see also *tête de nègre*.

NÉGRESSE   Lit.: 'negress'. Name for black potato (*pomme de terre noire*).
 Négresse/nègre en chemise: chocolate *mousse* or ice cream covered in cream or ice cream.

NEIGE   Lit.: 'snow', 'whiteness'. *Oeufs à la neige*: whites of egg poached in milk, served with vanilla custard.
 Neige de Florence: white pasta flakes, used in clear soups.

NELSON   See *côtelette* and *sole*.

NELUSCO   (Lorraine) Tiny cake with redcurrant jam.

NEMOURS   Town in *Ile-de-France*. Garnish of peas, carrots and potatoes.
 Small jam tartlet.

NÊNE   (Rouergue) Aniseed cake.

NÉRAC   Town in *Périgord*. See *terrine*.

NÉROLI   Neroli oil, extracted from orange blossom. Small almond orange-flavoured cake.

NESSELRODE   Rich ice cream with puréed chestnuts, often candied fruit and liqueur; created for the Comte de Nesselrode.

NEUFCHÂTEL   (Normandie) Soft small white cheese (*AOC*), with delicate flavour, or aged and stronger, best between August and November; made around Neufchâtel in *Bray*, mainly by farms, when it is packed in straw, in various shapes – square, brick, heart, cylinder (also known as *Bondon de Neufchâtel*).

(À LA) NEUVIC   In the style of Neuvic in *Périgord*. See *carpe*.

(À LA) NÉVA   River in Russia. See *poularde*.

NEVERS   Capital of the Nièvre department and *Nivernais*. *Soupe à la Nevers*: carrot and Brussels sprout soup.

NEWBURG   See *homard* for the lobster dish originally called Wenberg, after its creator, which became Newberg, then Newburg.

NICE   Capital of the Alpes-Maritime department in *Provence*; and the name of the former county equivalent to that department.

(À LA) NIÇOISE   In the style of *Nice*. With tomatoes, garlic, and anchovies, olives, capers, French beans, artichokes etc. *Salade niçoise*: famous salad usually including anchovy fillets, tuna, hard-boiled egg, peppers, lettuce, celery, tomatoes, black olives, and perhaps French or broad beans, potatoes, onions, capers, basil or other herbs, with *vinaigrette*. See also *caviar*, *courgette*, *farci*, *gnocchi*, *moule*, *pissaladière*, *poitrine*, *ravioli*, *rouget*, *stockfish*, *tarte* and *tripes*.

NID   Lit.: 'nest'. 'Nest' of potatoes or other ingredients.

NIELLE   Name for allspice (*toute-épice*).

NIEULLE   (Flandre) Round flat cake.

NIGELLE   Black cumin, the spice. Name for allspice (*toute-épice*).

NÎMES   Capital of *Gard*.

(À LA) NÎMOISE   In the style of *Nîmes*. *Potage de poissons à la nîmoise*: fish soup with eggs and *aïoli*. *Potée nîmoise*: leek, cabbage and celery soup with barley and basil. See also *carbonnade*.

NINETTE   See *artichaut*.

NIOLO/NIOLIN   (Corse) Square white sheep's milk cheese, with strong smell and flavour, also eaten fresh when creamy and mild; made by farms on the Niolo plateau, also known as *Asco*.

NIORT   Capital of the Deux-Sèvres department in *Poitou*.

(À LA) NIORTAISE   In the style of *Niort*. See *Jonchée, porcelet* and *poulet*.

(À LA) NISSARDE   See *sole*.

NIVERNAIS   Region equivalent to the department of Nièvre, in *Bourgogne*.

(À LA) NIVERNAISE   In the style of *Nivernais*. Garnish of glazed carrots and onions, perhaps turnips, braised lettuce and boiled potatoes. *Sauce nivernaise*: white wine, garlic and butter sauce. *Crème nivernais*: cream of carrot soup. *Omelette nivernaise*: flat omelette filled with sorrel, ham and chives.

(À LA) NOAILLES   See *pièce de boeuf*. The Duc de Noailles served under Louis XIV.

NOCE(S)   Lit.: 'wedding'. (Bretagne) Oat porridge. See also *bouillon*.

NOËL   Christmas. *Salade de Noël*: winter salad of dandelion leaves and lamb's lettuce (*mâche*). See also *bûche*, *cardon, estouffade, gibassier, sole* and *treize desserts*.

NOGUETTE   *Potage Noguette* (Bretagne): creamy fish soup.

(À LA) NOHANT   See *queue de boeuf*.

NOILLY PRAT   Brand of French *vermouth*. *Au Noilly*: with *vermouth* sauce (e.g. *sole au Noilly*).

NOIR(-E)   Black.

NOISETTE   Hazelnut. Nut-shaped/coloured. *Pommes (de terre) noisette*: small nut-shaped sauté potatoes. *Sauce noisette*: hollandaise sauce with *beurre noisette*. See also *beurre* and *café*.

Small coffee-flavoured sponge square topped with a hazelnut.

Small round steak like *médaillon*, usually of lamb (also known as *mignonette*), or veal. *Noisettes d'agneau des Tournelles*: sautéed lamb steaks with puréed onions, *vermouth* and sherry sauce. *Noisettes de veau à la Bénévent*: braised veal steaks with vegetables and madeira.

NOISETTINE   Small hazelnut-flavoured pastry.

NOIX Walnut; grown on a large scale, especially in *Dauphiné* and *Savoie*, where there is an *AC noix de Grenoble*, and in *Périgord*. Also a liqueur made from walnuts.

Nut. *Noix d'Amérique/du Bresil*: Brazil nut. *Noix d'acajou*: name for cashew nut (*anacarde*). (*Noix de*) *coco*: coconut.

Cushion, topside of veal, also known as *fricandeau*. *Noix pâtissière*: similar cut, also known as *sous-noix*. *Noix de veau à l'aixoise* (Savoie): with carrots, celery, chestnuts, onions; *à la caucasienne*: cold, with anchovy butter and tomato jelly; *à la suédoise*: cold, with tongue, mayonnaise, and horseradish butter.

NOMINOË (Bretagne) Creamy chestnut soup.

NON(N)AT (Provence) Tiny fish, either distinct species or very young *gobies*; deep-fried, or used in soups and omelettes.

NONNE(TTE) Lit.: '(small) nun'. *Nonnette*: small round iced ginger-bread cake, originally made in convents, now manufactured.

(Lorraine) Cream cheese cake. See also *pet de nonne*.

NONPAREIL(-LE) Lit.: 'matchless'. Variety of caper (*câpre*) from *Provence*, considered the best.

Variety of pear.

NOQUE (Alsace) Small *quenelle*. *Potage aux noques*: thickened broth from boiled beef with *noques*.

NORBERTE (Champagne) Plum jam.

NORELLE/NOROLLE (Normandie) Small cake sprinkled with cider.

(À LA) NORMANDE In the style of *Normandie*. With cream. With either or all of *Calvados*, cider, apples. *Sauce normande*: cream and white wine sauce, for fish. Garnish for fish of oysters, mussels, prawns, crayfish, sprats, truffles, mushrooms. *Omelette normande*: omelette with mushrooms, shrimps, sometimes oysters; or sweet omelette with cream, apples and *Calvados*. *Potage normand*: leek, potato and milk soup, perhaps with haricot beans. See also *cauchoise*, *ficelle*, *graisse*, *matelote* and *sole*.

NORMANDIE Normandy, province covering the departments of Manche, *Calvados*, Orne, Eure and Seine-Maritime.

(À LA) NORVÉGIENNE Norwegian-style. *Omelette norvégienne*: sponge cake filled with ice cream and covered with meringue, served hot; also known as *omelette surprise*. See also *saumon*. *Norvégien*: almond cake.

NOUGAT Nougat, soft nut sweet, for which Montélimar in *Dauphiné* is famous; from the Latin *'nux'* – nut/walnut. (S France) Walnut oil cake.

NOUGATINE Small chocolate-iced cake.

NOUILLES Long flat noodles.

NOUILLETTES Small noodles.

NOURET Name for variety of fungus (*pleurote*).

NOUVEAU (NOUVELLE) New. *Salade nouvelle*: warm spinach salad with *foie gras*. See also *primeur*.

NOUVELLE CUISINE Lit.: 'new cooking'. Movement in cookery which is characterized by a lighter, simpler style and the use of fine natural ingredients in such a way as to bring out their true flavours; it may be seen as a reaction to the heavy sauces, fancy garnishes and over-elaborate presentation of classical French cooking. Pioneered by Fernand Point in the 1950s, its major exponents include Bocuse, Chapel, the Troisgros brothers, Outhier, Gaertner, Vergé, and Haeberlin brothers, Girardet, Bise, Senderens, Faugeron, Clerc and Guérard.

Michel Guérard also introduced *cuisine minceur* to the public, with his book of the same name; he showed how slimming could be made compatible with good food by bending the rules of gourmet cooking – replacing fattening with non-fattening, and equally delicious, ingredients, and using smaller portions.

NOUVILLARDS/NOUZILLARD (Périgord, Anjou) Chestnuts with milk or sweet wine.

NOYAU Kernel, stone, of fruit. *Fruits à noyau*: stone fruit (e.g. apricots). *Noyau/crème de noyaux*: sweet liqueur flavoured with crushed kernels of cherries or apricots.

(À LA) NUITONNE In the style of *Nuits-Saint-Georges*. See *jambon*.

NUITS See *Côte de Nuits*.

NUITS-SAINT-GEORGES Major town of *Côtes de Nuits*, and one of the most famous communes of *Bourgogne*, producing fine red wine (*AC*).

NULLE Lit.: 'no one'. Light egg custard.

NUQUE (Périgord) Maize fritter.

NUREIO (Provence) Hard-boiled egg, anchovy and lettuce salad.

NYMPHES   Lit.: 'nymphs'. Name for frog's legs (*grenouilles*). *Nymphes à l'aurore*: poached in white wine, served cold in pink jellied sauce.

 Nymphe des montagnes: name for type of fungus (*faux mousseron*).

OBLADE   Saddled bream, type of sea bream; also known as *blade*.

(À L')OCCITANE   Occitan-style. With tomatoes and garlic. See also *estouffade* and *morue*. Occitan, or the *langue d'oc*, is the old language of S France.

OEDICNÈME   Stone curlew; bird like plover.

OEILLADE   Variety of black table grape.

OELENBERG   (Alsace) Smooth round mild cheese, made at the Abbey of Oelenberg; also known as *Trappiste d'Oelenberg*.

OEUF   Egg. *Oeuf du jour*: new-laid egg. *Oeuf de Pâques*: Easter egg. *Blanc/jaune d'oeuf*: egg white/yolk (see also *oronge*). For egg recipes, see under their distinguishing names (e.g. *oeufs à l'agenaise*: see *agenaise*). Major cooking methods are *oeufs brouillés*: scrambled; *en cocotte*: cooked and served in individual dishes with butter and often cream; *à la coque*: soft-boiled in the shell; *durs*: hard-boiled; *frits*: deep-fried; *mollets*: soft-boiled, shelled and used like poached eggs; *au plat/sur le plat/au miroir*: cooked in butter in a shallow dish, either in the oven or on top of the stove, served in the same dish; *pochés*: poached; *à la poêle*: fried. See also *omelette*.

OFFICIER   Lit.: 'officer'. Name for pout (*tacaud*).

OGNON   Alternative spelling for *oignon* (onion).

OGNONNADE   See *oignonade*.

OIE   Goose; the two main varieties are the common goose, for eating, and the large *Toulouse* or *Strasbourg* goose, specially bred and force-fed for its liver (*foie gras*). *Oie à l'alsacienne*: stuffed with sausage, roasted, with *choucroute*, pork and sausages; *à la flamande*: stuffed, braised with cabbage, carrots and turnips, *à la poitevine*: braised with onions, garlic, tomatoes, wine. See also *civet*, *confit*, *cou*, *langue* and *poitrine*.

OIGNON   Onion, also spelt *ognon*. *Soubise* indicates their presence.

OIGNONADE   Onion stew, also spelt *ognonnade*.

OILLETTE   See *huile*.

OISEAU SANS TÊTE   Lit.: 'headless bird'. See *paupiette*.

OISON   Young goose, gosling.

OLÉRON   See *Ile d'Oléron*.

OLGA   *Consommé Olga*: clear beef soup with celeriac, leeks, carrots and gherkins.

OLIVE   Olive. *Olives cassés* (Provence): cracked olives, steeped in water with salt and fennel.
     Wedge shell, type of clam; also known as *haricot de mer*.

OLIVET BLEU   (Orléanais) Small rich fruity cheese with bluish skin, sometimes wrapped in plane tree leaves; made by dairies, named after the market town.

OLIVET CENDRÉ   (Orléanais) Small firm ash-coated cheese with savoury taste; dairy-made, named after the market town.

OLIVETTE   Name for queen scallop (*pétoncle*).
     Olivette Blanche: variety of white table grape.

OLORON-SAINTE-MARIE   See *Esbareich*.

OLYMPIQUE   (Dauphiné) Walnut cake, created in *Grenoble* in honour of the 1968 Winter Olympics.

OMBLE CHEVALIER   Char, type of salmon, highly esteemed, found in lakes of *Savoie*; also known as *ombre chevalier*.

OMBRE   Lit.: 'shadow'. Grayling, rare freshwater fish similar to large trout. See also *omble chevalier* and *ombrine*.

OMBRINE   Umbrine, fish of meagre (*maigre*) family; also known as *ombre de mer, chrau, daine* and *lumbrina*.

OMELETTE   Omelette, savoury or sweet. See under their distinguishing names for the various types of omelette (e.g. *omelette à la toulonnaise*: see *toulonnaise*). The word is perhaps derived from 'oeufs meslette', from 'mêler' – to mix; or from Old French 'alumette' – tin plate; or from 'lamelle' – blade.

ONGLET   Flank, of beef, often grilled with shallots.

OPÉRA   Lit.: 'opera'. Garnish of chicken livers and asparagus tips. See also *gâteau*.

OPERNE   Small shellfish, eaten especially on the W coast.

OR   Lit.: 'gold'. See *Côte-d'Or* and *palet*.

ORANGE   Orange. *Orange givré*: orange sorbet in orange skin.

ORANGEAT   Candied orange peel.

ORDINAIRE   Ordinary, common. See also *Grand Ordinaire* and *vin*.

OREILLE   Ear, of pig or calf, usually prepared like trotters (*pieds*). Names of varieties of fungus. *Oreille de chardon/d'orme*: for *pleurote* (lit.: 'of thistle/elm'). *Oreille de chat/de Judas*: for *helvelle* (lit.: 'of cat/Judas'). *Oreille de meunier*: for *clitopile* (lit.: 'of miller').

OREILLE DE MER/DE SAINT-PIERRE   Name for ormer (*ormeau*).

OREILLETTE   Small prepared pig's ear, from a *charcuterie*. (Provence) Sweet fritter with orange blossom.

OREILLON   Ear, small ear. Ear-shaped (e.g. halved apricot).

ORGE   Barley. *Soupe d'orge* (Vivarais): barley and vegetable soup.

ORGEAT   Orgeat, sweet drink.

(À L')ORIENTALE   Eastern-style. With rice, saffron, peppers, tomatoes etc and sometimes okra (*gombo*).

ORIGAN   Origanum, oregano, herb.

ORLÉANAIS   Province corresponding to the departments of Loiret, Loir-et-Cher and Eure-et-Loir. Red, white and rosé wines made in Orléanais, known as *Vin de l'Orléanais* (*VDQS*).

(À L')ORLÉANAISE   In the style of *Orléanais*. Garnish of chicory and potatoes. See also *brochet*.

ORLÉANS   Capital of the Loiret department and of *Orléanais*. (*A la d'*) *Orléans*: Duke/Duchess of Orléans-style. *Consommé à la d'Orléans*: clear chicken soup with *quenelles*. See also *chou rouge*.

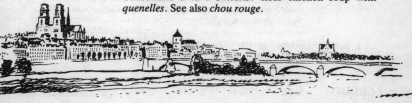

ORLOFF Prince Orloff, ambassador of Czar Nicholas I to France. With creamy onion sauce and cheese.

(À L')ORLY Of fish, filleted, dipped in batter, deep-fried, with tomato sauce.

ORMEAU/ORMIER Ormer, abalone, ear-shaped shellfish; also known as *oreille de mer/de Saint Pierre* and *six-yeux*.

ORONGE Group of fungi of *amanite* family, the most celebrated being *oronge vraie/des Césars*. Caesar's mushroom, found in late summer and autumn, especially in S and E France; varieties also known as *cocon*, *coucoumelle blanche*, *golmotte* and *jaune d'oeuf*.

ORPHIE Name for garfish (*aiguille*).

(LES) ORRYS (Foix) Large firm tangy cheese; made in mountain cottages around Les Orrys.

ORS See *Larron d'Ors*.

ORTIE Nettle, sometimes made into soup.

ORTIE DE MER Name for sea anemone (*anémone de mer*).

ORTOLAN Ortolan, bunting, small bird common in S France, especially in *Landes*, fattened in cages after capture; also known as *bénari*. *Ortolans à la Brissac*: roasted on skewers with ham, plus mushrooms, truffles, fried bread; *à la landaise*: spit-roasted in their own fat.

OS Bone, of meat. *À l'os*: with bone marrow (e.g. *entrecôte à l'os*). See also *tranche*.

OSCIETRE See *caviar*.

OSEILLE Sorrel, bitter spinach-like vegetable.

(L')OSSAU-IRATY-BREBIS-PYRÉNÉES (Béarn, Pays basque) *AOC* cheese, of sheep's milk, large, round with orange rind, pressed, salted, matured for at least 3 months; made by farms and dairies, and named after the Ossau river and Iraty forest. *Petit Ossau-Iraty-Brebis-Pyrénées*: smaller version.

(À L')OSTENDAISE In the style of Ostend, on the Belgian coast. With oysters, sometimes shrimps and mushrooms in cream sauce.

OUBLIE Wafer.

OUILLADE   (Languedoc, Roussillon) Soup of cabbage and haricot beans, cooked in two separate pots ('ouilles') and mixed at the end.

OUILLAT/OULIAT   (Béarn) Onion and garlic soup, with variations including tomatoes, leeks, broad beans, cheese, poured on slices of bread; also known as *soupe du berger* and *tourri*.

OULADE   (Languedoc, Auvergne) Cabbage and potato soup with salt pork and sausage.

OULIAT   See *ouillat*.

OURSIN   Sea urchin, whose corals or ovaries are eaten, either raw with lemon juice, or added to scrambled eggs; also known as *alisson* and *châtaigne de mer*.

OURSINADE   (Provence) Sea urchin soup.

OUSTET   See *Bethmale*.

OUTARDE   Bustard, large land bird, in season in April, usually served roasted; also known as *bastardeau* in *Berry*.

OUVERT(-E)   Open.

OXALIDE   Name for wood sorrel (*surelle*).

OYONNADE   (Bourbonnais) Goose stew with the blood and liver, wine and spirit.

PACHADE   (Auvergne) Sweet omelette with prunes.

PACHERENC DU VIC-BILH   White wine (*AC*), made in *Béarn*.

PAGEAU/PAGEL/PAGEOT   Pandora, type of sea bream; also known as *bézuque*.

PAGRE   Type of Mediterranean sea bream, also known as *acarne*. *Pagre royal*: larger rarer variety, also known as *sar royal*.

PAGURE   Name for hermit crab (*bernard l'hermite*).

PAILLARD   *Paris* restaurant. See *sole*.

PAILLARDE/PAILLARDINE (DE VEAU)   Grilled veal *escalope*.

PAILLASSON   Lit.: 'door-mat'. *Pommes* (*de terre*) *paillasson* (Lyonnais): flat potato cake.

PAILLE   Lit.: 'straw(-coloured)'. *Pommes* (*de terre frites*) *paille*: deep-fried straw potatoes. See also *vin*.

PAILLETTE   Lit.: 'spangle'. *Paillette dorée*: cheese straw. *Paillettes d'oignons frits*: crisp fried onion rings.

(À LA) PAIMPOLAISE   In the style of Paimpol in *Bretagne*. See *morue*.

PAIN   Bread, loaf. *Un pain*: a loaf. *Gros pain*: large crusty loaf, sold by weight. *Petit pain*: bread roll. *Pain d'antan* (Bretagne): keeping bread, of wheat and rye flour. *Pain*

azyme: unleavened bread. *Pain bis*: brown bread. *Pain brié* (Normandie): star-shaped loaf. *Pain brioché*: brioche loaf. *Pain de campagne*: large round white loaf. *Pain complet/entier*: wholemeal bread. *Pain grillé*: toast. *Pain de gruau*: wheaten bread. *Pain de mie*: sandwich loaf. *Pain mousseau*: fine wheaten bread. *Pain perdu*: French toast (lit.: 'lost'). *Pain rassis*: stale bread. *Pain de régime*: diet bread. *Pain de seigle*: rye bread. *Pain viennois*: Vienna loaf.

Cake, flavoured bread. *Pain à l'anis* (Alsace): aniseed-flavoured cake. *Pain doux* (Bretagne, Normandie): sultana bread. *Pain d'épice(s)*: spiced gingerbread. *Pain de Gênes*: Genoa cake.

Savoury loaf, of vegetables, fish etc, puréed, mixed with eggs and breadcrumbs, poached in a mould, served with sauce. *Pain à la reine* (Champagne): pike loaf with crayfish sauce. *Petit pain*: small savoury loaf. *Pain de sucre*: sugar loaf. See also *chicorée*.

PALAILLE/PALAILLETTE   (Nice) Tiny sardines and anchovies (bigger than larval *poutine*).

PALAIS DE BOEUF   Palate of beef, often served cold as *hors d'oeuvre*. *Palais de boeuf à la dunoise*: grilled squares with spicy *vinaigrette*.

(À LA) PALAISE   See *paloise*.

PALANGRE   Fishing line with lots of hooks and feathers; used in descriptions of fish so caught.

(À LA) PALAVASIENNE   In the style of Palavas in *Languedoc*. See *thon*.

PALEFOUR   (Champagne) Bacon tart.

PALERON   Part of the shoulder, of beef.

PALESTINE   Palestine. With Jerusalem artichokes (e.g. *purée Palestine*). See also *homard*.

PALET   Lit.: 'disk'. *Palet de boeuf*: round of minced beef.
Palet de dames: Small thin biscuit topped with a currant. *Palet d'or*: small chocolate.

PALETTE   Small vineyard area near *Aix-en-Provence*, producing red, white and rosé wines (*AC*). Bladebone, of pork etc.

PALMATA   (Corse) Local name for gilt-head bream (*daurade*).

PALMIER   Palm tree; see *coeur de palmier*.
Small sweet pastry puff, in the shape of a heart.

(À LA) PALOISE   In the style of *Pau*; (*à la*) *palaise* is an alternative form. *Sauce paloise*: *béarnaise* sauce flavoured with mint instead of tarragon. See also *tripes*.

PALOMBE Wild pigeon. *Palombes à la béarnaise*: marinated, braised in white wine and brandy, with puréed artichokes and the livers. See also *salmis*.

PALOMET Name for type of fungus (*russule*).

PALOMÈTE/PALOMINE Type of bonito (*bonite*). Or type of meagre (*maigre*).

PALOURDE Clam, carpet-shell; also known as *beuda*, *clam*, *chirlat*, *clovisse*, *coque rayée* and *rigadelle*. *Palourdes farcies* (Touraine, Bretagne): stuffed with shallots, cream and cheese, browned; *à la lorientaise*: cooked with white wine and shallots. See also *fausse palourde* and *verni*.

PALUS Marsh. See *vin*.

PAMPLEMOUSSE Grapefruit.

PANACHÉ(-E) Mixed. *Glace panachée*: mixed ice cream. *Salade panachée*: mixed salad. See also *haricot* and *tarte*. *Panaché*: shandy, also known as *bière limonade*.

PANADE Bread, milk and egg soup. Panada, mixture of eggs, flour, milk or water, for croquettes etc.

PANAIS Parsnip.

PAN BAGNA(T) (Provence) Long loaf or roll soaked in olive oil, filled with onions, anchovies, black olives, peppers, lettuce etc in *vinaigrette*.

PANCHOUSE See *pochouse*.

PAN COUDOUN (Provence) Quince pastry.

PANÉ(-E) Coated in breadcrumbs.

PANETIÈRE Lit.: 'small sideboard'. Cooked food placed in a pastry shell and baked golden (e.g. of small birds, sweetbreads).

PANETTE DOUCE (Corse) Raisin bread, an Easter speciality.

PANIER Basket.

PANISSE/PANISSO (Provence) Fried chick pea or maize cake, eaten with sugar.

PANIZZE (Corse) Chestnut flour cake.

PANNEQUET Pancake, more commonly known as *crêpe* or *galette*.

PANNES CENDRÉ (Orléanais) Thick round ash-coated cheese, very strong; made by farms and dairies around Pannes.

PANOUFLE   Cut of beef, from the sirloin.

PANTIN   Lit.: 'puppet'. Small pork pastry.

PANURE   Breadcrumbs.

PANZAROTTI   (Corse) Lemon cheese fritters.

PAPANAS À LA ROUMAINE   Fried cream cheese.

PAPETON   Corn cob.
    (Provence) Fried aubergines arranged in a crown; perhaps once created for a Pope at *Avignon*, also known as *aubergines des papes*.

PAPILLOTE   Greased paper or tinfoil pouch in which small cuts of meat, fish etc are baked *en papillote*.

PAPRIKA   Paprika, the spice; also known as *piment basquais*.

PÂQUES   Easter. See also *oeuf* and *pâté*.

PAQUETTE   Female lobster (*homard*), with fully formed eggs, highly esteemed.

PARAMÉ   Resort in *Bretagne*. See *hareng* and *poularde*.

PARC   Lit.: 'park'. Oyster bed.

PARFAIT   Lit.: 'perfect'. Rich *mousse*-like cream, usually coffee-flavoured and iced, or sometimes chocolate, praline or vanilla. See also *Fin-de-Siècle*.

PARFAIT-AMOUR   Lit.: 'perfect love'. Highly scented liqueur, usually violet in colour.

PARFUM   Perfume. Flavour of food, especially sorbets, ice creams.

PARILLADE   Mixed fried and grilled fish with garlic. From the Spanish *parillada*.

PARIS   Capital of France, at the heart of *Ile-de-France*. See also *cervelas*, *champignon* and *jambon*.

PARIS-BREST   Large *choux* pastry ring with almonds, butter cream.

PARIS-GÊNES   Lit.: 'Paris-Genoa'. Rich cake layered with rum-flavoured chocolate cream.

(À LA) PARISIENNE   Parisian-style. Garnish for fish, chicken etc of mushrooms, asparagus, truffles with white wine sauce. *Sauce parisienne*: see *allemande*. *Pomme (de terre) à la parisienne*: small nut-shaped sauté potatoes. *Consommé à la parisienne*: clear chicken soup with vegetables.

Potage parisien: vegetable soup. *Omelette à la parisienne*: omelette with onions, mushrooms and small sausages. *Salade parisienne*: cold boiled beef with potatoes, onions, gherkins, parsley and *vinaigrette*; or lobster or salmon salad with thick mayonnaise. See also *bouillabaisse*, *charlotte*, *gâteau*, *gnocchi*, *homard*, *hure*, *melon*, *morue*, *poulet* and *tendron*.
  Variety of walnut (*noix*).

PARME Parma, in Italy. See *jambon*.
  (Provence) Local name for amberjack (*sériole*).

PARMENTIER Antoine-Auguste Parmentier, (1737–1817), economist and writer on food, who converted the French to potatoes, previously thought to be dangerous. With potatoes. *Hachis Parmentier*: similar to shepherd's pie. *Potage Parmentier*: potato and leek soup. *Pommes (de terre) Parmentier*: cubed potatoes cooked in butter. See also *mousseline*.

(À LA) PARMESANE With Parmesan cheese.

PARSAC-SAINT-ÉMILION Outlying part of *Saint-Emilion*, *Bordeaux*, making red wines (*AC*).

PARTHENAY See *Jonchée*.

PASCADE (Auvergne, Rouergue) Sweet or savoury pancake.

PASCADO (Provence) Bacon omelette.

PASCAL(-E) Of Easter (*Pâques*). *Soupe pascale* (Provence): beef and chicken soup with eggs. See also *agneau*.

PASCALINE DE POULET Chicken and cheese *quenelle* with white sauce and truffles.

PASSARELLE Dried *Muscat* grape; from 'passarillage' – process of turning the grapes into raisins.

PASSE-CRASSANE Variety of pear.

PASSE-L'AN (Quercy) Large round hard yellow cheese, cured for at least 2 years (lit.: 'pass the year'), strongly flavoured; made by dairies, imitation of Italian Parmesan.

PASSE-PIERRES Lit.: 'pass-stones'. Type of seaweed, often pickled in vinegar in N France; also known as *cornichon de mer*.

PASSE-POMME Variety of apple.

PASSÉ(-E) Sieved, strained. Percolated. Lightly fried.

PASSE-TOUT-GRAINS Lit.: 'pass-all-grapes'. Red wine (*AC*) made in *Bourgogne* from mixed *Pinot Noir* and *Gamay* grapes.

PASTEGUE   Name for sea anemone (*anémone de mer*).

PASTÈQUE   Water melon.

PASTEURISÉ(-E)   Pasteurized, of milk, cheese.

PASTILLE   Small sweet (e.g. *pastille au miel*: honey drop).

PASTIS   Liquorice-flavoured aperitif, similar to *anis*; brands include *Berger* and *Ricard*.
    (Pays basque, Béarn) Yeast cake flavoured with orange blossom.
    (Gascogne) Prune pastry flavoured with orange blossom water and *Armagnac*; or apple pie with flaky pastry.
    (*Lou*) *pastis* (*en pott*) (SW France): pork and beef stewed with new red wine, repeatedly reheated and replenished.

PASTISSOUN   (Provence) Small pastry flavoured with orange blossom water; also known as *pâté de Beaucaire*.

PASTIZA   Name for *gâteau basque*.

PASTIZZU   (Corse) Macaroni with meat sauce.

(À LA) PASTOURELLE   Lit.: 'shepherd's style'. *Potage pastourelle*: leek, potato and mushroom soup. *Salade pastourelle* (Auvergne): green salad with herbs, cream blue cheese.

PATACLÉ   (S France) Local name for type of sea bream (*sparaillon*).

PATATE   Sweet potato, root similar to yam.
    Slang word for potato, spud.

PÂTE   Pastry; dough; batter. *Pâte brisée*: short (lit.: 'broken') pastry; *à chou*: choux; *feuilletée*: flaky, puff; *frolle*: almond; *levée*: yeast (lit.: 'raised'); *sablée/sucrée*: sweet crumbly.
    Paste. *Pâte d'amandes*: almond paste. *Pâte de coings*: name for quince paste (*cotignac*). *Pâte de fruits*: fruit jelly. *Pâte de guimauve*: marshmallow sweet.
    Pâte (*alimentaires*): pasta, noodles.

PÂTÉ    Pâté, rich mixture of meat, especially pork, game or fish, baked in a *terrine* or earthenware dish (correctly *pâté en terrine* and the same as *terrine*), or in a pastry case (*pâté en croûte*), usually eaten cold. Of 2 major kinds – coarse and crumbly (e.g. *pâté de campagne*: of pork, with herbs, mushrooms, pepper); and smooth (e.g. usually *pâté maison*: of pig's liver, fat pork, veal, with garlic, spices, brandy). *Pâté d'Angoulême/de Chartres*: partridge; *à la beauceronne/de Pithiviers*: lark, sometimes in pastry; *de Pâques* (Poitou): pork, chicken or rabbit with hard-boiled eggs; *vendéen*: rabbit.

Pastry, pie. *Petit pâté*: small pastry, patty. *Pâté de Beaucaire*: see *pastissoun*; *aux poires* (Bourgogne): pear tart; *de pommes de terre* (central France): potato pie with bacon, perhaps veal, and onions and cream, also known as *pâté bourbonnais/de tr(e)uffles/au tartouffe*; *à la viande sucré* (Languedoc): meat pastry with sugar and lemon peel, also known as *petit pâté de Pézenas*.

PATELLE   Limpet, small shellfish usually boiled or fried; also known as *alapedo*, *arapède*, *barnache*, *bassin*, *bernache*, *berniche*, *chapeau chinois*, *flie*, *jamble* and *venis*.

PATIENCE   Lit.: 'patience'. Dock, wild plant sometimes made into soup.

PÂTISSERIE   Pastries, cakes etc. Shop selling these. Art of pastry-making.

PÂTISSIER (PÂTISSIÈRE)   Pastry cook. To do with pastry-making. See also *crème* and *noix*.

PÂTISSON   Custard marrow, squash.

PATRANQUE/PATRENQUE   (Auvergne) Fried flat cake of bread-crumbs and cheese.

PATRICIEN   Lit.: 'nobleman'. (Nivernais) Almond meringue filled with chestnuts and rum.

PATRON   Patron. Proprietor, of a hotel.

PATTE   Paw; foot; leg. *Pattes rouges*: large imported crayfish (*écrevisses*) with red claws.

PAU   Capital of the Pyrénées-Atlantiques department, and of *Béarn*.

PAUCHOUSE   See *pochouse*.

PAUILLAC   Commune (*AC*) of *Haut-Médoc*, *Bordeaux*, containing many famous red wine vineyards (e.g. Lafite, Latour, Mouton-Rothschild, Lynch-Bages).

PAULINE   See *côte* (*de veau*).

PAUPIETTE   Beef/veal olive – a thin slice stuffed, rolled and braised; also known as *alouette/oiseau sans tête*. Rolled fillet of fish, especially *sole*.

PAUVRE HOMME   Lit.: 'poor man'. With onion, vinegar, mustard and tomato sauce.

PAVÉ   Lit.: 'paving stone'. Square type of cake (e.g. *pavé de Chartres*: spice bread).

Cold savoury mousse or similar set in a square mould. Thick slice of beef steak. *Pavé Villette*: fillet steak. See also below.

PAVÉ DE MOYAUX/D'AUGE (Normandie) Firm spicy slab-shaped cheese with yellow rind; made by farms and dairies in Auge, named after village of Moyaux, and also known as *Carré de Bonneville*.

PAVIE Clingstone peach.

PAVOT Poppy, also known as *coquelicot*. *Graines de pavot*: poppy seeds. See also *tourte*.

(EL) PA Y ALL (Roussillon) Slice of bread, fresh or fried, rubbed with garlic and olive oil.

PAYS Country, region. See also *jambon* and *vin*.

(À LA) PAYSANNE Lit.: 'peasant-style'. With vegetables, especially onions and carrots, sometimes bacon. *Potage paysanne*: mixed vegetable soup. *Pommes (de terre) à la paysanne*: sliced potatoes baked in stock with herbs and garlic. See also *tourte*.

PAYS BASQUE The Basque country, province covering about one third of the Pyrénées-Atlantiques department.

PAYS D'AUGE See *Auge*.

PAYS DE FOIX See *Foix*.

PEAU (pl. PEAUX) Skin. *Peau de goret*: pig's skin; see also *porcelet*. *Omelette aux peaux de canard*: omelette with bits of duck skin.

PÈBRE D'AI/D'AS/D'AZE (Provence) Local name for summer savory (*sarriette*). See also *Poivre d'Ane*.

PEBRONATA (DE BOEUF) (Corse) Beef stew with white wine and spicy tomato sauce.

PEC See *hareng*.

PÉCHARMANT District of *Bergerac* in *Périgord*, known for red wines (*AC*).

PÊCHE Peach, either white (*pêche blanche*) or yellow-fleshed (*pêche-abricot*, *pêche jaune/abricotée*). *Pêches Aiglon*: cold, poached, with ice cream; *Alexandra*: same, plus puréed strawberries; *aurore*: on strawberry *mousse*; *dame-blanche*: cold, poached, with ice cream, pineapple and whipped cream; *Maintenon*: hot, on sponge cake with meringue; *Melba*: cold, on ice cream with raspberry

purée; *Mistral*: cold, with puréed strawberries, almonds and whipped cream; *Pénélope*: with strawberry *mousse*; *à la royale* (Touraine): in creamy sauce.
Fishing, angling.

PÉCHÉ Lit.: 'sin'. Description for something tempting, delicacy etc.

PÊCHEUR Lit.: 'fisherman'. *Oeufs du pêcheur*: poached eggs with mussel stock. See also *civet* and *daurade*.

PEÏ (S France) Local name for various fish. *Peï coua*: corb. *Peï furco*: armed gurnard (*malarmat*). *Peï rei*: meagre (*maigre*).

PEIGNE Lit.: 'comb'. Name for scallop (*coquille Saint-Jacques*).

PELAMIDE Name for bonito (*bonite*).

PÉLARDON DES CÉVENNES (Languedoc) Small soft white goat's milk cheese with nutty flavour; made on farms in *Cévennes*, also known as *Pélardon d'Altier/d'Anduze/de Ruoms*.

PÉLERINE Lit.: 'pilgrim'. Name for scallop (*coquille Saint-Jacques*). *A la pélerine*: with scallops.

PÉLOU (Provence) Local name for small crab (*ériphie*).

PELURE D'OIGNON Lit.: 'onion skin'. Description for the colour of wine, rosé with a tawny tinge.

PELUSSIN See *Rigotte de Pelussin*.

PELVOUX See *Tomme de Chèvre*.

PÉNÉLOPE See *pêche*.

PEPPERPOT (Flandre) Mutton and pork stew with beer and vegetables.

PÉRAL (Rouergue) Sheep's milk cheese ripened in straw.

PERCE-PIERRE Lit.: 'pierce-stone'. Name for samphire (*bacile*).

PERCEUR Lit.: 'driller'. Small type of murex (*rocher*).

PERCHE Region bordering *Orléanais* and *Normandie*, once known for Percheron horses.
Perch, considered one of the best freshwater fish.
(*Perche*) *goujonnière*: name for pope (*gremille*).

PERCHE DE MER Name for sea bass (*bar*). Or name for type of comber (*serran*).

(À LA) PERCHERONNE   In the style of *Perche*. *Oeufs à la percheronne*: hard-boiled eggs and potatoes in white sauce.

PERCHETTE/PERCHOT   Young river perch.

PERDREAU   Young partridge. *Perdreau Alexis*: pot-roasted with grapes; *à la coque* (Orléanais): stuffed with *foie gras*, cooked in stock; *Lautrec*: split, flattened, grilled with mushrooms and parsley butter; *à la limousine*: stuffed with *cèpes* and chicken livers, casseroled; *Marly*: baked with mushrooms.

PERDRIX   Adult partridge. *Perdrix à l'auvergnate*: stewed in white wine; *à la catalane*: stewed in white wine with peppers and bitter oranges.

PÈRE LATHUILE   *Paris* restaurant, painted by Manet. See *poulet*.

PÈRE TRANQUILLE   Lit.: 'tranquil Father', perhaps a Capuchin monk. *Soupe du Père Tranquille*: lettuce soup; from the supposedly soporific effect of lettuce.

PÉRIGORD   Province based on *Dordogne*; sometimes loosely includes *Quercy* and *Agenais* to the south.

(À LA) PÉRIGOURDINE   In the style of *Périgord*. With truffles, sometimes *foie gras* as well. See also *cèpe*, *lièvre* and *fricassée*.

PÉRIGUEUX   Capital of the *Dordogne*, and of *Périgord*. *Sauce Périgueux*: truffle and madeira sauce. See also *foie gras*.

PÉRINETTE   See *côtelette*.

PERLANT(-E)   Lit.: 'in pearls', 'drops'. Slightly sparkling, of wine; the same as *perlé*.

PERLE   Lit.: 'pearl'. *Perles du Japon*: tapioca. *Perles du Périgord*: fanciful name for truffles.

PERLÉ(-E)   Lit.: 'polished', 'beaded'. Having a very slight sparkle, of wine; the same as *perlant*.

PERLON   Name for tub gurnard (*grondin galinette*).

PERLOT   (Normandie) Local name for small oyster.

PERNAND-VERGELESSES   Small commune of *Côte de Beaune*, *Bourgogne*, making red and white wines (*AC*), and containing part of two *grand cru* vineyards, *Corton* and *Corton-Charlemagne*.

PERNOD   Famous makers of *anis* and *pastis*, and the original inventors of *absinthe*.

PERNOLLET   *Salade Pernollet*: crayfish and truffle salad with mayonnaise.

PERPIGNAN   Capital of the Pyrénées-Orientales department, and of *Roussillon*.

PERRIER   Brand of sparkling mineral water from Vergèze in *Provence*; the sparkle comes from natural carbon dioxide gas obtained separately at the source and reintroduced during bottling.

(À LA) PERSANE   Persian-style. See *côtelette* and *sole*.

PERSIL   Parsley, the herb. *Persil commun*: single-leaved parsley. *Persil frisé*: curly parsley. *Persil à grosse racine*: turnip rooted parsley, vegetable.

PERSILLADE   Mixture of finely chopped parsley with shallot or garlic, added to various dishes.

PERSILLÉ(-E)   Sprinkled with parsley; parsleyed, e.g. *jambon persillé*.
  Marbled, with fat, of meat.
  Blue-veined, of cheese; see below.

PERSILLÉ DES ARAVIS   (Savoie) Tall cylindrical blue goat's milk cheese, supple to firm, very strong; made by farms and dairies in the Massif des *Aravis*, also known as (*Persillé du*) *Grand-Bornand* and *Persillé de Thônes*.

PERSILLÉ DU MONT-CENIS   (Savoie) Smooth strong blue cheese of cow's and goat's milk; made by farms and dairies in the *Mont-Cenis* region.

PERSILLÉ DE TIGNES/DE THÔNES   See *Bleu de Tignes* and *Persillé des Aravis*.

PESCAJOU   (Languedoc) Sweet pancake.

PESCIU GATTU   (Corse) Local name for dogfish (*roussette*).

PÉTAFINE   (Dauphiné) Cow's or goat's milk mixed with oil and brandy.

PET DE NONNE   (Lorraine especially) Lit.: 'nun's fart'. Small soufflé fritter; also known as *soupir de nonne* (lit.: 'nun's sigh').

PETERAM   (Bigorre, Languedoc) Stew of sheep's trotters and tripe, ham, vegetables and *Gaillac* wine.

PÉTILLANT(-E)   Slightly sparkling, of wine especially.

PETIT(-E)   Small, little.

PETIT BEURRE   Small dry biscuit.

PETIT-CHABLIS   See *Chablis*.

PETIT DÉJEUNER   Lit.: 'little lunch'. Breakfast.

PETIT-DUC   Lit.: 'little duke'. Garnish of mushrooms, perhaps truffles, with wine sauce.
  Cold dessert of poached peaches or pears with nuts, ice cream and jam.

PETITE CHAMPAGNE   See *Cognac*.

PETITE LINGUE   Name for rockling (*mostèle*).

PETITE-MARIÉE   Lit.: 'little bride'. See *poularde*.

PETITE MARMITE   Lit.: 'little pot'. Clear meat and vegetable soup, served in a small *marmite*.

PETITES   (Languedoc) Local name for mutton or veal tripe.

PETITES FONDUES   See *fondue*.

PETIT FOUR   Lit.: 'little oven'. Small biscuit, miniature sponge cake, often almond-flavoured, and including *cigarettes russes*, *tuiles*, *palets de dames*, etc. General term for these, plus sweets and candied fruits, served at the end of a meal.

PETIT GRIS   Lit.: 'small grey'. Small snail, known locally under many different names.
  Name for *chanterelle*.

PETIT-HOUX   Lit.: 'small holly'. Butcher's broom, shrub whose shoots are sometimes eaten; also known as *houx-frélon*.

PETIT LAIT   Whey, of milk.

PETIT LISIEUX   (Normandie) Small round cheese with glossy red rind, strong smell and flavour, packed in rushes; made by farms and dairies around Lisieux, one of the oldest cheeses of *Normandie*, also known as *Demi-Livarot*.

PETIT MARCELLIN   (Ile de France) Small almond pastry.

PETIT PAIN   Bread roll. Small savoury loaf.

PETIT PÂTÉ   Small pastry, patty.

PETIT PIED BLEU   Lit.: 'small blue foot'. Name for variety of fungus (*tricholome*).

PETIT POIS   Small young green garden peas; usual menu description for peas. *Petits pois à la française*: cooked with lettuce, small onions, parsley, butter, sugar.

PETIT POT DE CRÈME   See *pot-au-crème*.

PETIT POUSSIN   See *poussin*.

PETIT SALÉ   Salt pork, also known as *lard salé*.
Lightly salted roast pork, ready-prepared at a *charcuterie*.

PETIT-SUISSE   Lit.: 'little Swiss'. Fresh soft unsalted cheese of pasteurized milk and cream, packed in tiny cylindrical containers, usually eaten with fruit or sugar; invented in 1850 by a farmer's wife and Swiss cowherd in *Bray*, now made throughout France.

PETITS VENTRES   (Limousin) Lit.: 'little bellies'. Stuffed mutton belly.

PÉTONCLE   Queen scallop, smaller than the usual kind; also known as *cillette*, *olivette*, *vanneau* and *vanette*.

PETRO   (Provence) Local name for scaldfish (*fausse limande*).

(À LA) PÉTROCORIENNE   In the style of *Périgueux*.

PÉZENAS   Town in *Languedoc*. See *pâté*.

PFAMKUCHEN   (Alsace) Clear meat broth with eggs, onions, spinach and raisins.

PFLÜTTEN/PFLÜTTER   (Alsace) Small fried potato squares.

(À LA) PHARAONNE   Lit.: 'Pharaoh's style'. See *pintade*.

PHOLIOTE   Type of fungus, thick and orange, esteemed in S France; also known as *pivoulade*.

PHOLLADE   Shellfish, tough and tasteless but sometimes eaten in *Bordelais*, where it is also known as *gîte*.

PIBAL(L)ES   (Bordelais, Charentes) Local name for tiny young eels, usually fried.

PIBRONATA   (Corse) Spicy sauce, for meat etc.

PICADOU   (Périgord) Very strong sheep's or goat's milk cheese, wrapped in leaves and aged in crocks with wine or brandy.

PICANCHÂGNE/PIQUENCHÂGNE   (Bourbonnais) Pear tart.

(À LA) PICARDE   In the style of *Picardie*. *Soufflé picard*: leek soufflé. See also *ficelle* and *flet*.

PICARDIE   Picardy, province roughly covering the Somme department; loosely it includes *Artois*, *Boulonnais* and the *Cambrai* region.

PICAREL   Name for picarel (*mendole*).

PICAUT   (Normandie) Local name for turkey (*dindon*).

PICHEREL   Aniseed-flavoured spirit, a speciality of *Bretagne*.

PICHET   Jug, pitcher.

PICHOLINE   Large long olive.

PICODON   Name for family of cheeses with piquant flavour; see below.

PICODON DE DIEULEFIT   (Dauphiné) Small round goat's milk cheese soaked in white wine, with orange rind and sharp flavour; made by farms around Dieulefit.

PICODON DE L'ARDÈCHE   (Vivarais) *AOC* goat's milk cheese, small and circular with a natural flowery flavour; sold loose.

PICODON DE SAINT-AGRÈVE   (Vivarais) Small round strong goat's milk cheese; made by farms around Saint-Agrève.

PICODON DE VALRÉAS   (Provence) Small round semi-fresh goat's milk cheese; made by farms around Valréas.

PICON   Brand of aperitif, wine and spirit based, flavoured with orange and gentian; also known as *Amer Picon*.

PICOUS(S)EL/PIQUE-AOUSEL   (Rouergue) Meat *pâté*.

PICPOUL   Variety of white grape, grown mainly in the *Midi*.

PIÈCE DE BOEUF   Top rump, of beef, also known as *aiguillette* and *pointe de culotte*. *Pièce de boeuf à la Noailles*: larded, marinated, braised with red wine, brandy and onions, served with rice; *à la royale*: served cold in jelly.

PIECH   (Nice) Brisket of mutton or veal stuffed with rice and chard (*blette*).

PIED   Foot. Trotter, usually of sheep or pig, which may be bought ready prepared from a *charcuterie*. *Pieds de mouton à la rouennaise*: stuffed sheep's trotters, fried or grilled; *à la cherbourgeoise*: cooked slowly with onions and carrots. See also *Sainte-Menehould*.
    Head, of celery, lettuce etc. Stalk.

PIED DE MOUTON BLANC   Name for variety of fungus (*hydne*).

PIED-DE-CHEVAL   Lit.: 'horse's hoof'. Type of large oyster (*huître*), especially from Bassin de *Thau*.

PIEDS ET PAQUETS   (Provence) Mutton tripe rolled into packets, cooked with sheep's trotters and tomatoes in white wine.

PIEMONTA (Corse) Braised beef with juniper berries.

(À LA) PIÉMONTAISE In the style of Piedmont, N Italy. Garnish of white truffles, rice or maize, with tomato sauce and Parmesan cheese.

PIERRE-CHAPELLE See *Saint-Pierre*.

PIERRE-LE-GRAND Peter the Great of Russia. *Potage Pierre-le-Grand*: cream soup of mushrooms or celeriac.

PIERRE-QUI-VIRE (Bourgogne) Flat round cheese on straw with reddish rind, strong smell and taste, also eaten fresh; made at the Abbey of La Pierre-Qui-Vire. See also *Boulete de La Pierre-Qui-Vire*.

PIERREVERT See *Coteaux de Pierrevert*.

PIERRE-SUR-HAUTE See *Fourme de Pierre-sur-Haute*.

PIÈTRE (Normandie) Local name for sandsmelt (*athérine*).

PIEUVRE (W France) Local name for octopus (*poulpe*). *Pieuvre à la cocotte*: stewed in oil and white wine with shallots, garlic, tomatoes.

PIGEON Pigeon. See also *colombe*, *palombe* and *ramier*.

PIGEONNEAU Squab, young pigeon; menu description for pigeon. *Pigeonneau Gauthier*: 15 days to 3 weeks old pigeon, strangled.

PIGNON (DE PIN) Pine kernel, used especially in the cooking of *Landes* and *Provence*.

PIGOUILLE (Charentes, Poitou) Small fresh creamy white cheese on straw, of sheep's, goat's or cow's milk; it is a dialect word.

PILAF/PILAU/PILAW Dish of savoury rice. *Pilau à la marseillaise*: rice with seafood.

PILÉE (Bourbonnais) Lit.: 'crushed'. Oat and milk porridge.

PILET Pintail duck, small type of mallard.

PILLEVERJUS See *côte*.

PILON Drumstick, of poultry.

PILOT CANTEUX (Boulonnais) Name for whelk (*buccin*).

PILPIL (Pays basque) Salt cod with garlic.

PIMENT Capsicum, pepper. *Piment doux/basquais*: name for sweet pepper (*poivron*); see also *paprika*. *Piment fort rouge*: hot red pepper, chilli.

PIMENTÉ(-E)   Hot, spicy.

PIMPE(R)NEAU   (Bretagne) Local name for eel (*anguille*).

PIMPERNELLE   Salad burnet, slightly bitter salad green. See also *chou-fleur*.

PIN   Pine tree. See *champignon* and *pignon*.

PINAOU   (S France) Local name for grey gurnard (*grondin gris*).

PINCE   Claw, of lobster, crab.

PINEAU DE LA LOIRE   Name for *Chenin Blanc* grape variety.

PINEAU DES CHARENTES   Aperitif (*AC*) made in *Charentes* from fresh grape juice and *Cognac*.

PINÉE   Best quality dried cod.

PINOT   Variety of grape. *Pinot Blanc*: white grape grown in *Alsace*. *Pinot Chardonnay*: name for *Chardonnay* grape. *Pinot Gris*: grape grown in *Alsace*, where it is known as *Tokay d'Alsace*. *Pinot Noir*: black grape responsible for the great red wines of *Bourgogne* and important in *Champagne*; also grown in *Alsace* for light red or rosé wines.

PINSON ROYAL   Name for hawfinch (*gros-bec*).

PINTADE   Guinea fowl. *Pintade pharaonne* (Quercy): stuffed with truffles, roasted, flamed with spirit and served on fried bread with foie gras.

PINTADEAU   Young guinea fowl.

PINU   (Languedoc) Small aniseed cake.

PIOCHON/PIOCHOU   (Anjou) Small green cabbage.

PIPÉRADE   (Pays basque) Fluffy omelette or scrambled eggs with tomatoes, peppers, onions, often served with sliced *Bayonne* ham.

PIQUANT(-E)   Pungent; piquant; spicy. *Sauce piquante*: white wine sauce with vinegar, shallots, capers, gherkins, tarragon.

PIQUÉ(-E)   Spiked (with), larded.

PIQUE-AOUSEL   See *picousel*.

PIQUENCHÂGNE See *picanchâgne*.

PIQUE-NIQUE Picnic.

PIRE *Sauce de pire* (Alsace): pork lungs cooked in white wine and bound with blood.

PIROJKI Little savoury pies or croquettes; of Russian origin.

(À LA) PIRON Alexis Piron, 18th-century poet, native of *Dijon*. See *lièvre*.

PIROT (Poitou) Sautéed goat with garlic and sorrel.

(À LA) PISANE In the style of Pisa in Italy. See *sardine*.

(À LA) PISCÉNOISE In the style of *Pézenas*.

PISLICINE (Corse) Yeast cake with chestnuts and aniseed.

PISSALA/PISSALAT (Provence) Puréed anchovies with cloves, sometimes oil.

PISSALADIÈRE/PISSALADINA (NIÇOISE) (Provence) Flat open tart filled with onion, anchovies, black olives, sometimes tomatoes, like a pizza.

PISSALAT See *pissala*.

PISSALOT (Provence) Cold anchovy sauce.

PISSENLIT Lit.: 'piss-in-the-bed', alluding to the plant's diuretic qualities, Dandelion, also known as *dent-de-lion*, *grouin d'âne* and *laitue de chien*. *Salade de pissenlits au lard*: dandelion leaf salad with cubes of hot bacon, sometimes fried bread, and vinegar.

PISTACHE   Pistachio nut.
(*En*) *pistache* (Languedoc, Roussillon): leg or shoulder of mutton braised with ham, vegetables, white wine and fifty cloves of garlic, often served with white haricot beans; also known as (*à la*) *catalane*, sometimes applied to partridge or pigeon.

PISTICCHINI   (Corse) Chestnut soufflé.

PISTILS   (Provence) Flaky pastry filled with sheep's cheese, covered with cream and chopped mint and served warm.

PISTOLE   Type of prune (*pruneau*) from *Orléanais*.

PISTOU   (Nice) Local name for basil (*basilic*).
Sauce of basil, garlic and olive oil, sometimes tomato and cheese; adapted from 'pesto' sauce of Genoa in Italy. *Soupe au pistou*: vegetable soup similar to Italian 'minestrone', usually French and haricot beans, onions, potatoes, tomatoes, courgettes, and pasta, served with *pistou* mixed in or separately, and grated cheese.

PITHIVIERS   Town in *Orléanais*.
Rich puff pastry cake filled with almond- and rum-flavoured cream; in full *gâteau de Pithiviers feuilletée*. See also *pâté* and *Bondaroy au foin*.

PITTARA   (Pays basque) Dry cider.

PIVERUNATA   (Corse) Goat stew with peppers.

PIVOULADE   (S France) Local name for type of fungus (*pholiote*).

PLAISIR   Lit.: 'pleasure'. Small cone-shaped wafer.

PLANCHE   Board, platter. *Planche de charcuterie*: plate of assorted cold meats.

PLANTE   Plant. *Plantes potagères*: pot vegetables.

PLAT   Dish, literally and figuratively. Course, of a meal. *Plat du jour*: today's speciality, dish of the day.
Sur le plat: cooked in a shallow dish, either in the oven or on top of the stove, served in the same dish (e.g. *oeufs/sole sur le plat*).
Plat(-e): flat. Plain, of water.
Plate: relatively flat oyster; see also *huître*.

PLAT-DE-CÔTES   Flank, of beef, pork.

PLATEAU   Large platter, tray (also plateau). *Plateau de fruits de mer*: seafood platter. *Plateau à/de fromages*: cheese-board.

PLEUROTE   Family of fungi which grow on trees and bushes, with white firm flesh, the most highly esteemed called oyster mushroom; varieties also known as *nouret* and *oreille de chardon/d'orme*.

PLIE (FRANCHE)   Plaice; also known as *carrelet*.

(À LA) PLOËRMELAISE   In the style of Ploërmel in *Bretagne*. See *anguille*.

PLOMBIÈRES   Spa in *Lorraine*, and site of meeting between *Cavour* and Napoleon III, which perhaps led to the creation of the ice cream; see *glace*.

P'LOUSE   (Boulonnais) Local name for pout (*tacaud*).

PLUCHE   Small leaf (e.g. of chervil, parsley).

PLUVIER   Plover, type of wading bird; also known as *arpenteur*. *Pluvier guignard*: name for dotterel (*guignard*).

POCHADE   (Savoie) Stew of lake fish with crayfish, raisins, carrots.

POCHÉ(-E)   Poached.

POCHETEAU   Skate, deep-sea fish (technically different from *raie*: ray); also known as *raie capucin/grise*, *tire* and *tyre*.

POCHOUSE/PÔCHOUSE   (Bourgogne) Freshwater fish stew, of eel, burbot (*lotte*), bream etc with garlic and white wine; a speciality of a small area south of *Dijon*, also known as *panchouse* and *pauchouse*, probably from the fisherman's 'poche' or game bag.

(À LA) PODOTE   See *ponote*.

POÊLE   Stove.
  Frying pan. *Oeufs à la poêle*: fried eggs.
  See also *gâteau*.

POÊLÉ(-E)   Pot-roasted on a bed of vegetables, usually for tender cuts of meat.

POÊLON   Round casserole with lid, usually earthenware, for pot-roasting.

POGNE (DE ROMANS)   (Dauphiné) Large *brioche* cake filled with fruit, especially pumpkin, or jam.

POGNON   (Bourgogne) Flat cake.

POINGCLOS   Lit.: 'closed fist'. (Bretagne) Local name for large crab (*tourteau*).

(À) POINT   Medium-done, of steak. Just right for eating, of cheese. Ripe, of fruit.

POINTE   Tip. *Pointe d'asperge*: asparagus tip. *Pointe de culotte*: see *pièce de boeuf*.

POIRAT   (Berry) Pear tart.

POIRE  Pear. *Poires Alma*: poached in port; *belle-angevine*: cold, poached in red wine, or stuffed with ice cream; *(belle-)-Hélène*: cold, poached, with ice cream and hot chocolate sauce; *Brillat-Savarin*: hot, on rum-soaked sponge; *Madeleine*: with sponge, apricot jam and whipped cream; *Montreuil*: cold, poached, with ice cream, puréed apricots and raspberries; *religieuse*: cold, poached, with chocolate cream; *Richelieu*: poached in red wine, cold with redcurrant jelly and whipped cream; *Savoie*: cooked in cream; *vigneronne* (Bourgogne): poached in red wine and sugar. *Poires tapées* (Touraine): dried pears.

POIRÉ   Fermented pear juice, perry.

POIREAU   Leek. *Poireaux à la niçoise*: stewed in oil with tomatoes and garlic.

POIRE DE TERRE   Name for Jerusalem artichoke (*topinambour*).

POIRÉE (À CARDE)   Name for chard (*blette*).

POIRE WILLIAMS   Colourless pear spirit, speciality of *Alsace*.

POIS   Peas. See also *petit pois*. *Clamart* and *Saint-Germain* indicate the presence of green peas.
   Pois gourmands/princesse: *mange-tout* peas.
   Pois cassés: split peas.
   Pois chiches: chick peas (lit.: 'stingy'). *Pois chiches à la catalane*: with spicy sausages, tomatoes and garlic.

POISSON(S)   Fish.

POISSON JUIF   Lit.: 'Jewish fish'. Name for *corb*.

POISSON LIMON   Name for amberjack (*sériole*).

POISSON LUNE   Moonfish, large, rare Atlantic fish; also known as *poisson royal*.

POISSONNAILLE   Name for fry, young fish (*fretin*).

POISSONNERIE   Fishmonger's, fish shop.

POISSONIER (POISSONNIÈRE)   Fishmonger. Fish chef.
   Poissonnière: fish kettle.

POISSON PILOTE   Pilot fish, like mackerel; also known as *fanfre*.

POISSON ROYAL   See *poisson lune*.

POISSON SAUTEUR   Lit.: 'jumping fish'. Name for grey mullet (*mulet*).

POISSON VOLANT   Flying fish, also known as *exocet* and *hirondelle de mer*.

(À LA) POITEVINE   In the style of *Poitou*. *Salade poitevine*: haricot bean and lamb's lettuce (*mâche*) salad. See also *bifteck*, *chou*, *farci* and *oie*.

POITIERS   Capital of the Vienne department and of *Poitou*.

POITOU   Province equivalent to the Vienne and Deux-Sèvres departments. See *beurre*.

POITRINE   Breast, of lamb, veal etc; brisket, of beef. *Poitrine de mouton farcie à l'ariégeoise*: mutton breast stuffed with ham, cooked with white wine and vegetables, plus stuffed cabbage and potatoes. *Poitrine d'oie fumée* (Alsace): smoked goose breast, sold ready-prepared and eaten cold, often with *choucroute*. *Poitrine de veau farcie* (Gascogne): veal breast stuffed with sausage and herbs, cooked with vegetables; *farcie niçoise*: stuffed with salt pork, chicken livers, spinach, cheese etc, served cold with tomatoes and black olives.

(À LA) POIVRADE   With pepper and salt. *Sauce poivrade*: vinegar, marinade and pepper sauce, for hare or venison; or peppery *vinaigrette*.

POIVRE   Pepper. *Poivre blanc*: white pepper; *de Cayenne*: cayenne; *en grains*: whole peppercorns; *gris/noir*: black; *de la Jamaïque*: allspice, also known as *tout-épice*; *moulu/ en poudre*: ground; *rose/rouge*: red; *vert*: green peppercorns. See also *steak*.

POIVRÉ   Peppered, spicy. See also *menthe*.

POIVRE D'ÂNE   Lit.: 'donkey's pepper'. (Provence) Local name for savoury (*sarriette*), also known in dialect as *pèbre d'ai/ d'as/d'aze*. *Banon* cheese flavoured with savory; also known as (*Banon au*) *Pèbre d'Ai/d'As/d'Aze*.

POIVRETTE   Name for savory (*sarriette*).

POIVRON   Sweet pepper, red or green; also known as *piment basquais/doux*.

POJARSKI/POJARSKY   False cutlet, finely chopped meat or fish shaped into a cutlet, fried (e.g. *côte de veau Pojarski*, *côtelette de saumon Pojarski*).

POLENTA/POLENTE   (Nice) Maize meal porridge, with butter and grated cheese.
  Polenta di castagne (Corse): chestnut flour.

POLIGNAC   Reactionary minister of the early 19th century. Garnish of mushrooms and truffles.

(À LA) POLONAISE   Polish-style. Of vegetables (e.g. cauliflower, asparagus), cooked, sprinkled with chopped hard-boiled egg, breadcrumbs and parsley, finished with melted butter; sometimes applied to chicken etc. *Salade polonaise*: herring and vegetable salad with gherkins and hard-boiled eggs. See also *carpe* and *champignon*.
  Polonais: hot *brioche* layered with almond filling and candied fruit, covered in meringue.

POMEROL   Important red wine area (*AC*) of *Bordeaux*, containing the famous Château Petrus.

POMMADE   Thick smooth paste.

POMMARD   Commune of *Côte de Beaune*, *Bourgogne*, producing large quantities of red wine (*AC*).

POMME   Apple. *Pommes en l'air*: fried, served especially with sausages; *bonne-femme*: baked.
  Short for *pomme de terre*: potato.

POMMÉ(-E)   Firm, round, hearted, of cabbage, lettuce.
  (Normandie) Apple and/or pear syrup with cider.

POMME DE MADAGASCAR   See *pomme de terre*.

POMME DE TERRE   Potato, usually shortened to *pomme*, also known as *tr(e)uffe*, *trouffe* and *truche* in central France; *Parmentier* indicates their presence. See under distinguishing names for methods of cooking (e.g. *pommes de terre dauphine*: see *dauphine*).
  Pomme de terre noir: black potato, also known as *négresse* and *pomme de Madagascar*.

POMPADOUR   Mme de Pompadour, mistress of Louis XV. Of fish or cuts of meat, coated with onion, egg and breadcrumbs, fried or baked.

POMPE   Lit.: 'pomp', 'pump'. (Auvergne, Bourgogne) Fruit pastry. See also *gibassier*.
  Cake/pastry with frizzled cubes of pork and pork fat, especially *pompe aux grattons/graillons* (Bourbonnais), *pompe aux grignaudes* (Berry).

POMPONETTE   Small savoury pastry.

(À LA) PONOTE   In the style of *Le Puy*; *à la podote* is an alternative form. See *lentille*.

PONT-L'ÉVÊQUE   (Normandie) *AOC* cheese, small, square with yellowish rind, savoury smell and flavour; made by farms and dairies around Pont-L'Evêque in *Auge*, originally known as 'Augelot', then as the *Angelot* mentioned in the 13th-century *Roman de la Rose*. *Petit/Demi Pont-l'Evêque*: smaller versions.

PONT-NEUF   Lit.: 'new bridge', the oldest bridge in *Paris*. *Pommes (de terre frites) Pont-Neuf*: elegant term for French fried potatoes (*pommes frites*), originally sold on the Pont-Neuf.
   Small puff pastry almond tart.

(À LA) PONTOISE   In the style of Pontoise in *Ile-de-France*. See *longe*.

PORC   Pork. See *carré, côte, échine, épaule, longe, jambon, jambonneau*, for major cuts; and see also *fromage de porc. Porc aux pruneaux de Tours*: with *Vouvray* wine, cream and prunes.

PORCELET   Piglet, sucking pig. *Porcelet en gelée*: in jelly, ready-prepared at a *charcuterie*: *niortaise*: with potatoes and onions; *farci à la peau de goret* (Alsace): stuffed and roasted.

PORCHÉ   (Bretagne) Stewed pig's ears, feet etc.

PORCHETTA   (Nice) Whole young pig stuffed with its own offal and herbs, spit-roasted.

PORMONIER   (Savoie) Herb sausage.

PORPHYRÉE POURPRE   Laver, reddish seaweed.

PORQUA   (S France) Local name for grey mullet (*mulet*).

(À LA) PORTAISE   In the style of Port-en-Bessin in *Normandie*. See *barbue*.

PORTEFEUILLE   Lit.: 'portfolio'. *En portefeuille*: stuffed, wrapped in something.

PORTE-MAILLOT   One of the main entrances to *Paris* from the W. See *Maillot*.

(À LA) PORTIÈRE   Lit.: 'porter's style'. See *hareng*.

PORTO   Port (wine).

PORT-ROYAL   Religious community in *Paris*. *Salade Port-Royal*: potato, apple and French bean salad.

PORT-SALUT Variety of *Saint-Paulin* cheese, originally made by the Monastery of Port-du-Salut in *Maine*; the name is now owned by a commercial producer.

(À LA) PORTUGAISE Portuguese-style. Garnish of tomatoes, chopped shallots and mushrooms. With tomatoes, herbs and perhaps peppers, courgettes and rice. With tomato sauce. *Potage portugaise*: tomato soup with garlic, bacon and rice.

Portuguese oyster; see also *huître*.

POT Pot, jar, jug etc.

POTABLE Drinkable (e.g. *eau potable*).

POTAGE Soup, thickened (as opposed to clear *consommé*, and more elegant than *soupe*). *Potage crème*: cream soup, usually based on *béchamel* sauce and finished with cream. *Potage purée*: soup based on a purée, usually of vegetables. *Potage velouté*: soup based on *velouté* sauce and finished with egg yolks and cream, often of fish and shellfish. For the numerous soups, see under their distinguishing names (e.g. *potage/purée Crécy*: see *Crécy*; *crème Argenteuil*: see *Argenteuil*).

POTAGER (POTAGÈRE) Culinary, to do with the kitchen. *Herbes/ plantes potagères*: pot herbs, vegetables.

POT-AU-CRÈME Lit.: 'pot-with-cream'. Creamy cold dessert, of egg yolks flavoured with vanilla, chocolate or coffee, in a little individual pot; also known as *petit pot de crème*.

POT-AU-FEU Lit.: 'pot on the fire'. Boiled beef (*bouilli*) with vegetables and beef broth (*bouillon*), two dishes in one; sometimes also with chicken, salt pork and sausage, with many regional variations. *Pot-au-feu carcassonnais*: beef, mutton, bacon with stuffed cabbage, haricot beans etc; *gascon*: mutton, veal, preserved or fresh goose.

POTÉE Lit.: 'potful'. Substantial soup of various meats and vegetables, typically (salt) pork, cabbage, beans/lentils, sausages; with many regional versions (e.g. *potée auvergnate*, *potée champenoise*). *Potée à la tête de porc* (Poitou): chopped pig's head cooked in broth, which is first drunk, the head then eaten with vinegar and rock salt.

POTIQUET Individual stoneware dish.

POTIRON Pumpkin, larger variety than *citrouille*.

POTJE FLESH/POTJE VLEESCH/POTJEVLEISCH (Flandre)
Veal, chicken and rabbit *pâté*.

POTTIOCK Small wild horse from the Pyrenees; mostly used for *charcuterie*.

POUCE-PIED Lit.: 'big toe-foot'. Goose-necked barnacle, type of shellfish.

POUDING Name for plum pudding (*pudding*).

POUDRE Powder. *En poudre*: powdered, ground.

POUILLARD Young partridge or pheasant.

POUILLY-BLANC-FUMÉ White wine (*AC*) made from the *Sauvignon* grape (known locally as *Blanc Fumé*), at *Pouilly-sur-Loire* in *Nivernais* (not to be confused with the *Pouilly* of the *Mâconnais* – see below); the commune also produces, under its own name, a less distinguished white wine (*AC*) from the *Chasselas* grape.

POUILLY-FUISSÉ Commune of *Mâconnais* producing, with its neighbours *Pouilly-Loché* and *Pouilly-Vinzelles*, fine white wines (*AC*).

POUILLY-LOCHÉ See above.

POUILLY-SUR-LOIRE See *Pouilly-Blanc-Fumé*.

POUILLY-VINZELLES See *Pouilly-Fuissé*.

POULARDE Fattened hen; roasting chicken, in practice often interchangeable with *poulet*, and with *chapon* and *coq*. *Poularde à la bayonnaise*: with onions soaked in lemon juice; *belle aurore*: with white wine, cream sauce, and morels in puff pastry; *au blanc*: poached, with cream sauce; *Chanteclair*: stuffed, with artichokes, asparagus and white sauce; *à la chevalière*: in flan case with mushrooms and truffles; *dauphinoise*: stuffed with *foie gras*, truffles etc, poached in a pig's bladder; *demi-deuil/ de la Mère Filloux* (Lyonnais): poached, with truffles under the skin and white sauce; *à l'impératrice*: poached, with sweetbreads and brains; *Mireille*: sautéed, with morels and cream; *à la Néva*: cold in jellied white sauce; *Paramé*: pot-roasted with vegetables; *petite-mariée*: poached with vegetables; *à la reine*: stuffed, poached with truffles and white sauce;

Rosière: stuffed, poached, with sweetbreads, mushrooms, cream sauce; *Tosca*: pot-roasted, with fennel; *Véronique*: poached, with cream sauce and grapes; *en vessie* (Lyonnais): stuffed, poached in a pig's bladder, with vegetables.

POULE Hen. (Boiling) fowl. *Poule au pot*: stuffed chicken poached with vegetables; *poule au pot d'Henri IV* (Béarn especially) supposedly originated from the King's wish that every family in the land should have a chicken in the pot each Sunday.

POULE DE MER Name for John Dory (*Saint-Pierre*).

POULE DES BOIS Name for hazel grouse (*gélinotte*).

POULET

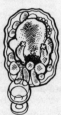

(Young) chicken, in practice interchangeable with *poularde*, *chapon* and *coq*. *Poulet fermier/de grain*: free-range/corn-fed chicken. *Poulet jaune*: free-range chicken fed on maize, raised especially in *Landes*. *Jambon de poulet*: leg of chicken. Many areas are known for fine poultry, including *La Flèche*, *Le Mans*, *Barbezieux* and, most famous, *Bresse*, with its own *appellation*. *Poulet de Bresse*: free-range chicken fattened on maize and buckwheat, killed and plucked by hand, with ruff of feathers as trademark, bathed in milk.

Among numerous dishes, with the chicken often jointed first and sautéed, are *poulet sauté Alexandra*: with cream and onion sauce; *farci ariégeoise*: cooked in broth with salt pork, served first as soup, followed by the bird with stuffed cabbage and potatoes; *en barbouille* (Berry): in red wine or cream sauce thickened with the blood; *basquaise*: with tomatoes, peppers, *chorizo* sausage, mushrooms and wine; *sauté Beaulieu*: with olives, artichokes, potatoes, white wine sauce; *sauté à la biarrotte*: with white wine and tomato sauce, *cèpes*, aubergines etc; *sauté Boivin*: with artichokes, onions and potatoes; *Céléstine*: with tomatoes, mushrooms, wine and cream; *César* (Auvergne): with wine, bacon, mushrooms and spirit; *à la corsaire* (Bretagne): stuffed with sausage, prunes, raisins and spices; *sauté dauphinoise*: with whole garlic cloves; *à la gannatoise*: with cheese sauce; *sauté grenobloise*: with white wine, tomatoes and garlic; *à l'hôtelière*: stuffed with sausage and mushrooms, pot-roasted; *Katoff*: split, grilled, on potato nest; *à la Kiev*: deep-fried chicken breasts stuffed with herb/garlic butter; *sauté à la livonienne*: with mushrooms and cream; *(sauté à la) Marengo*: with tomatoes, garlic and mushrooms, plus authentically, but rarely, fried eggs, fried bread and crayfish tails; *en matelote* (Nivernais): with onions, bacon, and sliced eel cooked in red wine; *à la nazairienne*: with cream, tomato and tarragon sauce; *sauté à la niortaise*: with fried onions and potatoes; *sauté à la parisienne*: with white wine sauce, potatoes and asparagus; *sauté Père Lathuile*: with potatoes and artichokes; *sauté Rivoli*: with potatoes, truffles, sherry sauce; *rouilleuse* (Périgord): with garlic and white wine, the sauce thickened with blood; *au sang* (Bourgogne): with its own blood, also known as *jau au sang/à la Vauclan*; *au gratin à la savoyarde*: browned with cheese sauce; *farci à la mode de Sorges* (Périgord): stuffed, poached, with carrots, turnips and spicy *vinaigrette*; *vauclusienne*: casseroled with tomatoes, bacon, white wine, plus aubergines and olives; *Vichy*: stuffed with *foie gras*, truffles, ham etc, braised with cream sauce; *au vinaigre* (Lyonnais): with shallots, tomatoes, white wine, vinegar and cream; *vivandière*: stuffed with white pudding (*boudin blanc*), with *Calvados*, cream and apples; *sauté yvetois*: with apples and *Calvados*.

POULETTE   Pullet, young chicken.
    Sauce poulette: rich white sauce, sometimes with button onions, mushrooms, white wine.

POULIGNY-SAINT-PIERRE   (Berry) Goat's milk cheese (*AOC*), shaped like a small pyramid, with bluish rind, light smell and strong tang, best between April and October; farm-made around Pouligny.

POULIOT   Pennyroyal, type of wild mint; also known as *menthe pouliot*.

POULOUD   (Bretagne) Buckwheat dumplings poached in milk.

POULPE   Octopus; also known as *minard*, *pieuvre*, *pourpre* and *tripe de mer*.
    Poulpe rouge: smaller type of octopus, also known as *poupresse* and *pouprihon*.

POUNTARI   (Auvergne) Cabbage stuffed with bacon and sausage.

POUNTI   (Auvergne) Hash or soufflé of bacon and Swiss chard (*blette*), sometimes with eggs, cream, grapes and prunes.

POUPART   Name for large crab (*tourteau*).

POUPELIN   Rich pastry cake filled with whipped cream, *mousse* or ice cream.

POUPETON   Meat roll, usually braised.
    (Provence) Fish *pâté* with cheese and cream.

POUPRESSE/POUPRIHOUN   (Provence) Local name for small octopus (*poulpe rouge*).

POURLY   (Bourgogne) Smooth nutty goat's milk cheese, made by small dairies; named after nearest village.

POURPIER   Purslane, salad green.

POURPRE (Provence) Lit.: 'crimson'. Local name for octopus (*poulpe*). See also *porphyrée pourpre*.

POURRI(-E) Lit.: 'rotten'. See *gigot*.

POUSSE-CAFÉ Lit.: 'push-cafe'. Small glass of spirit taken after coffee.

POUSSE-RAPIÈRE Lit.: 'rapier thrust'. Aperitif of sparkling wine mixed with *Armagnac*, a speciality of *Gascogne*.

POUSSIN Young spring chicken, very small chicken; also known as *petit poussin*. *Poussins Cendrillon*: split, flattened, grilled, with truffle sauce; *Hermitage*: as above but sautéed, plus fried potato balls and peas.

POUSTAGNACQ (Landes) Fermented sheep's milk cheese.

POUTARGUE See *boutargue*.

POUTASSOU Blue whiting, Mediterranean fish.

POUTINA/POUTINE/PUTINA (Nice) Tiny larval sardines and anchovies, used for fritters, omelettes and to make fish paste.

POUYTROLLE (Vivarais) Baked pork and vegetable sausage.

PRAIRE Warty Venus, type of small clam. See also *fausse palourde*.

PRALIN(E)/PRASLIN Praline, powdered mixture of caramel and toasted nuts, usually almonds, used in pastries.
    Almond coated with caramel, sweet invented by the chef to the 17th-century Duc of Plessis-Praslin.

PRALINÉ(-E) Praline/almond-flavoured. (*Gâteau*) *praliné*: almond sponge cake with praline.

PRASLIN See *pralin(e)*.

PRATELLE Name for type of fungus (*psalliote*).

PRÉALABLE Preliminary; first.

PREGA-DIOU (S France) Local name for mantis shrimp (*squille*).

PRÉPON Name for sweet melon (*sucrin*).

PREMIÈRES CÔTES DE BORDEAUX Area of *Bordeaux*, making mainly white wines (*AC*).

PRÉ(S) Meadow(s). *Pré-salé*: salt marsh; see *agneau*.

(À LA) PRESSE/PRESSÉ(-E)   Pressed, squeezed (e.g. *citron pressé*: freshly squeezed lemon juice). See also *caneton*.

PRESSION   Lit.: 'pressure'. See *bière*.

PRESSKOPF   (Alsace) Pig's or calf's head brawn with shallots and gherkins in *Riesling*-flavoured jelly, often served with *vinaigrette*; also known as *tête roulée*.

PRÊTRE   Lit.: 'priest'. Name for sandsmelt (*athérine*).

PRÉVAT   Name for variety of fungus (*russule*).

(LES) PREUSES   See *Chablis*.

PRIMEUR   Lit.: 'first'. *Primeurs*: early fruit and especially vegetables.
      The first or new wine, also known as *nouveau*; *Beaujolais Nouveau*, usually released on the 3rd Thursday of November, is the most familiar, but *primeurs* are also made in other regions.

(À LA) PRINCESSE   Lit.: 'princess-style'. Garnish of asparagus tips, truffles and white sauce; or of stuffed artichokes and potato balls. See also *mange-tout*.
      Variety of almond grown in *Provence*.
      Princesse berrichonne: almond pastry.

(À LA) PRINTANIÈRE   Lit.: 'spring-style'. With spring vegetables (e.g. *navarin printanier*).
      Printanier: thin sponge slice covered with multicoloured icing.

PRINTEMPS   Spring.

PRISULTRE/PRISUTTE/PRIZZUTU   (Corse) Raw ham.

PRIVAS   Capital of *Ardèche* and of *Vivarais*.

PRIX   Price. *Prix fixe*: set price (menu/meal).

PRIZZUTU   See *prisultre*.

PROFITEROLE   Profiterole, small *choux* pastry with sweet or sometimes savoury filling.

PROPRIÉTAIRE   Proprietor, owner, especially of vineyards.

PROPRIÉTÉ   Property, estate. Vineyard estate. See also *mise*.

(À LA) PROVENÇALE   In the style of *Provence*. With tomatoes, garlic, often onions, olives, aubergines, anchovies etc. See also *artichaut*, *grenouille*, *morue*, *tomate* and *tripes*.

PROVENCE   Large southern province covering the departments of *Vaucluse*, Bouches-du-Rhône, *Var*, Alpes-de-Haute-Provence (formerly Basses-Alpes) and Alpes-Maritimes. See *Côtes de Provence*.

PROVIDENCE   Lit.: 'providence'. See *Bricquebec*.

PRUNE   Plum. Also plum brandy.
Prune de Damas: damson (lit.: 'of Damascus').

PRUNÉ   (Poitou) Plum pastry.

PRUNEAU   Prune, dried plum, those of *Touraine* and *Agenais* being well known. *Pruneau d'Agen*: prune from a *prunier d'ente* (lit.: 'grafted') plum tree, of a type dating from the Crusades. Other varieties include *brignole*, also known as *pruneau fleuri*, and *pistole*.

PRUNELLE   Sloe, tiny sour plum, often wild. Also liqueur made from sloe stones.

PRUNIER   Famous *Paris* fish restaurant, opened in 1870's. See *sole*.
Plum tree.

PSALLIOTE   Family of fungi, whitish and firm; also known as *pratelle*. Varieties include the cultivated *champignon de couche*, and wild types also known as *champignon rose des champs* and *boule de neige*.

PUANT(-E)   Lit.: 'stinking'. *Puant de Lille*, *Gris Puant*, *Puant Macéré*: names for *Gris de Lille* cheese; also for *Maroilles* cheese soaked in brine and sometimes beer.

PUCE   Lit.: 'flea'. Name for small crawfish (*langouste*).

PUDDING   Plum pudding; also known as *pouding*.

PUISSEGUIN-SAINT-ÉMILION   Satellite area of *Saint-Emilion*, *Bordeaux*, making red wine (*AC*).

PUITS D'AMOUR   Lit.: 'well of love'. Small round pastry filled with cream, jelly or fruit.

PULENTA   (Corse) Thick chestnut flour porridge, often made into cakes.

PULIGNY-MONTRACHET   Commune of *Côte de Beaune* renowned for its white wines (*AC*), containing the *grand cru* vineyards *Bienvenues-Bâtard-Montrachet* and *Chevalier-Montrachet*, and parts of *Le Montrachet* and *Bâtard-Montrachet*.

PUNCH À LA ROMAINE   Frothy water ice of wine and egg whites with rum added.

PURÉE   Purée. *Purée de pommes* (*de terre*): mashed potatoes.

(*Potage*) *purée*: soup based on a purée, usually vegetable. For soups of this kind, see under their distinguishing names; e.g. *purée Crécy*: see *Crécy*.

PUTINA   See *poutine*.

(LE) PUY   Capital of the Haute-Loire department, on the *Languedoc-Auvergne* borders. See also *brochette* and *lentille*.

PYRAMIDE   Lit.: 'pyramid'. See *Valençay*.

QUART   Quarter. *Quart de poulet*: quarter of chicken. *Quart de vin*: quarter litre bottle of wine.
      Cheeses which are smaller versions of their parents – *Quart Livarot, Quart Maroilles*.

QUARTIER   Quarter. Piece, portion. Segment, of fruit. Hind-, forequarter, of an animal. *Quartier de mouton à la champenoise*: larded with bacon, marinated and braised in white wine.

QUARTS-DE-CHAUME   Area of *Coteaux du Layon*, making the finest sweet white wine (*AC*) of *Anjou*.

QUASI (DE VEAU)   Lit.: 'almost'. Chump, thick part of loin, of veal; also known as *cul*. *Quasi de veau bourgeoise*: casseroled with calf's foot, pork and vegetables.

QUATRE-ÉPICES   Lit.: 'four spices'. Finely ground mixture of cloves, ginger, white pepper and nutmeg.
      Name for allspice (*toute-épice*).

QUATRE MENDIANTS   Mixed hazelnuts, figs, almonds and raisins, the colours supposed to resemble the dress of the 4 orders of mendicant friars; also known as *mendiants*.

QUATRE-QUARTS   Lit.: 'four quarters'. Pound cake, made of equal quantities of eggs, flour, butter and sugar; originally from *Bretagne*.

QUEMEU   See *tarte*.

QUENELLE   (especially Lyonnais, Bugey, Alsace) Quenelle, type of small *mousse*, poached and very light in consistency; *quenelles de brochet* (of pike) and *de volaille* (of chicken) are perhaps the most common. From German 'Knödel' – dumpling.

QUERCY   Region equivalent to the departments of Lot and Tarn-et-Garonne, S of *Périgord*. See also *Bleu du Quercy*.

(À LA) QUERCYNOISE   In the style of *Quercy*.

QUETSCH(E)   Variety of plum. Also a colourless spirit distilled from *quetschs*, principally in *Alsace*.

QUEUE (DE BOEUF)   Oxtail. *Queue de boeuf à l'auvergnate*: braised in white wine with bacon, onions, chestnuts; *Cavour*: braised, with chestnut purée; *à la charolaise*: braised with carrots, turnips, bacon and potatoes; *à la Nohant*: braised with vegetables, sweetbreads, tongue; *des vignerons* (Bourgogne): stewed with white grapes.

QUICHE   (Lorraine, Alsace especially) Flat custard tart, usually savoury, especially *quiche lorraine*: with bacon, eggs, cream, sometimes cream cheese but not, correctly, Gruyère cheese; also spelt *kiche*, known locally as *féouse* and *flon*, probably from German 'Kuche' – cake.

QUICHÉ/QUICHET   (Provence) Large slice of bread soaked in oil, covered with anchovies, toasted.

QUIGNON   See *grignon*.

QUILLET   Large cake filled with rich butter cream.

QUIMPER   Capital of the Finistère department in *Bretagne*.

(À LA) QUIMPERLAISE/QUIMPÉROISE   In the style of *Quimper*. *Salade quimperlaise*: fish and shellfish salad. See also *cabillaud*, *hareng*, *maquereau* and *terrine*.

QUINCY   Village in *Berry*, making dry white wine (*AC*) from the *Sauvignon* grape.

QUINQUINA   General name for wine-based aperitifs flavoured with quinine (e.g. *Dubonnet*, *Byrrh*).

QUINTAL   Variety of white cabbage, used in the *choucroute* of *Alsace*.

RÂBLE Saddle, of hare, rabbit (*lièvre*, *lapin*) (as opposed to *selle* of larger animals).

RABOT(T)E (Champagne, Picardie) Whole apple in pastry; also known as *boulot* and *talibur*.

RACHEL 19th-century actress. Garnish of bone marrow and artichoke hearts with wine sauce. *Purée Rachel*: puréed artichoke hearts.

RACINE Root. Root vegetable. See also *persil*.

RACLETTE (Savoie) Melted cheese and jacket potatoes, accompanied by ham, salami, bread and tea or white wine. From 'racler', to scrape, when the cheese was warmed by the fire and scraped onto the potatoes.

RADIS Radish.

RADISSE (Lyonnais) Large long *brioche*.

RAFRAÎCHI(-E) Chilled. Cool. See also *fruit*.

RAGOT 2-year-old wild boar.

RAGOÛT Light stew, white or brown, with small amount of sauce; from 'ragoûter' (re-à-goûter), to stimulate the appetite. *Ragoût bigoudenn*: casserole of sausages, bacon and potatoes; *de volaille à l'étouffée* (Béarn): chicken stew with garlic, potatoes and carrots; *de Vic*: stew of calf's tongue, muzzle and brains.

RAIE Ray, skate, flat sea fish, often served with black butter (*raie au beurre noir*). Major types are *raie bouclée*: thornback ray (lit.: 'curled'), the best and commonest, also known as *clavelado*; *raie batis*: common ray; *raie blanche*: white skate, also known as *bec-pointu*; *raie douce*: spotted ray; *raie miroir*: smaller type.
  Raie capucin/grise: name for skate (*pocheteau*).

RAIFORT Horseradish. *Sauce raifort*: creamy horseradish sauce.

RAINETTE See *Reinette*.

RAÏOLES (Nice) Local name for ravioli.

RAIPONCE Rampion, plant whose leaves and roots may be eaten.

RAISIN Grape.
  Raisin sec: raisin. *Raisin de Corinthe*: currant; *de Malaga*: Muscat raisin; *de Smyrne*: sultana.

RAISINÉ (Charentes, Bourgogne especially) Thick grape jam or jelly, often with pears or quinces.

RAITEAU/RAITON   Small skate.

RAÏTO/RAYTE   (Provence) Red wine sauce with garlic, tomatoes, nuts, for fish (e.g. *merlan en raïto*); believed to have been brought to *Marseille* by the Phoenicians.

RAITON   Small skate, also known as *raiteau*.

RAKI   Name for *arack*.

RÂLE   Rail, marsh bird.
 Râle de genêt: name for corncrake (*roi de cailles*).

RAMBOUR(G)   Variety of apple, originally from Rambures in *Picardie*.

RAMEQUIN   Ramekin, individual dish. Food cooked in this. *Ramequin (au fromage)*: cheese tartlet. (Franche-Comté) Cheese *fondue* with red wine, garlic, mustard. *Ramequin douaisien*: baked bread rolls stuffed with calf's kidneys. See below.

RAMEQUIN DE LAGNIEU   (Bugey): Small hard goat's milk cheese, with nutty flavour; made by farms around Lagnieu.

RAMEREAU   Young wood pigeon.

RAMIER   Wood pigeon.

RANCIO   Description for fortified sweet wine (e.g. *Banyuls, Rasteau, Rivesaltes*) which has become oxidized with age; from Spanish for 'rancid, rank'.

RÂPÉ(-E)   Grated. Short for *fromage râpé*: grated cheese.
 Râpée/rapis (Morvan, Lyonnais): thick pancake of grated potato.

RAPURE   Large overgrown oyster; see also *huître*.

RAQUETTE   Grey partridge.

RASCASSE   Scorpion fish, hog fish, essential ingredient of *bouillabaisse*; also known as *badasco, capoum, chapon, cordonniero, crapaud, diable de mer, garde-écueil, scorpion, sébaste chèvre* and *truie de mer*.

RASOIR   Lit. razor. Name for razor shell (*couteau*).

RASPAIL   Yellow herb liqueur, named after its inventor.

RASSIS(-E)   Lit.: 'calm'. Stale, of bread.

RASTEAU   Commune of *Vaucluse* known for its red fortified sweet wine (*AC*) from the *Grenache* grape; also making red wine sold as *Côtes-du-Rhône-Villages-Rasteau* (*AC*).

RASTÈGNE   Name for sea anemone (*anémone de mer*).

RAT   Lit.: 'rat'. Name for star-gazer (*boeuf*).

RATAFIA   Liqueur made by infusing fruit or nuts in brandy; originally served at the ratification of a treaty. *Ratafia de Bourgogne/de Champagne*: mixture of unfermented grape juice and brandy.
  (Provence, Lyonnais) Small macaroon.

RATATOUILLE/RATATOUIA   (Provence) Stew of aubergines, tomatoes, onions, peppers, courgettes and garlic in oil; probably from dialect 'touiller' – to stir and crush.

RATE   Spleen, of ox, pig etc, sometimes used in soups and stews.

RATON   Lit.: 'young rat'. Cream cheese pastry.

RAVE   Name for turnip (*navet*).

RIVIER   Small dish of *hors d'oeuvres*.

RAVIGOTE   *Sauce ravigote*: spicy *vinaigrette* with mustard, gherkins, capers etc; from 'ravigoter', to enliven. See also *beurre*.

RAVIOLE   (Dauphiné) Small goat's milk cheese pastry.

RAVIOLI(S)   Ravioli, also known as *raïoles* in *Nice*. *Ravioli à la niçoise*: filled with meat, Swiss chard (*blette*) and grated cheese.

RAYOLES   (Provence) Small pasta squares filled with vegetables, in walnut sauce.

RAYON (DE MIEL)   Honeycomb.

RAYTE   See *raïto*.

REBLOCHON   (Savoie) *AOC* cheese, smooth, round, pale ivory, with mild creamy flavour; made by farms and dairies, using milk from cows of the *Abondance* breed. For many years an unknown cheese, because originally made from 'lait de rebloche' – undeclared milk which the herdsmen kept back for themselves, instead of milking the cows dry when the yields were inspected. *Reblochonnet/Demi-Reblochon/Petit Reblochon*: smaller version.

(À LA) RÉBOULETO   See *tripes*.

RECET   See *lard*.

RECETTE   Recipe.

RÉCHAUD   Hot plate; chafing dish; small portable stove.

RÉCHAUFFÉ(-E) Reheated. Dish made with cooked meat.

RÉCOLLET (Lorraine) Factory-made cheese similar to *Carré de l'Est*; brand name.

RÉCOLTANT Grower, especially of wine; owner who harvests his own crop. *Récoltant-manipulant*: term in *Champagne* for vineyard owner-grower, who also makes the wine himself.

RÉCOLTE Harvest, crop, especially of wine.

RÉCOLTÉ(-E) Harvested (by), especially of grapes; grown (by).

RECUIT(-E) Recooked. *Recuite*: version of Italian Ricotta cheese, made by reheating the whey.

RÉDUCTION Reduction, of sauce concentrated by boiling.

RÉGAL DE MARCHOIS Lit.: 'treat of an inhabitant of *Marche*'. See *fondu*.

RÉGAL DE SANG (Périgord) Fried cake of poultry blood, served with vinegar and garlic.

RÉGENCE Lit.: 'regency'; and café in 19th-century *Paris*. Elaborate garnish of *quenelles*, truffles etc. See also *filet* and *ris*.

RÉGIME Diet. See also *pain*.

RÉGION Region.

RÉGIONAL(-E) Local, regional, of the district.

RÉGLISSE Liquorice.

REGUIGNEU (Provence) Fried sliced raw ham.

(À LA) REINE Lit.: 'queen's style'; often connected with Louis XV's queen, Marie Lesczinka, known to appreciate her food. With chicken or puréed chicken. *Consommé à la reine*: clear chicken soup. See also *bouchée*, *pain* and *poularde*. Short for *poulet de reine*.

REINE-CLAUDE Greengage, after Queen Claude, wife of François I.

REINE DE SABA Queen of Sheba. See *gâteau*.

REINE DES GLACES Iceberg lettuce.

REINE DES REINETTES Variety of apple, similar to Cox.

REINE PÉDAUQUE *Paris* restaurant. *Omelette Reine Pédauque*: sweet apple omelette in meringue. *Salade Reine-Pédauque*: lettuce, cherry and orange salad with cream.

REINETTE   Variety of apple, also known as *Rainette*; including *Reinette du Canada*, *Reinette Gris*, *Reinette du Mans* and *Reinette Clochard*.

RÉJANE   19th-century actress. Garnish of potatoes, spinach, artichokes and bone marrow. *Potage Réjane*: chicken, leek and potato soup. See also *saumon*.

RELAIS   Lit.: 'relay', 'change of horses', derived in the same way as post-house, coaching inn in English. Inn, hostelry.
Relais routier/des routiers: transport café, offering a full and often excellent menu at reasonable prices, used by lorry drivers and travellers generally.

RELIGIEUSE   Lit.: 'nun'. Elaborate cake made of éclairs, supposed to resemble a robed nun. Also jam tart latticed with pastry strips. See also *poire*.

(À LA) RÉMOISE   In the style of Reims in *Champagne*. Sometimes with *Champagne*.

RÉMOULADE   Sharp mayonnaise flavoured with mustard, gherkins, capers etc, served especially with celeriac (*céleri rémoulade*).

(À LA) RENAISSANCE   Lit.: 'Renaissance-style'. Garnish of mixed spring vegetables.

RENNES   Capital of the Ille-et-Vilaine department and of *Bretagne*.

(À LA) RENNAISE   In the style of Rennes. See also *casse*.

RENNE   Reindeer, whose meat might be encountered in a Swedish restaurant.

REPAS   Meal.

REQUIN (MARTEAU)   (Hammerhead) shark, sometimes eaten as steaks; also known as *chien de mer*.

RÉSERVE   Lit.: 'reserve'. Term indicating the age of *Armagnac*, *Calvados* and *Cognac*. See also *grande/vieille réserve*.

RESTAURANT   Restaurant; originally fortifying broth, restorative.

RESTES   Left-overs.

REUILLY   Small area in *Berry*, known mainly for dry white wine (*AC*) from the *Sauvignon* grape.

REVARD   See *Tomme de Savoie*.

RÊVE D'AMOUR   Lit.: 'dream of love'. See *truffe*.

RÉVEILLON   Late supper, taken after Midnight Mass on Christmas Eve, and on New Year's Eve.

REVENIR   Lit.: 'to return'. *Faire revenir*: to brown, gently fry.

REVESSET   (Provence) Fish soup of sardines, smelts, and other small fish, spinach and sorrel. It is a speciality of Le Revest.

(À LA) REVINOISE   In the style of Revin in *Champagne*. *Pommes (de terre) à la revinoise*: potatoes baked in layers with shallots.

RHÔNE   Department in *Lyonnais*.

The river *Rhône*, flowing from Lake Geneva in a roughly SW direction through the *Jura* mountains to *Lyon*, where it meets the Saône, then S to the Mediterranean. The *Côtes-du-Rhône* vineyard area stretches from Vienne to *Avignon*, divided in the middle by the Montélimar plain. The general *AC Côtes-du-Rhône* applies to red, white and rosé wines produced throughout the valley (see also *Côtes-du-Rhône-Villages*). Many fine wines are produced in the region, including *Côte Rôtie*, *Hermitage* and *Saint-Joseph* from the N section, and the famous *Châteauneuf-du-Pape* from the S.

RHUBARBE   Rhubarb.

RHUM   Rum, distilled from molasses (*rhum industriel*) or sugar cane juice (*rhum agricole*); most coming from the W Indies (*Les Antilles*) and island of Réunion (Indian Ocean). *Rhum vieux*: matured for at least three years in oak. *Rhum grand arome*: molasses-based rum with pungent smell.
(S France) Local name for brill (*barbue*).

RIBOT   See *lait*.

RICARD   Brand of *pastis*.

(LES) RICEYS   (Champagne) Flat round ash-coated cheese, with fruity flavour; made by dairies around Les Riceys, also known as *Cendré de Champagne/des Riceys*. See also *Rosé des Riceys*.

RICHE   Lit.: 'rich'; also fashionable restaurant in 19th-century Paris. *Salade riche*: warm *foie gras* and spinach, salad. *Sauce Riche*: fish sauce with lobster and brandy, for sole especially; also known as *sauce diplomate*. See also *bécasse*.

RICHEBOURG   See *Vosne-Romanée*.

(À LA) RICHELIEU   Lit.: 'in the style of Cardinal Richelieu', 17th-century statesman. Garnish of stuffed tomatoes, mushrooms, braised lettuce and potatoes. Coated in egg and breadcrumbs, fried, with herb butter, sometimes truffles, of fish fillets, chicken breasts.
Type of large iced cake. See also *poire*.

RIESLING   Variety of white grape, considered the finest of *Alsace*.

RIGADELLE   (Bretagne) Local name for clam (*palourde*).

RIGODON   Lit.: 'rigadoon' (dance). (Bourgogne) Large *brioche* flan, savoury with diced bacon, or sweet with nuts or fruit, served warm or cold.

RIGOTTE DE CONDRIEU   (Lyonnais) Small mild cheese with reddish rind; made by dairies around Condrieu.

RIGOTTE DE PELUSSIN   (Auvergne) Nutty goat's milk cheese; made by farms and small dairies around Pelussin.

RILLAUDS   See *rillons*.

RILLETTES   (Loire valley) Cubed pork cooked in its own fat with herbs, pounded in a mortar, preserved in jars; derived from the Old French 'rille' – slice. *Angers*, *Le Mans*, *Tours*, *Amboise*, *Blois*, *Saumur* and *Vendôme* have their own versions, differing mainly in consistency and in-gredients added (e.g. pork liver and goose).

RILLONS (Loire valley) Pork pieces prepared like *rillettes* but cooked until well browned and left whole not pounded; also known as *rillauds*.

RIMOT(T)ES (SW France) Sweet maize meal porridge.

RINCE COCHON See *Kir*.

RIPPELE (Alsace) Pork chop with red wine sauce; traditional grape harvesters' dish.

RIS Sweetbreads (thymus gland), of calf or lamb. *Ris de veau Régence*: calf's, braised with port, cream, mushrooms, truffles and *foie gras*.

RISOTTO/RIZOTTO Risotto, creamy rice cooked in stock, with grated cheese, tomato, saffron etc; of Italian origin.

RISSOLE Small filled pastry puff or fritter, deep-fried, usually savoury. *Rissoles de Bugey*: filled with tripe, turkey and currants, traditionally served at Christmas.

RISSOLÉ(-E) Browned, fried. *Pommes (de terre) rissolées*: fried potatoes.

RITZ César Ritz, founder of the Ritz in *Paris* and with *Escoffier*, of the Savoy and Carlton in London. See also *fraise*.

RIVESALTES Area in *Roussillon*, known for its fortified sweet wine (*AC*) from the *Muscat* grape.

RIVIÈRE River.

RIVOLI Rue de Rivoli in *Paris*. See *poulet*.

RIZ   Rice. *Riz à la bayonnaise*: cooked in stock, served with
                  cheese. *Riz à la grecque*: with sausage, onions, peas,
                  peppers. *Riz créole*: with peppers and tomatoes; or
                  sweet orange-flavoured rice. *Riz à l'impératrice*: mixed
                  with custard, crystallized fruit and thick cream, a basis
                  for fruit desserts (e.g. *poires à l'impératrice*). *Riz à
                  l'indienne*: plain boiled (savoury) rice. *Crème de riz*: rice
                  flour.

RIZOTTO   See *risotto*.

ROAIX   See *Côtes-du-Rhône-Villages*.

(À LA) ROANNAISE   In the style of Roanne in *Lyonnais*. See *Côte
                  Roannaise*.

ROBATE   See *rouyat*.

ROBE DE CHAMBRE/DES CHAMPS   Lit.: 'dressing   gown'/'field
                  dress'. *Pommes (de terre) en robe de chambre*: jacket
                  potatoes, baked or steamed.

ROBERT   *Sauce Robert*: onion sauce with mustard, vinegar and
                  white wine, often served with pork chops; perhaps
                  corruption of roebuck.
                      Pommes (de terre) Robert: fried potato cake with
                  chives.

ROBINET   Tap.

ROBINETTE   Name for scad (*saurel*).

ROBLOT   Name for small mackerel (*maquereau*).

ROCAMADOUR   See *Cabécou de Rocamadour*.

ROCAMBOLE   Type of onion similar to shallot.

(LA-)ROCHE-AUX-MOINES   See *Savennières*.

ROCHEFORT   See *Cantalon*.

(À LA) ROCHELAISE   In the style of *La Rochelle*. Of fish, with red
                  wine. See also *moule* and *sole*.

(LA) ROCHELLE   Capital of the Charente-Maritime department in
                  Charentes.

ROCHER   Lit.: 'rock'. Murex, small southern shellfish, also known
                  as *escargot de mer* and *murex*; in Roman times, a source
                  of dye for imperial purple, with *Toulon* an important
                  centre.

(LA) ROCHE-SUR-YON   Capital of *Vendée*.

ROCROI (CENDRÉ)   (Champagne) Fruity ash-coated cheese; made by farms around Rocroi in *Ardennes*, also known as *Cendré des Ardennes*.

RODEZ   Capital of *Aveyron*, and of *Rouergue*.

ROGERET DES CÉVENNES   (Languedoc) Small round soft goat's milk cheese, with strong smell and flavour; made by farms in *Cévennes*.

ROGNE   (Bordelais) Paste of mullet and other fish roe.

ROGNON   Kidney, usually of lamb or calf. *Rognons Beaugé* (Bordelais): with red wine, madeira, mustard; *à la berrichonne*: with red wine sauce, onions, mushrooms, on fried bread; *à la charentaise*: with white wine and mushrooms; *à la lyonnaise*: with cream and *cognac*. *Turbigo*: with mushrooms, sausages, white wine and tomato sauce; *Viéville*: similar to *Turbigo*, with madeira sauce.
     Rognons blancs: euphemism for testicles (*animelles*).

ROGNONNADE (DE VEAU)   Saddle of veal, with kidneys.

ROI   Lit.: 'king'. See *galette* and *Saint-Gildas-des-Bois*.

ROI DE CAILLES   Lit.: 'king of quails'. Corncrake, similar to quail; also known as *râle de genêt* (lit.: 'rail of broom').

ROLLOT   (Picardie) Small round cheese with glossy yellow rind, spicy smell and flavour; made by small dairies, named after the village of Rollot, also known as *Coeur d'Arras* when heart-shaped.

(À LA) ROMAINE   Roman-style. Garnish of spinach, anchovies, potato cakes and tomato sauce. *Sauce romaine*: sweet-sour sauce with nuts and currants, for venison. See also *anguille*, *caille*, *gnocchi* and *punch*.
     Short for *laitue romaine*: cos lettuce.

(LA) ROMANÉE/ROMANÉE-CONTI/ROMANÉE-SAINT-VIVANT   See *Vosne-Romanée*.

RAMANOFF/ROMANOV   Ruling house of Russia until 1917 Revolution. Often denotes a classic luxury dish. See *fraise*.

ROMANS(-SUR-ISÈRE)   Town in *Dauphiné*. See *pogne* and *Tomme de Romans*.

ROMARIN   Rosemary, the herb.

ROMBOU   (S France) Local name for brill (*barbue*).

ROMORANTIN   See *Selles-sur-Cher*.

ROMSTECK/RUMSTEAK   Rump steak.

RONCE   Blackberry bush. *Baie/mûre de ronce*: blackberry.

RONCIN   (Lorraine) Flat potato and bacon cake.

ROND DE GIGOT   Thick slice with bone, of leg of mutton.

ROQUEFORT   (Rouergue) *AOC* cheese, of sheep's milk, in the shape of large cylinder, packed in foil, with firm buttery feel, evenly marbled with mould, distinctive smell and strong flavour; aged for at least three months in the natural caves of Cambalou, although sometimes originating in *Corse*. In 1411 the French king signed a charter granting the inhabitants of Roquefort-sur-Soulzon 'the monopoly of curing cheese as has been done in the caves of the aforesaid village since time immemorial'.

ROQUETTE   Rocket, salad green; used especially in southern France for *mesclun*.

ROQUILLE   Candied orange peel.

ROSALIE   See *maquereau*.

ROSBIF   Roast beef.

ROSCOFF   Port in *Bretagne*. See *sole*.

ROSÉ(-E)   Rosy, pink. Of wine, rosé, very light red. See also *champignon*.

ROSÉ DES RICEYS   Rosé wine (*AC*) grown in Les Riceys in *Champagne*.

ROSETTE   (Lyonnais) Lit.: 'rosette'. Large dry pork sausage, eaten cold in slices.
      Semi-sweet white wine (*AC*), made around *Bergerac* in *Périgord*.

ROSIÈRE   Lit.: 'innocent maiden'. See *poularde*.

ROSQUILLA/ROUSQUILLE   (Roussillon) Almond cake.

ROSSINI   19th-century Italian composer; perhaps the inventor of *tournedos* (lit.: 'turnback'), at first greeted with the objection that it would be an unsightly dish. See *tournedos*.

ROSSOLIS   Rosolio, brandy and fruit liqueur, usually home-made.

ROTENGLE   Red-eye, rudd, freshwater fish; also known as *gardon rouge*.

ROTHINAGO   (Normandie) Fried eggs with ham, sausages and tomato sauce; from Latin for *Rouen*.

RÔTI   Roasted. Roast (joint of meat).

ROTISSON   Name for chub (*chevaine*).

ROUCAOU   (Provence) Local name for wrasse (*vieille*).

ROUELLE   Round slice. *Rouelle de veau*: boned fillet of veal.

ROUEN   Capital of the Seine-Maritime department in *Normandie*.

(À LA) ROUENNAISE   In the style of *Rouen*. With red wine, duck liver and shallot sauce. With puréed duck liver (e.g. *omelette rouennaise*). Of fish, poached in red wine, with shellfish, smelts, mushrooms etc. *See also canard, caneton* and *pied*.

(À LA) ROUERGATE   In the style of *Rouergue*. See also *manouls*.

ROUERGUE   Province equivalent to *Aveyron*, often included in *Languedoc*.

ROUGAIL   Spicy seasoning used in Creole dishes.

ROUGE   Red. Red wine.

ROUGE DE RIVIÈRE   Lit.: 'red of river'. Wild shoveller duck.

ROUGEOT   Smoked wild duck fillet.

ROUGE-QUEUE   Lit.: 'red tail'. Redstart, robin-like bird.

ROUGERET   See *Mâconnais*.

ROUGET (DE ROCHE)   Red mullet, excellent sea fish; also known as *apogon, barbarin, bécasse de mer* (because it may be cooked ungutted, like woodcock), *surmulet* (*rouget*) and *mallette*. *Rouget-barbet*: less good type. *Rouget Baron Brisse*: grilled, with potato balls and parsley butter; *à la bordelaise*: grilled, with shallot and white wine sauce; *Montesquieu*: fried fillets; *à la nantaise*: grilled, with sauce of the livers, shallots and white wine; *à la niçoise*: grilled, fried or baked, with puréed anchovies, fried tomatoes, black olives; *Théodore*: stuffed with mushrooms, poached in white wine; *à la trouvillaise*: stuffed with the roes, poached in white wine.

    Rouget(-grondin): name for red gurnard (*grondin rouge*).

ROUILLE/ROULHO   Lit.: 'rust'. (Provence) Spicy mayonnaise with red pepper and garlic, served with fish soups.

ROUILLEUX (ROUILLEUSE)   Lit.: 'rusty'. See *poulet*.

ROULADE   Rolled meat, sometimes fish or omelette, often stuffed.

ROULÉ(-E)   Rolled. Meat roll. Swiss roll; pastry roll. See also *hareng* and *presskopf*.

ROULHO   See *rouille*.

ROULOT(TE)   See *rouyat*.

(À LA) ROUMAINE   Romanian-style. See *papanas à la roumaine*.

ROUMANILLE   See *tournedos*.

ROUMBOU/ROUN   (S France) Local name for brill (*barbue*).

ROUQUAS/ROUQUIER   (Provence) Local name for wrasse (*vieille*).

ROUSQUILLE   See *rosquilla*.

ROUSSE   Feminine of *roux*.

ROUSSEAU   Lit.: 'red-haired person'. Name for red sea bream (*dorade*).

ROUSSELET   Russet pear.

ROUSSEROLLE   (Berry) Cream fritter.

ROUSSETTE   Dogfish, rock salmon; also known as *chien* (*de mer*), *saumonette*, *squale* and *vache*, and *cata*, *gat*(*oulin*) and *pesciu gattu*.
   Variety of white grape, used in the wines of *Savoie*, especially around *Seyssel*.
   Sweet fritter.

ROUSSILLON   Province equivalent to the Pyrénées-Orientales department, sometimes included in *Languedoc*. See also *Côtes du Roussillon*.

(À LA) ROUSSILLONNAISE   In the style of the *Roussillon*. See *aubergine*.

ROUSSIN   (Provence) Spinach sauce, to accompany hard-boiled eggs.

ROUTIER (ROUTIÈRE)   Of roads. Lorry driver. See *relais*.

ROUX (ROUSSE)   Lit.: 'red', 'russet'. Mixture of butter and flour used to thicken sauces.

ROUY   (Bourgogne) Smooth square cheese with strong smell and flavour; made by dairies in *Dijon*, trade name.

ROUYAT   (Lorraine) Whole apple in pastry, also known as *roulot* (*te*) and *robate*.

ROVE   See *Brousse*.

(À LA) ROYALE   Lit.: 'royal-style'. Poultry, brains or fish, poached, coated in cream sauce, finished with truffles, often as a garnish or filling. *Consommé à la royale*: clear soup garnished with savoury custard shapes. See also *ananas*, *caramote*, *choucroute*, *dorade*, *Kir*, *lièvre*, *pagre*, *pêche*, *pièce de boeuf* and *poisson lune*.
Name for *langouste*.

ROYAN   Port in *Charentes*, which has given its name to esteemed type of *sardine*.

RUBANÉ(-E)   Ribboned, striped.

RUCHE   Lit.: 'beehive'. Ice cream, meringue and sponge dessert (*omelette norvégienne*) in the shape of a beehive.

RUCHOTTES-CHAMBERTIN   See *Gevrey-Chambertin*.

RUFFEC   (Poitou, Charentes) Small round goat's milk cheese with bluish rind and fruity flavour; made by farms around Ruffec.

RULLY   Commune in *Côte Chalonnaise*, making some red but mainly white wines (*AC*), much of it going into the production of *Bourgogne Mousseux*.

RUMSTEAK   See *romsteck*.

RUOMS   See *Pélardon des Cévennes*.

(À LA) RUSSE   Russian-style. *Salade russe*: mixed diced vegetables with mayonnaise. See also *bitok*, *charlotte*, *cigarette*, *hareng*, *homard* and *sole*.

RUSSEROLE   (Touraine) Sweet pastry.

RUSSULE   Family of fungi with firm flesh, of different colours, often with pleasant flavour; varieties also known as *berdanel*, *bisotte*, *blavet*, *bordet vert*, *charbonnier*, *palomet*, *prévat*, *verdette* and *vert bonnet*.

RUTABAGA   Name for swede (*chou-navet*).

(À LA) RUTHÉNOISE   In the style of *Rodez*.

SABARDIN (Lyonnais) Pork and beef offal sausage, cooked in red wine.

SABAYON Frothy mixture of egg yolks and wine, as a warm dessert, or sweet or savoury sauce; from the Italian 'zabaglione'.

SABLE Sand. See *vin*.

SABLÉ(-E) Lit.: 'sanded'. (Normandie, Maine) Shortbread, perhaps created at Sablé-sur-Sarthe in *Maine*. See also *pâte*.

SABLET See *Côtes-du-Rhône-Villages*.

SABODET (Lyonnais, Dauphiné) Pig's head sausage, eaten hot in thick slices; originally sabot-shaped.

SABOT Lit.: 'clog'. One ingredient enclosed in another (e.g. *laitances en sabot*: soft roes in baked potatoes).

SABRE Lit.: 'sabre'. Scabbard fish, long thin sea fish.

SACRISTAIN Lit.: 'sacristan'. Small twisted pastry.

SAFRAN Saffron, yellow spice.

SAFRANÉ(-E) Flavoured or coloured with saffron.

SAGOU Sago.

SAIGNANT(-E) Lit.: 'bleeding'. Rare, underdone, of steak.

SAIGNEUX(-SE) Lit.: 'bloody'. (*Bout*) *saigneux*: scrag end, of mutton etc.

SAINDOUX Lard, melted pork fat, used especially in SW France instead of butter or oil.

SAIN-GORLON Blue cheese, imitation of Italian Gorgonzola.

SAINT(-E) Lit.: 'saint'. Holy.

SAINT-AGRÈVE See *Picodon de Saint-Agrève*.

SAINT-AMOUR See *Beaujolais*.

SAINT-ANTOINE St Anthony, patron saint of swineherds. Sometimes used in descriptions of pork dishes.

SAINT-AUBIN Commune of *Côte de Beaune*, *Bourgogne*, producing red and white wines (*AC*).

SAINT-BENOÎT/SAINT-BENOIST (Orléanais) Round fruity cheese, made by farms around Saint-Benoît-sur-Loire.

SAINT-BRIEUC Capital of the Côtes-du-Nord department in *Bretagne*. See also *huître*.

SAINT-CHINIAN Red wine area of the *Languedoc*, north of Beziers (*AC*).

SAINT-CLOUD Park and suburb of *Paris*. *Potage Saint-Cloud*: puréed pea and lettuce soup with fried bread cubes.

SAINT-CYR Town in *Ile-de-France*. See *Délice de Saint-Cyr*. (Poitou) Factory-made goat's milk cheese; brand name.

SAINTE-ALLIANCE Lit.: 'Holy Alliance'. See *faisan*.

SAINTE-CROIX-DU-MONT Small district in *Bordeaux*, making mainly sweet white wines (*AC*).

SAINTE-FOY See *Bleu de Sainte-Foy*.

SAINTE-FOY-BORDEAUX Area next to *Bergerac*, growing white wine, mainly sweet, and some red (*AC*).

SAINTE-MAURE (Touraine) Long cylindrical goat's milk cheese, with powerful smell and flavour; made around Sainte-Maure, also in *Anjou*, *Charentes*, *Poitou*. *Sainte-Maure Fermier*: farm-made, unwrapped, with straw through the middle. *Sainte-Maure Laitier*: factory-made, regular in shape, packed in paper, sometimes with straw at the centre; also known as *Chèvre Long*.

SAINTE-MENEHOULD Town in *Champagne*, noted for its method of preparing pig's trotters and ears, cooked slowly, rolled in breadcrumbs, grilled or fried. *Sauce Sainte-Menehould*: spicy white wine sauce with shallots, vinegar, mustard etc.

SAINT-ÉMILION Important area (*AC*) of *Bordeaux*, containing famous châteaux (e.g. Ausone and Cheval Blanc).
Saint-Emilion au chocolat: cold macaroon and chocolate dessert.

SAINTE-ODILE (Alsace) Fresh cheese flavoured with cumin.

SAINT-ESTÈPHE Commune (*AC*) of *Haut-Médoc*, *Bordeaux*, with the prestigious vineyards of Cos d'Estournel, Montrose, Calon-Segur etc.
Aperitif made in *Nice* of red, white or rosé wine mixed with vanilla, chicory, sugar and spirit.

SAINT-ETIENNE Capital of the *Loire* department, in *Lyonnais*.

SAINT-FLORENTIN (Bourgogne) Flat round cheese with shiny rind, spicy smell and flavour; made by farms and dairies around Saint-Florentin. See also *truite*.

SAINT-FLORENTINE   *Pommes* (*de terre*) *Saint-Florentine*: potato croquettes with ham and *cèpes*.

SAINT-FLOUR   Town in *Auvergne*. *Pomme* (*de terre*) *Saint-Flour*: sliced potatoes baked with cabbage and bacon. See also *friand*.

SAINT-FORTUNAT   7th-century bishop of *Metz*. See *cochon*.

SAINT-GEORGES-SAINT-ÉMILION   Outlying district of *Saint-Emilion*, *Bordeaux*, growing red wine (*AC*).

(À LA) SAINT-GERMAIN   In the style of Saint-Germain in *Ile-de-France*, like *Clamart*, once famous for peas. With peas, fresh or dried, and sometimes artichokes. *Potage Saint-Germain*: pea soup. With *béarnaise* sauce (probably invented at Saint-Germain) and potatoes.

SAINT-GILDAS-DES-BOIS   (Bretagne) Triple cream cheese of pasteurized milk, white, mild and creamy; made at Saint-Gildas-des-Bois, also with the trade name *Le Roi*.

SAINT-HONORAT   Perhaps connected with the Ile-Saint-Honorat, off the coast of *Nice*. See *sardine*.

SAINT-HONORÉ   Patron saint of pastry cooks. (*Gâteau*) *Saint-Honoré*: rich *choux* pastry ring filled with confectioner's custard.

(À LA) SAINT-HUBERT   Patron saint of hunters. *Potage Saint-Hubert*: pheasant and lentil soup. See also *marcassin*.

SAINT-JACQUES   St James. Short for *coquille Saint-Jacques*: scallop. Variety of table grape.

SAINT-JEAN(-DE-LUZ)   Tuna-fishing port in *Pays basque*. See *thon*.

SAINT-JEAN-DE-MINERVOIS   Commune in *Aude*, making fortified sweet wine (*AC*) from the *Muscat* grape.

SAINT-JOSEPH   Area of the *Rhône*, producing red and white wines (*AC*).

SAINT-JULIEN   Commune (*AC*) of *Haut-Médoc*, *Bordeaux*, containing many famous vineyards (e.g. Ducru-Beaucaillou, Beychevelle and the Léoville châteaux).
    Potage Saint-Julien: leek and potato soup, with slices of bread and cheese. See also *herbe*.

SAINT-LIZIER   See *Bethmale*.

SAINT-LÔ   Capital of the Manche department in *Normandie*.

SAINT-LOUP   (Poitou) Factory-made goat's milk cheese; trade name.

SAINT-MACAIRE See *Côtes de Bordeaux-Saint-Macaire*.

SAINT-MALO Port in *Bretagne*. *Sauce Saint-Malo*: white wine, mustard and anchovy sauce, for fish. See also *tripes*.

SAINT-MANDÉ *Paris* suburb. Garnish of peas, French beans and potatoes.

SAINT-MARC See *marcassin*.

SAINT-MARCELLIN (Dauphiné) Small round mild cheese, formerly farm-made from goat's milk, but now commercially produced from cow's milk; also known as *Tomme de Saint-Marcellin*, after the largest market town.

SAINT-MARS See *caille*.

SAINT-MARTIN Roman legionary and bishop of Tours; Saint-Martin-le-Beau in *Touraine* is known for fine table ducks. See *caneton*.

SAINT-MICHEL Layered sponge cake with coffee butter cream.

SAINT-NECTAIRE (Auvergne) Flat round firm cheese (*AOC*), with purplish grey rind, mouldy smell, mild but aromatic flavour, often ripened in the Monts-Dore caves; made by dairies and farms, named after the town of *Saint-Nectaire*.

SAINT-NICHOLAS-DE-BOURGUEIL See *Bourgueil*.

(À LA) SAINTONGEAISE In the style of *Saintonge*.

SAINTONGE Province covering most of the Charente-Maritime department in *Charentes*.

SAINT-PAULIN Large round smooth mild cheese, with orange rind; made from pasteurized milk throughout France, especially *Maine*, *Anjou* and *Bretagne*. *Port-Salut* is well-known variety.

SAINT-PÉRAY Commune of the *Rhône*, making still and sparkling white wines (*AC*).

SAINT-PIERRE St Peter. John Dory, spiny fierce-looking fish with large mouth and dark spots on each side of its back (the thumb marks of St Peter), good to eat; also known as *dorée*, *jean-doré*, *gal*, *horrible* and *poule de mer*. *Filets de Saint-Pierre Pierre Chapelle*: fried fillets with curried rice, tomatoes and onions.
  Name for haddock (*aiglefin*), which also has the 'thumb marks'. See also *ormeau* and *herbe*.

SAINT-POURÇAIN-SUR-SIOULE Area of *Bourbonnais*, growing red, white and rosé wines (*VDQS*).

SAINT-RAPHAËL   Wine-based aperitif flavoured with quinine.

SAINT-RÉMY   (Lorraine) Smooth square cheese with reddish rind, strong smell and flavour; made by local dairies; trade name.

SAINT-ROMAIN   Commune of *Côte de Beaune*, *Bourgogne*, making red and white wines (*AC*).
Town in *Normandie*, famous for *boudin*.

SAINT-SAVIOL   (Poitou) Factory-made goat's milk cheese; brand name.

SAINT-SYLVESTRE   New Year's Eve. *Salade Saint-Sylvestre*: celeriac, artichoke, mushroom and truffle salad.

SAINT-VAAST-LA-HOUGUE   Port in *Normandie*. See *huître*.

SAINT-VARENT   (Poitou) Factory-made goat's milk cheese; trade name.

SAINT-VÉRAN   Commune of *Mâconnais*, *Bourgogne*, making white wine (*AC*) similar to that of its neighbour, *Pouilly-Fuissé*.

SAISON   Season.

SAISONNIER (SAISONNIÈRE)   Seasonal, of vegetables etc.

SALADE   Salad. Salad green – lettuce, endive etc. *Salade composée*: substantial mixed salad. *Salade panachée*: mixed salad. *Salade simple*: plain salad. *Salade verte*: green salad. For the many types of salad, see under their distinguishing names (e.g. *salade cauchoise*: see *cauchoise*).

SALADIER   Salad bowl. Large mixed salad. *Saladier lyonnaise*: salad of calf's head, pig's and sheep's trotters, ox muzzle, sausage etc with *vinaigrette*.

SALAISON   Salted food (e.g. anchovies, salt herrings, olives), as an *hors d'oeuvre*.

SALAMBO   Small filled *choux* bun, iced or dipped in caramel.

SALAMIS DE STRASBOURG   Smoked beef and pork sausage.

SALCICCA/SALCISSIA   (Corse) Soft pork sausage.

SALDA   (Béarn) Soup of bacon, sausage, cabbage, beans etc.

SALÉ(-E)   Salted, salt. Salted food. See also *petit-salé*.

SALERS   (Auvergne) Large cylindrical cheese (*AOC*), pressed, uncooked, with blotchy golden rind, firm yellow inside and savoury taste, matured for 3 months to a year in natural caves; named after the city in the *Cantal* mountains, also known as *Fourme de Salers*.

SALIADE/SALURGUE   (Béarn, Pays basque) Bacon fat.

SALIGNY   See *Epoisses*.

SALMIGONDIS   Hotchpotch; stew of reheated meat.

SALMIS   Salmi, dish with ancient pedigree, of game or poultry, first half-cooked by roasting, then finished in wine sauce. *Salmis des palombes* (Béarn, Pays basque, Bordelais): pigeons in red wine sauce with small onions, diced ham, mushrooms.

SALON   Lit.: 'sitting-room'. *Salon de thé*: tearoom.

SALOPE   Lit.: 'slut'. (Boulonnais) Local name for megrim (*limandelle*).

SALPICON   Preparation of meat or fish and diced vegetables in sauce, as a stuffing or garnish.

SALSIFIS   Salsify, long white root vegetable wth delicate flavour; also known as *barberon*.
  Name for scorzonera (*scorsonère*), very similar to salsify but with blackish skin.

SALURGUE   See *saliade*.

SAMPIGNY-LES-MARANGES   Commune of *Côte de Beaune*, *Bourgogne*, growing mainly red wines (*AC*).

SANCERRE   Town and vineyard area (*AC*) in Berry, known for dry white wines from the *Sauvignon* grape; also making red and rosé from the *Pinot Noir*.
  (Berry) Family name for three cheeses, *Chavignol*, *Crézancy* and *Santranges*.

SANCIAU/SAUCIAU   (central France) Thick sweet or savoury pancake or fritter; also known as *chanciau*, *crapiau*, and *grapiau*.

SANDRE   Pike-perch; river fish with delicate flavour.

SANDWICH   Sandwich; usually made with a long loaf (*baguette*) or crusty roll (*petit pain*), often filled with ham.

(À LA) SANFLORAINE   In the style of *Saint-Flour*. See *friand*.

SANG   Blood. See also *poulet*.

SANG-CUIT   Lit.: 'cooked blood'. See *sanguet*.

SANGLIER   Mature wild boar, as opposed to young *marcassin*.

SANGUE   (Corse) Black pudding, often with grapes or herbs.

SANGUET(TE)/SANGUINE/SANQUETTE   (central and W France) Seasoned cooked blood, of chicken, goat, rabbit or pig; also known as *sang-cuit*.

SANGUIN   Type of fungus found in pine woods.

SANGUINE   Blood orange. See also *sanguet*.

SANQUETTE   See *sanguet*.

SANSIOT   (Bourgogne) Calf's head.

SANSONNET   Name for small mackerel (*maquereau*).

SANTÉ   Lit.: 'health'. *Potage santé*: potato and watercress/leek soup. (*A votre*) *santé*: your good health, cheers.

SANTENAY   Important commune of *Côte de Beaune*, *Bourgogne*, producing chiefly red wines (*AC*).

SANTRANGES-SANCERRE   (Berry) Small white goat's milk cheese, shaped like a flattened ball, with strong flavour; made by farms around Santranges.

SAOUQUENO   (S France) Local name for gilt-head bream (*daurade*).

SAPEUR   Lit.: 'sapper', 'fireman'. See *tablier de sapeur*.

SAPIN   Fir tree, sometimes used to flavour *liqueur de sapin*. See also below.

SAPINDOR   Greenish liqueur made from fir cones, kept in wooden bottles; speciality of *Franche-Comté*.

SAR   Fish of the sea bream family, found mainly in S waters, some types being good to eat. Varieties include *sar* (*commun*), also known as *sargue* and *sar rayé*; *sar doré*; *sar à grosse lèvres* (lit.: 'with big lips'); *sar tambour*, also known as *mouré pountchou* and *mourre agut*. *Sar royal*: see *pagre*.

SARAH BERNHARDT   19th-century actress, with many dishes, often including *foie gras*, named after her.

SARCELLE   Teal, type of small wild duck.

(À LA) SARDE   Sardinian-style. Garnish of mushrooms, French beans, croquettes and tomato sauce. See also *Sartena*.

SARDINE   Sardine (young fish), pilchard (adult); also known as *cardeau*, *celan*, *haranguet*, *royan*. See also *demi-sel* and *poutina. Sardines à l'antiboise*: fried, with tomatoes, garlic; *à l'escabèche* (Provence especially): fried with onions, cold as a first course; *farci aux épinards* (Provence): stuffed with spinach, baked; *à la havraise*: stuffed, poached, with wine sauce, mussels, *à la hyéroise*: as above, with leeks instead of mussels; *à la pisane*: stuffed, baked with white wine, spinach, anchovies, tomato sauce; *Saint-Honorat*: fried, with tomatoes and mint-flavoured *béarnaise* sauce; *à la toulonnaise*: same as *havraise*; *à la vivandière*: poached, with mushrooms, cucumber, tomato sauce.

SARGUE   Name for type of sea bream (*sar*).

(À LA) SARLADAISE   In the style of Sarlat in *Périgord*. With truffles. *Pommes (de terre) à la sarladaise*: baked sliced potatoes and truffles.

SARMENT (DE VIGNE)   Vine shoot, sometimes used on grills.

SARRASIN   Saracen. Buckwheat, also known as *blé noir*. *Farine de sarrasin*: buckwheat flour, used especially in *Bretagne* for pancakes (*galettes*).

SARRASON   (Languedoc) Buttermilk mixed with water and milk, served with potatoes.

SARRIETTE   Savory, bitter herb; also known as *herbe de Saint-Julien* and *poivrette* and in *Provence* as *poivre d'âne* and *pèbre d'ai/d'as/d'aze*.

SARTADAGNANO/SARTAGNADE/SARTAÑADO   (Nice)   Mixture of small fish fried in oil and seasoned with vinegar.

SARTASSOU   (Vivarais) Whey with potatoes.

SARTENA/SARTENAIS   (Corse)   Ball-shaped cheese of goat's, sheep's milk, or a mixture, with a sharp flavour; probably dating back to Roman times, and made by farms around Sartène.

SASSENAGE   (Dauphiné) Large loaf-shaped smooth blue cheese of cow's milk plus a little goat's milk, with spicy flavour; made by dairies in the Sassenage region, also known as *Bleu de Sassenage*.

SAUCE   Sauce. For the numerous sauces, see under their distinguishing names (e.g. *sauce gribiche*: see *gribiche*).

SAUCIAU   See *sanciau*.

SAUCISSE Sausage, the type that must be cooked before eating, usually grilled or fried; also including smoked or dried sausages which may be poached. *Saucisse de bière* (Alsace): mixed meat and fat, but no beer; *à la boudine* (Poitou): pork and sorrel or chard (*blette*); *croquante*: dried, smoked, of pork and beef, tied together in pairs; *de Francfort*: Frankfurter; *au gruau*: pork and wheat-meal; *madrilène*: small, of veal, pork fat and sardines, tied into rings; *rouge*: of pork, with red pepper; *de Strasbourg*: smoked beef and pork, eaten especially with *choucroute*; *de Toulouse*: long and rough.

SAUCISSON Large slicing sausage, eaten cold as a first course; of 2 main kinds – *saucisson sec*: dried sausage (i.e. hung up to dry naturally) usually of coarsely chopped pork (e.g. *saucisson de montagne/de campagne*, *rosette* and *jésus*), although *saucisson d'Arles* is made of pork and beef; and *saucisson* which is not dried but cooked (e.g. *saucisson à l'ail*: garlic sausage), usually softer. *Saucisson noir*: see *schwarzwurst*.

Large saveloy type of sausage, poached and eaten hot with various garnishes. *Saucisson chaud à l'alsacienne*: with horseradish; *à la lyonnaise*: with hot potato salad.

SAUCLET Name for sandsmelt (*athérine*).

SAUGE Sage, the herb.

SAULIEU Town in *Bourgogne*. See *jambon*.

SAUMON Salmon. *Saumon froid à la norvégienne*: cold, jellied, with prawns, cucumber etc; *en pain de Caudebec*: cold loaf, *à la parisienne*: cold, mayonnaise; *Réjane*: baked cutlets with white wine sauce. *Darne de saumon à la danoise*: poached slice with boiled potatoes, anchovy and butter sauce.

SAUMON BLANC Name for hake (*colin*).

SAUMONÉ(-E) Salmon pink. Treated like salmon. See *truite de mer* and *veau*.

SAUMONEAU Grilse, young salmon, also known as *tocan* in *Béarn*.

SAUMONETTE Name for dogfish (*roussette*).

SAUMUR City of *Anjou*, famous for dry white wines (*AC*), both still and sparkling, made principally from the *Chenin Blanc* grape, and sold as *Saumur*, *Saumur Mousseux* or, *Crémant de Loire*; also making red wines and dry rosé. See also *rillette*.

SAUMUR-CHAMPIGNY Red wine (*AC*) grown in the *Saumur* region.

SAUMURÉ Food salted or pickled in brine ('saumure').

SAUPE Type of sea bream.

SAUPIQUET Piquant red wine and vinegar sauce; served with roast hare or venison, especially in *Foix*, and with ham in *Bourgogne* and *Bourbonnais*.

SAUQUET (Languedoc) Cooked chicken's blood with garlic and vinegar.

SAUR/SAURET (Flandre, Picardie) Name for *hareng saur*.

SAUREL Horse mackerel, scad, different species from ordinary mackerel and less good; also known as *carringue*, *chien*, *chinchard*, *cudaspru*, *estrangle-belle-mère*, *robinette*, *séveran* and *sévereau*.

SAURET See *saur*.

SAUSSIGNAC Town, west of *Bergerac*, producing red and white wines (*AC*).

SAUSSON (Provence) Almond, anchovy and mint paste; also known as *sauce aux amandes*.

SAUTÉ(-E) Lit.: 'jumped', 'tossed'. Sautéed, lightly fried or browned. Sautéed food (e.g. *sauté de poulet*).

SAUTERELLE (DE MER) Lit.: '(sea) grasshopper'. Name for mantis shrimp (*squille*). (Boulonnais) Or local name for shrimp (*crevette*).

SAUTERNES Small area of *Bordeaux*, famous for sweet white wines (*AC*), including Château Yquem, *premier grand cru*. Other fine vineyards of *Sauternes* and neighbouring *Barsac* are classified into 11 *premiers crus* and 12 *deuxièmes*.

SAUVAGE Wild; uncultivated (e.g. mushroom); undomesticated (e.g. duck).

SAUVIGNON Variety of white grape, present in all the great white wines of *Bordeaux*, and on the *Loire* for *Sancerre* and *Pouilly-Blanc-Fumé*; wines may be sold as *cépage Sauvignon*, and are usually dry and crisp.

SAUZE-VAUSSAIS (Poitou) Factory-made goat's milk cheese; trade name.

SAVARIN Light ring-shaped yeast cake soaked in rum or *kirsch*; originally known as *Brillat-Savarin*.

SAVAGNIN Variety of grape, used in *vin jaune*.

SAVARON (Auvergne) Large round cheese, with grey mildewy rind, strong smell and flavour; made by dairies.

SAVENNIÈRES Area in *Anjou*, making full dry white wine (*AC*) from the *Chenin Blanc* grape; *Coulée de Serrant* and *La-Roche-aux-Moines* may add their names to *Savennières* (*AC*).

SAVIGNY-LES-BEAUNE Commune of *Côte de Beaune*, *Bourgogne*, making mainly red wines (*AC*).

SAVOIE Savoy, province divided into the *Savoie* and Haute-Savoie departments.
White wine, still and sparkling (*AC*), made from the *Chasselas* grape in *Savoie*, known as *Vin de Savoie*. See also *Roussette*.

(À LA) SAVOYARDE In the style of *Savoie*. With cheese and potatoes (e.g. *omelette à la savoyarde*, and *pommes de terre à la savoyarde*, also known as *gratin savoyard*). *Soupe savoyarde*: vegetable soup with cheese and milk. See also *croûte*, *escalope* and *poulet*.

SCARE Parrot-fish, Mediterranean fish.

SCAROLE Scarole, Batavian endive, salad green; also known as *escarole*, and sometimes *chicorée*.

SCHALETH (À LA JUIVE) (Alsace) Large baked apple dumpling.

SCHANKELAS (Alsace) Almond pastry roll.

SCHIFELA/SCHIFFALA (Alsace) Hot smoked shoulder of pork, often with potato and onion salad or pickled turnips.

SCHNITZEN Dried apples and pears, served with game.

SCHWARZWURST (Alsace) Smoked pork and onion sausage; also known as *saucisson noir*.

SCIACCE (Corse) Sweet cheese pastry.

SCIÈNE Name for meagre (*maigre*).

SCIPION Name for small cuttlefish (*sépiole*).

SCORPION Lit.: 'scorpion'. Name for *rascasse*.

SCORSONÈRE Scorzonera; see also *salsifis*.

SÉBASTE CHÈVRE Name for *rascasse*.

SEC (SÈCHE) Dry. Dried (e.g. *raisin sec*: raisin). Dry, of wine, but of *Champagne*, leaning towards sweetness, midway between *extra-sec* and *demi-sec*.

SÈCHE (Franche-Comté) Sweet tart. See also above and below.

SEICHE/SÈCHE Cuttlefish; also known as *casseron*, *sépi(a)* and *supi*. *Seiche à l'agathoise*: stuffed and boiled. *Blanc de seiche grillé* (Charentes): grilled over charcoal, served with butter.

SÉGURET See *Côtes-du-Rhône-Villages*.

SEIGLE Rye. See also *farine* and *pain*.

SEL Salt. *Sel gemme*: rock salt (lit.: 'gem'). *Sel gris*: coarse rock or sea salt; also known as *gros sel*. *Sel marin*: sea salt. *Sel raffiné/fin/de table*: table salt. See also *croque au sel* and *demi-sel*.

SELLE Saddle, back. *Selle d'agneau Mirabelle*: roast saddle of lamb with vegetables. *Selle de veau Metternich*: braised saddle of veal with creamy paprika sauce and rice. See also *chevreuil*.

SELLES-SUR-CHER (Orléanais, Berry) Goat's milk cheese (*AOC*), small round, flat, dusted with charcoal, ripened for three weeks, white inside with light smell and mild flavour; named after the nearest town, also known as *Romorantin*.

SELON According to. *Selon arrivage*: available according to arrival, especially of fish. *Selon grosser/grandeur*: priced according to size, especially of lobster.

SELTZ See *eau*.

SEMILLON Variety of white grape, used in the wines of *Bordeaux* and the SW.

SEMOULE Semolina. See also *sucre*.

SÉNANCOLE Bright yellow herb-flavoured liqueur, from Salon in *Provence*.

SÉPI(A) Lit.: 'sepia' (cuttlefish ink). (S France) Local name for cuttlefish (*seiche*).

SÉPIOLE/SÉPIOU/SEPIOUN/SUPIOUN/SUPPION Small cuttlefish, popular in S France; also known as *muscardin* and *scipion*.

SEPT HEURES Lit.: 'seven hours'. See *gigot*.

SEPTMONCEL See *Bleu de Gex-Haut-Jura*.

SEPT TROUS/YEUX Lit.: 'seven holes/eyes'. Name for lamprey (*lamproie*).

(À LA) SERBE   Serbian-style. See *aubergine*.

SÉRIOLE   Amberjack, large sea fish; also known as *parme* and *poisson limon*.

SERPOL(ET)   Wild thyme, name used especially in *Provence*. *Serpolet du Canada*: name for lemon thyme (*thym-citron*).

SERRAN   Comber, small type of sea bass, Varieties include *serran écriture*: lettered (lit.: 'writing') perch, also known as *perche* (*de mer*) and *serran chevrette*.

SERRE   Greenhouse.

SERRÉ(-E)   Lit.: 'tight', 'compact'. Cheese made from whey.

SERVANT   Lit.: 'servant'. Variety of white table grape.

SERVI(-E)   Served. See also *garniture*.

SERVICE   Service, service charge. The percentage of the bill which is either included (*service compris*) or extra (*service non compris*), in which case you should add 12–15%.

SERVIETTE   Napkin. *A la serviette*: presented in a napkin (e.g. jacket potatoes, rice, truffles). See also *caneton*.

(À LA) SÉTOISE   In the style of Sète in *Languedoc*. See *langouste*.

SÈVE   Lit.: 'sap'. Sloe and brandy liqueur, from *Berry*. *Sève d'angélique*: angelica liqueur, from *Niort*.

SÉVERAN/SÉVEREAU   (Provence) Local name for scad (*saurel*).

SÉVÉRINE   Garnish of lettuce, mushrooms and potatoes.

SÈVRE-ET-MAINE   See *Muscadet*.

SEVRUGA   See *caviar*.

SEYOT   (Boulonnais) Local name for monkfish (*lotte*).

SEYSSEL   Town straddling the upper *Rhône*, making the best-known white wines (*AC*) of *Savoie*, from the *Roussette* grape, some of them sparkling.

SG   *Selon grosseur/grandeur*. See *selon*.

(À LA) SIBÉRIENNE   Siberian-style. See *asperges*.

(À LA) SICILIENNE   Sicilian-style. With pasta, cheese, pistachio nuts, sometimes chicken livers. See also *céleri-rave*.

SIG(UI)   Russian fish, smoked, pickled or fresh, as a first course.

(À LA) SILÉSIENNE   Silesian-style. Garnish of stuffed tomatoes and rice. See also *anchois*.

SILURE   Wels, freshwater fish similar to burbot.

SIMPLE   Plain, unadorned.

SIOUCLET   Name for sandsmelt (*athérine*).

SIRÈNE   Lit.: 'siren'. (Poitou) Sweet pastry in a serpent shape.

SIROP   Syrup.

SIX-YEUX   Lit.: 'six eyes'. Name for ormer (*ormeau*).

SMITANE   *Sauce smitane*: white wine and sour cream sauce, for game.

SOBRONADE   (Périgord) Soup of fresh and salt pork, haricot beans, root vegetables, poured on slices of bread.

SOCCA   (Nice) Thin flat cake of chick pea flour; sold in the street and eaten with salt or sugar.

SOJA   Soya bean.

(À LA) SOISSONNAISE   In the style of *Soissons*. With white haricot beans.

SOISSONS   Town in *Ile-de-France* known for large white haricot beans, which are sometimes called (*Belles de*) *Soissons*.

SOLANGE   *Consommé Solange*: clear soup with pearl barley, lettuce and chicken.

SOLE   Dover sole (called 'solea' by the ancients, as being worthy footwear for an ocean nymph). Smaller relatives include *sole de Klein/tachetée* (lit.: 'of Klein', 18th-century naturalist/'speckled'); *sole ocellée*; *sole panachée*: thickback sole; *sole pélouse/pôle*: sand sole (lit.: 'lawn'); *sole velue* (lit.: 'hairy').

Among innumerable recipes for sole, fillets of sole, and *paupiettes* (stuffed and rolled fillets) are *sole Albert*: sautéed, finished with *vermouth*; *arlésienne*: poached, with tomatoes, courgettes, onions, cream; *Caprice*: grilled, with fried banana; *cardinal*: stuffed, poached, with lobster sauce; *Condé*: poached, with wine and tomato sauce; *Coquelin*: poached in white wine, with boiled potatoes; *Cubat*: poached, with puréed mushrooms and white sauce; *Déjazet*: fried, with tarragon butter; *Dominique*: stuffed, baked with wine, cream, mushrooms and cheese sauce; *Dubois*: fried strips with white wine sauce; *Dugléré*: poached, with white wine, tomatoes, onions, herbs and cream sauce; *à la Duse*: stuffed, poached, with rice, shrimps and cheese sauce; *fécampoise*: same as *trouvillaise*; *Floréal*: stuffed, poached, with asparagus and white wine sauce; *au glui* (Normandie): grilled with straw, old recipe; *Héloise*: poached, with mushrooms; *Hermitage*: stuffed, baked, with butter and cream sauce; *Isidore*: baked with shallots, tomatoes and white wine; *à la Jacques*: poached in white wine with onions, mushrooms, potatoes; *Jean-Bart*: poached, with shrimps, mussels, mushrooms and cream sauce; *Lutèce*: fried, on spinach bed with artichokes, onions, fried potatoes; *Marguéry*: poached, with mussels, shrimps and rich egg sauce; *Miramar*: fried, with rice, aubergines; *Murat*: fried strips (*goujons*) with artichokes, tomatoes, potatoes; *Nelson*: poached, with soft roes, potatoes and white wine sauce; *à la nissarde*: poached with courgettes; *Noël*: similar to *Jean-Bart*; *normande*: poached in cider, with mussels, shrimps and cream sauce, or in the *Paris* version using white wine and adding elaborate garnish of oysters, crayfish, truffles etc; *Paillard*: stuffed, poached in white wine, with mushrooms, onions; *persane*: poached, with peppers, rice, paprika and lobster sauce; *Prunier*: poached, with oysters, truffles and cream sauce; *à la rochelaise*: poached in red wine, with soft roes, oysters, mussels; *Roscoff*: poached, with lobster, paprika, tomato and cream sauce; *à la russe*: poached, with butter sauce; *Tivoli*: poached in red wine, with soft roes, oysters, mushrooms, noodles; *à la trouvillaise*: poached, with shrimps, mussels, mushrooms, also known as *fécampoise*; *Véronique*: poached in white wine, with grapes; *Walewska*: poached, with scampi, truffles and cheese sauce.

Sole d'Ecosse: lit.: 'Scottish sole'. Name for *fausse sole*. *Sole limande*: lemon sole, also known as *limande (sole)*. *Sole maudite*: lit.: 'cursed sole'. Name for scaldfish (*fausse limande*).

SOLETTE   Small sole, slip; also known as *céteau* and *langue d'avocat*.

SOLFÉRINO   Battle in N Italy (1859) between French and Austrians. *Potage Solférino*: cream of tomato soup with leeks and carrots.

SOLOGNE   Wooded region in *Orléanais*. See also *gigot*.

SOLILEM/SOLIMÈME   (Alsace) Yeast cake, served hot with butter.

(À LA) SOLOGNOTE   In the style of *Sologne*. See *caneton*, *lamproie*, *lapin* and *tarte*.

SOPHIE   See *escalope*.

SORBAIS   (Flandre) Smaller version of *Maroilles* cheese, named after a village.

SORBE (ALISIER)/SORBIER Sorb apple/sorb tree, similar to rowan and *alisier*. Also a clear spirit of sorb apples, a speciality of *Alsace*.

SORBET Sorbet, water ice. *Sorbet de milieu*: taken between courses as a refresher.

SORGES Town in *Périgord*. See *poulet*.

SORGHO Sorghum, kind of millet, used in porridges etc.

SOSPEL See *Tomme de Sospel*.

SOT-Y-LAISE Oyster, of chicken.

SOUBISE With puréed onions; dedicated to the Prince de Soubise, friend of Louis XV.

SOU-FASSUM/SOUS FASSOUN (Provence) Boiled cabbage stuffed with meat, rice etc: also known as *fassum*.

SOUFFLÉ Lit.: 'puffed', 'blown up'. Soufflé, sweet or savoury, usually hot (as opposed to cold *mousse*). *Soufflé glacé*: iced soufflé.

SOUPE Substantial soup (as opposed to more refined *potage*), usually based on vegetables, especially cabbage, leeks, roots, with bread in some form and sometimes salt pork or sausage; from *souper*: supper. For different kinds, see under their distinguishing names (e.g. *soupe au pistou*: see *pistou*).

SOUPER Supper. To sup, have supper.

SOUPIR DE NONNE Lit.: 'nun's sigh'. See *pet de nonne*.

SOURCE Source, spring. See also *eau minérale*.

SOURDON (Charentes) Name for cockle (*coque*).

SOUS Under.

SOUS FASSOUN See *sou fassum*.

SOUS-NOIX See *noix*.

(À LA) SOUVAROFF/SOUVAROV Of quail, pheasant etc, casseroled with *foie gras*, truffles, brandy and madeira; originally served in a pastry crust, cracked open at table. Iced *petit four*.

SOUVIGNY See *Chevrotin du Bourbonnais*.

SPARAILLON/SPARLOT Annular bream, type of sea bream; also known as *pataclé* and *squirlu*.

SPÄTSEL/SPÄTZEL (Alsace) Type of noodle.

SPÉCIAL(-E) Special. *Spéciale*: short for *huître spéciale*.

SPÉCIALITÉ Speciality.

SPÉCULOS (N France) Spiced buns, of Belgian origin.

SPET Name for barracuda (*brochet de mer*).

SPETZLI (Alsace) Rich dumplings, poached then fried, served with butter.

(À LA) SPINALIENNE In the style of *Epinal*.

SPOOM Frothy water ice of wine or fruit juice with egg whites.

SPRAT Name for sprat (*esprot*).

SQUALE Name for dogfish (*roussette*).

SQUERU (Corse) Local name for angel fish (*ange*).

SQUILLE Mantis shrimp; resembles praying mantis insect; also known as *mante* (*de mer*), *sauterelle de mer*, and *pregadiou*.

SQUINADO (S France) Local name for spider crab (*araignée de mer*).

SQUIRLU (Corse) Local name for type of sea bream (*sparaillon*).

(À LA) STANISLAS Stanislas Lesczinski, king of Poland, last duke of *Lorraine* and father-in-law of Louis XV. See *caille*.

STANLEY With creamy curry sauce. See also *artichaut*.

STC *Service et taxe comprise*: service and tax included.

STEA(C)K Steak, beefsteak; see also *bifteck*. *Steak au poivre*: fried steak covered in crushed peppercorns, sometimes flamed with brandy; *tartare*: raw minced steak mixed with raw egg, onions, capers. When ordering – *bleu*: very rare; *saignant*: rare; *à point*: medium; *bien cuit*: well done.

STEENWOORDE (Flandre) Trade name of dairy producing mainly Dutch-style cheeses.

STELLA Variety of potato.

(À LA) STEPHANOISE In the style of *Saint-Etienne*.

STERLET   Sterlet, fish related to sturgeon.

STOCAFICADA   See below.

STOCKFISH/STOCAFICADA/STOFICADO/STOFINADO   (Provence, Nice especially) Dried cod, opened out and flattened; also known as *badoche*, *estocaficada*, *estofica-do*, *estofinado* and *morue plate*. Stew of dried cod with garlic, tomatoes, potatoes, olives.

STORZAPRETI   (Corse) Spinach or Swiss chard (*blette*) with eggs.

STRASBOURG   Capital of the Bas-Rhin department in *Alsace*. See also *boudin*, *cervelas*, *foie gras*, *salamis* and *saucisse*.

(À LA) STRASBOURGEOISE   In the style of *Strasbourg*. With *chou-croute*, *foie gras* and salt pork. *Consommé à la stras-bourgeoise*: clear soup with red cabbage, sausage, horseradish, juniper berries.

STROMATÉE   Name for pomfret (*fiatole*).

STUFFATU   (Corse) Onion, tomato and wine sauce, to accompany beef, mutton, goat etc.

SUBRIC   Small fried ball, often of vegetables or sweetbreads.

(À LA) SUÇARELLE   Lit.: 'sucking'. See *escargot*.

SUCÉE   Lit.: 'sucked'. *Petit four* with chopped candied fruit.

SUCETTE   Lollipop.

SUCRE   Sugar. *Sucre brun/roux*: brown sugar; *de canne*: cane; *cristallisé*: granulated; *filé*: spun; *glace*: icing; *d'orge*: barley; *en morceaux/pain*: loaf, cube; *en poudre/semoule*: caster. *Sucre de pomme* (Normandie): sugar apple. See also *chicorée*.

SUCRÉ(-E)   Sweet, sweetened. Soft, of drinks.

SUCRIN   Sweet melon, especially from *Touraine*; also known as *prépon*.

(À LA) SUÉDOISE   Swedish-style. See *caneton*. *Suédoise*: jelly of puréed fruit.

SUFFREN   See *anguille*.

SUFFRIGE   (Camargue) Version of *bouillabaisse*.

SUGGELI   (Nice) Home-made pastry.

SUISSE   Swiss. Larger version of *Petit Suisse* cheese, also known as *Gros Suisse*.

Small sponge round with *kirsch*-flavoured icing. See also *gendarme* and *tartine*.

SUIVANT   According to.

(À LA) SULTANE   Lit.: 'sultan's style'. Garnish of red cabbage and potatoes.
Large elaborate pastry.

SUPÉRIEUR   Lit.: 'superior, higher'. Of wines – generally indicates a higher degree of alcohol than the simple appellation.

SUPI   (S France) Local name for cuttlefish (*seiche*).

SUPIOUN/SUPPION   Name for small cuttlefish (*sépiole*).

SUPRÊME (DE VOLAILLE)   Lit.: 'supreme'. Breast and wing fillet of chicken (or sometimes game), also known as *blanc/côtelette/filet de volaille*.
Suprême de volaille Françoise: cooked in butter, with cream sauce and asparagus; *Gabrielle*: sautéed; *Jeannette*: cold, jellied, in white sauce, surrounded with ice. See also *Fin-de-Siècle*.
Sauce suprême: creamy sauce.

SUR   On. *Sur lie*: see *Muscadet*. See also *commande* and *plat*.

SUREAU   Elder tree. Also a clear spirit made from elderberries, a speciality of *Alsace*.

SURELLE   Wood sorrel, wild plant sometimes eaten as salad or vegetable; also known as *oxalide*.

SURFIN(-E)   Superfine, extra fine.

SURMULET (ROUGET)   Name for red mullet (*rouget*).

(EN) SURPRISE   Lit.: 'in surprise'. Could mean anything; see also *melon* and *norvégienne*.

(EN) SUS   In addition, extra.

SUZE   Brand of yellow aperitif, spirit-based, flavoured with gentian.

SUZETTE   Mystery person dining with the Prince of Wales (future Edward VII), for whom the famous pancake was created. See *crêpe*.

SYLPHIDE (DE VOLAILLE)   Lit.: 'sylph'. Rich chicken *quenelle* in boat-shaped pastry, with cheese sauce.

SYLVANER   Variety of white grape, grown mainly in *Alsace*.

SYRAH   Variety of black grape grown in *Rhône* valley and S, producing full-bodied wines (e.g. *Cornas*, *Hermitage*).

TABLE　　　　Table. See also *eau minérale* and *vin*.

TABLE D'HÔTE　Lit.: 'host's table'. Meal of several courses at fixed price. Originally, arrangement where everyone sat at the same table and nearest thing to a restaurant; you might find something similar today, eating with the family at a farmhouse or small hotel.

TABLETTE　　　Tablet, small bar (e.g. of chocolate, almonds).

TABLIER DE SAPEUR　Lit.: 'sapper's (fireman's) apron'. (Lyonnais) Slab of ox tripe coated with egg and breadcrumbs, grilled, served with snail butter, tartare sauce or spicy mayonnaise.

TACAUD　　　　Pout, type of cod; also known as *gode*, *morue borgne*, *officier* and *p'louse*.

(LA) TÂCHE　　See *Vosne-Romanée*.

TAGLIARINI　　(Corse) Pasta strips.

TAILLEVENT　　14th-century royal chef, author of the first French cookery book.

TALIBUR　　　　See *rabotte*.

TALLEYRAND　　Charles-Maurice de Talleyrand-Périgord, Prince de *Bénévent* (1754–1838), statesman and gourmet, with *Carême* his cook for a time; the only master he never betrayed was *Brie*, so it was said. Garnish of truffles, with mushrooms, cream sauce, goose liver, Parmesan cheese or macaroni. *Sauce Talleyrand*: white sauce with truffles and tongue. *Consommé Talleyrand*: clear chicken soup with sherry and truffles. See also *caille*.

TALMOUSE　　　Pastry shell with cheese filling.

TAMBOUR　　　Lit.: 'drum'. Variety of comber (*serran*). See also *sar* and *baguette de tambour*.

TAMIÉ　　　　　(Savoie) Smooth round cheese with strong milky flavour, made at the Abbey of Tamié; also known as *Trappiste de Tamié*.

TANCHE　　　　Tench, small freshwater fish.

TANTOUILLET　See *gigoret*.

TANUDO　　　　(Provence) Local name for black bream (*griset*).

TAOUTEN(N)O　(Provence) Local name for squid (*calamar*).

TAPÉ(-E)　　　Dried. See also *poire*.

TAPENADE   (Provence) Thick anchovy paste with capers (*tapéno*), olives and tuna fish.

TAPÉNO   (Provence) Local name for capers (*câpre*).

TAPINETTE   (Orléanais, Bourgogne) Cheese tart, sometimes with saffron.

TAPIOCA   Tapioca, also known as *perles du Japon*.

TARARE   (Lyonnais) Small cylindrical cream cheese, farm-made.

TARBES   Capital of the Hautes-Pyrénées department and of *Bigorre*.

TARDETS   See *Esbareich*.

TARTARE   Tartar. *Sauce tartare*: mayonnaise with onions, herbs, capers, mustard. See also *steak*.
   (Périgord) Rich herb-flavoured cream cheese, factory-made.

TARTE   Tart, flan, usually sweet; from *tourte*. *Tarte alsacienne*: different jams in sections with latticed top and almond pastry; *bourbonnaise*: cheese; *Bourdaloue*: pear and custard; *au canelle*: fruit, with cinnamon pastry; *à la courge* (Provence): pumpkin and orange; *à l'écoloche* (Flandre): apple, with vanilla custard; *aux épinards* (Provence): sweet spinach, Christmas speciality; *flambée*: see *flammerkueche*; *maison*: usually large open fruit tart, probably home-made and often not on the menu, but worth asking for; *au m'gin/megin/mougin/mengin* (Lorraine): cream cheese; *niçoise*: spinach or chard (*blette*) with sardines or olives; *panachée mirliton*: upside-down, mixed fruit; *au quemeu* (Champagne): custard; (*des demoiselles*) *Tatin* (Orléanais especially): upside-down-apple pie, invented at La Motte-Beuvron, also known as *tarte solognote*.

TARTELETTE   Tartlet, savoury or sweet.

TARTIBAS   (Bourbonnais) Raisin pancake.

TARTINE   Slice of bread and butter, or jam etc. Small tart. *Tartine suisse*: of flaky or puff pastry filled with vanilla cream.
   (Picardie) Large round white loaf with raisins.

TARTINER   To spread. *Fromage à tartiner*: cheese spread.

TARTINETTE   (Alsace) Soft spreading sausage of beef and pork; also known as *weiche mettwurst*.

TARTISSEAU   (Charentes) Sweet fritter.

TARTOUFFE   Old name for potato. See also *pâté*.

TARTOUILLAT   (Bourgogne) Apple tart.

TASSE   Cup.

TASSERGAL   Blue fish, similar to mackerel.

TASTEVIN   Shallow silver cup for wine-tasting, especially in *Bourgogne*. *Confrérie des Chevaliers du Tastevin*: brotherhood founded in 1930s to promote *Bourgogne* wines, based at the château of *Clos de Vougeot*; it awards labels to approved wines.

TATIN   See *tarte*.

TÂTRE DES ALLYMES   (Lyonnais) Onion flan.

TAUPE   Porbeagle shark, sometimes eaten as steaks; also known as *chien de mer*.

TAUTENNE   (Provence) Local name for squid (*calamar*).

TAVEL   Village of the *Rhône*, making well-known rosé wine (*AC*), mainly from the *Grenache* grape.

TELLINE   Type of small clam with long flat shell, common in *Camargue*.

TÉNARÈZE   See *Armagnac*.

TENDRE DE TRANCHE   Name for silverside of beef (*gîte à la noix*).

TENDRON (DE VEAU)   Small strip of meat from the rib, of veal, containing cartilage, usually braised or pot-roasted; also known as *côtelette parisienne*.

TERÉE (DE MOULES)   See *éclade*.

TERFEZ   Large white truffle from N Africa.

TERGOULE / TEURGOULE / TORD-GOULE / TORGOULE / TERRINÉE   (Normandie) Rice pudding with cinnamon.

TERRAPÈNE   Terrapin, small turtle, rare in Europe.

TERRE   Earth, soil.

TERRINE   Cooking dish, usually rectangular with a lid and of earthenware (Latin 'terra' – earth). Technically correct name for pork-based *pâté*, cooked in a *terrine* and eaten cold; but see also *pâté*. *Terrine berrichonne*: rabbit and calf's foot; *de campagne*: coarse pork *pâté*, often a

speciality of the house; *de lapin aux pruneaux* (Touraine): rabbit with *Vouvray* wine and prunes; *de Nérac*: partridge; *quimpéroise*: rolled pork with onions and herbs. See also *anguille*.

TERRINÉE   Lit.: 'dishful'. (Bretagne) Pork and vegetables baked in a *terrine*. See also *tergoule*.

TESTARD   Name for chub (*chevaine*).

TÊTE   Head, especially calf's, often served hot with *vinaigrette*, and pig's, also used for brawn (*fromage de tête/hure de porc*). *Tête de veau à l'anglaise*: boiled calf's head with bacon and parsley sauce; *grosse nounou* (Charentes): stuffed with pork, veal, *Cognac*, mushrooms, truffles, served hot or cold with brains and gherkins. See also *presskopf* and *tortue*.

TÊTE D'ALOYAU   Lit.: 'head of sirloin'. Part of rump nearest the sirloin, of beef.

TÊTE DE CUVÉE   Lit.: 'top of vatful'. See *cuvée*.

TÊTE DE NÈGRE   Lit.: 'negro's head'. Fungus of the *cèpe* family.

TÉTINE   Udder, usually cow's, which may be braised or fried, or salted and smoked.

TÉTON DE VÉNUS   Lit.: 'Venus's breast'. Variety of peach.

TÉTRAGONE   New Zealand spinach, similar to the ordinary kind.

TÉTRAS   Grouse; often called *grouse* on French menus, but rare.

THAU   Bassin de Thau, lagoon on *Languedoc* coast, with the port of Sète at the entrance; centre for oyster and mussel cultivation.

TEURGOULE   See *tergoule*.

THÉ   Tea, the drink. *Thé au citron*: lemon tea, the most common method of serving. *Thé au lait*: tea with milk, often in a glass. *Thé à la menthe*: peppermint tea.

THÉODORE   See *rouget*.

THERMIDOR   Eleventh month of Republican calendar, 20 July–18 August. Lobster *Thermidor* was created during the Third-Republic, after the revival of a historical play; see *homard*.

THIÉZAC   See *Bleu de Thiézac*.

THIONVILLE   (Lorraine) Strong processed cheese, made from *Mattons*.

THON   Tuna, tunny fish; found in Mediterranean and warmer parts of Atlantic, eaten fresh or canned. *Thon (rouge)*: largest type; also known as *toun* in S. *Thon (blanc)*: long-fin tuna, smaller, fished as far N as *Bretagne*; also known as *germon*. *Thon concarnois*: baked with onions, vinegar, herbs, or with white wine, carrots, peas, rice; *froid sauce bretonne*: cold, with herby *vinaigrette*; *à la marinette*: salad with tomatoes, onions, potatoes, as a first course; *de Saint-Jean*: with peppers, tomatoes, white wine. *Tripes de thon en daube* (Languedoc): tuna tripe stewed in white wine with peppers, onions; *à la palavasienne*: fisherman's recipe for tuna tripe, with wine, sea water, herbs.

THÔNES   See *Persillé des Aravis*.

THONINE/THONNA/THOUNA/THOUNINA   Small Mediterranean tuna.

THOURINS   See *tourin*.

THOURSAIS   Area of NW *Poitou* around Thouars, making red, white and rosé wines (*VDQS*), known as *Vins du Thoursais*.

THYM   Thyme, the herb. *Thym-citron*: lemon thyme; also known as *serpolet du Canada*.

TIAN   (Provence) Shallow earthenware dish. Food baked in a *tian*, often of vegetables, plus eggs, rice, garlic etc, similar to *gratin*.

TIÈDE   Tepid. Warm.

TIGNARD/TIGNES   See *Bleu de Tignes*.

TILLEUL   Lime tree, whose flowers are used in herb tea.

TIMBALE   Round mould, originally designed to imitate pastry crust. Food cooked in a *timbale* (e.g. *timbale de macaroni*: lined with macaroni, with forcemeat filling). Modern *timbales* are often of fish or vegetable purées or small *mousses*, unmoulded, served with sauce (similar to *mousseline*). *Timbale vésulienne*: pike *quenelles*, veal sweetbreads and mushrooms.

TINTAINE   Aniseed-flavoured liqueur, bottled with a sprig of fennel.

TIORO   See *ttoro*.

TIRE   (Boulonnais) Local name for skate (*pocheteau*).

TIRER SUR LIE   See *Muscadet*.

TISANE   Herbal tea.

TIVOLI   Garnish of stuffed mushrooms and asparagus. See also *sole*.

TOCAN   (Béarn) Local name for young salmon (*saumoneau*).

TOKAY D'ALSACE   Name in *Alsace* for *Pinot Gris* grape variety.

TOMATE   Tomato, essential ingredient of Mediterranean dishes, and of many garnishes (e.g. *catalane*, *marseillaise*, *niçoise*, *portugaise*); used raw or cooked, or as purée or *concassée*. *Tomates à l'antiboise*: with anchovies, tuna, garlic, browned; *à la génoise*: with peppers, anchovies, potatoes; *à la monégasque*: stuffed with tuna and hard-boiled eggs; *à la provençale*: halved, sprinkled or filled with herbs, breadcrumbs and garlic, fried or baked.

TOMATE DE MER   Red sea anemone, sometimes used in fish soups in the S; also known as *actine*.

TOMBE   Lit.: 'grave'. Name for tub gurnard (*grondin galinette*).

TOM(M)E   Name for large number of cheeses, mainly from the Alps, usually mild, of cow's or goat's milk; see below. Dialect for cheese in *Savoie*.

TOMME ARLÉSIENNE   See *Tomme de Camargue*.

TOMME AU FENOUIL / AU MARC / AUX RAISINS / BOUDANE / DE BAUGES / DE BELLEVILLE / DU REVARD   See *Tomme de Savoie*.

TOMME D'ABONDANCE / D'ALIGOT (FRAÎCHE) / D'ANNOT / D'ARÊCHES   See *Abondance*, *Aligot*, *Annot* and *Grataron d'Arêches*.

TOMME D'AUVERGNE/DE CANTAL   General name for small goat's milk cheeses (e.g. *Brique du Forez*).

TOMME DE BEAUFORT / DE BELLEY / DE COMBOVIN / DE CORPS /DE COURCHEVEL / DE CREST / DES ALLUES/DU PELVOUX   See *Tomme de Chèvre*.

TOMME DE BRACH   (Limousin) Firm cylindrical sheep's milk cheese, with strong flavour, farm-made; dialect name, also known as *Caillada de Vouillos*.

TOMME DE CAMARGUE   (Provence) Fresh square herb-flavoured cheese, of sheep's milk, with mild creamy taste, stronger with age; made by small dairies, also known as *Tomme Arlésienne*.

TOMME DE CANTAL   See *Tomme d'Auvergne* (not to be confused with *Fourme de Cantal*).

TOMME DE CHÈVRE   General name for large number of goat's milk cheeses, usually made by mountain farms, ranging from mild to strong in flavour, named after the place of origin. These include (Savoie) *Tomme des Allues/de Beaufort/ de Courchevel*; (Dauphiné) *Tomme de Combovin/de Corps/de Crest/du Pelvoux*; (Franche-Comté) *Tomme de Belley*, also known as *Chevret*.

TOMME DE LIVRON/DE MAURIENNE   See *Livron* and *Chevrine de Lenta*.

TOMME DE ROMANS   (Dauphiné) Factory-made round cheese on straw, originally of goat's milk, with light smell and flavour; produced at Romans-sur-Isère.

TOMME DE SAINT-MARCELLIN   See *Saint-Marcellin*.

TOMME DE SAVOIE   (Savoie) Large round smooth cheese with grey dotted rind, mouldy smell, mild flavour, made by farms and dairies; similar versions or varieties, named according to the place of origin, include *Tomme de Bauges/de Belleville/Boudane/du Revard. Tomme au Fenouil*: flavoured with fennel. *Tomme au Marc/aux Raisins*: steeped in grape *marc*.

TOMME DE SOSPEL   (Nice) Sheep's or goat's milk cheese with fruity flavour; made around Sospel.

TOMME DE MONT-VENTOUX/FRAÎCHE   See *Cachat* and *Aligot*.

TOPINAMBOUR   Jerusalem artichoke, also known as *artichaut d'hiver/du Canada* and *poire de terre. Palestine* sometimes indicates their presence.

TORCHON   Cloth, napkin.

TOR(D)GOULE   See *tergoule*.

TORPILLE   Lit.: 'torpedo'. Large fish similar to skate; also known as *tremble* in *Charentes*.

TORTA CASTAGNINA   (Corse) Chestnut flour tart with nuts, raisins and rum.

TORTE   Sweet filled flan. Rich cake layered with cream. From the German.

TORTILLON   (Gascogne) Ring-shaped aniseed biscuit.

TORTUE   Turtle (imported); the flippers (*nageoires*) are prized. *Potage à la tortue*: clear soup of meat stock and turtle pieces.
    Sauce tortue: herby tomato and madeira sauce. *En tortue*: with *quenelles*, mushrooms, truffles, olives,

gherkins, tongue and brains, bound with *sauce tortue*, for calf's head.

TOSCA   See *poularde*.

(À LA) TOSCANE   Tuscan-style. Of chicken pieces, steaks, etc, fried with Parmesan cheese, plus truffles, *foie gras* and macaroni. See also *carré*.

TÔT-FAIT   Lit.: 'soon-made'. Sponge cake.

TOUL   See *Côtes de Toul*.

TOULIA   (Bigorre) Onion soup, sometimes with cheese, tomatoes, leeks and garlic.

(À LA) TOULONNAISE   In the style of Toulon in *Provence*. *Omelette à la toulonnaise*: omelette with fried artichokes. See also *barbue*, *moule*, and *sardine*.

TOULOUSE   Capital of the Haute-Garonne department in *Languedoc*. See also *foie gras* and *saucisse*.

(À LA) TOULOUSAINE   In the style of *Toulouse*. Garnish of truffles, *foie gras*, sweetbreads, cockscombs and kidneys in cream sauce. Filling for pastries etc of white meat in white sauce. *Pommes (de terre) à la toulousaine*: sliced potatoes cooked with goose fat, garlic and stock. See also *aïllade* and *gâteau*.

TOUN   (S France) Local name for large tuna (*thon*).

TOUPIN   Earthenware cooking pot, bulbous at the base, narrow at the top; used in the SW especially for *garbure* and *daubes*. Food cooked in a *toupin*.

TOUPINEL   Vaudeville show of late 19th century. *Oeufs à la Toupinel*: poached eggs in baked potatoes.

(À LA) TOUQUETTOISE   In the style of Le Touquet in *Picardie*.

TOURAIN   See *tourin*.

TOURAINE   Province roughly equivalent to the Indre-et-Loire department. The general *AC Touraine*, sometimes with a village name (e.g. Mesland, *Amboise*) added, covers red, white, rosé, still and sparkling wines.

(À LA) TOURANGELLE   In the style of *Touraine*. With mixed haricot and French beans. With prunes. *Salade tourangelle*: haricot and French bean salad with potatoes. See also *beauchelle*, *fève* and *matelote*.

TOUR D'ARGENT   *Paris* restaurant, in the quai de la Tournelle, dating from 1582; famous for its system, started in the

1890s, of numbering the ducks consumed. See *caneton*
and *noisette*.

TOURDRE   (S France) Local name for type of wrasse (*labre vert*).

TOURIN   (SW France) Onion and milk soup, poured over slices of
bread, sometimes with grated cheese; also known as
thourins and *tourain*.

TOURMETA   (Nice) Heart-shaped pastry with sheep's milk cheese.

TOURNEDOS   Lit.: 'turn-back'. Small round steak, from thickest part
of the fillet, of beef; see also *Rossini*. *Tournedos de
Cambo*: with aubergines, shallots, peppers and potatoes; *Cendrillon*: sautéed, with stuffed artichokes;
cordon rouge: larded with ham and *foie gras*, sautéed,
with brandy and port sauce; *Curnonsky*: sautéed, with
grilled tomatoes, bone marrow, *Cognac*, port and truffle
sauce; *Marguéry*: sautéed, with stuffed artichokes, port
and cream sauce; *à la monégasque*: sautéed, with aubergines, tomato sauce, black olives; *Rossini*: with truffles,
foie gras, madeira sauce; *Roumanille*: sautéed, with
tomatoes, aubergines, anchovies, olives, cheese sauce.

TOURNELLES   See *Tour d'Argent*.

TOURNESOL   Sunflower. See also *huile*.

TOURNON-SAINT-PIERRE   (Touraine) Mild goat's milk cheese;
made by farms around Tournon.

TOURON/TTOURON   (S France) Almond pastry with hazelnuts, pis-
tachios, crystallized fruit; of Spanish origin.

TOURRI   See *ouillat*.

TOURS   Capital of the Indre-et-Loire department, and of
Touraine. See also *marcassin*, *porc* and *rillette*.

TOURTE   Pie, covered tart, usually savoury (as opposed to *tarte*,
generally sweet); from Latin 'torta' – round. *Tourte/
tourton de blettes* (Nice): Swiss chard, eggs and cheese.
Tourte aux grenouilles (Lorraine): frog's legs with egg

custard; *à la lorraine*: veal and pork with custard; *aux pavots* (Lorraine): sweet, poppy seeds and custard; *paysanne* (Franche-Comté): pork, served hot; *de truffes à la périgourdine*: truffles and *foie gras* with brandy; *à la viande* (Auvergne): pork and veal.

(Corse) Chestnut porridge with pine nuts, aniseed and raisins.

TOURTEAU   Large crab, also known as *dormeur*, *poupart* and *poing-clos*.

Oilcake. *Tourteau fromagé* (Poitou): cheese cake.

TOURTEREAU/TOURTERELLE   Turtle dove.

TOURTIÈRE   Pie dish; flan case. Food cooked in a *tourtière*, especially *tourtière* (*au poulet et aux salsifis*) (Périgord, Angoumois): chicken and salsify pie.

TOURTISSEAU   (Poitou) Orange-flavoured fritter.

TOURTON/TOURTOU   (Limousin) Thick buckwheat flour pancake, also known as *galetou*. See also *tourte*.

TOUT(-E) (pl. TOUS, TOUTES)   All, every etc.

TOUTE-ÉPICE   Allspice; also known as *nielle, nigelle, poivre de la Jamaïque* and *quatre-épices*.

TRADITIONEL(-LE)   Traditional.

TRAIN   (Hind)quarters. *Train de lièvre*: saddle of hare including hind legs.

Train de côtes: rib, of beef; also known as *côte de boeuf*.

TRANCHE   Slice, of bread, cheese etc.

Rasher, steak, chop, of meat.

Tranche grasse: thick flank, of beef. *Tranche au petit os*: cut of beef, from the silverside.

Tranches napolitains: Neapolitan ice cream, layers of plain ice and *mousse*.

TRANG'NAT   (Lorraine) Soft salted and peppered cheese, home-made; used mainly in *Gueyin*.

TRAPPISTINE   Greenish-yellow liqueur, based on *Armagnac*, herb-flavoured, made especially in *Franche-Comté*.

TRAVERS DE PORC   Pork spareribs.

(LOU) TRÉBUC   (Pays basque, Béarn) Preserved goose, pork, turkey or duck, often added to *garbure*; also known as *tromblon*.

TREIZE DESSERTS DE NOËL   (Provence) Lit.: '13 desserts of Christmas'. Mixture of fresh, dried and candied fruit, nuts, small cakes, sweets etc; traditionally served on Christmas Eve in memory of Christ and the 12 Apostles.

TREMBLE   (Charentes) Local name for torpedo (*torpille*), whose liver is often eaten on toast.

TREMPETTE   Slice of bread soaked in soup before serving; 'tremper' – to soak.

TRÉNELS   See *manouls*.

TREUFFE   (central France) Local name for potato (*pomme de terre*). See also *pâté*.

TREVISE   Red chicory, salad vegetable with bitter taste.

TRIANON   Château in *Paris*. Cold dessert of peaches, apricots, nectarines or pears on vanilla *mousse*, with liqueur-soaked macaroons and puréed strawberries.

TRICASTIN   See *Coteaux du Tricastin*.

TRICHOLOME   Family of fungi with firm flesh, of different colours, including *mousseron*; other varieties also known as *chevalier* and *petit pied bleu*.

TRIGLE   Name for gurnard (*grondin*).

TRIPA   (Corse) Sausages of lamb's tripe and vegetables.

TRIPAILLES   Name for tripe (*tripes*).

(À LA) TRIPE   *Oeufs* (*durs*) *à la tripe* (Normandie especially): hard-boiled eggs with stewed onions and milk; also known as *oeufs à la lyonnaise*.

TRIPE DE MER   (Provence) Local name for octopus (*poulpe*).

TRIPÉE   (Picardie) Pig's offal stewed in white wine.

TRIPES   Tripe, stomach; of ox, technically all 4 stomachs (as opposed to *gras-double* – 3 stomachs). *Tripes à l'alésienne*: (ox) with carrots, celery, tomatoes; *à la mode d'Angoulême*: (ox) plus trotters wth white wine, tomatoes, garlic; *au Banyuls* (Roussillon): (ox) with *Banyuls* and white wine, tomatoes, garlic etc; *à la cadurcienne*: (ox) with saffron; *à la mode de Caen*: perhaps the most famous dish, made with 4 stomachs of ox, cooked with trotters, cider, *Calvados*, carrots, onions, herbs in an earthenware 'tripière'; *à la cambraisienne*: (ox) plus trotters with herbs and fried potatoes; *de la Ferté-Macé*: small packets (ox) on skewers; *à la niçoise*: (ox) with white wine, onions, carrots, garlic; *à la paloise*: (veal) with white wine and *Bayonne* ham; *à la provençale*: (ox, pig) with pig's head and tomato sauce: *à la rébouleto*

(Provence): (mutton) with *vinaigrette* dressing; *rouergates*: see *manouls*; *à la mode de Saint-Malo*: (ox) cooked in cider with calf's foot and salt pork; *à la mode de Vannes*: as above with carrots and leeks. See also *civet* and *thon*.

TRIPETTES   (Corse) Sheep's tripe.

TRIPLE-CRÈME   Lit.: 'triple cream'. Legal name for cheese containing more than 75% butterfat (e.g. *Fontainebleau*).

TRIPLE SEC   Lit.: 'triple dry'. White orange-flavoured liqueur, originally made by the firm of *Cointreau*.

TRIPOTCH(KA)   (Pays basque) Spicy black pudding of mutton/veal.

TRIPOUS/TRIPOUX   (S and central France) Small cushions of mutton/veal tripe, stuffed and heavily seasoned.

TROGNON   Edible part of fruit or vegetable (e.g. apple, cabbage).

TROIS FRÈRES   Lit.: 'three brothers'. Rich cake, created by the 3 Julien brothers, 19th-century pastrycooks.

TROMBLON   See *trébuc*.

TROMPETTE DES MORTS   Lit.: 'trumpet of death(s)', 'horn of plenty'. Name for type of fungus (*craterelle*).

TRONÇON   Thick cut, chunk, of meat, fish, especially salmon. *Tronçon de milieu*: middle cut (e.g. of salmon).

TROO   See *Montoire*.

TROUCH(I)A   See *trucca*.

TROUFFE   (central France) Local name for potato (*pomme de terre*).

TROUVILLE   Town in *Normandie*. Trade name for farm-made *Pont-l'Evêque*.

(À LA) TROUVILLAISE   In the style of *Trouville*. See *rouget* and *sole*.

TROYES   Capital of the Aube department in *Champagne*. See also *andouille*, *andouillette* and *Barbery*.

TRUCCA/TRUCHA (CANNOISE)   Swiss chard (*blette*) or spinach omelette; also known as *trouchia*.

TRUCHE   (Berry) Local name for potato (*pomme de terre*).

TRUFFADE/TRUFFADO   (Auvergne) Potato cake with *Cantal* cheese, perhaps bacon and garlic.

TRUFFE Truffle, prized underground fungus growing on oak and hazel tree roots, scented out by dogs or pigs. The best – black, rough, strongly scented – are found in *Périgord*, *Quercy* and elsewhere; other types are violet, or white (from N Italy, *terfez* from N Africa). *Truffes rêve d'amour*: cooked in *Champagne* with herbs, eaten cold; *à la serviette*: cooked in madeira or *Champagne*, presented in a dish in a folded napkin; *sous la cendre*: wrapped in bacon and paper, cooked in ashes, or baked in pastry.

Old name for potato (*pomme de terre*), still used in parts of central France. See also *pâté*.

Chocolate truffle (sweet).

TRUFFÉ(-E) Truffled – garnished, studded or stuffed with truffles.

TRUFFIAT (Berry) Thick potato pancake, or potatoes wrapped in pastry; also known as *bourre-chrétien*.

TRUIE DE MER Lit.: 'sea sow'. Name for *rascasse*.

TRUITE Trout. *Truite arc-en-ciel/de rivière*: rainbow/river (often brown) trout. *Truite des gaves*: trout from mountain rivers in the Pyrenees. *Truite à la beauvaisienne*: baked with peppercorns; *Cléopâtre*: cooked in butter, with lemon juice, parsley, shrimps, capers, soft roes; *Gavarnie*: baked in papercases with parsley butter; *aux lardons* (Rouergue): with bacon; *à la Mantoue*: stuffed, poached in white wine, with tomato and mushroom sauce; *à la montbardoise*: stuffed with spinach and shallots; *à la Mont-Dore*: cooked in butter with cheese and *vermouth*; *à la Saint-Florentin*: cooked in *Chablis* wine with nutmeg and cloves; *à la d'Ussel*: coated in breadcrumbs, browned in the oven, then poached; *à la vauclusienne*: fried in olive oil. See also *bleu*.

TRUITE DE MER Salmon trout, also known as *truite saumonée/de Dieppe*.

TRULET (Nice) Pork and vegetable black pudding.

TRUMEAU Leg, shin, of beef.

(À LA) TSARINE/TZARINE Lit.: 'czarina-style'. Garnish of cucumber or mushrooms cooked in butter, and sometimes cream.

TTORO (Pays basque) Fish stew with onions, tomatoes, garlic; also known as *tioro*.

TTOURON See *touron*.

TUILE Lit.: 'tile'. Small almond biscuit shaped like a curved tile.

TUILLARD   See *millat*.

TULIPE   Lit.: 'tulip'. Tulip-shaped glass, of ice cream, *mousse*, fruit etc.

TULLE   Capital of *Corrèze*.

(À LA) TURBALLOISE   In the style of La Turballe in *Bretagne*. See *morue*.

TURBAN   Lit.: 'turban'. Food arranged in a ring, or turned out of a ring mould.

TURBIGO   See *rognon*.

TURBOT   Turbot, large white fish with delicate flavour; also known as *bretonneau* and *cailletot*. *Turbot à la Bréval*: braised, with tomatoes, mushrooms and cream sauce.

TURBOTIN   Small/chicken turbot.

TURBOT LISSE   Name for brill (*barbue*); lit.: 'smooth' (as opposed to the warty turbot).

TURINOIS   Sponge cake covered with almond paste.

(À LA) TURQUE   Turkish-style. See *aubergine* and *côtelette*.

TURQUIE   Turkey. See *blé*.

TURSAN   Area of the *Landes*, producing red and white wines (*VDQS*).

TUSSET   See *mourtaïrol*.

TYRE   (Boulonnais) Local name for skate (*pocheteau*).

(À LA) TYROLIENNE   Tyrolean-style. With tomatoes and onion rings. *Sauce tyrolienne*: *béarnaise* sauce made with olive oil instead of butter. See also *caneton*.

(À LA) TZARINE   See *tsarine*.

URSULINE   Lit.: 'Ursuline' (nun). *Ursuline de Nancy*: chicken *quenelle* in pastry with *foie gras*, truffles, asparagus.

URT   Brand name of *Saint-Paulin* cheese, made in *Béarn*.

USSEL   Town in *Limousin*. See *anguille* and *truite*.

UZÈS   Town in *Languedoc*. *Sauce d'Uzès*: *hollandaise* sauce with anchovy essence and madeira. *Consommé d'Uzès*: clear hare soup. See also *chevreuil*.

Ù ZIMINU   See *aziminu*.

VACHARD   (Auvergne) Round cheese with strong smell and flavour, made by farms.

VACHE   Cow.
Name for variety of fungus (*lactaire*).
Name for dogfish (*roussette*).

VACHERIN   Alpine cheese usually of thick pancake shape, soft or runny, with smooth pink rind and mild creamy flavour, made by mountain farms; the name refers to the type of milk used. Varieties include (Savoie) *Vacherin d'Abondance/des Aillons/des Bauges*; (Franche-Comté) *Vacherin Mont-d'Or* (*AC*).
Meringue ring filled with whipped cream, ice cream, strawberries etc.

VACHOTTE   Name for variety of fungus (*lactaire*).

VACQUEYRAS   See *Côtes-du-Rhône-Villages*.

VAIRON   Minnow, small freshwater fish.

VALENÇAY   (Berry) Small, pyramid-shaped goat's milk cheese, named after the town. *Valençay Fermier*: farm-made, dusted with charcoal, with light smell and flavour. *Valençay Laitier*: factory-made, also in *Touraine*, *Anjou*, *Charentes* and *Poitou*, with strong smell and taste; also known as *Berrichon*, *Châteauroux*, *Levroux* and *Pyramide*. VDQS wines grown in the region.

VALENCE   Capital of the Drôme department in *Dauphiné*.
Spanish orange.

(À LA) VALENCIENNES   In the style of Valenciennes, capital of *Hainaut*, once a Spanish town. Garnish of rice with peppers and white wine or tomato sauce, for chicken especially. *Consommé Valenciennes*: clear chicken soup with *quenelles* and chervil. See also *chou rouge* and *lapin*.

(À LA) VALENTINOISE   In the style of *Valence*.

VALLÉE D'AUGE   Region in *Normandie*, where the best cider and *Calvados* come from, also known as (*pays d'*) *Auge*. Of chicken and veal especially, with *Calvados* and cream.

(LA) VALLIÈRE   See *Lavallière*.

VALMUR   See *Chablis*.

VALOIS   Ruling house of France until 1589. Garnish of artichokes and sauté potatoes. *Sauce Valois*: see *Foyot*.

VALRÉAS   See *Côtes-du-Rhône-Villages* and *Picodon de Valréas*.

VALVINS   See *brocheton*.

VANDOISE   Name for dace (*dard*).

VANETTE   Name for queen scallop (*pétoncle*).

VANILLE   Vanilla. *Crème de vanille*: sweet vanilla-flavoured liqueur.

VANNEAU   Lapwing, type of plover.
                Name for queen scallop (*pétoncle*).

VANNES   Capital of *Morbihan*. See also *tripes*.

VAPEUR   Steam. *Pommes (de terre) vapeur*: plain boiled/steamed potatoes.

VAR   Department in *Provence*.

VARÈCHE   Seaweed.

(LA) VARENNE   See *La Varenne*.

VARLET DE VILLE   Lit.: 'town varlet'. (Provence) Local name for picarel (*mendole*).

VARIÉ(-E)   Assorted.

(À LA) VAROISE   In the style of *Var*. See *caillette*.

VASQUE   Shallow round bowl, of glass, china or silver, for elegant presentation of cold foods.

VAUBAN   17th-century economist and builder. See *galimafrée*.

(À LA) VAUCLAN   See *poulet*.

VAUCLUSE   Department in *Provence*, the same as *Comtat Venaissin*.

(À LA) VAUCLUSIENNE   In the style of *Vaucluse*. See *écrevisse*, *poulet* and *truite*.

VAUDÉSIR   See *Chablis*.

VDQS   *Vin Délimité de Qualité Supérieur*. See *vin*.

VEAU   Veal. See *côte*, *cul*, *escalope*, *grenadin*, *longe*, *noisette*, *noix*, *ris*, *selle*, *tendron*, *tête*, for major cuts. *Veau saumoné angoumois*: leg of veal, salted, marinated and boiled, served cold with anchovy sauce and mayonnaise.

VEILLÉE   Lit.: 'evening'. See *gâteau*.

VELAY   Range of mountains in *Languedoc*. See also *Bleu de Loudes* and *verveine*.

VELOUTÉ   Lit.: 'velvety'. Creamy white sauce made with white stock. Soup based on *velouté* sauce, finished with egg yolks and cream. See under their distinguishing names for soups of this type (e.g. *velouté Eugénie*: see *Eugénie*).

VENACO   (Corse) Firm square goat's or sheep's milk cheese, cured in rock caves, with strong smell and flavour; made in mountain cabins around Venaco.

VENAISON   Venison, more often called *chevreuil*. *Sauce venaison*: peppery game sauce with redcurrants and cream.

VENDANGE   Grape harvest. *Soupe des vendanges* (Bordelais): substantial beef, veal and vegetable soup.
    Vendange tardive: late harvest (i.e. grapes harvested late when extra ripe and rich; same as German 'Spätlese').

VENDANGEUR/(À LA) VENDANGEUSE Lit.: 'in the style of the grape harvester'. With grapes; see also *vigneron*. *Salade des vendangeurs* (Bourgogne): wild chicory, dandelion and lamb's lettuce (*mâche*) salad with fried bacon cubes.

VENDÉE   Department and region N of *Poitou*.

(À LA) VENDÉENNE In the style of *Vendée*. See *fressure* and *pâté*.

VENDÔME   Town in *Orléanais*, known for *rillettes*.

VENIS   (Bretagne) Local name for limpet (*patelle*).

(À LA) VÉNITIENNE Venetian-style. *Sauce vénitienne*: white sauce with vinegar and herbs. See also *foie*.

VENTOUX   See *Côtes de Ventoux*.

VENTRE   Belly, breast. *Petits ventres* (Limousin): stuffed mutton belly.

VENTRÈCHE (Rouergue) Salted or smoked breast of pork.

VENTRISIO (Provence) Salt breast of pork.

VERDETTE   Name for type of fungus (*russule*).

VERDI   19th-century Italian composer. Garnish of macaroni and truffles.

VERDIER   Greenfinch, small bird; sometimes eaten in *Provence*.

VERDURE   Greenery. Green vegetables.

VERDURETTE *Sauce verdurette*: herby *vinaigrette*.

(À LA) VERDURIÈRE Lit.: 'greengrocer's style'. With sorrel, lettuce, herbs (e.g. *omelette verdurière*).

VERJUS   Verjuice, acid juice of unripe grapes, used in medieval times instead of vinegar; also known as *vin vert*.

VERMICELLE   Vermicelli, very thin pasta used in soups.

VERMOUTH   Aperitif, red, white or rosé, wine-based with the addition of sugar, alcohol, herbs and plants; from German 'Vermut' – wormwood, one of the ingredients. The French style is generally dry (e.g. *Noilly*, *Chambéry*).

VERNEUIL   (Touraine) Brand name of factory-made goat's milk cheese from Verneuil.

VERNI   Lit.: 'varnished'. Venus shell, type of clam with shiny shell; also known as *grande/grosse palourde*.

VERNON   Garnish of stuffed artichokes, turnips and potatoes.

VÉRONIQUE   See *poularde* and *sole*.

VERRE   (A) glass.

VERSAILLES   Capital of the Seine-et-Oise department in *Ile-de-France*.

VERT(-E)   Green. *Sauce verte*: green herb mayonnaise. See also *anguille*.
   Verte (*de Marennes*): green oyster from *Marennes*; see also *huître*.

VERT BONNET   Lit.: 'green bonnet'. Name for type of fungus (*russule*).

VERT-PRÉ   Lit.: 'green meadow'. Garnish, for grilled steak and kidneys, of straw potatoes, watercress, parsley butter. Of cold chicken, fish etc, coated with green mayonnaise. Garnish of peas, French beans, asparagus.

VERTUS   Variety of turnip, long and carrot-shaped; originally from Vertus in *Champagne*.

VERVEINE   Verbena, often used for herb tea. Also verbena-flavoured liqueur, green or yellow; *Verveine du Velay* is well known.

VESOUL   Capital of the Haute-Saône department in *Franche-Comté*.

VÉSUBIE   River in *Provence*. See *Brousse*.

(À LA) VÉSULIENNE   In the style of *Vesoul*. See *brochet*, *coquelet* and *timbale*.

VESSIE　　Pig's bladder. See also *caneton* and *poularde*.

VÉZELAY　　(Bourgogne) Strong goat's milk cheese; farm-made around Vézelay.

VIANDES(S)　　Meat.

VIC-EN-BIGORRE　　Town in *Bigorre*. See *ragoût*.

VICHY　　Brand of mineral water, slightly sparkling, from the ancient spa of the same name in the Massif Central, *Bourbonnais-Auvergne* borders. See also *carotte* and *poulet*.

(À LA) VICHYSSOISE　　In the style of *Vichy*. Short for *crème vichyssoise*: potato and leek soup, served cold or hot; invented by a French chef in New York in 1917.

VICTORIA　　Garnish of stuffed tomatoes, artichokes, macaroni etc. *Sauce Victoria*: white wine sauce with lobster and truffles.
　　Strawberry ice cream filled with ice cream mixed with crystallized fruit and chestnuts; or vanilla ice cream filled with whipped cream and redcurrants.

VIEILLE　　Feminine of *vieux*: old. Wrasse, sea fish with coarse flesh; also known as *labre*, and *roucaou*, *rouquier*, *rouquas* and *vras*. *Vieille coquette*: cuckoo wrasse (lit.: 'old flirt'), also known as *demoiselle*.

VIEILLE CURE　　Lit.: 'old cure'. Yellow herb-flavoured liqueur based on *Cognac* and *Armagnac*, made near *Bordeaux*.

VIEILLE RÉSERVE　　Term indicating age, of *Calvados*. Also used for high-quality matured vinegar.

VIEILLE TÊTE　　Lit.: 'old head'. See *Gris de Lille*.

(À LA) VIENNOISE　　Viennese-style. Coated in egg and breadcrumbs, fried, especially veal *escalope*; sometimes garnished with hard-boiled eggs, olives, anchovies. See also *pain*.

VIERGE　　Lit.: 'virgin'. See *Chantilly* and *huile*.

VIEUX (VIEILLE)　　Old. See also *Calvados* and *rhum*. *Vieux (Lille)*: see *Gris de Lille* and *Mimolette*.

VIÉVILLE　　See *rognon*.

VIGNE　　Vine. Vineyard. See also *escargot*.

VIGNEAU　　Name for winkle (*bigorneau*).

VIGNERON/(À LA) VIGNERONNE   Lit.: ('in the style of the) wine-grower'. With grapes, vine leaves, wine, *marc* or brandy. See also *escargot* and *vendangeur*.

VIGNETTE   Name for winkle (*bigorneau*).

VIGNOBLE   Vineyard, vineyard area.

VIGNOT   Name for winkle (*bigorneau*).

(À LA) VILLAGEOISE   Lit.: 'village-style'. *Sauce villageoise*: rich white sauce with onions and mushrooms. *Potage villageoise*: leek and cabbage soup with pasta.

VILLAGES   Villages; added to the name of a wine-growing area, gives greater definition to the general *AC* and implies higher quality.

VILLEBERNIER   See *escargot*.

VILLEROI/VILLEROY   Coated with white sauce, egg and breadcrumbs, deep-fried. Probably after Maréchal de Villeroy in Louis XV's reign.

VILLE SAINT-JACQUES   See *Brie de Montereau*.

(LA) VILLETTE   Suburb in N *Paris*, considered the meat capital of France. See *pavé*.

VILLIERS-SUR-LOIR   See *Montoire*.

VIN   Wine. Under EEC regulations, wines are divided into two categories: quality wines produced in a defined region; and ordinary table wines. In France, each category is further subdivided, the first comprising *AOC* and *VDQS*; the second *vins de pays* and *vins de table*. *AOC* or *AC* (*appellation d'origine contrôlée*) wines are those of highest quality, produced in a strictly defined region, using grape varieties and methods closely regulated by INAO (Institut National des Appellations d'Origine). *VDQS* (*vins délimités de qualité supérieure*) are wines of superior quality from a defined area, not good enough to be in the highest rank of *AC*, but subject to INAO controls. *Vins de pays* must be made from recommended grape types and produced in the region indicated by their name. *Vins de table* may be made by blending the produce of several regions; priced according to alcoholic strength, which must be given on the label, and usually sold under brand names.
   Vin blanc: white wine. *Vin blanc cassis*: see *Kir*.
   Vin chaud: mulled wine.
   Vin cuit (Provence): homemade dessert wine.
   Vin doux naturel: sweet fortified wine, red or white, often from the *Muscat* grape, made especially in *Rhône* and *Languedoc-Roussillon*: used as aperitifs and with dessert.

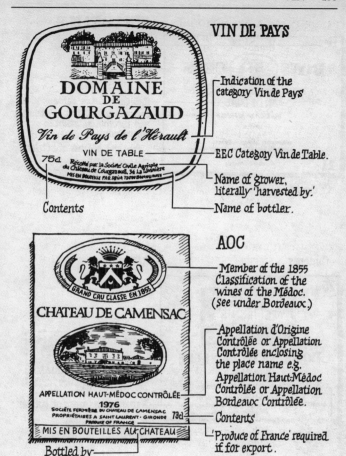

VIN DE PAYS

- Indication of the category Vin de Pays

DOMAINE DE GOURGAZAUD
Vin de Pays de l'Hérault
VIN DE TABLE

- EEC Category Vin de Table.
- Name of grower, literally 'harvested by.'
- Name of bottler.

Contents

AOC

- Member of the 1855 Classification of the wines of the Médoc. (See under Bordeaux.)

CHATEAU DE CAMENSAC

APPELLATION HAUT-MÉDOC CONTRÔLÉE

- Appellation d'Origine Contrôlée or Appellation Contrôlée enclosing the place name e.g. Appellation Haut-Médoc Contrôlée or Appellation Bordeaux Contrôlée.
- Contents
- 'Produce of France' required if for export.

Bottled by

Vin gris: grey wine (i.e. of a light rosé colour), especially from around *Arbois*.

Vin jaune: yellow wine, made in *Franche-Comté*, especially at *Château-Chalon* and *Arbois*, using the *Savagnin* grape; aged in oak casks.

Vin de liqueur: strong sweet wine.

Vin nature: still, as opposed to sparkling, wine.

Vin ordinaire: ordinary wine, sold in bulk, priced according to alcoholic strength.

Vin de paille: straw wine, in which the grapes are dried on mats of straw before pressing; made chiefly in *Franche-Comté* but rare.

Vin de palus: wine grown on the marshes bordering the rivers of *Médoc*.

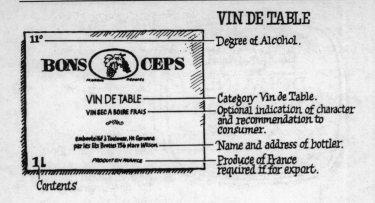

VIN DE TABLE

11° — Degree of Alcohol.

BONS CEPS

VIN DE TABLE — Category Vin de Table.

VIN SEC A BOIRE FRAIS — Optional indication of character and recommendation to consumer.

Embouteillé à Toulouse, Ht Garonne par les Ets Brottes 156 place Wilson — Name and address of bottler.

PRODUIT EN FRANCE — Produce of France required if for export.

1L

Contents

Contents

75 cl

VDQS

— Place of origin.

DOMAINE DE LA SALLE
corbières
VIN DELIMITE DE QUALITE SUPERIEURE

VDQS — VDQS stamp of guarantee and control number.

M. Roussille viticulteur à Comigne (Aude) Embouteillé et distribué par S.A.Sofip, 3 rue du Chai, Paris 5° — Name and address of bottler.

PRODUIT EN FRANCE — Produce of France required if for export.

Category VDQS

Vin de/du pays: regional wine. See above.

Vin rosé: rosé wine.

Vin rouge: red wine.

Vin des sables: wine, made from vines grown on sand especially in *Camargue* and *Landes*.

Vin de table: table wine. See above.

Vin vert: name for verjuice (*verjus*).

For wines with the word *vin* in the title, see under their distinguishing names (e.g. *Vin de Blanquette*: see *Blanquette).

VINAIGRE Vinegar (lit.: 'sour wine' – *vin aigre*), made of red or white wine, cider, sherry or fruit like raspberries and

cherries, often flavoured with shallots or herbs, especially tarragon.

VINAIGRETTE   Cold dressing for salads of oil and vinegar with salt
and pepper; herbs, lemon juice, mustard or hard-boiled
egg yolks may be added.

VINCENT   *Sauce Vincent*: green herb mayonnaise.

VINIFICATEUR   Wine-maker.

VINSOBRES   See *Côtes-du-Rhône-Villages*.

VIOGNIER   Variety of white grape, used especially in the *Rhône* for
the wines of *Château Grillet* and *Condrieu*.

VIOLET   Lit.: 'purple'. Small sea creature resembling a knobbly
potato outside and scrambled egg inside, which is the
edible part, eaten raw; also known as *figue de mer*.

VIOLETTE   Violet, whose petals are often candied. *Crème de violette*: sweet liqueur flavoured with violets.

VIOLON   Lit.: 'violin'. Violin-shaped fish of the skate family; also
known as *guitare*.

VIRE   Town in *Normandie*, known for *andouille*.

VIRGOULEUSE   Variety of pear, originally from Virgoulée in
Limousin.

(À LA) VIROFLAY   Town in *Ile-de-France* once known for spinach.
Garnish of spinach balls, cheese sauce, artichokes,
potatoes. See also *épinards*.

VISAN   See *Côtes-du-Rhône-Villages*.

VISE EN L'AIR   (Bretagne) Local name for type of clam (*mye*).

VISITANDINE   Lit.: 'nun of the Visitation order'. (Lorraine) Small
round almond cake, probably invented by nuns.

VITALON   (Picardie) Sweet pastry dumpling, poached in milk.

VITICOLE   To do with wine.

VITICULTEUR   Wine-grower.

VITELOTTE   Kidney potato.

VITTEL   Brand of mineral
water from the spa
of the same name
in *Vosges*.

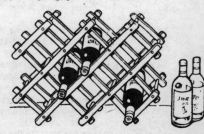

(À LA) VIVANDIÈRE Lit.: 'in the style of the *vivandière*' (woman attached to a regiment selling provisions and liquor). See *poulet* and *sardine*.

VIVARAIS Province equivalent to *Ardèche*. See also *Côtes du Vivarais*.

(À LA) VIVARAISE In the style of *Vivarais*. See *chou*.

VIVE Weever, sea fish with poisonous spines. Types include *vive rayée* (lit.: 'striped'); and (*vive*) *araignée*, also known as *aragno*, *dragena* and *iragno*.

VIVEROLS See *Brique du Forez*.

VIVEUR Lit.: 'fast liver'. Seasoned with cayenne, paprika etc (e.g. *potage des viveurs*).

VIVIER Fish tank/pond.

VLADIMIR Garnish of courgettes and cucumbers, with sour cream, paprika and horseradish sauce.

VO See *VSOP*.

VOILIER PORTE-GLAIVE Lit.: 'sailing sword-bearer'. Name for trumpet fish (*bécasse de mer*).

VOISIN Lit.: 'neighbour'; also *Paris* restaurant. *Pommes* (*de terre*) *Voisin*: flat cake of sliced potatoes and grated cheese.

VOITURE Trolley, of desserts etc.

VOLAILLE(S) Poultry, fowl. Chicken, on a menu. See also *blanc*, *chapon*, *coq*, *jambonneau*, *poularde*, *poule*, *poulet*, *poussin* and *suprême*.

VOL-AU-VENT Lit.: 'flight-with-the-wind'. Light puff pastry ring with a hat, variously filled; small ones are often known as *bouchées à la reine*.

VOLNAY Commune of *Côte de Beaune*, *Bourgogne*, known for delicate red wine (*AC*).

VOLNAY SANTENOTS Red wine (*AC*) made adjacent to *Volnay*, in the commune of *Meursault*.

VOLVIC Brand of still mineral water from town of same name in *Auvergne* mountains.

(À LA) VONNASSIENNE In the style of Vonnas in *Bresse*. See *crêpe*.

VOSGES   Department of *Lorraine*, and mountainous region dividing *Alsace* and *Lorraine*.

(À LA) VOSGIENNE   In the style of *Vosges*. See *côte* and *hogue vosgien*.

VOSNE-ROMANÉE   Commune of *Côte de Nuits* producing some of the finest red wines (*AC*) of *Bourgogne*; it contains the celebrated *grand cru* vineyards – *La Romanée*, *Romanée-Saint-Vivant*, *Richebourg*, *La Tâche* and *Romanée-Conti*.

VOUGEOT   Commune of *Côte de Nuits*, *Bourgogne*, making mostly red wines (*AC*); containing the renowned vineyard, *Clos de Vougeot* (*grand cru AC*).

VOUVRAY   Important commune of the *Loire*, making distinguished white wines (*AC*), both still and sparkling, generally dry but with a tendency to sweetness.

(À LA) VOUVRILLONNE   In the style of *Vouvray*. With *Vouvray* wine, applied to chicken, pike *quenelles* etc. See also *andouillette*.

VRAI(-E)   True.

VRAS   (Normandie) Local name for wrasse (*vieille*). *Vras à la cherbourgeoise*: large wrasse stuffed with a smaller one, baked with cider.

VRILLE DE VIGNE   Vine tendril, sometimes marinated in vinegar and eaten cold as an *hors d'oeuvre*.

VS   See below.

VSOP   Very Special/Superior Old Pale; used in various combinations – *VO*, *VS*, *VSOP* – to indicate the age of *Armagnac*, *Calvados* and *Cognac*.

WAFFELPASTETA   (Alsace) *Foie gras* in pastry.

WALDORF   *Salade Waldorf*: apple, celeriac and walnut salad.

WALEWSKA   Son of Napoleon's Polish mistress and 19th-century government minister. See *sole*.

WAMS   (N France) General name for smoked fish.

WASHINGTON   With sweetcorn, especially of chicken.

WASSEWECKE   (Alsace) Bread roll.

WATERFISCH   Freshwater fish in general; from the Dutch.
  Sauce waterfisch: cold jellied or hot sauce with gherkins, capers etc, for freshwater fish, especially perch.

WATERZO(O)Ï/WATERZOOTJE   (Flandre) *Waterzooï(de poissons)*: freshwater fish stew with herbs. *Waterzooï de poulet/de volaille*: chicken stewed with leeks and cream sauce. Of Belgian origin.

WATTIEU   See *gâteau*.

WEICHE METTWURST   See *tartinette*.

WHISKY   Whisky.

WILHELMINE   See *fraise*.

WILLIAMS   Short for *poire Williams*: variety of pear. Also a clear spirit made from pears, especially in *Alsace*.

WITLOOF   Name for chicory (*endive*).

XAVIER   Comte de Provence, later Louis XVIII. *Consommé Xavier*: clear beef soup with madeira and pancake strips. *Potage Xavier*: cream of rice soup.

XÉRÈS   Sherry.

XO   See *Cognac*.

YAOURT   Yoghourt.

YERBILHOU   See *broye*.

(À LA) YONNAISE   In the style of *La Roche-sur-Yon*.

YORK   See *jambon*.

YPORT   Town in *Normandie*. *Tarte au sucre d'Yport*: apple tart with *calvados*.

(À LA) YVETOISE   In the style of Yvetot in *Normandie*. See *poulet*.

YVETTE See *Annette*.

YVONNE *Velouté Yvonne*: cream of chicken soup with lettuce.

 ZÉBRINE Variety of aubergine, with a striped skin.

ZEPHYR Lit.: 'zephyr'. Fanciful name for light frothy preparation.

ZESTE Rind, peel, of orange, lemon.

ZEWELMAI/ZEWELWAÏ (Alsace) Onion and cream flan.

ZIMINU See *aziminu*.

ZIMMET-KUCHE (Alsace) Cinnamon cake.

(À LA) ZINGARA Lit.: 'gypsy-style'. Garnish of ham, tongue, mushrooms and truffles with tomato sauce. With tomato sauce.

ZIZI Aperitif of *Champagne*, blackcurrant and raspberry liqueurs; named after a mayor of *Lyon*, rival of *Kir* in *Dijon*.

ZUCCATA (Corse) Vegetable pastry.

ZUNGENWURST (Alsace) Black pudding of ox or pig's tongue; also known as *boudin de langue*.

ZWIEBACK Rusk.

ZWIEBEL KUCHE (Alsace) Onion tart; from German 'Zwiebel' – onion.

ENGLISH–FRENCH INDEX